STANDING FIRM

STANDING FIRM

A Vice-Presidential Memoir

DAN QUAYLE

HarperCollins*Publishers*
Zondervan

HarperCollins books may be purchased for educational, business, or sales promotional use. For information please write: Special Markets Department, HarperCollins Publishers, Inc., 10 East 53rd Street, New York, NY 10022.

Designed by Nancy Singer

Photo inserts researched, edited, and designed by Vincent Virga

Library of Congress Cataloging-in-Publication Data
Quayle, Dan, 1947–
Standing firm : a vice-presidential memoir / by Dan Quayle.—1st ed.
    p.   cm.
Includes index.
ISBN 0-06-017758-6
1. Quayle, Dan, 1947–   . 2. Vice-Presidents—United States—Biography.
3. United States—Politics and government—1989–1993. I. Title.
E840.8.Q28A3   1994
973.928'092—dc20
[B]   94–4174
94 95 96 97 98 ❖/HC 10 9 8 7 6 5 4 3 2

I dedicate this book to the people I love the most,
my family, who lived these pages with me:
Marilyn, Tucker, Benjamin, and Corinne

Where the Spirit of the Lord is, there is Liberty

II Cor. 3:17

Contents

PART FIVE: LOSING AND WINNING (1992)

(Photo sections follow pages 114 and 242)

Acknowledgments

Writing these acknowledgments may be the most difficult part of producing this memoir, since so many people have helped me over the years, not only with this book but in living the events it describes. I know that there will be omissions from the list that follows, and I can only hope that anyone I've forgotten will forgive me.

Richard Nixon was one of the people I spoke with before writing this book. As usual, he gave me his honest and unvarnished views, suggesting that I not try to curry favor with my critics. I considered that good advice.

In writing *Standing Firm* I was assisted by a great team who made invaluable contributions. First and foremost, I must credit my "Editor-in-Chief"—not just for this book but for all my life's endeavors—Marilyn. As usual, she proved indispensable. Researcher Sallie Motsch was indefatigable in checking the factual content of the manuscript. My dear friend, Don Wade, made insightful comments along the way, as did author Nancy Northcott, who took time away from her book to help me finish mine. Special friend Fran Pirozzolo made suggestions for improvements that proved essential. Carol Shookhoff devoted long hours to interview transcription, going the extra mile to meet all deadlines. A very close friend for many years, Jack Vardaman, not only helped launch this book but gave me valuable counsel at critical times. And my good friend and former national security adviser Karl Jackson supplied important background information as the book was being completed.

No less important was the contribution of my talented assistant Anne Hathaway, who kept all the plates in the air. John McConnell, my trusted speech writer and good friend, was helpful in organizing volumes of material from my years in office. Doug

McCorkindale was the first of many friends who suggested I write a book about my years as Vice President. Family friend and super book lawyer Bob Barnett got this project started.

I'd also like to thank the press (well, some of them), specifically Bob Woodward, Michael Barone, David Broder, Brit Hume, Ann Devroy, Dan Rather, Mark Shields, and Len Downie. All of them sat down with me as I worked on this book, offering valuable reflections upon my unique experience with the fourth estate. Tom Mallon, who wrote an evenhanded essay about me while I was in office, provided a great deal of help for which I'm grateful.

The HarperCollins team was composed of my editor, Rick Horgan, whose criticisms were both constructive and essential and added great value to this book; publishers Bill Shinker and Jack McKeown; and their colleagues Joseph Montebello, Vincent Virga, Steve Sorrentino, Chris McLaughlin, and golfing ace Brenda Marsh. All were absolutely fantastic to work with. The Zondervan team, led by editor John Sloan and publisher Scott Bolinder, made a significant contribution.

When I ran for Congress in 1976 at the age of twenty-nine, against a sixteen-year incumbent, many thought I was pursuing a pipe dream. But others put their confidence in me and helped me toward victory. Among those I gratefully remember are the late Ernie Williams, Jim Loomis, Marge Meeks, Orvas Beers, Helen Peare, Jill Emmert, the late Ann Pfister, Don Purviance, Annie Echrich, Paul Seitz, Mary Morrill, Betsy Shoppy, Les Gerig, and Bob Bolenbaugh. No book about my life in politics would be complete without thanking my hometown friends in Huntington, Indiana, whose steady and faithful support carried me through good times and bad. I'm especially grateful to Marj Hiner and David Brewer and the friends who today run The Dan Quayle Center & Museum.

Once in the House, I was lucky to have a staff who not only helped make my two terms there a success but also positioned me for an uphill run for the Senate in 1980. Special thanks to Cynthia Ferneau, who was with me from my first day in public office until the last one sixteen years later; Les Rosen; Dan Coats, who followed me as a Congressman and Senator and gave outstanding service throughout; Les Novitsky; Myrna Dugan; and Karen Hoppe.

That 1980 race against Birch Bayh—another longtime incumbent who looked unbeatable—was won with the help of a great staff and volunteers. I still owe a debt of gratitude to Tom Moses, Bud Tucker, Dave Griffiths, Dan Evans, Bill Watt, Ray Rizzo, J. B. King, Joe Morrow, Bob Orr, Steve Chancellor, Bill Neale, Doc Bowen, the late Frank McKinney, Kathy Hubbard, Mark Miles, Van Smith, Dick Lugar, Ian Rolland, Chris Schenkel, Ilsa Koch, Jim and Sherry Tucker, and Steve Nix. The hundreds of volunteers who worked their hearts out all over Indiana are too numerous to mention here but have my profound gratitude.

My Senate staff of Tom Duesterberg, Jeff Nesbit, Peter Lincoln, Henry Sokolski, Greg Zoeller, Bob Guttman, Rob Goodling, Alice Davidson, Marian Kelly, Bob Rowe, Dave Juday, and Eva Marie Grace worked hard for both me and my constituents and helped to put me into the running for Vice President in 1988. Thanks to all of them. Ken Khachigian was a bright spot as speech writer and confidant during the 1988 campaign.

Bill Kristol, a skilled strategist and a man with a passion for ideas, headed my vice-presidential office. Al Hubbard, my good friend, who was my able deputy chief of staff offered some keen insights to this book. I was never short of talented people. Prominent among them were Bill Gribbin, Spence Abraham, Glen Tuit, Ccce Kremer, Richard Porter, Marguerite Sullivan, Dave Beckwith, Dan Murphy, Tom Fleener, Craig Whitney, Denise Balzano, Randy Wilson, Karl Jackson, Carnes Lord, Jon Glassman, Kathy Fauster, Kim Walsh, Jeff McKittrick, David McIntosh, Barbara Edgerton, Judy Volchko, Jean Thompson, and Mark Albrecht.

Many thanks to my true friends in the House and Senate— those who stood by when others didn't have the courage to do so.

Then there are friends to thank, longtime ones like my college roommate Mark Rolfing, fellow DePauw alum Randy Reifers, Dick and Deanna Freeland, the late Kent Frandsen, Ken and Carol Adelman, Tom Kyhos, Zora Brown, Frank Russell, Henry Kissinger, Rae and Dave Evans, Jon Kraushar, Mary Howell, Fred Fielding, Bob Scheerschmidt, Don Rice, Richard Perle, Roger Ailes, Jeane Kirkpatrick, Cap Weinberger, Mort and Harriet Moss, Jerry Edgerton, David Woodward, Terry Morrow, Bob Allen, Jerry Bepko, Tom Clancy, John Snow, John Whitehead, Randy Tobias, Tom Kelley, and some from the last five years, like Mark Mulvoy, Steve Forbes, George Zahringer, Henry Kravis, Wayne Huizenga, John Taylor, Hank Greenberg, Jim Wolfensohn, Norm Augustine, Ernie Ransome, Joe Schuchert, Mano Kampouris, Norm and Nancy Brinker, Jim McClean, Kent Cayce, Bonnie Newman, Charles and Margo Rathell, Van Batchelder, Phil Edlund, Bob Simonds, Richard Starr, Dick Heckmann, Howard Marguleas, Carl Lindner, Tom Selleck, Debi Rolfing, John Piper, Adele Hall, Nancy Dickerson, George Klein, Lucy Billingsley, Gerald McRaney, Roger Penske, Lou Sullivan (a good Cabinet secretary), Karen and Wes Williams, Walter and Lenore Annenberg, David Rockefeller, and Karen Phebus.

I have been blessed with loving parents—Jim and Corinne Quayle—who have stood by me during the best and worst of times. My siblings—Chris, Mike, and Martha—have always loved and defended their older brother, and he's indebted to all of them. Thanks, in fact, to all of my family—the Quayles, the Pulliams, Suzanne Murphy (whose house I used while beginning this book), the Schultes, the McDanielses, the Tuckers, the Northcotts, the Hoards, and especially President and Mrs. Bush, who will always seem like family to me.

PART ONE

Winning and Losing

1988

1 | Pushing Through the Plaza

New Orleans was full of conventioneers, and at 2:00 on that hot August afternoon we looked no different from most of them. I was wearing casual clothes, and Marilyn had on a denim dress. We were walking up Bourbon Street, making our way back to our hotel after lunch at Sammy's, trying to enjoy the sun and the street noise of New Orleans. I think we were holding hands, though Marilyn reminds me I've never been big on public displays of affection. There's one thing we both remember for sure, though: the moment the beeper went off.

That morning we'd been given it to carry by Mary Moses Cochran, who had worked in my Senate office and campaigns and whose dad, Tom Moses, had been an early supporter when I ran for the Senate eight years earlier. Bob Kimmitt, who was handling the vice-presidential selection process, had told me that I would receive a call around 2:00 P.M. He never said who would call, only that a call would be coming.

As soon as we heard the thing beep, Marilyn and I stopped in our tracks and looked at each other, and I said, as calmly as I could, "Now we'll find out." I remember thinking, "This is the moment. I'm either going to be the vice-presidential nominee, or I'll be joining my Indiana delegation and enjoying the drama of our national convention with friends."

Sammy's restaurant hadn't been all that crowded—the convention proceedings were in their second day, and many of the delegates were already making their way to the riverfront area called Spanish Plaza, where a big rally was being organized to coincide with George Bush's arrival in town that afternoon, by riverboat. Neither Marilyn nor I had much of an appetite, though I managed to get down a steak sandwich. For months the two of us had speculated about my being chosen as Bush's running mate. He'd already asked if I'd let myself be considered, and over the last few days some people in the press realized that I was emerging as a surprise selection. By Tuesday morning Marilyn and I were beginning to climb the walls a bit; that's the main reason we decided to go out for lunch that day.

Now, as we walked the last block back to the hotel, we knew that one way or another the suspense would be over. For the last few days I'd let myself dream about the headlines that might greet my own selection—BUSH PICKS HOOSIER RISING STAR FOR VEEP. Ever since George Bush called me after the Democratic Convention, I had a feeling it just might be me. I had done what every politician attempts to do—put myself in a win-win situation. If I'm chosen, I win; if not, I'm still young and the speculation will have been good for my career.

When we got up to our floor, Tom Duesterberg, my administrative assistant, handed me a phone number and said I was supposed to call Jim Baker, Bush's campaign chairman. So, while Marilyn and I walked down the hall to our room, I said, "Well, I guess I didn't get it." Since Baker was calling and not the Vice President, I just assumed I wasn't going to get the nod. I felt both excited and disappointed—excited that I had come this far but disappointed that I wasn't able to push it across the goal line. Still, that morning, Mary Moses Cochran had told us she'd seen some Secret Service around, and Greg Zoeller, who ran my Senate office in Indiana, thought he could "just smell it." Once in the room, we turned on the television with the volume down low. Marilyn sat beside me on the edge of the bed and I made the call. Jim Baker answered, and as soon as I identified myself, he said, "Hang on for the Veep." The next voice I heard was George Bush's, asking me if I would like the job he himself had held for the past eight years. I turned to Marilyn and gave her a thumbs-up.

Only hours before Bush had said good-bye to President Ronald Reagan at the Belle Chase Naval Air Station. The President was leaving New Orleans after having addressed the convention the

night before. There was a symbolic aspect to his departure—he
was turning leadership of the party over to George Bush, and one
of the last things Bush did before Reagan boarded *Air Force One*
was whisper in the President's ear the name of his own choice for
Vice President. Now Bush was calling to tell me. Those who were
with him—including close aides who had advised him on the vice-
presidential choice—were also hearing the news for the first time.

I accepted without hesitation. I told him I would do my best
and that we'd be a great team. And then our attention turned to
the moment at hand, the way it always does in campaigns: you
deal with whatever scheduling or setback or spin needs immediate attention. Politics is supposed to be strategic, but it is almost
always tactical. In this case, the chosen tactic was to maximize
news interest in the choice of a running mate by keeping the
selection a secret for as long as possible. There the next President
was, telling me about his desire for suspense, while from the foot
of my hotel room bed I could hear the TV newsman saying he
now knew it was not going to be Bob Dole or Jack Kemp. I told
the Vice President what I was hearing, and how it didn't seem as
if it would take the media much longer to figure out what was
going on. He responded that the campaign was still going to try to
withhold my name for as long as possible, and that he wanted me
to appear with him at 3:30 in the Spanish Plaza for the surprise
announcement. He'd soon be boarding the SS *Natchez* for the
short trip downriver.

When Marilyn heard me repeating the location, she gave me a
poke and turned my attention to the TV, which was showing that
very spot—already mobbed with thousands of people. I expressed
my doubts about the feasibility of our getting down there and
through the crowd in time, and when it became apparent that
Bush didn't have much else for me in the way of details and directions, I asked him to put Jim Baker back on.

I told him about the crowds we were seeing on the TV, and I
asked how I was supposed to get there. Was he going to send a
driver? "No, no," he said, the surprise factor still very much on his
mind. He just wanted me to show up, and to keep this a secret.
Okay, I told him, we'd figure out how to get down there. He
reminded me that this was my first assignment and I'd better not

blow it. "Remember," he joked, "this decision is revocable." We both laughed. It was the last laugh I would have for a long, long time.

This was not the best-planned episode in political history, and it certainly had its comic aspects. In her organized way, Marilyn quickly began to make the best of a chaotic situation, getting out the clothes we'd need and plugging in her electric rollers. Having decided that the one person I should tell was Tom Duesterberg, I went down the hall to get him. But I found him with a room full of other staffers and realized there was no way I could get him out of there without giving the whole thing away. So, after a moment's hesitation, I went back to my own room. We decided it would be easier for Marilyn to get him. So she took the rollers out of her hair and went down to see Tom. She told him, "Tom, Dan needs to speak to you," and said nothing else to anyone in the room. Tom and the rest of them were sure it was bad news.

Marilyn brought Tom back to our room. After we told him it was good news and he offered his quiet congratulations, we went about planning this little mission to Spanish Plaza. We decided that, if we were going to get through that crowd, Andy Buroker, a staff member who now practices law in the same firm as Marilyn, would have to drive us. So, we told Andy the news (the secret was already getting out), and Tom went back and told the rest of the staff that he had to go out for a while and that, given all the crazy speculation, they should just avoid answering the phones.

There were a few other people who, we decided, had to know right away. First and foremost were our children, whose lives we knew were about to change abruptly (actually, we didn't know the half of it). They were back at our home in McLean, Virginia, being minded by Marilyn's aunt, Janet Craig, a wonderful woman who never married but acted as a surrogate grandmother to our kids after Marilyn's mother died. Ben, our eleven-year-old son, answered the phone; he said he already knew his dad would be picked because Tom Brokaw had just called up trying to find out if he knew anything! We told Ben to get his brother and sister on the extensions. They greeted the news with a sort of dead silence, but there was no time to reflect. I instructed them that they absolutely could not tell anyone until they heard it announced on television. I knew I could count on them. After that, I called my parents in Huntington, Indiana, and they immediately began making plans to come to New Orleans. (Tom Brokaw, who was having as busy an afternoon as I was, would soon get the local operator to cut in on a phone conversation between my mother and a friend of hers.)

All of this happened in a great rush. Our families had no more time to let the news sink in than we had to ponder it ourselves. I jumped into the shower, where I focused my thoughts on getting through the next hour or two. We'd been told nothing about the platform arrangements at Spanish Plaza, and I had no idea what sort of speech I was expected to give. I decided I would just make the kind of remarks I'd been making at political appearances over the past few months: talking about "George Bush's America" and the leadership he could bring to our world. In my congressional career, I was used to speaking without a prepared text in front of me—and even if there had been time to write anything down, I don't think I'd have bothered.

When we arrived at the Plaza we realized that, if anything, the impression we'd gotten from the TV pictures barely approached the reality. It was a mob scene—hot and loud and friendly, but not something you wanted to push your way through. Andy got us as close as he could, and Tom got out of the car, scouting for a spot where he and I and Marilyn might have the best chance to start moving in on foot. We got out and started trying to make it through the folks who had been waiting in the broiling sun for hours. You can imagine how popular these three people pushing their way to the front became. We got plenty of who-the-heck-do-you-think-you-are looks and remarks, and we could hardly blame the people who were making them. I can remember one guy recognizing me and saying, "Oh, that's Senator Quayle!"—only to be answered by somebody else, "I don't care who he is! I've been waiting here for a long time!" I wished I could have told him I was going to be the vice-presidential nominee and he could do me a favor by letting me through.

Most of the Bush campaign brass—Lee Atwater, Roger Ailes, and Craig Fuller—had been pacing up and down the platform and scanning the crowd, looking for us. We started waving to them, doing whatever we could to get their attention as we tried to get through the crowd. They didn't see us, but fortunately, a group of politicians up front—including Wisconsin Governor Tommy Thompson and Senator Strom Thurmond—recognized us and figured out what was going on. (Even then it occurred to me that at least one or two of them were probably thinking: Why isn't it me? Thompson let the press know afterwards that he'd wanted to be considered.) They started pointing to us and yelling, trying to get the campaign people to recognize and rescue us.

Finally Craig Fuller spotted us, and the second he did—boom!—the Secret Service got the crowd to open up and we walked straight through. This was a startling sign of what life was soon to be like, although my memories of the 1988 campaign, which was beginning for me at that moment, remain closer to ones of drowning than of having waters part at my approach. In the excitement of the moment, I tried to operate on instinct. I told myself that, after all, my instincts had already taken me far in life. Trust yourself, I kept saying. At forty-one years old I was considered by many a rising star in the Republican Party, someone who'd served four years in the House and eight in the Senate, all the time getting very favorable press. I figured (naively, I soon came to realize) that my instincts would get me through this new experience on the national stage, too. Some people might call this chutzpah; to me it was just self-confidence.

We were finally up on the platform and able to appreciate the reasons they'd chosen the setting. A big riverboat and the mighty Mississippi were behind us, and George Bush, standing in shirt-sleeves under the bright sun, looked like the great campaigner and vigorous leader we knew he was. Since the Democratic Convention we'd remained down in the polls, but people with faith in our message and our nominee—and no one had more of that than I did—were convinced that we could leave our own convention with the situation in rapid turnaround.

I had my own jacket off now and was responding to the roar that greeted Bush's announcement that I was his choice. While I did get the chance to say how honored I was to have been picked, and did make those remarks about "George Bush's America," I managed, in all the excitement, to create the video clip that would be played over and over during the next few days, the one that has me excitedly punching George Bush on the arm and telling the crowd, "Let's go get 'em!"

Looking back, I realize that the speech was too hot. I was talking like a junior Senator in campaign overdrive. I was picked, in part, for my youth, but this was a little too youthful—not vice-presidential nor, given the nature of that office, potentially presidential. (Several years later, the *Washington Post*'s Ann Devroy told me the picture looked wrong to her: "A Republican doesn't hug George Bush.") But I was energized and proud, and I was wearing my emotions on my shirtsleeves. During the next couple of weeks, many people went out of their way to tell both Marilyn and me that they thought the campaign had required some fire at that point. Governor Jim Thompson of Illinois, himself presidential timber, said that punch on the arm helped give George Bush just the kind of jump start he needed.

But that's not how most of the media played it. I was a stranger to most Americans, and that night the commentary they heard included the memorable line (historians should note it as the first Quayle joke) that up there on the platform in Spanish Plaza I looked like the guy on the game show who'd just won the Oldsmobile.

2 | The Short List

"Tell me about Dan Quayle." On the night of August 16, this was the question hundreds of newspeople in New Orleans were asking any acquaintance of mine they could find—because it was the same question millions of Americans were asking. It's a question George Bush had also asked, several months earlier.

He'd been in Indiana in the spring, shortly after his nomination for President seemed assured, and was on his way to tour the AM General plant where they manufacture the HumVee. (That's the all-terrain successor to the Jeep, one of the American-built marvels that a couple of years later would help us win the Gulf War. I'd helped to save it several years earlier, rallying my Senate colleagues in the middle of the night to vote against an amendment to kill it, which Delaware Senator William Roth had proposed in response to a misguided ABC News investigation.) With Bush in his limousine were Indiana Governor Bob Orr; the state party chairman, Gordon Durnil; and Congressman Jack Hiler. Bush took the opportunity to ask them about their fellow Hoosier: "What kind of Senator has Dan Quayle been?"

They were willing to give him a positive review of me. In fact, Gordon Durnil went so far as to tell him that in a recent statewide poll, my approval rating was even higher than that of my senior Senate colleague, Dick Lugar. Since his victory over Bob Dole in the New Hampshire primary, George Bush had been plotting the selection of his future running mate, and now he was gathering valuable information.

*   *   *

Unlike many politicians, I was never much of a student government type. My family's moves from Indiana to Arizona and back again, and the number of times I changed schools (5 grade schools, 2 high schools), had something to do with that. But from early childhood I never lacked exposure to politics. My maternal grandfather, Eugene Pulliam, the son of a Methodist minister, became a highly successful and respected newspaper publisher. He was a strong, smart, self-made man who relished challenges and never backed down from a good fight. He had a tremendous influence on his children as well as his grandchildren. Fiercely distrustful of government interference, he sold some of the radio stations he owned rather than let Washington regulate them.

Both my parents served on precinct committees and were heavily involved in Republican party politics. My dad worked in the newspaper business everywhere we lived, and our house was always filled with discussions about local and national politics. I'd often go down to the paper with him. I can still remember the excitement, when I was about eleven years old, when Barry Goldwater called our house in Phoenix. In Arizona, Goldwater was an icon.

Throughout my life I've loved beating the odds. I switched elementary schools five times. Whenever I arrived at a new one, the teacher would put me in the last row, which was reserved for the slow kids. Within a matter of weeks I'd make it to the front of the room. I was small and developed late, which made it more difficult to play sports, but most of the time I'd work my way from the bench to the starting team. I was never an all-star, but I could mix it up with the best of them.

I headed off to DePauw University as a freshman in the fall of 1965, and while the four years that followed were politically tumultuous for a lot of campuses, ours in Greencastle, Indiana, remained a sleepy place, where the handful of student radicals were never taken seriously.

By the summer of 1968, just before my senior year, Nixon was running for President. I would cast my first vote for him, partly because I thought he would end the Vietnam War sooner and more honorably than anyone else. I went down to the Republican convention in Miami and worked as a driver for some of the

Nixon staffers. Once there, like a lot of other young people, I was captivated by the charisma of Ronald Reagan, who was making a last-minute bid for the nomination.

After six months of Army basic training as part of my National Guard obligation, I went to work in the Indiana attorney general's office in 1970, where my natural interest in politics really accelerated. That fall I entered Indiana University as a law student where I started the student newspaper.

I then worked my way up and became an administrative assistant in the Governor's office. That's where I met another young law student, Marilyn Tucker, when we worked together on a capital punishment brief. I had a hard time getting a date with her, since she was seeing somebody else. But I soon managed to cook her a few dinners at my apartment, and within a matter of months we were married. After the Governor's office and my short stint with the state's Department of Revenue, Marilyn and I both passed the bar exam and moved back to Huntington. There I published the family newspaper, set up a law practice with Marilyn (Quayle & Quayle) and began my career in politics.

In the summer of 1974, when we were looking at places to live in Huntington, I had already scoped out a state-rep district where I thought I could make a run in 1976.

As it turned out, I did run that year, but not for the state legislature. After joining the Fort Wayne Press Club, I became good friends with Ernie Williams, editor of the *Fort Wayne News-Sentinel,* and he suggested me as a candidate for Congress to Orvas Beers, the GOP county chairman. In February 1976, Orvas came up to me at the end of a press club meeting and said, "I want you to run for Congress and be our candidate."

"Well," I said, "that's really interesting. But what about Walt Helmke?" He had run in 1974 but was no longer interested, Orvas assured me.

"Then what about Phil Gutman?" (Phil was the powerful state Senate majority leader.) They'd already talked to him, said Orvas, and Gutman wasn't interested either. Nor were a couple more people I mentioned. Most of them had already taken a failed shot at the longtime incumbent, Ed Roush, who was considered unbeatable.

Orvas was serious, and before long so was I. Marilyn supported my decision but gently reminded me that I'd once said I wouldn't run for Congress until our children were older. My parents were traveling in Australia, and I called them from a newspaper conference in Williamsburg, Virginia, to talk about it. "Fine," said Dad. "Run. But you won't win. Nobody can beat Ed Roush" (the popular Democrat who had represented the Fourth District for sixteen years). Dad was just relieved that there hadn't been a death in the family, which is what he'd been expecting to hear when he returned the phone call in Australia and heard my voice.

Our newspaper group was invited to the White House, and Marilyn and I had our picture taken with President Ford, who'd just beaten Ronald Reagan in the New Hampshire primary. "I'm going to be running for Congress in the Fourth Congressional District," I told him. "Great!" he said, still pumped up from his victory. "We'll be running together!" Which is what we did (even though I voted for Reagan in the Indiana primary).

As one reporter boiled it down, I ran on a platform of less government, less spending, and less taxation. My opponent and I both stuck to the issues. Ed Roush was a decent, hard-working family man who had simply been in Washington too long. On critical issues like welfare, defense, and the federal bailout of New York City, he had traded a Hoosier perspective for a Potomac one. He was unable to embrace reform. Jerry Ford, though he would manage to carry Indiana against Jimmy Carter, wasn't especially popular at the time, and I didn't mention him much. In fact, after Watergate and the Nixon pardon, I didn't even put the word *Republican* on my campaign literature. But I did attack the Democratic Congress, where Ed Roush had always been in the comfortable, complacent majority.

He was also too complacent at the beginning of the campaign. He made the mistake of accepting a series of debates, which he could have ducked and which gave me the exposure I needed in front of newspaper reporters and business leaders.

The Christian community also provided crucial support. Les Gerig, the head of Mutual Security Life Insurance, was very helpful in rallying that support, even though many in the Christian community were supporting Jimmy Carter for President that year.

About the only things Carter and I had in common were strong religious faith and the fact that we were new faces. Being a new face from a new generation, I attracted new volunteers fed up with politics as usual. We relied heavily on them to do our precinct work, and, because of the new federal election laws, we set up our own organization, separate from (and not to the liking of) the regular Republican Party. Our volunteers worked long hours—licking envelopes, making phone calls, and getting the vote out. It was a tremendous effort, and it sank deep roots into Indiana politics. For example, once I was elected, Gerig suggested that I get a fellow named Dan Coats to run my district office, which I proceeded to do. In 1981, Dan would succeed me in the House, and eight years later he'd be appointed to fill my Senate seat. He'd win reelection to both positions with the help of the same family-oriented volunteers who came through for me in 1976.

When I was sworn in, in January 1977, I was twenty-nine years old, full of youthful enthusiasm and idealism. I wanted to change the country. But I soon awoke to the realities of being in a minority that had existed since 1954. Republicans in the House get mauled by the rules, mauled by committee assignments, and mauled in floor vote after floor vote. I had some memorable, even enjoyable, fights—trying to defeat the establishment of another huge bureaucracy in the Department of Education; attempting to keep a liaison office on Taiwan—but most of my experience in the House was reactive and frustrating, something that's still true for Republicans two decades later.

Almost as soon as I was in, I wanted out—or up. I spent most of my last two years in the House running for the Senate. This time I didn't wait for the opening to come to me. I made it clear that I wanted the chance to take on Birch Bayh, the Democratic incumbent, who'd run for President and was considered a political giant. A number of people let me know that it wasn't my turn and that I should defer to more senior members of the Indiana congressional delegation. I called Governor Otis "Doc" Bowen to tell him that if he ran, I'd work all-out for him; otherwise, I'd declare my own candidacy. On May 8, 1979, Bowen announced that he wouldn't run, and on May 14, I put myself in the race.

It was a contest I had to win. Indiana's other Senate seat belonged to a Republican, Dick Lugar, and he'd be holding it for a long time. If I gave up my House seat now and lost, I wouldn't have another crack at Bayh until six years later, during which time I'd be forgotten, a footnote to the history of the Fourth Congressional District. So it was make or break, and that attitude made the difference. Although we were just getting settled in Washington and losing would mean another move, Marilyn was all for it.

Of course, Jimmy Carter's being challenged by Ronald Reagan made a difference, too. I attacked the President's gasoline tax while, in front of the cameras, I pumped gas at a filling station. I went into a McDonald's with a chart showing what the hundreds of federal regulations governing the making of a hamburger did to its cost. I argued that we needed a new generation of leadership because Birch Bayh was simply out of touch after eighteen years in Washington. In that time, 399 federal agencies had been created—and never once did he vote against creating one.

Birch Bayh was a vulnerable politician, and he only made himself more so by accepting seven different debates with me. He was a good debater and thought he would chew me up. I can assure you, by the last of them, in South Bend, when I kept hammering him with his liberal voting record, he wished he'd never accepted those invitations. He outspent us by several hundred thousand dollars, but we beat him, 54 percent to 46 percent, with a good grassroots campaign.

I came in with the first Republican Senate majority in a generation, and for the next few years we went about cutting taxes, curtailing regulation, building up our defenses, and effecting what would come to be known as the Reagan Revolution. We had the gavel and we set the agenda. It was easy to be cocky, easy to let success go to your head, and as someone who had come so far so fast I was probably especially vulnerable to the seductions of Washington. But my faith, my family, and my friends kept me centered. I can remember Oregon's Mark Hatfield taking me aside and telling me, when I first arrived, "Look, you're young and you've got a family. Make time for them." If I was smart, he counseled, I wouldn't let the Senate and the Washington party circuit consume me. It was good advice, and I stuck to it. What little I saw of Washington society didn't impress me much in any case. I attended very few Washington dinners or social events unless our children were included. If we'd wanted to, Marilyn and I could have gone out every night, but we rarely did. One of those times was a dinner at the home of Katherine Graham, publisher of the *Washington Post*. I found myself talking to Sally Quinn, the former *Post* reporter and wife of *Post* editor Ben Bradlee. She asked me, "Did you ever think you'd be among so many important people?" It was clear that she considered people like herself—the capital's permanent social and media government—to be the truly important ones in the room. I knew then how right I was to put my family first.

The Senate's hours were notoriously late but I made it home for dinner with Marilyn and the kids whenever I could; often they would hold off having dinner until 8:00 P.M., which is late for young children. When I couldn't make it at all, they sometimes came to the Senate and had dinner with me there. Our children became familiar with many famous faces, and I don't think I'll ever forget the day when Benjamin, who couldn't have been seven, shouted a friendly "Hi, Bob!" to Senator Dole. When Dole was majority leader, Corinne (age seven) even wrote him a note asking if he could possibly arrange things so her dad might get home on the night of her school play in time to see it. He was so tickled with the note that he read it into the record—and fiddled with the schedule. Being a father is not just showing up at home, it's being there for your children when and where they need you. I loved making the time to coach Tucker and Ben in basketball, for example. (I may even have overdone it. After a game, the boys would tell me my comments were too hard on them. When the game was over, they didn't even want to think about it, whereas I'd watch the film clips of it throughout the weekend.)

My two big committee assignments were Armed Services, chaired by John Tower, and the Labor Committee's employment subcommittee, which I got to chair. I saw an opportunity there, since CETA, the 1973 Comprehensive Employment and Training Act, was due to be reauthorized. I'd spoken out against it, often and loudly, as a gross example of mismanagement by the federal government. Now I had a chance, instead of just carping from the conservative sidelines, to help replace it with a federal program that would be cheaper and more efficient because it reflected my philosophy of a limited government. The Job Training Partnership Act (JTPA) would bring business and government into real partnership at the local level and set up performance-based standards that program recipients had to work toward. JTPA was my most comprehensive legislative achievement in the Senate, and it came about through an unlikely alliance I formed with Ted Kennedy, who on this occasion was willing to inject a little pragmatism into his usual big government inclinations. I knew there was no love lost between Ted and Ohio's Howard Metzenbaum, the ranking Democrat, so I did an end run around Metzenbaum and corralled Ted into supporting my bill. I knew our alliance would make news.

It also made some people in the Reagan administration uncomfortable. Ed Meese, then a presidential assistant, actually threatened a veto of the bill. I bluffed him and said that I'd spoken with the President about it and that Reagan seemed to be for it. In fact, I'd only mentioned it in passing, when Reagan called me to make sure of my support for the MX missile; I was pretty sure that until then he'd never really heard of JTPA. When the bill passed and got some good publicity, they decided to sign it—but since they were displeased with the ink and airtime I'd gotten from it, they conveniently had the signing ceremony on a day I was out of town.

The important outcome was the program itself, which over the years has provided millions of Americans with marketable skills and jobs with good wages. JTPA has proven that there's a role for government in the economy, when it can get away from its know-it-all paternalism and constant tendency to micromanage.

In 1986 I had a relatively easy reelection campaign against Jill Long, a Valparaiso councilwoman who today represents my old congressional district. The campaign got help from some early appearances by Vice President George Bush, whom I called shortly after his 1984 reelection to ask if he'd come into Indiana and help raise money for me. He had campaigned for me in 1978 and 1980. This time, when he and Barbara came to Fort Wayne, the biggest city in my old congressional district, we raised the unexpectedly large sum of more than $100,000, even though at the time of the fundraiser that city's mayor, Winfield Moses, was expected to be my Democratic opponent. We did three events in a single evening. Our arrival at Fort Wayne was exciting because Marilyn, the kids, and I rode on *Air Force Two* with the Bushes.

My win in 1986 was so lopsided, and the Reagan–Bush administration soon found itself in such hot water over Iran-contra, that I briefly contemplated making a run for President myself in 1988. I never seriously discussed it with anyone but Marilyn and a few close friends, but none of them opposed the idea. When it became clear, however, that the administration was bouncing back, and that George Bush would be running in 1988, I shelved the idea.

Even so, I was restless throughout 1987. The Republicans had lost their Senate majority, and life in the upper body began to resemble what it had been in the House ten years earlier. We could help the administration only by getting Democrats to support us, and we often fell back into the minority mentality—simple obstructionism. Sam Nunn took over the Armed Services Committee from John Tower, and Ted Kennedy, now that he headed up Labor, was back to proposing the kind of big government, antibusiness solutions I couldn't support.

By 1988 I was ready for lightning to strike. There were plenty of strengths I could bring to a ticket headed by George Bush. The first was generational. Lee Atwater and I had had lengthy discussions about generational politics. The first party to nominate someone from the huge baby-boom voting bloc would help itself capture elections for years to come. The question was which party would go first. Another strength was geographical. As a Texan transplanted from New England, George Bush could only be helped by a Midwesterner, especially since Michael Dukakis had failed to name Ohio's John Glenn as his running mate. Finally, there was ideology. I was a strong champion of conservative causes, especially national defense, and that, too, would be an asset to George Bush, a onetime rival to Ronald Reagan, who, even after eight years as his loyal Vice President, had to contend with the suspicions of some right-wing elements in the party.

The vice-presidency isn't an office you can campaign for—in fact, any demonstration of eagerness for it is more likely to hurt than help—but I had tried, as subtly as I could, to make it clear I was both qualified and available. That spring I started to give more speeches, particularly ones warning about inadequacies in the INF treaty the administration had just concluded with the Soviets. I spoke at a McKinley Day dinner in Congressman Ralph Regula's district in Ohio, after which Ralph wrote George Bush a letter suggesting he should think about me for the number two spot. I made myself more available to the press than usual, and jumped into the debate on plant closings—offering a compromise to the Democrats' insistence on the mandatory notification of workers by business. I suggested a plan for voluntary notification, and one of the people who took notice and thought it a good idea was George Bush.

I kept up these efforts through the summer, and when I met with the Vice President about the defense bill I told him I thought he should try to persuade President Reagan to veto it. I strongly argued that the Democrats had drained it of strategic weaponry and loaded it up with their own prescriptions for arms control. George Bush knew I was serious about these matters, and whenever we spoke I think he was comfortable with the quality of the advice I gave and the manner in which I gave it. On one occasion we spoke at the Vice President's residence. John Tower, Arizona's John McCain, and California's Pete Wilson were among those present. Pete and I were the ones most strongly in favor of a veto. I'd prepared a short paper on national defense, which Bush quickly read and made some favorable comments about. I felt my arguments were persuasive and made a strong impression. Bush had asked me to sit next to him, and I think I was already on his mind as a possible running mate.

So I can't say I was completely surprised when, on the Monday after the Democratic Convention, George Bush called my Senate office. As it happened, I wasn't there to take the call. That summer I was trying to get my children involved in junior golf, and on Monday mornings I'd be on the course at 7:00 A.M., keeping score for them and the other kids. On the morning of July 25, I was out with my nine-year-old daughter, Corinne, and didn't get into the office until about 10:30. As soon as I entered, I could see how excited my longtime secretary, Cynthia Ferneau, appeared to be. "The Vice President has called," she told me. "Not once, but three times." I thought it was still a bit early for him to be making his own vice-presidential choice, and if I were being sounded out in the usual preliminary way, I didn't expect the call to come from him directly. But I didn't waste any time in returning it. I apologized for not being available when he first phoned, and we had a quick, pleasant conversation about a number of things, including defense matters and the Democratic Convention that had just nominated Governor Dukakis and Senator Bentsen.

Then he asked if it would be all right for him to consider me as a running mate. "I'm flattered," I told him, before asking if it would be okay to talk it over with my wife and then sleep on it. He said that was fine, and that I should call him back directly. (Bob Teeter and Bob Kimmitt, his top campaign aides, were coordinating the selection process, but as it went on, I realized that George Bush, old CIA director that he was, had set things up so that he was the only one who ever had all the information at once. Teeter, Lee Atwater, Craig Fuller, Roger Ailes, Bob Mosbacher, Sheila Tate, and Treasury Secretary Nick Brady each gave him three recommendations on paper. Jim Baker presented his suggestions in person.) As soon as I got off the phone, I jotted him a note, apologizing once more for the difficulty he had in reaching me. I told him about the junior golf and that Corinne had shot a power 70 for four holes. (She's since given up the game, but back in 1988 I was convinced she had great potential—she still does but doesn't know it.)

That night I sat at the dinner table with Marilyn and our three children (Tucker was fourteen, Ben was eleven, and Corinne was nine), and we went through the pros and cons of being Vice President. Marilyn and I added up all the pluses I could bring to the ticket: youth, conservative perspective, my Senate record on national security matters, and my role in creating the Job Training Partnership Act and authorizing the Adult Education bill, which included funds for literacy training, a special concern of Barbara Bush's. I would be a bold choice for George Bush—a cautious man by nature—but in the end we realized that this reach across the generations made political sense.

But did I *want* to do it? Marilyn asked me. I knew the answer was yes. I had a coherent, conservative vision of the country's course, both domestically and in foreign affairs, and the necessary experience—four years in the House and eight in the Senate—to take over the presidency if the need arose. I admired George Bush and knew I could serve him well. If we won, my ideas would be heard in the Oval Office and I would do my best to change things.

All of this was true, but I don't mean to say that personal ambition was absent from my thinking. It wasn't. When you're in the Senate, there are only two more elective places to go: the presidency and the vice-presidency. People have always joked about the latter ("not worth a pitcher of warm spit," according to Franklin Roosevelt's first Veep, John Nance Garner), but I know that almost every Senator wants it, even those who publicly express reluctance to be considered. It remains the most likely route to the presidency, and the idea that ambitious politicians scorn the office is a myth. They don't turn it down. They may say no in advance, but only if they know it won't be offered. When it *is* offered, they take it. There are very few people who really want to stay in the Senate decade after decade. The truth is that the level of job satisfaction and the quality of life there are dwindling. Under George Mitchell it's a much more partisan place than it was under majority leaders like Mike Mansfield and Howard Baker. Collegiality is not what it once was. The hours and scheduling—voting on nickel-and-dime amendments at midnight—make less and less sense as the years go by. Senators spend more time harassing one another with amendments and parliamentary dodges than they do in honest compromise or genuine debate. Campaigns are longer, nastier, and more expensive than ever before, and the battles over nominations like those of John Tower, Robert Bork, and Clarence Thomas are much more bloody and partisan than they used to be. For all the prestige associated with "the club," more and more of its best members (people like Jack Danforth from Missouri) are trying to make graceful exits. I won't say I had reached that level of frustration, but in the summer of 1988 I was young and ambitious and felt I had plenty to offer my party and country.

My kids may have had their doubts. Corinne—perhaps with an intuition of what lay ahead—said she hoped it would be Bob Dole. Tucker tried to ignore most of the talk. And Ben said he didn't think George Bush would pick me, because I was "not even a famous Senator." He was right about that, but a fresh face might be one of the qualities Bush was looking for. Marilyn and I had thought of that too, and by the time we were through with our family dinner, I'd decided I would call George Bush in the morning and tell him that I would be delighted to be considered.

When I did, he asked me to keep all this confidential. I asked who would be handling the process, and he told me I'd be dealing mostly with Bob Kimmitt, a West Point graduate and Vietnam veteran whose father had been the Secretary of the Senate. Bob had grown up around politics, and he'd be the one going over my record, my finances, my personal life—doing the sort of scrutiny that became the norm after the Eagleton fiasco back in 1972. At this point I could hardly be sure I'd be the one to get it, but I knew Bush's consideration had to be serious. For one thing, he didn't owe me anything. I'd remained neutral during his recent campaign against Dole. (With Indiana's late primary, we're not a much sought-after state in any case.)

During this background check, I worried a little about a college arrest for underage drinking, which I made sure to tell Kimmitt, and I became somewhat nervous about how my grandfather's wealth might be perceived. The investigation is designed to avoid "gotcha" journalism, which these days blows up any minor, long-ago mistake into a potential catastrophe. Because of all the new scrutiny, the kind of quality people who even twenty years ago were willing to enter politics no longer do. They simply won't put up with all the invasions of their privacy.

I kept my word when it came to secrecy. I never acknowledged to friends and colleagues that I was under consideration, but of course this was a period when any political conversation eventually turned to the question of whom George Bush might pick as a running mate. People commented that the *perception* I was being considered, even if I wasn't finally picked, could only be good for my career. Had I not been hemmed in by my promise of confidentiality, I would still have wanted to "low-ball" it with them. After all, not getting it would be a setback if I looked as if I was trying hard to be picked.

Most of the people I talked to seemed pretty sure that in the end Dole would be chosen, but one who didn't was New Hampshire's Warren Rudman, who had been an important Dole supporter during the primaries. He was well respected in the Senate. Candid, outspoken, a bit of a know-it-all, he came up to me during this period and said he was convinced that for several reasons George Bush was going to pick me. I downplayed it, of course ("*Oh, well, Warren . . .* "), because I didn't want to raise expectations. I knew that as soon as I raised my head, somebody would start shooting. I wanted to be a little bit under the water, with just a snorkel sticking up. Let the focus be on Dole, or Kemp; the more time there was to focus on *their* negatives, the better for me.

I instructed my staff not to do any talking; lie low and let these other guys get the publicity. They went along with me, but some of them were almost apoplectic. They wanted to rush out with the rumors. If he does get it, they thought, that will be terrific; but if he doesn't, we need to take advantage of this *now*, because it will be great for building his career. This was, after all, a golden opportunity to get me on television and call the press in. But I told them they just couldn't treat this as an image-builder or reputation-enhancer. There was too good a chance I'd get the job, and I wanted nothing to put that opportunity in jeopardy.

The weekend before the start of our convention was the first time that I received serious press attention. That Saturday Marilyn and the kids and I were in Indiana for a Hoosier History Days celebration of Lincoln's boyhood. (That's right. I never tire of reminding Illinois friends that Lincoln spent his truly formative years across the border in Indiana.) I could feel things building a day or two before, when I'd been in Huntington and Indianapolis, and then on Saturday the *New York Times* ran an article saying that I was one of six candidates on the short list, and that "surprisingly strong support" had emerged for me. The media interpreted this article by Gerald Boyd as a leak from Baker's people that Quayle was under consideration, and that anyone with objections should come forward now. Baker wasn't trying to shoot down my candidacy (if he'd wanted to kill the nomination he could have gone directly to his friend George Bush and insisted); he was trying to test the appeal of my candidacy. I actually welcomed this. In fact, I wish the story had come a week earlier. If it had, some of the chaos in New Orleans might have been avoided.

We were staying at Marilyn's brother and sister-in-law's, on their fold-out couch, and that night I put in a call to Jim Baker about the *Times* article. He said, "Yeah, I don't know who leaked that," and I told him I wasn't really calling about that. I just wanted to let him know that if it was going to be me, I hoped things were being taken care of. He had to remember that I didn't have a big staff, that I hadn't been in a national campaign nor dealt with the national press. And he said to me—I'll never forget it—"Don't worry. We've got the best staff available for whomever the Vice President chooses to be his running mate." He mentioned Stu Spencer, a California campaign consultant, and assured me that he would be able to take care of everything no matter who was picked. "So just don't worry about it," he said. And I replied, "Okay, fine."

I had another phone conversation that night. George Will called and asked me to appear the following morning on "This Week with David Brinkley." In keeping with my low-profile strategy, I didn't really want to do it, but he told me that both Dole and Kemp were going to be on, so I wound up making a spur-of-the-moment decision to appear, on a live hook-up from Evansville. I decided I had earned the right to take one shot on my own behalf, and I was glad I did. I was later told that neither Dole nor Kemp—both of whom had run against Bush in the primaries—came off that well. On the program I stressed my understanding of how a vice-presidential candidate had to conduct his campaign at the direction of the top man on the ticket. I later learned that Bob Kimmitt showed Bush a tape of the show, and I'm sure it was a factor that helped to make up his mind. I'm confident this became part of the mix of things he was considering. So I had reason to be grateful for that crucial phone call from George Will—as I would for another one a couple of months later.

Marilyn's Aunt Janet came down to Evansville to fly back to Washington with the children while Marilyn and I left for New Orleans. Before coming out to Indiana, Marilyn had made sure the kids would be ready to join us at the convention if I was picked. She'd left behind packed suitcases for them, just in case. And, since we might find ourselves thrust into a campaign, with no time for anything else for the next two and a half months, she'd already done all of their school shopping.

We arrived in New Orleans to the same terrific local welcome the convention organizers arranged for each arriving delegation—greeters and a jazz band playing when you got off the plane. We went to a dinner that first night hosted by *Washington Post* editor Meg Greenfield and George Will. Kay Graham was there, along with David Broder. The *Post* people were hoping to have the next Vice President there, and some of those still being mentioned (like Arizona's John McCain and New Mexico's Pete Domenici) attended. During the next two days Marilyn and I made the rounds of some state delegations, and I talked to some of the newsmagazines. I can remember just feeling the momentum continuing to break in my direction. Dole had gone out of his way to say he found the selection process demeaning, and while he had not exactly withdrawn his name, he hadn't helped his prospects.

Bob Dole is a complicated man. He's in constant motion. Like many Senators, he gets his information from briefings rather than reading. The Senate totally consumes his life, and his relaxation is campaigning. He is a smart political pro who is not driven by ideology. The media dwells on his toughness but he has an emotional side too. I've seen Bob Dole, who was scarred by battle in World War II, fight back tears during an after-dinner speech when he talked about George Bush's wartime experience.

By Monday night I was feeling more and more confident that I would be the choice. Diane Sawyer and Joe Peyronnin, a CBS executive, came around asking me how I felt. "On the end of your fingertips, do you think it's going to be you?" Sawyer asked playfully. The truth is I did, but there was no way I could tell her. On Tuesday morning Bob Kimmitt came around to our hotel room with one final set of questions, and I figured that it was going to be me. By that point there wouldn't have been time to make one last check with everyone. But I still didn't know for sure, and the suspense was beginning to build. Marilyn and I were both beginning to pace the floor, so we went out to Sammy's—and you already know about the next few hours.

Since the media didn't know of my month-long discussions with the Bush campaign, they were surprised by my selection. I wasn't. My name had only been floating around in the national papers and on TV for about seventy-two hours, and it was never out there alone. That was partly because I had done my best to play by George Bush's rules of secrecy and my own political instincts. I don't think I'd have been picked if I'd played it otherwise and encouraged all the speculation. But in the years since, I've sometimes wished that my name *had* been out there more conspicuously in those two or three weeks before the convention. If I had had some really serious scrutiny by the press, if I had taken off the snorkel and emerged above the water line, I might have avoided some of what followed. By Tuesday night I was beginning to realize just how far from shore I was—and to notice the pack of very hungry sharks heading my way.

3 | Feeding Frenzy

We left Spanish Plaza with George and Barbara Bush. Back in their hotel suite, we met their family and some of the campaign people. We were pumped up, excited—too excited to do much substantive planning. The main piece of business, I learned, was that Baker wanted Bush and me to have a joint news conference the next morning, and that seemed fine, routine.

Very swiftly, in a way that was hard to notice—much less combat—I was being cocooned, shut off from the political and personal life I'd always known. Marilyn and I were soon moved to a different hotel, away from our own staff, and turned over to a whole new cast of operatives provided by the Bush campaign. I kidded Marilyn that our lunch at Sammy's was the last meal we were ever going to have without a bunch of people around, a light remark that proved only too prophetic. Back in Huntington, the press had descended on my parents. Dozens of reporters filled their house on a sweltering day. My dad kept his sport coat on despite the heat: though he's a proud Marine who served in World War II, he was afraid that the big bulldog tattoo on his forearm might somehow embarrass me. I wish he'd let them see it—it might have helped people realize we were a little more down to earth than the press were saying.

That night Marilyn and I went to dinner with Stu Spencer and Joe Canzeri, who from then on were to be in charge of our campaign. They were, in political slang, our "handlers." Spencer was a campaign consultant from California, and Canzeri was a public relations guy out of Washington. Both were old friends of the

Reagans (Spencer had been involved in Ronald Reagan's gubernatorial campaigns twenty years earlier) and they were placed with
us as a diplomatic favor to the Reagans. They were in this for the
short haul and were pretty much indifferent to our personal interests. They were really Rockefeller people who had gone to work
for Reagan without being Reaganites. They had no ideology and
could probably have worked for Democrats as well as Republicans. In this one respect they were like David Gergen, who started
out working for Nixon, later worked for Ford, and after that for
Reagan—and now works for Clinton. These people make up a
part of politics I don't enjoy. Their loyalty is to themselves, the
media they leak to, and the insider lobbyists who through their
financial clout have extraordinary access. They are only interested
in self-promotion and proximity to power.

It was unfortunate that I didn't feel in any position to complain
about Spencer and Canzeri. I owed my place on the ticket entirely
to George Bush, and if these were the people his campaign had
chosen, then I would make the best of it. My belief in Bush, my
certainty that we could turn the polls around and win in November, was what counted. My campaign—as I'd said Sunday on the
Brinkley show—would be completely subordinate to his; and, in
any case, how much could go wrong with it? In my past campaigns, I hadn't needed a lot of high-powered help. In 1976 a volunteer housewife ran my operation, and four years later the
Republican Senate campaign committee was annoyed that I
didn't hire an outside political consultant in my uphill race
against Birch Bayh.

Even on that first night, there were indications of just how
much could go wrong. If you listened to the television reporters,
you must have thought I was personally "worth" $650 million.
What was lost in this exaggeration of the fortune my grandfather
made in the newspaper business was that he believed in people
having to earn their own living. He knew the dangers of inherited
wealth. My parents made their own way through the middle class,
and I attended public schools. My dad became sick with lupus
when I was growing up, and he was in and out of hospitals for
two years. I can remember my mother, when I was about ten or
eleven, telling me that I was now "the man of the house." I

changed a lot of diapers and helped my mother through some very difficult times. I had jobs throughout college and law school. I've always lived off my salary and paid a mortgage. After both my mother and stepgrandmother die, I will receive some income from a small portion of the trust my grandfather set up, but the principal won't be distributed to his heirs for nearly a hundred years. I don't think of myself as wealthy, because I'm not. My total income was my Senate salary plus about $10,000 in interest and dividends. My net worth in 1988, including my house, was $854,000, a tiny fraction of Lloyd Bentsen's, but you would have had a hard time figuring that out from all the stories about the "$600-million man." The press could have gone to the financial disclosure forms from my twelve years in the House and Senate. Instead, the first bricks in my caricature were quickly being laid, and the Bush campaign—from both a feeling that these stories weren't important and an old-style Republican disdain for talking about money—never fought the stereotype very hard. (After I became Vice President and by law subject to IRS tax audits, Marilyn and I wondered what was taking the auditors so long. My lawyer told us that, because of all the press stories, they couldn't believe we weren't hiding income.)

The networks and newspapers did run some flattering comments about my selection—mostly from conservative foreign policy specialists like Jeane Kirkpatrick and Richard Perle. But the question of my wealth and my "lightweight" status was dominating the coverage. (The assertion by a couple of Republican strategists that my supposed "good looks" played well with female voters was dumb and condescending, and didn't help matters.) There was a hostile edge to the coverage, and some of that may have sprung from the fact that the press had been caught off guard. I wasn't the choice they were expecting, and some of them sounded as if George Bush had let them down by not picking one of the people they were prepared to talk about in detail.

I didn't sleep at all that first night, not because of any of this— the real firestorm had yet to begin—but from a pinched nerve in my shoulder that I'd gotten playing tennis the week before. Weeks would pass before I got rid of it, and on that Tuesday night it was killing me. When I got up on Wednesday, I was exhausted, and I had no idea just how rough a day it would turn out to be.

That morning I went to George Bush's hotel, and up in his suite, the two of us sat on a couch while Jim Baker and others went over questions that might come up at the joint press conference we were about to hold. Over the next four years, I would learn that George Bush generally called big meetings, but I was surprised by the number of people at this one (there may have been twenty) and by the chaotic atmosphere. I remember Baker asking me, "You served in the National Guard?" and my telling him yes. But the subject was just left hanging in the air. There was no follow-up, no anticipation of questions that might arise from it. Maybe this was because we all believed what I still believe: that my service in the Indiana National Guard was honorable. No strings were pulled on my behalf to get in. In retrospect, I realize that I was naive (as were my handlers) not to assume that, in the heat of a presidential campaign, somebody might try to twist all this into something sinister.

Most of the mock questions were for Bush. Somebody even managed to anticipate one being asked about how he'd recently called the grandchildren born to his Hispanic daughter-in-law "the little brown ones." This throwaway remark was made with obvious affection and pride (there is no more attentive grandfather in the world than George Bush) but in these crazy, hypersensitive times, the campaign people thought somebody might try to make a "gaffe" or even an "issue" out of it. As expected, it came up—to be batted away by George Bush, whose disgust for whatever the questioner was trying to imply was so obvious that no one dared take the matter any further.

I would have plenty of chances over the next four years to see how some innocent phrasing could turn into a week of press stories, and I was about to get my first taste of that now. Sure enough, my military service came up, and I was asked if I didn't now regret having joined the Guard instead of going to Vietnam. I replied: "I did not know in 1969 that I would be in this room today, I'll confess." What I meant was that I hadn't been especially reflective about that decision back then—I just pursued an option that was available to me. I didn't view the decision in the larger historical context, as the media seemed to think I should have. Unfortunately my answer seemed to imply that, if I'd been more politically calculating at the time, I would have made a different decision. I sounded vaguely apologetic about my service with the Guard, and that is absolutely the last thing I felt then or feel today. I also sounded as if I had joined the Guard to escape the war.

The fact is, yes, I knew, like everyone else, that by joining the Guard I was less likely to go to Vietnam. Having just graduated from college, I wanted to go to law school, and I knew I could do that while I served here at home. But when I joined the Guard I was also fully aware that my unit could be called up and sent overseas. Company D, the most highly decorated Army unit in Vietnam, happens to have been a National Guard Unit from Muncie, Indiana. If my own outfit had been summoned (and Marilyn and I both knew this was a possibility), I would have gone and served, proudly. In the end, my unit wasn't called, but I did complete a total of six years' service and fulfilled every obligation—without ever thinking, until August 17, 1988, that there were some people who thought I should feel this service was less than honorable, that there was some sort of taint to it. I never felt that, and I don't now.

I do take some blame for being no better prepared for this question than the campaign people were. Jim Baker and his colleagues could certainly have made a lot more positive information about me and my Senate record available to the reporters at the press conference—Kimmitt had brought to New Orleans bundles of papers on me. He wanted to do a thorough grilling, not a quick prep, before any press conference, and he wanted to distribute lots of clips to the media. But Baker didn't seem interested in any of this, and as a result, I think the reporters got fed more background information by the Democrats' Bob Squier than by our own people. (Squier was seeking political revenge because he was the media consultant to Birch Bayh, whom I had defeated in 1980.) I still don't know why Jim Baker didn't pay more attention to Kimmitt, who had worked with him at Treasury and would go on to become a top official with Baker at State. Among other things, Bob was a Vietnam vet, and would have had interesting, credible ideas about how to deal with the Guard issue.

But I could have been more savvy myself. After all, this was the first time anyone of my generation would be on a national ticket, and we all should have anticipated that Vietnam, a key shaping experience for those in their forties, was going to be an issue. Four years later, Bill Clinton would be hammered over his draft record, and a lot of comparisons would be made between his situation and mine. I resented them, because there's not much of a parallel. Clinton, who during his college years wrote a letter admitting that he "loathed the military," sought every way to get out of serving; I did not. I did not base my choices on some hypothetical future political career, whereas he did. As his letters home from Oxford show, with their references to future "political viability," Clinton clearly *was* thinking about standing before a press conference twenty years later. And when he did, and was finally called upon to explain his actions, he was evasive; I was not.

The implication of the Vietnam question was: "Quayle's hypocritical. He supported the Vietnam War, but he joined the National Guard—a cop-out." Wrong on both counts. National Guard service is never a cop-out, and in 1969 almost *nobody* supported the war, myself included. Like many in my generation, I supported the goal of preventing a communist military takeover in Southeast Asia, but I became opposed to the way the war was being conducted by the Johnson administration. I can remember in the fall of 1968, when I was a senior at DePauw, and John Scali, the UN ambassador and ABC commentator, came to speak. Compared to other campuses in the late sixties, DePauw wasn't a politically active school but Scali drew a big crowd, and I managed to be the first one recognized during the question-and-answer session. My question was this: "Who will get us out of Vietnam sooner, Richard Nixon or Hubert Humphrey?" And to the chagrin of my liberal friends, Scali said Nixon—because Nixon would come in fresh, with clean hands, and be able to turn away from Johnson's policies in a way that Humphrey might not be comfortable doing. We went out that night and had a long discussion about the war and the election, and I kept pushing the case that college students ought to get behind Nixon, who would honorably end the war sooner than the Democrats could. But twenty years later, the essence of the press conference was that I had "evaded service," whereas in fact I served six years in the National Guard.

The media brought up other subjects, too, of course. Questions were raised about my academic record at DePauw and then in law school. It wasn't stellar at either, but it certainly wasn't embarrassing. There were numerous rumors about failure and plagiarism—all of them subsequently disproved—but I refused to release my transcripts. I thought that they were irrelevant and that being asked to release them was demeaning, since no other candidate was being asked to do so.

Quite frankly, I didn't think the press conference went that badly. And nobody else I was around did either. On the way out, Senator Phil Gramm of Texas shook my hand and said, "You did a damn fine job." Back upstairs in George Bush's suite, Roger Ailes also complimented me. Bush turned to me and asked how I felt about it, and I said fine. He said he was pleased, too. Marilyn had watched it on television with Joe Canzeri, and neither of them saw any problems. There was a sense of relief, in fact. After all, vice-presidential nominees, who tend to come upon the national scene in a sudden burst, frequently run into a buzzsaw: think of Nixon in 1952, Eagleton in 1972, Ferraro in 1984. The Spanish Plaza introduction and the press conference hadn't been especially elegant affairs, but there had been nothing terribly wrong with them either. We thought we had come through twenty-four hours of chaos and that the focus would now return to the place it ought to be—the top of the ticket, and to the speculation about whether George Bush would give "the speech of his life," finally emerging from the giant shadow of Ronald Reagan and catching up with Michael Dukakis in the polls.

That afternoon we made an appearance before the California delegation, and then Marilyn and I had dinner with our children and my parents, all of whom by now had arrived in New Orleans. The family, who were not watching all that much television, were still pretty high with excitement. After dinner, my main duty was to tour the four network anchor booths in the convention Superdome. Sophisticated observers like Mark Shields—a political columnist with strong Democratic ties—told me years later that he could see I hadn't prepared myself for the inevitable tough questions that would come my way. Once more some careless phrasing made my troubles worse. Tom Brokaw asked me about how I'd enlisted in the Guard, and I said that some "phone calls were made." Well, that's true: I was talking about phone calls made in search of information about openings, not phone calls made to use "influence," which is how the remark was interpreted. Soon things would be much worse; the issue of favoritism had arisen, and even my Republican Senate colleague, John McCain, a POW during the Vietnam War, was saying that if such charges were true, he would be disturbed by them. They were *not* true, but late that night I realized just how far out of control this whole thing was getting. I also noticed I was not recovering the way I should have. Years later, David Broder would tell me that even some of my Republican colleagues were beginning to say this nomination would not fly.

At this point I was still more puzzled than angry, and I had no real idea of the growing panic within the Bush campaign. I was isolated; I noticed that even some GOP friends here in New Orleans hadn't called. Maybe they couldn't get through, or maybe they just didn't know what to say.

I needed sleep, but I wasn't going to get much more this night than last. Sometime after midnight, Joe Canzeri came knocking on my door. He told me I had to take a phone call. I said I was tired, but he wasn't going to take no for an answer. It was Jim Baker calling, and it was an emergency. "Now what?" I thought, on my way to the phone. "Look," said Baker, "there's a total meltdown on this National Guard thing. It's absolutely coming unglued. We've got to talk to you. I'm sending over Kimmitt and Darman."

And that's just what he did, in the middle of the night. Dick Darman, who would become President Bush's director of OMB (Office of Management and Budget), took charge of this crazy, groggy grilling. Poor Bob Kimmitt, who'd had the job of vetting the backgrounds of all the VP choices on the short list, was starting to take on some heavy water, and he looked about as uncomfortable as I did. It was obvious what Baker and the others had been asking him: Why didn't you know about this? Why didn't you check this thing out?

It was now imperative that we know every detail about a routine National Guard enlistment from nineteen years ago. So my dad was awakened, too, and brought to help piece together the story. This was no easy matter. In fact, four years later, when Bill Clinton's draft record became an issue, this was the one facet of his experience with which I could sympathize: the way the press expected him to recall a chain of events, every phone call and piece of correspondence, from a period decades earlier.

The basic story of my enlistment is this. In 1969, President Nixon ended draft deferments for graduate students, so that spring I talked to several people about National Guard openings in Indianapolis (where I would be going to law school). I was told of three: one at Stout Field, another in the 38th Division, and another one somewhere else. Through my family I'd come to know Wendell Phillippi, who'd once been a general in the Guard. For years, Phillippi had acted as a first screener of Guard candidates; any number of people in my generation from the north side of Indianapolis had people call him up to inquire on their behalf. It's what today we might call "networking." Far from trying to secure some special treatment for myself, I told other DePauw students that they, too, should call Phillippi to see if there were openings. If he looked you over and thought you were a good possibility for a slot that existed, then you would likely get in; if he didn't think you were up to snuff, you wouldn't. But he was the man you went to, and he advised me to go see Colonel Alfred F. Ahner, which I did. There was an opening, and on May 19, 1969, I joined the HHD (Headquarters and Headquarters Detachment) unit in Indianapolis.

The bottom line: Wendell Phillippi, as he would himself confirm, did nothing out of the ordinary. He was performing a public service by sending qualified recruits to the Guard's attention. And Colonel Ahner would tell people, during the campaign and afterwards, that there was indeed an opening and that I didn't jump ahead of anybody to get it.

Checking this out and piecing it together took some time, and on Wednesday night—or I should say Thursday morning—those of us in my hotel room decided we would say nothing until we had the whole story. In fact, I said no more about "the issue" until the weekend. I managed to get just three hours' sleep before I had to get ready for the last day of the convention.

There was a big luncheon rally scheduled. The Bush and Quayle families were making their grand entrance, but I can remember Sam Donaldson charging across the hall like a Santa Ana wind, trying to fan the flames that were engulfing me. "Are you going to get off the ticket? Are you going to get off the ticket?" He was more or less screaming, hysterical, and I can remember Barbara Bush turning to her husband and saying, serenely, "Gee, I've never seen Sam so exercised." I didn't know Sam that well. He's a bit of a loudmouth, but he can be charming enough in a social setting. Right then I was just mentally trying to block out his braying.

Anyway, that was the buzz in the room: that I might be forced off the ticket. The media frenzy was reaching its peak, but we remained determined to say nothing more. I was just going to get through my own speech and try to bring the focus back to George Bush. For the rest of the day, everywhere I went, no matter how big the press pack pursuing me, I said the same thing: "I'll be willing to answer questions about the National Guard or anything else beginning tomorrow, but tonight we're going to nominate George Bush as our presidential candidate, and I wish you'd extend him the courtesy of covering what he has to say." They would shout and scream for something more, but I insisted that I'd have nothing—except for my own speech—until tomorrow. On our way into the Superdome for a rehearsal at the podium, some of our advance people actually had to push some reporters out of the way in order to get through. I can remember that Canzeri proudly made a gross remark about where he'd managed to elbow Connie Chung, so in the middle of everything else I'm thinking, Geez, this is the guy they give me for staff.

My main anxiety was that I might really be hurting George Bush. More than anything I wanted that not to be the case, and when the evening came around and I was getting ready to go on, I knew that this was one of the most crucial moments of my life. I was not unseasoned in political drama. I'd had make-or-break debates with my opponents in 1976 and 1980; I'd addressed the national convention in Detroit eight years before. But I couldn't pretend I'd ever been through anything like this. I tried to eat, but couldn't. So I just drank water and paced the floor and talked a little bit to Marilyn. We tried to cheer up the kids, but they were as upset as everyone else, my parents included.

Jim Baker was in the ABC booth. As I was coming into the hall, he pulled out a piece of paper and told the eagerly attentive correspondents, almost verbatim, what I was going to say to the reporters gathered to ask me questions. The intended effect was to show them that he was in charge of me. Baker wanted to signal to the media that I was not really his choice, and that he was making the best of a bad situation. He was putting himself in a win-win position. If I sank the ticket, it was somebody else's fault, not Baker's. If I didn't, it was because Baker had taken charge of me. Years later, Dan Rather confirmed to me that Baker's demeanor in answering questions (as well as off-the-record comments by some of his people) seemed to indicate that he wasn't comfortable with my selection and that he was trying to distance himself from it.

This was presidential politics, a high-stakes, sometimes vicious game, and I reached that podium knowing there were countless people, not just in the press but in the public at large, who wanted to see me crumble right in front of them. But I also knew there were just as many who were rooting for me, who had faith in me, chief among them George Bush. So I got up there and—drawing strength from my faith and the sight of my family—I accepted my party's nomination to be the forty-fourth Vice President of the United States. And I accepted it with pride. I was proud to be running with George Bush, proud to be running on our platform, and proud, as I made a point of saying to thunderous cheers, to have been a member of the Indiana National Guard.

The newspeople conceded that I'd done all right. Dan Rather said that "whatever you think of the nomination . . . this young fellow gave a good speech." David Brinkley was even more generous, and I tried to hope that things might now be on the upswing, that a reaction might be setting in against the excesses of the press, which were visible to anyone who'd seen the television people chasing my every step all day.

George Bush made a terrific speech. "Read my lips" may have been the best sound bite, but its whole theme, about his being a man who saw his life in terms of missions and duty, was moving and true. I was determined to be worthy of his confidence—determined to leave New Orleans with my head held high. I was ready to get on with the campaign, which sure enough was already turning around. The first polls after the convention showed that we had wiped out Dukakis's lead and were already pulling ahead. George Bush had gotten exactly the convention "bounce" every presidential candidate hopes for.

What I didn't realize was that I was still in free fall.

4 | The Battle of Huntington

Indiana's great basketball coach, Bobby Knight, used to say that the best offense can never beat a really good defense. But this doesn't apply to politics. Staying on the offense, and not allowing anyone else to set the agenda—not your opponents, not the media—is absolutely crucial to winning. It's something Ronald Reagan understood, and something, as I'll show later on, that the Bush administration eventually forgot. Before the summer of 1988, I thought I had the offense principle down cold. Certainly no one could accuse me of being timid in my races to unseat Congressman Ed Roush in 1976 or Senator Birch Bayh in 1980. In fact, those who came to know me only after my selection as the vice-presidential nominee were sometimes stunned by video clips of my debates with Bayh from eight years earlier. During those contests I displayed an aggressiveness—a good offense—that I later exhibited too seldom.

By the time Marilyn and I left New Orleans, I was finding it difficult to trust myself. Scores of reporters were frenetically digging into my personal past back in Indiana, and I had become a gold mine for editorial cartoonists and the late-night comics. The press had gone into a "feeding frenzy," as the title of Larry J. Sabato's later book on "attack journalism" referred to it. In fact, Sabato called my experience a "megafrenzy" and noted that a number of important journalists later acknowledged the media's excesses. "Our pursuit of Quayle was relentless," Peter Jennings would say, "and our demeanor was terrible." The *Washington Post*'s Richard Harwood eventually declared that "the Quayle matters were pursued almost irrationally; the coverage was based on presumptions and perceptions more than a solid foundation of real information." In the days after the convention the media were out for blood—mine. I was reduced to a defensive crouch.

On Friday, August 19, we traveled with George and Barbara Bush to my hometown of Huntington, Indiana. I was looking forward to the big rally my friends and neighbors had planned to welcome back a local boy made good. It was just the kind of emotional support I needed. I looked out upon the twelve thousand people gathered near the steps of the town's courthouse and felt profoundly grateful. They were a kind of reality check: these people, who had four times elected me to office, knew the kind of man I was, and the kind of record I had. They knew I was not the pampered peabrain the media had been making me out to be for the past seventy-two hours. During those three days of the convention, these folks had been watching that caricature grow, in print and on their television screens, and they were angry. Just how angry would soon become apparent.

The campaign was now finally telling a coherent story about my enlistment in the Guard, and it was based on the simple truth. "I got into the National Guard fairly," I told the reporters who came to Huntington with us. "I did not ask anybody to break the rules, and as far as I know, nobody did break the rules." I said I resented the insinuations against not only my patriotism but the patriotism of all the men and women who'd served in the Guard with me. That morning I'd even tried mocking the media's charges by picking up on a TV comic's recommendation that I try a little humor. I recited my name, rank, and serial number—a joke that fell absolutely flat. I recognized that I was no Johnny Carson, and I dropped the act.

I didn't need sarcasm anyway. On Friday afternoon in Huntington, the press was booed getting off the bus. George Bush and I then delivered our stump speeches to a wildly enthusiastic crowd. After that my much anticipated press conference began. Some in the media wanted to go for the kill and their questions grew more combative. The harder they pushed, the madder the crowd got. I was standing on a hill on the courthouse square, positioned so precariously that one of the Secret Service men had to hold onto me. The campaign people decided to crank up the microphones so the crowd would hear all of the give-and-take between me and the press. We wanted to create a little healthy antagonism, to force the press to recognize that not everyone was buying into the media-created image.

The little skirmish we were hoping for turned into a battle royal. The press's questions were often outrageous. Ellen Hume of the *Wall Street Journal,* for example, screamed at me, wanting to know how I had felt when "people were dying in Vietnam while [I was] writing press releases" (one of my desk duties in the Guard). This absurdity was answered by angry shouts and name-calling from the crowd, who followed my own replies with deafening cheers. It continued on like this, a wild scene.

I loved every minute of it. For three days I'd been a punching bag, and suddenly I had twelve thousand troops punching back on my behalf. Three years later, when I returned to those court-house steps with Marilyn and our children to make a Fourth of July speech, the town unveiled a plaque commemorating the "bat-tle"—an event that's become part of Huntington folklore. But even as it was raging on that August afternoon in 1988, I knew there would be some bad consequences. The press—which as a profes-sion has at least as much vanity as politicians—was furious. They had *arrived* in town with bad feelings. After I left office, ABC's Brit Hume, who was on the press bus that day, told me he had heard some of his colleagues make ugly personal attacks, of a kind he had never really heard before, against both me and Bush. Now they thought they'd been had, and they were determined not to let us use them like this. So with the real campaign getting under way, they had a reason to stay hostile toward us, a reason to stick with their caricature and to make the antagonism personal. Len Downie, the *Washington Post*'s executive editor, told me years later that the media's "searing" experience in Huntington was one factor keeping them closed-minded about me during the years of my vice-presidency. They were not used to feeling the public's scorn.

I didn't have much chance to be reflective in those days of cri-sis, but six years later, I think it's important to consider why the press was so dead set against me from the start, and why that feeding frenzy continued—even after they'd found nothing scandalous to feed on. Part of the reason was simple liberal bias. The press corps remains overwhelmingly liberal, and they were hardly going to be well-disposed toward a vice-presidential nominee further to the right than a presidential candidate already too conservative for their tastes. But there was something else, something new, going on in 1988.

I was the first of my generation—the much written about baby-boomers—to be on a national ticket, which meant I was part of the same generation as a huge portion of the working press, including the men and women standing in front of their cameras and portable tape recorders that afternoon in Huntington. From their point of view, we shared age and nothing else. I was conservative and had never subscribed to the radical views of the sixties which many of them so cherished.

The media felt more comfortable with liberal candidates (like Bill Clinton in 1992) with whom they could identify. They could tolerate conservatives like George Bush or Ronald Reagan who reminded them of their fathers, but they couldn't abide a conservative of their own age who might occupy the White House and dominate the national scene for years to come.

Michael Barone has told me that the media "couldn't stand the fact that the first baby boomer wasn't a Doonesbury generation figure." I was *not one of them*, Chris Matthews, the Washington correspondent of the *San Francisco Examiner*, explained to me. I wasn't, from their standpoint, politically correct. Having the first national candidate from their generation be so alien led them to create a caricature full of elements they loved to hate or mock: I was the wealthy, lucky, good-looking WASP, an avid golfer who'd never done any harder work than cashing his trust fund checks at the bank. To Ellen Goodman of the *Boston Globe* I was "The Pretty Face: Danny Quayle, Young and Handsome, conservative and cute, right-winged and blue-eyed," a cross between Vanna White and the William Hurt character in *Broadcast News*. This is the same Ellen Goodman who referred to Senator Paul Tsongas as "the former male Senator" and when mentioning a blunder wrote "gaff" (no *e*, imagine that). The truth of this cartoon—just about none—didn't matter. It was the way the media felt I somehow *ought* to be. They loved my upper-class-sounding names (J. Danforth). Dukakis would emphasize it whenever he mentioned me, obscuring the fact that everybody has always called me Dan and, more important, that I was given my name, James Danforth, in memory of my dad's dearest friend, who was killed in World War II. (George Bush did a nice job pointing out this inconvenient fact during one of the debates.) Some reporters (especially Dan Rather) and some printed press accounts (as late as 1992!) would refer to me as J. Danforth Quayle *III*, I suppose because I seemed to them the sort of man who *ought* to carry a numeral after his surname. A *New York Times* reporter assigned to me in 1992 added the numeral—the same reporter who told me he was an admirer of Mario Cuomo and could provide me with a private channel of communication to him.

The media did not know me, and since they didn't, I had no business running for Vice President of the United States. Perhaps I should have made more attempts to get to know the national media while I was in the Senate. Many Senators do that; they arrive in the capital and begin taking members of the national press out to dinner, having them over to their homes and so forth. There's nothing wrong with that, but it just never appealed to me. One reporter said I had the "Joe Biden problem," referring to the way the Delaware Senator commuted home on Amtrak every night. My life after hours was reserved for my family. If I wasn't doing Senate work, I was home with my wife and kids. I just didn't make much effort with the press. If I had, things might have been smoother in 1988. But once I was thrown into the national glare, it was too late. The media quickly invested so much in their caricature of me that not even personal acquaintance could modify it.

I mean "invested" literally. Today, working journalists write their supposedly objective stories during the week. When the weekend comes, they supplement their incomes by appearing on the political talk shows, where they're encouraged to present their opinions with as sharp an edge as possible. (Think of Eleanor Clift, of *Newsweek* and "The McLaughlin Group," or Al Hunt, of the *Wall Street Journal* and "The Capital Gang.") Then these same people, who always complain about legislators taking honoraria

for speeches, get booked by lobbying groups and trade associa-
tions that pay them big fees for giving their "inside" point of view.
It is blatant hypocrisy for the media to complain about congressional honoraria but to take all they can get themselves.

Most people who actually know me say I'm easygoing in a
casual Midwestern way. We get the job done without the need for
fanfare. I've got a pretty good sense of humor—I knew how to
joke about myself long before Quayle jokes came along. When
reporters spend time with me, they generally come away liking
me well enough and, more important, respecting my knowledge
of issues. But it doesn't make any difference. I have actually heard
a couple of them remark afterwards that "I probably shouldn't
have met the guy, because I sort of like him. It would be a lot easier for me to write these stories without ever having met him."
You can't win! Or at least I couldn't.

After that Friday in Huntington, the press and I were at war,
and as the weekend wore on they came close to winning. Sunday
found Marilyn and me in Ohio, still with the Bushes, attending
church services in a town outside Cleveland. I was grateful for the
chance to worship and for a time of quiet in which to gather
strength, which I was going to need in abundance. As a Christian,
prayer is a constant in my life; not a day goes by when I don't conduct some kind of conversation—no matter how quiet and
casual—with God. That day I had to believe that He, and the family He'd blessed me with, would help me keep my head high.

But even as we worshipped, things were getting worse. Coming
out of church, we could hear reporters shouting questions over a
fence. We couldn't make out exactly what they were saying, so we
asked Sheila Tate, who was George Bush's press secretary, to go
over and find out what they wanted. She came back saying their
questions were all about a story, supposedly set to run in the *Plain
Dealer*, that I had gotten into law school the same way people
were saying I got into the Guard—through preferential treatment.

I just shook my head. Things had reached rock bottom, and I
didn't even know that, while I was at church, some members of
my own party were zinging me on the national talk shows. When
Bob Dole was told that Senator John Heinz of Pennsylvania (part
of the Heinz Foods family) had made supportive remarks about

me, he responded: "I'll bet he was chauffeured to kindergarten, too." (Remarks like this are one reason Bob Dole has never moved from the Senate to the White House.) This wasn't just the worst day of the whole campaign; it was one of the worst days of my life. I realized once and for all that this was not going to go away quickly. The media-created caricature was going to stick—if not forever, then for the length of the campaign. The stories and the jokes and the contempt were going to keep coming, and I was going to remain an issue.

Marilyn and I left the Bushes and returned to Washington. We were by ourselves; we'd left the kids with my folks in Huntington the day before, and I remember noticing how for the first time in their lives they were glad to say good-bye to their mother and father. They were totally cooked, shell-shocked by the week they'd been through, sick of the crowds and the press and hurt by all these things being said about a father who wasn't the one they knew and loved. They would rejoin us in Washington that night, but their absence on that flight from Ohio only increased my feelings of loneliness and frustration. This storm had come down so hard and heavy—the complete opposite of those headlines I had let myself fantasize about. Why had things gone so wrong? I kept asking myself. Was there *any* way to turn this nightmare around?

I was exhausted and my pinched nerve was killing me, and I wanted to stop the free fall. I thought there was only one sure way to do that, and that was to get off the ticket. For the last several years, when people have asked me whether I ever considered quitting, I've dodged the question, but the truth is I came close.

If I were hurting George Bush, I told myself, then I had an obligation to get off. That alone would have answered the question, but the evidence was not there. As I've said, polls since the convention showed that we were on the upswing, despite all the uproar over me. So the decision had to be made on another basis—whether I didn't owe it to myself and my family to put an end to what had become a miserable ordeal.

When Marilyn and I got back to our home in McLean, we found the press massed at the bottom of our driveway. They were conducting a kind of death watch, wondering about the same question I was wrestling with, determined to be there if word came I was throwing in the towel. Aware of their presence—able to hear them, in fact—Marilyn and I went up to our bedroom. She was sitting on the edge of the bed, while I stood between her and the television—that symbol of all I was up against. She later told me she had never seen me look as low as I did at that moment.

Finally, I asked her: Should I quit?

Her response was immediate and definite, and it brought reality into focus. For one thing, Marilyn was certain that my getting off would hurt George Bush more than it would help. He would be admitting poor judgment, be forced to apologize for a decision he did not in fact regret. "Have you done anything wrong?" she asked me. "Is anything that they're saying, is one single allegation, true?"

"No," I answered.

"Well, if you get out now, everyone for the rest of your life will believe it *is* true." That would include the media, my constituents, and, for all I knew, my children. "You have to stay," she told me, "and you have to fight."

I knew she was right. From that point on, any discussion of quitting was closed. All doubts were put aside, and I committed myself to winning the campaign. I knew I could fight as an underdog and come out on top. I'd done this my whole life, from the back of the class to the front, most notably in my elections in 1976 and 1980. This time, I knew, we would have to shut ourselves off from what was being said about me. For the next several weeks, we kept the television turned off, and we ignored most of the newspapers. This probably sounds absurd for a candidate running for national office but only by such extreme measures could I maintain a focused and rational outlook. I could not subject myself to all of the hateful ridicule that was being printed and broadcast about me and still walk out the door in the morning.

Forget the press, I thought; I'm going to weather this hurricane and be the next Vice President of the United States. I'm going to be there, and my critics are not.

The next morning I brought the garbage down from the house to be picked up by the truck. Visible amid the trash were some newspapers containing one more rehash of the Paula Parkinson lie (some in the media tried to suggest that I had a relationship with this female lobbyist), and I remarked to the press that the trash was where these belonged. They cynically assumed I'd done this as a planned "photo op." The fact is, I normally took out the trash and Monday was pickup day.

After my conversation with Marilyn, I once again focused on the campaign ahead. For one thing, our children had returned. But glad as I was to see them, I was more worried about what they would have to endure than anything I had to put up with. Fortunately, they're pretty resourceful. They are all intensely competitive, even shy Corinne, who'd sometimes been treated more like a kid brother than a kid sister by Tucker and Ben. They knew how to depend on one another, as well as on their parents, and I was counting on that now.

Eleven-year-old Ben had been hired by our neighbors down the street to walk their rottweiler. That night, while he was with the dog, a pack of reporters, still in their death-watch mode, followed him down the street and peppered him with questions.

"How's your dad doing? What's going on in your home? Has he made a decision?"

When the press got a closer look at the rottweiler they inquired, "Is that dog dangerous?"

Ben noticed they were backing away.

"You come near me," he said, "and I'll sic my dog on you."

Smart kid.

5 | Being "Handled"

Once we were committed to seeing the race through, we decided to isolate our kids from the next few weeks of media frenzy. A brother of Marilyn's friend Harriet Moss owned a camp in upstate New York whose most appealing feature was its lack of television. We were able to send the kids there with Harriet, her husband, Morty, and their three children, knowing they'd be protected from the worst of the press coverage. Having been shaken up by New Orleans, they were glad to go. We were hoping that by the time they got back, Labor Day weekend, the firestorm would have started to die down.

I had been so focused on the INF treaty over the past several months that what I would have liked most was to take a week off and do nothing but study the full array of campaign issues—from the perspective of a national candidate instead of a Senator. But there was no time for that. I had to plunge in, so on that first Monday after the convention I accepted an invitation from Governor Jim Thompson of Illinois to address a VFW convention in Chicago. The thinking behind this was obvious: if I could get a good reception from a veterans group, during a week when the papers remained full of commentary about my Guard enlistment, with more than one editorial urging me to get off the ticket, then the controversy might run out of steam.

My speech was well received, and it did have some bit of the desired effect, though the media-created Guard "issue" would haunt me during the campaign. I'd see occasional placards that said things like "Did your Daddy get you this job too?"

I was learning that every offhand remark I made would be subject to severe scrutiny. This is something any national candidate
experiences, but in my case it was particularly fierce. My image
was so bad that our opponents—and the press—were just waiting
for me to stumble. I could almost see them rubbing their hands in
gleeful anticipation. During that VFW appearance, I was aware
that my vote against the new Cabinet-level department of Veterans Affairs was unpopular with my audience. I decided to joke
about it. I said I was "older and wiser" now. Without realizing it,
I'd just punched two hot buttons in my case—youth and intellect—and a mini-flap was born. The press was turning into what
the *Wall Street Journal*'s Paul Gigot called the "Gaffe Patrol," just
looking for missteps—and sometimes even trying to provoke
them.

I'm most comfortable making off-the-cuff remarks or speaking
from notes instead of a prepared text. I'll admit, my thoughts
sometimes get ahead of my tongue. It happens to all public speakers at one time or other. The real problem is created when the
people thrusting portable recorders at you have their ears open
for nothing *but* gaffes. I was "quizzed" in a way other candidates
weren't. I can remember one reporter asking me who the head of
the South Florida Task Force was. In fact, this was an arm of the
antidrug program then being overseen by Vice President Bush,
but the word *drug* was not included in the name of the task force.
I was puzzled. Let's face it: the federal government is a blizzard of
bureaucracies and acronyms, and without a key word or context,
anyone, from the President on down, might mistake one vague-
sounding name for another. But this wasn't "anyone" making the
mistake. It was me, and to the media that made a difference.

When Al Gore made a reference to the leopard changing his
stripes instead of his spots, misstated the name of President
James Knox Polk, and botched our nation's motto (*e pluribus
unum*) people took it for what it was: a natural mistake. If I'd
done it, there would have been a week of Quayle jokes on the late-
night shows and three dozen editorial cartoons set inside zoos.
According to MediaWatch, the famous potato(e) incident received
six stories from CNN, NBC, and CBS over four days and thousands of newspaper articles. When Gore mangled our nation's

motto there was no network coverage and of the major newspapers only the *Washington Post* made passing reference to it. The last thing I want to do is duck responsibility for the mistakes, small and large, that I've made over the years: I gave the media plenty of ammunition during the campaign and later. But there was an obsession with my small verbal blunders that went beyond the bounds of fairness. Remember how the media loved to catch President Ford tripping or stumbling or hitting a wild golf shot? Those things only happened a few times, but as some fair-minded people have pointed out, the public was left thinking that one of the most athletic presidents ever to occupy the White House was a chronic stumblebum. Michael Dukakis spoke with great precision, but did this finally make him a more able politician? Would it have made him a good President?

I was not one of the most skilled orators ever to adorn the Senate chamber, but I was better than average. In the Senate, it was considered unimpressive to read from a prepared text. I learned to speak for an hour or more without notes. I might jumble my syntax from time to time, but my strength, both in the Senate chamber and out on the campaign trail, was in connecting with people and getting them to understand complex issues. But now, whenever I tripped on one sentence in a ten-page speech, it made the evening news.

The time I referred to Bobby Knight's maxim about the importance of a good defense, I was ridiculed for using a sports metaphor for as serious a subject as military preparedness. Instead of being praised for speaking on a complicated subject without notes, and in a manner that connected well with the audience, I was ridiculed for the supposedly sophomoric reference. And the campaign staff, who didn't like my ignoring the speech they'd prepared for me, said, "See. This is what happens when he goes it alone." (Never mind that I received two standing ovations.) After this I threw in the towel and started giving prepared speeches.

I began to fear spontaneity and to speak with unnatural deliberateness. I wound up sounding stiff and programmed. In fact, one of the surest ways to make a gaffe is to try to hear every word before it comes out of your mouth. You wind up like the nervous person being told to "RELAX!" Things only get worse.

Another thing I had to realize was that the media wanted me to make the kind of news that suited *them*. Let me give you an example. Early in the campaign I talked to state legislators in Ohio and Kentucky about my work on the Job Training Partnership Act. These were real nuts-and-bolts speeches that not only explained an important piece of domestic legislation—one of the most important of the Reagan years—but also showed my command of the legislative process, which would serve me well when I was eventually asked to "carry the President's water" up on Capitol Hill. But how were these speeches reported by the *Boston Globe*? "Bland and lacking in any partisan criticism." They must have decided my role that week was to be campaign pit bull, a sort of Spiro Agnew, and when I had something else in mind, they weren't interested.

As those first weeks went by, I think I got a little better, but not much. Aside from my own limitations, there were two main problems. One was the nature of the office I was running for. Vice-presidential candidates, like Vice Presidents, are not permitted what Lee Atwater called "defining moments"—occasions when the public gets a lasting impression of their having accomplished something. Presidents get them (think of Reagan posing with those vote-tally sheets back in 1981, when he forced bill after bill through a Congress still dominated by Democrats) and presidential candidates get them, too (remember Bill Clinton receiving cheers as the "Comeback Kid" on the night of the New Hampshire primary in 1992, when he came in second). The second man on the ticket doesn't have these opportunities, and they're not something he can create.

My second big problem was the staff that had been imposed upon me—my handlers, who made it nearly impossible for me to talk directly to the press. I take responsibility for not insisting on my own people. I should not have allowed my loyal Senate staff to get shut out. I should have taken my complaints directly to George Bush, but I didn't want to burden him with my problems. As our years together unfolded, I learned that this was exactly the sort of complaint I could have taken to him; he would have listened carefully and told me to take whatever action I thought was required.

So, throughout September, I was on a very unhappy campaign plane whose itinerary and atmosphere were largely created by Stu Spencer and Joe Canzeri. Some members of the press even referred to them as my "keepers," taking note of the extent to which they tried to coach and control me—and how I put up with it. Spencer and Canzeri were exceptionally cooperative with the press, but the only ones who benefited were Spencer and Canzeri, who did everything they could to create the impression that they were making the best of an impossible job (i.e., me, the burden they were saddled with). Late in September Spencer stopped traveling with me. Stories about his having received a $330,000 lobbying fee from Manuel Noriega were making him a potential embarrassment. (I knew I would get a question about whether he should resign, and I could have said he should go, because Noriega was so bad. But I didn't.) Nearly a month after he'd last been on the campaign plane, Spencer was still talking up his own skill at managing me. POLITICAL PRO IS PULLING ALL THE STRINGS was the headline of a *Los Angeles Times* story in which Spencer said his job was "a killer." He made himself sound like some put-upon babysitter, emphasizing all the work he was doing on me, all the teaching he was hoping I'd absorb. This was incredible stuff for a campaign staffer to be saying about his own candidate. The reporter asked why I did so much campaigning in safe Republican venues, and Spencer answered that "Dan Quayle doesn't know about cities" but that eventually he'd teach me. The fact is I could have shown Stu Spencer plenty of urban neighborhoods he'd never been to—places where my JTPA program was helping hard-core unemployed find jobs—but he was more interested in reinforcing the media's caricature than in refuting it.

I wasn't completely friendless in the press. During the campaign I was especially grateful to Michael Barone, who every other year produces *The Almanac of American Politics* and also writes for *U.S. News & World Report*. He knew my Senate record in detail and wrote a column saying that press coverage of me was very distorted. But more typical were journalists who knew virtually nothing about my record and loved summing me up in wild and wounding ways. A couple of weeks into September, Mike Barnicle (the *Boston Globe* again) wrote that I was "super rich, super tanned, about as smart as your average house plant." Try living with this kind of thing day after day; I don't recommend it. As I've said, I shut myself off from whatever coverage wasn't essential to keeping informed on the issues and conducting the campaign, but there was so much of that stuff out there that it was hard to avoid.

The press could have worn me down, but I took much solace— not to mention perspective—from the ordinary citizens who wrote letters of support and thronged our appearances along the campaign trail. They were wonderful; they gave me the strength to continue. I was constantly in touch with crowds of middle Americans—thirty thousand folks at a Georgia crafts fair, to take just one example—and just like the people in Huntington (if a little less vocally), they would tell me they hated what the media was doing. Every time I'd get a little bit down, somebody would come up and put an arm around me and say, "Our church is praying for you, we're praying for you. Don't let it get you. There are lots of people who love you." It was tremendous, because I believe in the power of prayer. Marilyn and I pray every day, not just in crises like this one, because faith has to be more than a crutch and more than an emergency measure. There was no denying, however, the testing, stressful nature of the campaign, and I remain grateful for every prayer that was offered in my behalf at this time.

One of the first trips Marilyn and I took after the convention was to the North Carolina–South Carolina football game. We stayed with our good friends, South Carolina Governor Carroll Campbell and his wife, Iris, and we rode with them to the game. Outside the stadium there were at the most a dozen protesters. Everywhere else, inside and out, we were cheered. We got into the Governor's box, and I was told that I'd be introduced at half-time. Meanwhile, we could sit back and enjoy the game. Well, all of a sudden, during the first quarter, in the middle of play, the announcer jumped the gun and started to introduce me. Marilyn, with her good political instincts, looked horrified: they're going to interrupt a big game just to introduce a politician! I got ready for some heavy booing, but figured I just had to go through with it. So I stood up and waved, and braced myself for the worst. And seventy thousand people stood up with me—to cheer and applaud. They will never know how much that meant to me; if I could have shaken every hand in the stadium, I would have.

But the media only picked up on the handful of protesters. They never mentioned the cheering crowds.

The next day Marilyn and I went to the Darlington Raceway for the Darlington 500. The local paper said the crowd reaction there would be a referendum, a good indication of how the election might go in that area. The paper also made some dire predictions about how I might get my comeuppance. As it turned out, there was just about nothing but cheering—more cheers than Strom Thurmond could ever remember hearing at Darlington.

The next day the paper never followed up on its predictions.

Despite crowds like these, there were stories about how I was being "hidden," not allowed to see the public. For all the unhappiness within our campaign operation, the fact is that I *was* out and about and getting a great response. There were times when I felt as if I were living in a separate world from the one being reported. Even within the media you could distinguish between ordinary folks and the opinion-making elite. Marilyn and I both had the experience of being talked to by TV technicians, make-up artists, and camera people, as we got ready for what we knew might be hostile interviews. These wonderful people often told us not to worry, that they were supporting us and that they knew their bosses in the press had gone off the deep end. Local reporters were often more sympathetic than their national counterparts—until they found themselves standing next to them at a press conference and were seized with the desire to impress their more famous colleagues by mimicking their most biased questions.

In the beginning, Canzeri and Spencer resisted Marilyn's going out and campaigning on her own, but she knew it was foolish to have the two of us in the same place when we could cover twice as much ground traveling separately. That's what we had always done in our Senate campaigns. Back in 1980, all summer, she traveled around with our three children in a Winnebago, stopping at seventy-two different county fairs. The kids were very small—Corinne just a year old—so Marilyn made a game out of it with the boys: once they'd passed out a certain number of brochures at the Republican booth, they got to go on a ride at the midway.

The 1988 campaign was different. All three were old enough to be hurt by what was going on, and we didn't want them to be part of it. So before Marilyn could do any campaigning, with me or on her own, she had to get someone to stay with the children, and the fact is we couldn't easily afford a sitter. On Labor Day weekend, we were in New Jersey getting ready to do an event on Ellis Island. Marilyn had previously mentioned her need of a sitter to Joe Canzeri and had asked if the campaign could pay this expense or find a volunteer to help out. Canzeri now had a response. He took her aside and reached into his pocket and pulled out a large roll of money. She looked at him as if he were crazy, and told him in no uncertain terms that this was inappropriate and to put the money away. Afterwards she told me about this and said that we had to watch this guy. Actually, we needed to get *rid* of this guy, but at that point in the campaign I didn't want to rock the boat.

The sitter we hired didn't work out, so Marilyn ended up calling her Aunt Janet to ask her to come to McLean and stay with the kids. She agreed to come right away, and we thought everything would be fine from there on. But one night Marilyn called home from California, and Tucker got on the phone to say that there was something wrong with Aunt Janet: she didn't feel well and she couldn't eat. Our friend, Dr. Morton Moss, went over to take a look at her, and he said she needed some tests. She wanted to be treated at home, so we had a friend drive her to Indiana. A plane ride would have been too uncomfortable for her. The tests showed she was suffering from cancer.

Janet lived long enough to attend the inauguration, but her death in 1990 was a terrible blow to Marilyn and me and the children. In the chaos of a campaign you don't have time to absorb the personal tragedies life brings your way. Your emotions are always being sidetracked, put off, and this is how it was when Aunt Janet became ill. Fortunately, we had my parents to turn to. My mom and dad did a terrific job taking care of our children for the rest of the campaign, and they became closer to them than they'd ever been before. Marilyn would fly home on weekends, shop for food, cook it, and put it away in the freezer to make their life a little easier.

Once the child-care situation stabilized, Marilyn looked forward to solo campaigning, but our handlers, those supposed experts, made the situation as difficult as possible for her. For a while they had her flying commercial, which is impractical in a campaign, and sure enough, flight delays and mechanical breakdowns would cause her to miss events. Canzeri finally got around to chartering some prop planes, little puddle-jumpers that bore no resemblance to the jets he hired for his own errands and travels.

Our anxieties about Tucker, Ben, and Corinne continued. Once they were back home from camp, they were exposed to the full malice of the campaign coverage. Marilyn had always been involved with the children's schools, and in return the schools turned out to be very supportive. The principals and teachers began watching our children a bit more closely, to help out if need be.

Tucker, our oldest (a high school freshman then), developed a real perspective on the whole ordeal. He and a friend even annotated one negative article he saw, offering a point-by-point refutation of all the things he knew weren't true about his dad. Throughout the campaign and administration, he would serve as the family's monitor of Quayle jokes on the late-night talk shows and "Saturday Night Live," telling us at breakfast which ones he thought were actually funny and dismissing the ones that just seemed stupid or mean-spirited. Among people who actually knew the children, kindness was always more frequent than cruelty. During the campaign, Tucker got a truly remarkable letter from a friend of his, a girl whose father had been in the Reagan administration and had withstood the horrors of a press-created character assassination. At a very young age she had seen what the media could do to someone she loved, so she told Tucker that it was important to remember that *he* knew his father better than they did, and that what was in his heart was more important than anything in the newspapers. It was an extraordinary letter for a thirteen-year-old to write, and it made a big difference to him. As the campaign went on, my mom used to ask if our children would join her in watching the evening news so that they could lean on one another.

We tried never to let our children see us upset. If we had

moaned and groaned about the way we were being portrayed, they would have picked up those signals and been miserable themselves. So we grinned and bore it, and told them we were sure the truth, the real story, would come out someday and replace the caricature.

But there was one time, on national TV several weeks into the campaign, when Marilyn couldn't hide her feelings. Stories were floating around about how she was a devoted follower of a supposedly controversial minister. On the day I was to debate Senator Bentsen, Marilyn did the morning talk shows on a remote hook-up from the auditorium in Omaha where the debate would take place. Jane Pauley (a fellow Hoosier who had worked at Indiana Democratic headquarters for two years and who has never forgiven me for unseating her friend Birch Bayh) asked Marilyn a question about her supposedly far-out religious beliefs and her father's faith. Marilyn looked shocked and said, "My father is a wonderful gentleman, he has nothing to do with Dan's campaign. I don't understand any of this. I'm a Presbyterian. I go to Fourth Presbyterian Church. I really didn't know that wasn't acceptable." In fact, our first pastor at Fourth Presbyterian, Dr. Richard C. Halverson, was the chaplain of the U.S. Senate, and he continued to send us letters of prayer and to counsel me when I was Vice President. That's how far-out we are.

Christianity is central to our lives, but to many in the media and the entertainment industry, Christianity is something that consists chiefly of corrupt televangelists and "redneck" rabble-rousing, something to be cartooned and ridiculed. Jane Pauley could have asked Marilyn about the time and effort we'd put into our children's actual religious education, about the wonderful Sunday School programs at Fourth, or the adult Bible classes Marilyn and I had both attended. But that wouldn't have interested them the way their cartoons did. Back in McLean, my mother was watching that interview with Ben, whom she remembers turning to her and asking, "Is my mom going to cry?" His mom was ready to, from sheer anger at Pauley's attack on her father, and I don't blame her.

In a conversation we had after I left office, ABC's Brit Hume characterized the national media as the most secular group of individuals in the world. Religion is not something many of them have frequent contact with. At the White House we used to joke that George Bush, a Christian who usually attended private services (especially at Camp David, where he and Barbara built a beautiful chapel), should go to a public church more often, because then the media would be forced to go, too. It would do them some good—certainly in broadening their perspective. Writing about the 1993 Virginia Lieutenant Governor's race, Michael Barone pointed out how no one in the general news media was criticizing the ridicule directed at conservative Christians in television ads being run against a conservative Christian candidate, Republican Mike Farris. What if, Barone wondered, those ads had mocked an Orthodox Jew or a Moslem? There would have been, quite properly, outrage.

But conservative Christians are considered fair game for caricature and abuse, and the result has been severe public prejudice against them. A 1989 Gallup poll showed that, while only 3 percent of those surveyed would mind Catholics as neighbors and 5 percent would mind Jews, a staggering 30 percent said they would not want to live near a fundamentalist Christian. That figure was almost triple what it had been a decade earlier. During the 1980s the news and entertainment media had turned legitimate scrutiny of the abuse of preachers like Jim Bakker into an opportunity to make sinister cartoons of Christians. Sadly, prejudice against conservative Christians is probably the only acceptable form of bigotry in today's America.

My faith in God and belief in the Bible is an important part of my life but it is nothing for others to fear. Faith in God is personal and cannot be mandated by a government. Our pastors lead us and help us to understand the Word, but the Bible always remains, eternal and unchangeable. Its words would be my solace and strength in the weeks and years ahead.

6 | "You're No Jack Kennedy"

The vice-presidential debate, scheduled for Omaha on October 6, would actually be my second televised debate with Senator Bentsen. Earlier in the year, before either of us knew we would be on our parties' national tickets, we had briefly gone head-to-head, when "The MacNeil/Lehrer Newshour" asked us to debate the Democrats' plant-closing-notification bill. Most people thought I'd gotten the best of that exchange, so the chance to debate him for ninety minutes before a huge national audience, just a month before the election, didn't fill me with anxiety; it struck me as a golden opportunity to come out from under the pounding I'd taken for a month and a half. If all went well, I would reemerge as the man I had been, not the one seen leaving New Orleans in August.

I knew Lloyd Bentsen; you might even say Lloyd Bentsen was a friend of mine. We had a cordial relationship in the Senate, and I'd been to both his home in Washington and the farm he had in Virginia. Both of those social occasions involved only very small groups, and on one of them I was probably the only Republican in the room. Bentsen is not someone who's easy to get close to but his charming wife, B.A., and Marilyn had been friends for years.

At one of these affairs Jack Valenti, a former Lyndon Johnson aide, told me a story about my grandfather that may interest political trivia buffs. My grandfather was a friend of Johnson's, and when he wanted to get a ticket to Douglas MacArthur's farewell speech to a joint session of Congress, it was Bentsen, a young Representative, who gave up one of his—probably at the couldn't-be-ignored request of LBJ. In fact, my grandfather was friendly enough with LBJ that he didn't back Barry Goldwater, as would be normally expected in his Indiana papers in 1964. As a rabid seventeen-year-old Goldwater man, I took vigorous exception and wrote my grandfather a letter protesting the endorsement. My mother, trying to put family harmony above the political fray, gently dissuaded me from mailing it. Years later, when I had a small dustup with Barry on the Senate's Indian Affairs Committee, he would tell me: "You're just like your grandfather, stubborn." I accepted it as a compliment.

Like the primaries, our presidential and vice-presidential debates are really all about the "expectations" game. If you can beat the point spread, you're generally declared the winner— regardless of the substance that was exchanged. In the days leading up to my debate with Bentsen, most of the handicapping was based on the abysmal picture of me that had been out there for a month and a half. A California pollster was quoted as saying, "Expectations are so low that if he's still standing after the debate, he looks good." I suppose I could have taken some political pleasure in that, but only if I had as little self-esteem as most of those in the media felt I was entitled to. I also had to remember that some of them were so eager to see me self-destruct that they would stack the expectations deck in just the opposite way. "Better than expected," wrote Tom Wicker in the *New York Times*, "will not be good enough." More reasonably, his colleague, E. J. Dionne, wrote that this debate "could have more impact on the campaign" than any earlier one between candidates for the vice-presidency, and that it was certain to "be one of the defining events of the 1988 campaign." I certainly wanted it to be one of those "defining moments" Lee Atwater talked about. It wound up being one of them—not for me but for Bentsen.

In order to prepare, I had numerous meetings to discuss issues. I sat down with foreign policy specialists like Henry Kissinger, Larry Eagleburger, and Jeane Kirkpatrick. "Doc" Bowen, the former Indiana Governor who was now President Reagan's Secretary of Health and Human Services (HHS), briefed me on health care matters. Mike Boskin, who would become Bush's top economist, shared his ideas. I enjoyed these give-and-take discussions much more than the later rehearsals and cram sessions, when I felt less as if I were preparing to debate the important issues before the country than as if I were studying for a test—a short-answer, fill-in-the-blanks one. The object was to hit hard, create sound bites, and avoid the gaffes that are frequently the only real news the media sees in the confrontations. (Everyone preparing for one of these events has on his mind what happened to Jerry Ford in 1976, when a careless choice of words made it seem as if he really believed the Poles didn't live under Soviet tyranny.)

We had two rehearsals, each conducted in a small room, with Margaret Tutwiler, Jim Baker's longtime aide, as the moderator and a couple of staff people acting as the questioners. Bob Packwood was Bentsen's stand-in for both rehearsals. Dick Darman and the campaign people felt he didn't come at me hard enough during the first—they were sure Bentsen would come on strong— and so Bob became more aggressive, and frequently interrupted in the second. But the questions were all rather stiff, policy-oriented ones, and I knew my stuff. I remember the handlers remarking that they thought I had an even better grasp of some of these issues than George Bush. If that were the case (which I doubt), it shouldn't have been a surprise: I'd been dealing with them in the House and Senate, in a nuts-and-bolts way, for twelve years.

The real problem with the questions they anticipated was that they were *too* issue-oriented. The staff didn't seem able to imagine the more general, reflective questions that have become a part of these debates. No one came up with anything like the question Senator Bentsen and I would both be asked about the advice and experiences that had formed our character and ideas of public service. (The from-the-heart answer I gave to that one during the actual debate—about my grandmother's saying I could do anything I set my mind to—would be widely mocked as unsophisticated and clichéd. If people stop to give that remark some serious thought, as I did when I applied it to my life, they might realize it has plenty of shaping power.) During the preparation no one ever asked any question like the climactic one of the actual debate— namely, what I would do if I actually had to assume the presidency. Though he was only around the debate prep for about ten minutes, Phil Gramm came closest to the question when he told me to emphasize how I had more relevant experience for being President than Dukakis had. Yes, I could have done more to anticipate these questions on my own, but over days of cramming and rehearsal there was only one general idea being pounded into me: don't plow any new ground. Don't make a mistake. If you feel unsure of an answer, just fall back on old rhetoric. In other words, don't trust yourself. This was the mistake I made throughout the campaign.

Marilyn and I arrived in Omaha the night before the debate, and we went to dinner with our good friend Roger Ailes. I had a hard time sleeping, and spent most of the next day just endlessly replaying those rote answers in my mind. It was not any way to come into the debate relaxed or spontaneous, and I wound up paying a price for it. In the afternoon we had a walk-through in the studio, where I asked for information about the positions of the cameras and so forth. Ailes, for all his media savvy, had surprisingly few tips on body language and facial expression for me, other than to avoid looking too much in Bentsen's direction. Just do what makes you feel comfortable, he said, but don't smile too much. It's not vice-presidential.

Four years later I would be very comfortable (I remember being casual about the same sort of dry run in 1992, whereas Al Gore even rehearsed the way he would kiss his wife after the debate). But the night of that 1988 debate, I was awkward and stiff.

Back in 1960, a survey of people who heard the Kennedy–Nixon debates on radio instead of seeing them on TV found that a majority thought Nixon had won. They were focused on the words, on the substance of what was being said, and not on the imagery, which worked so powerfully in Kennedy's favor. I had a slight taste of this discrepancy myself, when George Shultz and Henry Kissinger, who were both traveling outside the country and unable to watch the debate, read a verbatim transcript. Now, I'm not pretending these were totally unbiased observers, but they both were struck by how the text they'd read didn't square with what the media and the polls were saying. "You won this debate," George Shultz told me. "Don't let anybody tell you any differently." And George Shultz was not somebody who indulged in hyperbole.

Whether I won or lost overall—the way a debate might be scored on points—is something serious observers can still argue about. A number of people not normally too friendly to me (like liberal commentators Chris Matthews and Hodding Carter) didn't think I'd done badly. But overall judgments were beside the point, because the debate that was written about in the morning papers, and the debate that went, in its small way, into American political history, consisted of a single exchange. I'm talking, of course, about the one that included Senator Bentsen's declaration that I was "no Jack Kennedy."

Oddly enough, this is one of the things we did anticipate during our rehearsals. I was told not to make any reference to Kennedy, was warned that it could backfire. In the end I probably should have avoided it, but I only brought it up to make a single, valid comparison about our experience in the Congress. Because I was young and such a new face on the national scene, my opponents were arguing that I lacked the qualifications for the vice-presidency. When they made this argument, they often weren't talking about stature or vision (legitimate matters for debate where any candidate is concerned) but were trying to indicate that I lacked any basic experience in government. And this was ridiculous. I had served four years in the House of Representatives and eight in the Senate—a considerably longer and more challenging stretch than that served by the Democrats' 1984 nominee for Vice President, Geraldine Ferraro, whose genuine lack of experience had been a non-issue. The comparison of myself and Kennedy on this point was relevant, because by 1960 he had served six years in the House and eight in the Senate, almost exactly what I had, and he was running for the presidency itself.

I made the comparison out of frustration, in response to a question the panel kept asking over and over: What would you do if you suddenly found yourself having to assume the presidency? Bentsen was never asked this question, but I was asked it three times. I felt I had answered it satisfactorily the first two. I responded that the first thing I would do is say a prayer (a truthful answer that many in the media tried to ridicule), and then I talked of the necessary meetings (National Security Council) I would convene and so forth. But they wouldn't let go of this. It was, ironically enough, ABC's Brit Hume who first raised the question. (I say "ironically" because it was Brit who, some time before, in anticipation of the debate, told me that all I would have to do with Bentsen is stand there and look like the newcomer, the fresh hope for the future. That would be great for the Republicans and for George Bush.)

So here comes the what-would-you-do-first question for the third time. Trying to answer it in some new way, one that would put it to rest, I said what was true: that at the heart of the question lay qualifications and experience. And that's when I mentioned Kennedy—strictly to compare our length of service in the Congress. I didn't say I was like President Kennedy, a man of great talents and great flaws, in any other respect. But Bentsen came back with his "You're no Jack Kennedy" line, and I, stung by its excess, could only more or less mutter what I (and many others) thought: that it was uncalled for.

The line would, over and over, be described as a "knockout" punch, and it was replayed endlessly on the TV news shows. Politically, it *was* a good line, so good I'm convinced that Bentsen would have found some way to use it whether I gave him an opening or not.

Surveys showed that I lost the debate. The Associated Press had 51 percent of viewers calling Bentsen the winner and only 27 percent naming me as the winner; 22 percent called it a tie. I was disappointed with these numbers, but I was more interested in another set—the ones about which ticket people intended to vote for. The debate, for all its hoopla, didn't really move those numbers at all; we maintained our lead, and we were headed into the final lap. And if the Dukakis people wanted to keep focused on me instead of George Bush, that was just fine. I was willing to be the lightning rod—or, to use Lee Atwater's image, the rabbit they could chase. Such a strategy wasn't going to get them anywhere. Our message about growth, low taxes, and a strong defense— maintaining the Reagan revolution—was getting through, and we were going to win. A piece in the Gannett newspapers drew the bottom line: "Michael Dukakis is going to have to find another way to beat George Bush. Dan Quayle isn't going to do it for him. . . . Any Democratic hopes that Quayle, Bush's much maligned boyish-looking running mate, would self-destruct on national television, dragging down Republican election hopes, evaporated in the only 90 minutes that will matter in the campaign of the junior Senator from Indiana." This is not exactly a politician's dream coverage, but it had its eye on the ball, and that's where I was keeping mine. There would, I thought, be time enough later to cope with any long-term damage—the lingering image, coined by Meg Greenfield, that I had looked like "a deer caught in the headlights." (CBS's Lesley Stahl tells me that the camera sometimes does peculiar things to people's eyes. In my case, she says, it captures some look of uncertainty, even though my demeanor in person reflects otherwise.)

The place where I could have used some strong support right away was in my own campaign, and I didn't get it. George Bush himself was terrific—insisting in his post-debate phone call to me with real force that he was pleased with how I'd done and that he remained completely behind me. But my handlers (Spencer and Canzeri and the campaign crowd that had been imposed on me) began their hand-wringing. I was told later that the campaign team boarded the plane after the debate thinking we'd acquitted ourselves pretty well, but by the time we landed they had bought into the press's agenda—something they were always too willing to do—and convinced themselves the debate had been a disaster. And these were the people I was counting on to support me, to do their job and "spin" the debate in my favor. No wonder the press was ready to begin another death watch. Later in the month, Jim Baker himself, in looking back on the debate, would say: "When you think about what might have happened, we have to be pretty happy."

The one piece of coverage that bothered me most came from George Will, somebody I considered a friend: "Quayle was so over-programmed it seemed that someone backstage was operating a compact disc." He said my handlers had stuffed me with "itsy-bitsy slivers of ideas—notions really, ideological lint," and that the conservatism I'd demonstrated was "less a creed than an absorbed climate of opinion, absorbed in a golf cart." If Bush won, he predicted, I would "not be trusted to handle even the more serious foreign funerals."

Bad as this seems, it was a blessing in disguise. I read it and did something I'd needed to do for almost two months: I exploded. I called Will from Atlanta and asked, "George, what is this all about?" He responded: "Well, this is what your friends are saying—that you're not the same person they knew." This is also what he truly felt himself; he had been one of the people saying Bush should consider me for the second spot on the ticket, and now that I had it, he couldn't recognize the man he was seeing.

Throughout the campaign I would encounter many otherwise intelligent people who were easily swayed by the media into abandoning reality. That some of these people were friends was especially difficult.

George Will and I had first met early in 1976 at a newspaper conference in Williamsburg, Virginia. I told him that the *Huntington Herald-Press* would now be taking his column. We got to know each other when I was in the Senate, and at one time we talked about the possibility of his running for one of Maryland's Senate seats. He told one breakfast meeting of the House Republicans' Chowder and Marching Society and SOS group that I'd make a good Vice President. We went to each other's houses on occasion. It wasn't until after the election that I realized the bitter feelings between George Bush and Will, who once wrote that Bush was a "lapdog" to Ronald Reagan. This mutual dislike eventually put a strain on my own friendship with Will.

Paul Gigot had written something similar to Will's column for the *Wall Street Journal* just before the debate ("For anyone familiar with Senator Quayle before he became national cannon fodder, his unnaturalness is disconcerting. He wasn't always like this . . . "), but it was this conversation with Will that had the real impact on me. I had to admit the truth: I had surrendered my independence and my instincts to people in whom I had no confidence and who certainly had interests other than mine front and center in their minds. I had always been willing to take responsibility for my own mistakes—and I made plenty of them on my own in 1988. But my biggest mistake was allowing myself to be put in a position where I couldn't take responsibility for *anything*—my schedule, my press availability, my own words and movements. I realized, when I slammed the phone down in Atlanta, that I was on my way to winning the vice-presidency but in danger of losing myself. I had three weeks left to try and change things, and that night I told myself what I was going to tell the press: "From now on, *I'm* Doctor Spin."

7 | Winning and Losing

The press corps following our campaign had swelled in the three or four days after the debate—a half-hearted death watch. They didn't really expect that I'd be leaving the ticket at this late date, but having so exaggerated my "loss" of the debate, they now wanted to be around to see me crumble in public. Most of them were bored within a few days of Omaha, but there were still plenty of them around for my personal rebellion on October 12.

Rich Bond, a high-level member of the Bush campaign, was on the plane that day, and I told him what I was going to do just before I went back to talk to the press. The noisy, raucous session that I started took them by surprise—after all, the story they would have to write was that, instead of crumbling, I was getting up from the mat. "I'm my own handler," I told them. "I've done it their way thus far and now it's my turn." I let them know that I would be speaking my own mind and using my own judgment—for good reason: "I'm the one who's been elected to office. . . . I know how to get votes, and I know how I can best help George Bush, and that's what I'm going to do." I was beginning to trust myself once again.

And George Bush knew what was best for me. I called him shortly after this, stressing my loyalty and telling him that I wouldn't do anything that would hurt him but that I'd reached a snapping point and just had to do things my own way. He knew what I'd been through and had thought the debate coverage was almost crazy, so he told me to go ahead and do whatever I was comfortable with.

By contrast, Baker felt nervous enough to call me in Indianapolis—one of only two calls from him that I can remember during the campaign. He told me I should be careful and not reject the advice I was getting, not do too much on my own. I told him, "I've had all the advice I can take, and none of it has been any good. I've talked to the Vice President and said I'm going to do things my way." And that was that. Baker had little choice but to endorse my decision when he talked to the press himself. He said I was "justified at being steamed" by what I'd been through and, according to *Newsweek,* he "threaten[ed] to dismiss any Bush aide who trashes Quayle," a remark that made the magazine ask: "Will he fire himself?" That was overstating it, but I didn't mind seeing the irony noted.

The personal effects of my "declaration" were clear and liberating. The last three weeks of the campaign were exciting and I was enjoying myself. The plane was a happier place. Stu Spencer had left it, and Mitch Daniels had come aboard to replace him. Some Indiana friends and some colleagues from the Senate, like Strom Thurmond and John Tower, also made trips with us. Their presence buoyed my spirits. It began to feel—however late—like my own campaign. Soon B. Drummond Ayres of the *New York Times* was reporting that Dan Quayle had had his best week, having "finally eased into a campaign stride that he seemed comfortable with, so comfortable that he even began to deal a little in the ultimate in political ease and confidence—self-deprecation." He went on to note that "the stylish change, along with increasingly smooth advance work . . . resulted in a series of appearances that left some crowds hoarse from cheering and the candidate beaming from ear to ear."

For the most part, and properly, I receded into the status of a background issue. The press became preoccupied at last with the real story—Dukakis's declining fortunes. The voters were becoming more aware that he represented nothing different from the tax-and-spend liberalism they had rejected eight years before. George Bush absolutely blew him away in their second debate, which was marked by the first questions Bernie Shaw put to both candidates. George Bush, in his response to a query about me, offered an emotional defense, whereas Dukakis, asked to tell how he'd react to the rape and murder of his own wife, remained mechanical. (Shaw was so tough that four years later the Clinton people would reject his participation in the 1992 debates.)

Dukakis had said that the election was about competence, not ideology. He was trying to sell himself to the voters as a sort of high-tech manager, and I knew this was not going to work for him. The election *was* about ideology: we were conservatives, and he was just as much a liberal as those the Democrats had been nominating with little success for the past twenty years and more. The electorate was going to make its choice on precisely this ideological basis, and I mocked the "competence" talk at almost every campaign stop. "Competence" was Dukakis's sheep's clothing, and it didn't fit him any better than that army helmet he had on when he took his infamous tank ride. The real irony of the situation is that four years later we'd be using their playbook, trying to win reelection by portraying ourselves as good managers of the country and world and letting ourselves be perceived as out of ideas. But in 1988 we had it right.

In those last couple of weeks a Bush–Quayle victory seemed certain. Our phone conversations were positive. We took pleasure in the polls and talked about how we couldn't wait for the campaign to be over. Early one morning Bush tracked down Marilyn and gave her a call, out of the blue, just to cheer her on with the same message—that the whole ordeal would soon be over. It was the kind of considerateness that defined the man, and over the years it extended to the thoughtful notes he wrote our children.

There was one last rumor that flared up in those last weeks, and it involved drug use. The media had been tantalized from the beginning by the possibility—I'd even call it their certainty—that I had used drugs when I was in college. After all, this was part of the boomer profile. The truth is I hadn't used them. During the years I was there (1965–69), drugs weren't much in evidence. Had I gone to school a few years later, I would have been much more exposed to them. While I am adamantly opposed to the legalization of even so-called soft drugs like marijuana, it's foolish to think we should write off a whole generation for having flirted with the stuff when it was all around them. Four years later I never cared much about whether Clinton had inhaled or not.

Still, the press felt there *had* to be some drug story about the first boomer candidate, and in the last weeks of the campaign a convicted felon bent on exploiting the system cooked up just the story some of them wanted. Brett Kimberlin was a perjurer doing a fifty-one-year federal prison sentence for terrorizing the town of Speedway, Indiana, by planting eight bombs in seven days. The explosions maimed several people, including a Vietnam veteran, the father of two young children, who lost his leg. Suddenly, just before the election, he was claiming to have regularly sold me marijuana. He said he wanted to show how "hypocritical" my antidrug positions were.

There was not a shred of truth to his bizarre accusation, nor a single witness to back it up, and if anyone could have less credibility I have a hard time imagining who it would be. (CBS's "60 Minutes" would eventually spend two years looking into this story before deciding that there was nothing there.) But the media in the frantic final days of the campaign didn't care about facts and ran with the story anyway. On the Friday before the election Kimberlin scheduled a press conference. Before he could manage to hold it, the Federal Bureau of Prisons put him into administrative detention. He was in and out of solitary for the next ten days, partly for violating prison rules and partly, according to the bureau director, out of concern for his personal safety. There was a controversy, inevitably, over whether the Reagan administration or the Bush campaign pulled some strings to keep him quiet until the election was over. Whether they did overreact and exert pressure, I don't know, but Kimberlin's story was so ridiculous that it should never have made its way into the mainstream media. Even assuming the worst, I'll let Larry Sabato have the last even-handed word about this incident. In *Feeding Frenzy* he says that "the responsible federal officials, if not the Bush/Quayle campaign itself, have only themselves to blame for elevating Kimberlin to martyr status. But there is also a pitiful quality to the way in which the press let itself be manipulated by an apparently public-ity-hungry federal prisoner guilty of heinous crimes."

We finally reached the finish line—and home. On Saturday, November 5, we'd celebrated Ben's twelfth birthday on a plane between West Virginia and Washington (he'd rather have been elsewhere), and on Monday, the 7th, Marilyn and the kids linked up with me in Indiana. Monday night, election eve, we had a rally in Fort Wayne, which is near Huntington, where I was joined by the gubernatorial candidate, John Mutz, and Dan Coats, who was running for reelection to my old House seat. My family and I went back to my parents' house for dinner.

The next morning, November 8, 1988, Marilyn and I got up and had coffee with my Dad at Nick's Kitchen, a local café, and walked through Huntington to the courthouse to vote. On election day there is a feeling of fatigue and relief. One way or another, the whole thing is over. Life is going to be more normal, more the way you want it to be. There's a chance to go about some of your ordinary business again. On Election Day 1988 I went down to Dr. John Regan's office to get my teeth cleaned, as I have every election day. (He's a good dentist but a lousy pundit—back in 1980 he told me I'd lose to Bayh, and twelve years later he predicted Bush over Clinton!)

Marilyn and I would have preferred to spend election night in Indiana, but the campaign staff and I agreed that we should return to the national headquarters in Washington. George Bush was planning to spend election night in Houston, and without us neither of the candidates would be there to thank the national campaign staff and volunteers. So the family flew back to D.C. and went over to the Washington Hilton to watch the returns. Marilyn and I spent the evening with family and friends. There wasn't too much doubt about the outcome, but the forty-state victory was not quite the landslide people remember. Pennsylvania and Illinois turned out to be very close, and Ohio reasonably so; there were enough toss-ups to give the beginning of the evening just a little bit of suspense. Dukakis's concession came early, and we were soon down in the ballroom receiving cheers and thanking the army of campaign workers for helping to produce a come-from-behind victory. It was easy to forget how far behind we had been just three months before.

We don't have pictures from that night (in a last bit of strange campaign economics, we were told Canzeri wouldn't pay the photographer), but if you look at news footage of our appearance before the crowd, you'll probably see more jubilation than I was really feeling. After the fatigue and relief comes an inevitable election-night numbness, and it would be a while before I could really enjoy our win.

I could not pretend that I had come out of this campaign without significant problems. I had suffered more humiliations and ridicule than I ever expected to receive in a lifetime, let alone twelve weeks. If anybody in the national press still thinks I've had a charmed life, with everything silver-spooned my way, let them read through my clip file from the 1988 campaign. Six years later it's a folder I can't look through without wincing.

For my strength I had depended on my wife and my children and my faith, and none of them had let me down. Whatever had happened was God's will, however mysterious His workings. Even at the darkest moments I had not veered from my walk with Him, not questioned His plan for me. For that I am thankful.

Now I couldn't wait to get on with being Vice President. I told myself that we would shut the door on the campaign. Politics is politics, I reminded myself, and now that the campaign was over everything would change.

Little did I know.

8 | Transition

The press usually has its own story line for events that unfold over weeks or months, a narrative that may or may not coincide with reality. In my case, the theme of the story now changed to The Education of Dan Quayle, which in fact became the title of a *New York Times Magazine* article in the summer of 1989. But the shift to this kind of story got under way almost at the beginning of the transition from the Reagan to the Bush administration. The underlying drama of the story was: okay, the American people have saddled themselves with this guy, now is there any way he can be brought up to speed?

The result was a series of stories that I was undergoing some kind of unusual, almost remedial, education. *Time* did a piece on the cram courses in foreign and domestic policy that were supposedly being fed me. Actually, I initiated leisurely meetings, usually breakfasts, with people in and out of government whom I already knew or wanted to know. I met with members of the congressional leadership—Bob Dole, George Mitchell, Bob Michel—as well as various policy experts and scholars. Most important, I had daily meetings with George Bush where we planned the future of his administration. The day after the election, I'd met him and the Reagans on the South Lawn of the White House, where the outgoing President and First Lady congratulated the four of us on winning. Afterwards, Bush took Marilyn and me into his office, and he told me that from now on I'd be kept informed of everything I would need to know if I had to serve as President. From that point on I was in on all the meetings having to do with the selection of the Cabinet and other key arrangements for the new administration. But I knew that the real test of what kind of Vice President I'd be would only come after the inauguration. That's when I would see if I was a player.

I met with some of my predecessors in the vice-presidency, an office the first Vice President, John Adams, once described as "the most insignificant . . . that ever the invention of man construed or his imagination conceived." One of these predecessors, who in modern times had helped enlarge the office and turn it into a political springboard, was Richard Nixon. He stressed the need for loyalty to the President and recommended that I do a great deal of international travel, as he had done for President Eisenhower in the 1950s. He also suggested I stay in touch with all of the state party chairmen; the President wouldn't have time to do that himself, and it was important for the off-year elections we'd face in 1990, not to mention any reelection campaign in 1992.

It turned out that the day we scheduled for him to come to Washington coincided with a planned visit by former Presidents Ford and Carter: they were due to present the outgoing President with a report they had put together called *The American Agenda.* When I learned that they would be in town, I called Nixon to ask if it bothered him that all these other Presidents would be at the White House while he was on the other side of Pennsylvania Avenue, at the little transition office in Lafayette Square. It didn't bother him at all. By this point I don't think he much cared about whatever symbolism the press might see in something like that. He just seemed pleased to be of service—to be able to get on with whatever job presented itself. This wasn't such a bad piece of advice in itself, however indirectly it came my way. I was going to try not to be obsessed with the press, to do the job in front of me without worrying about every little item and twist in the coverage. As it was, accounts of my meeting with Nixon were dominated by a goofy picture of him and me entering the office. I noticed that the rain had stopped, so I pointed up to the sky and uttered some pleasantry like, "See, the skies are clearing." The gestures and our expressions resulted in a silly-looking picture that overwhelmed whatever story ran with it. You can't control these things, and you'll go crazy if you worry about them. Afterwards, Nixon's comment to the press was something about how I wasn't the dunce they made me out to be—helpful, I suppose, but less than one might have hoped for.

Fritz Mondale, who came across as not having been especially happy as Jimmy Carter's Vice President, had some interesting ideas. He stressed the number of people who would try to cut you off—put you "out of the loop," as the phrase goes—and he advised me against accepting any line-item authority (that is, responsibility for any particular program). The Space Council is now the statutory responsibility of the Vice President, so I was going to be involved in space policy, and publicly identified with the program, whether I wanted to be or not. But Mondale warned that, while identification with a specific area of policy might sound like a good idea for a Vice President in search of visibility and recognition, the office doesn't really provide the kind of authority that lets him carry out the task. He finds himself blocked by Cabinet members and competing power centers within the administration, and winds up being both frustrated and blamed by the public for failure in an area that he never really had the clout to influence—despite its having been "given" to him.

I gave his advice careful consideration, but in the end I set it aside. I went out of my way to seek responsibility for the White House Council on Competitiveness—for two reasons. First, I had been impressed with the Reagan administration's whole deregulatory thrust, and I didn't want to see any reversal of the powerful eight-year trend they had begun. Second, and perhaps most important, this kind of responsibility would make me a key player in the administration. President Bush, from the moment he took office, made it clear to everyone in the West Wing that I was to have all the access that I wanted. He hoped that that would make me conversant with all aspects of the presidency, the only way I could be properly prepared in the event of suddenly having to assume the office. The need for this broad, general involvement in the administration makes it unwise, I think, for the Vice President, as some have proposed, to head up a department of the Cabinet. Line-item responsibilities like the Space Council are one thing, but spending all one's time in one special area is not the best preparation for the presidency.

I turned most of the transition operation over to two trusted friends, Indianapolis lawyer Dan Evans and Washington insider Fred Fielding, who had been counsel to the Bush–Quayle campaign. Ken Adelman supplied us with valuable help from time to time. Most of our work involved picking a staff, and the bitter experience of the campaign left me determined to get just whom I wanted. Selecting a chief of staff, somebody both savvy and loyal, was my top priority, and the job proved hard to fill. One person I would have liked was Joe Wright, who was then directing OMB and has since become an executive with W. R. Grace, but that didn't work out. I ended up falling back on Bob Guttman, who'd been on my Senate staff for years and had done innovative work for me on JTPA. Bob had keen interests in education and job training, but he simply didn't have the stomach for partisan politics. Within a matter of months he told me he wanted to move on. He always served me loyally and was a great help in getting our operation going.

I was in a difficult situation vis-à-vis other members of my Senate staff. Most people around me, politicians and those in the press, naturally assumed that I would bring a lot of my staff people with me, but that wasn't so. There were many good people who'd served me with distinction, but the office of Vice President is executive in nature and requires different skills than the legislative side.

Marilyn had become so insistent on loyalty that after the election she strongly objected to my having Stu Spencer over to the house. He'd called to say he wanted to give me some advice on the transition, and Marilyn couldn't understand how I could stand seeing him. I argued to her that if I could turn him around a little bit, stroke his ego, then he might stop attacking me behind my back. My instincts ran toward conciliation, but Marilyn knew better. Don't give this guy the satisfaction of thinking you need his advice, she said, because he'll just go back and talk about how important he is and how needy you still are. Spencer did come over, and he did brag about how much in need of advice I was. In hindsight, I realize that Marilyn was right again. On matters like this, I should have listened to her more than I did. She was always my strongest and most loyal adviser.

During the last month of the campaign stories had circulated about how Marilyn was really the power behind the scenes, the person who did my thinking and made my decisions. These stories were mostly just one new spin on the caricature the media wanted to portray. But *she* was now being caricatured. The truth—that she has always been my closest adviser, someone with excellent political skills and a broad awareness of issues—got lost in the dragon-lady cartooning. Right after the election she was being pulled in opposite directions. There were those who thought she should keep herself as much in the background as possible, so that an image of me as independent and in charge would be strengthened. But there were others urging her to accept an appointment to fill out the remaining four years of my Senate term. Governor Bob Orr of Indiana wanted to know if Marilyn wanted to be considered for the seat. If Marilyn had said yes, it probably would have been hers for the asking, and she got all kinds of letters and phone calls from people back home pressing her to take it. She would have done an excellent job, but after some discussion of it at home she concluded that it really wouldn't work. I thought the press would be looking at her every single day, searching for the smallest traces of disagreement between her and the Bush–Quayle administration. By the time she was scheduled to have lunch with Governor Orr, she'd asked our old friend Mary Moses Cochran (the woman who'd given us that beeper a few months before in New Orleans) to call her husband, who was Bob Orr's administrative assistant, and just tell the Governor not to ask. In the end my former employee and good friend, Dan Coats, who was then a Congressman, got the nod.

We talked about Marilyn resuming her law career as she had planned to do before my nomination got her sidetracked. But considering the possibilities for apparent conflict of interest, it didn't even seem possible. Also, we had three children who needed the attention of their mother at this difficult time of transition. Fortunately, there were other reasons to stay out of legal practice for a while—namely, the opportunities she would have in her role as Second Lady, the chance to make a real difference in fields like breast cancer awareness and disaster preparedness. From the day we took office, Marilyn was determined to have an impact in those areas, and she did. She was going to set her own course, which suited me—as well as Barbara Bush—just fine. She and Marilyn had a friendly relationship. Mrs. Bush had considerable influence on her husband, much more than the public perceived. She had great political instincts and could tell which people were loyal and which ones weren't serving her husband well. Over the next four years, George Bush and I should have listened to our wives even more than we did.

That Christmas before the inauguration we managed a family ski vacation in Vail, Colorado. This was a much needed family break away from Washington. As the New Year approached it was time for us to get ready for the big day. The new Congress was taking office a few weeks before George Bush and I would be sworn in, and I resigned my Senate seat effective January 1 so that my successor would not be at a disadvantage because of seniority. This meant that I would be "unemployed," or at least without a paycheck, for three weeks, which was an awkward prospect. I was not the $600-million man. I was a Senator living off my salary, and I had a mortgage payment to make. So I asked the President-elect if I could go onto the transition office's payroll for a few weeks. After all, I was working every day to get my part of the new administration ready for its duties. Bush told me it was fine with him. That took care of the mortgage. When it came to buying Marilyn's and the children's inaugural clothes, she had her own solution: she sold the family van.

"Transition" was a word that applied to every aspect of our lives. It wasn't just a case of changing jobs; it was a matter of watching *everything* change. We would be leaving our house in McLean and moving across the river to the vice-presidential residence on the grounds of the old Naval Observatory in Washington, D.C., where the Secret Service would be a constant presence in our lives.

Would the press change too? Marilyn and I now both realize we were naive to think it might. We figured that if I did a good job, and was perceived to be working closely with George Bush, then the situation would turn itself around: the truth would come out. We still didn't realize what a vested interest the media had in the caricature they had drawn, and we didn't believe what lengths they would go to cement it. There were already warning signs that the tone of the campaign coverage would continue. The *Washington Post* began its "Quayle Watch" column—a regular report on virtually every sighting of me, all of it reinforcing the feeling that I was some sort of bizarre phenomenon that bore constant watching. Still, I had hopes that things would change.

First I had to be sworn in—and make sure I avoided the ultimate gaffe, stumbling over some word in the oath of office. It was going to be administered by Justice Sandra Day O'Connor, who was a friend from Arizona, and before inauguration day I thought about calling her to make sure we had exactly the same version of the vice-presidential oath. I decided against it, finally, because I knew how these things get out (talk about a perfect item for the "Quayle Watch"). Still, I remained uneasy, and I'll never quite forget the sounds I heard as I raised my right hand at the lectern on the Capitol steps: those hundreds of whirring, clicking cameras and microphones. And sure enough, there was a small mistake—Justice O'Connor's, not mine. She was trying to recite the oath from memory, and she ended up leaving out a few words. I knew the words by heart, and I could hardly believe what I was hearing. I thought to myself, how could this happen? I repeated the words she gave me and shortly after noon on January 20, 1989, became the forty-fourth Vice President of the United States.

My parents were somewhat overwhelmed by my new circumstances but looked forward to the excitement that would come with them. (They also learned to put up with the inconveniences: at times they would give a different name when making dinner reservations.) As an inaugural present they gave me a beautiful silver model of the *Mayflower*, the ship that had carried my distant ancestor Miles Standish, a "servant of God and country," to the shores of America. The small plaque inside the model's glass case was inscribed to commemorate this important day in my life and to remind me of the ship as a "Symbol of Freedom and Courage." I did not yet know what opportunities and perils would befall America in the next four years, or just how my service to her would be rendered, but as I turned away from the lectern where I had sworn my oath, I was ready, humbly, to step into my country's history.

PART TWO

The Quayle Model

1989

9 | Setting Up Shop

The Vice President officially resides in the admiral's house on the grounds of the Naval Observatory in northwestern Washington. It's a wonderful old house that was finished in 1893. At the beginning of the Bush administration it symbolized the peculiar new life the Quayle family would be leading. We were living near telescopes that could see to the edge of the solar system, yet we couldn't open our own windows, these huge bulletproof affairs installed during the 1970s when the house was renovated for its new role as the "Veep's" residence. I didn't want to be a complainer, but I did want to keep hearing the simple sounds of the real world, like cars driving by and crickets at night—the same things I'd always heard on Union Church Road in McLean, our home for the previous twelve years. I finally convinced the Secret Service to relax security a little and put in some screens and let us open things up a bit.

With the aid of donations, we remodeled the third floor and put in some bedrooms for our children. Eventually this great old place began to feel like home, but we never lost the sense that all of it was temporary. We did expect to stay for eight years instead of four, but even so we tried to remember that in this house we were really the guests of the Navy, whose stewards were even available to cook dinner.

If the Navy was our landlord, the Secret Service was our protector, which took some getting used to. At the beginning the agents stood guard right outside the front door, all the time, until I persuaded them to move a little off to the side. This sounds like a small thing, but just being able to walk out the front door without feeling a protective blanket being immediately thrown over me made a big psychological difference. At the beginning, I'd walk on the grounds with Marilyn, and the Service would follow along less than thirty feet behind us. Finally, I had to say, "Look, guys, we're just trying to take a walk in our own yard!" Throughout the four years I worked to get more freedom on the premises, and by the end things were somewhat more relaxed. Hubie Bell's by-the-book detail gave way to Joe Petro's somewhat more accommodating one. But I was never permitted to resume my old habit of jogging on the Washington mall—something I see Bill Clinton has managed to do! For exercise I golfed at the Congressional Country Club and ran on the quarter-mile track that Vice President Bush had installed at the Naval Observatory. I also played basketball with my kids on a half-sized court we shared with naval personnel. When we got to Vail at Christmastime, we'd go out on the slopes with both the Secret Service and the Ski Patrol. Before we left office, my lead agent, Ralph Basham, told me that the Secret Service experience with the young Quayle family would help them serve the Clintons and Gores.

We just had to remember that the Secret Service had a job to do. It was their business to think up worst-case scenarios, like a terrorist raid on the house. There were threats to deal with—on average, over a hundred a week, most of them directed to the office in letters and phone calls. During the Gulf War we would have to take extra precautions: different routes for me, a closer watch on the kids at school. Once in a while there would be a threat that especially concerned the agents, and they'd calmly tell me about it: "We're going to stand very close to you when you give your speech today, and if there are any shots, please get down behind the podium, which is bulletproof." Not exactly words to relax somebody, especially one who, to begin with, prefers a stand-up mike to a podium. I just tried not to dwell on any nightmarish possibilities. If I had, I couldn't have done my job and lived my life as a husband and father. Besides, I knew I was in God's hands as well as the capable ones of the Secret Service. (And on one occasion they were in good hands with me. When the family went white-water rafting along the Colorado River, I was the one who pulled Joe Petro out of the water!)

Even on ordinary days the agents had their plates full, dealing with a young and sometimes rambunctious family, the most physically active to occupy the house in the fifteen or so years it had served as the Vice President's home. By the time the Bushes moved in back in 1981, their kids were grown, and even when he was President, I noticed, George Bush did not chafe against the restrictions imposed by the Secret Service. He seemed able to accept them with a greater resignation than I could.

My kids didn't like the new security any more than they did the new limelight. The combination was putting them through huge changes. Out in McLean, where they were part of the gifted-and-talented programs of the Fairfax public schools, they had lived very anonymously—I'm sure some of their friends didn't even know I was a Senator. Now they were attending private schools in Washington, to which the Secret Service would drive them. Tucker used to complain that, when he went through the iron gates surrounding the residence, he felt as if he were being locked into jail. During the first weekend after we moved in, he had a friend over, and they tried to go out to a drugstore on Wisconsin Avenue. Before they got there a car from the uniformed division of the Secret Service pulled up alongside of them and asked the two boys if they wouldn't prefer to ride. The boys were a little put out at this intrusion.

Marilyn and I soon began to travel a lot. She would make most of the foreign trips with me, and she had her own domestic destinations. However, we had a firm rule about doing everything possible to see that one of us could be home with the kids. From time to time we wound up in comic situations, where the two of us would be communicating with each other through our children. But we'd always call them from the road. A phone call is not like having a mom or dad at home, but it's a substitute of sorts. We also called each other. The traveling spouse would initiate the call; if we were both away from home, it was up to me.

Our children are all good-natured, and they were very aware of all the new privileges and opportunities that went along with the restrictions. But in those first few months, if you'd given them the chance to go back to Virginia, they'd have packed their bags in a flash.

Still, there were plenty of compensations. For one thing, the children got to see more of their grandparents than they used to. My mother and father started coming to Washington more frequently than they had in my congressional days, and they would stay with the kids when Marilyn and I were on some of the foreign trips. And when I wasn't traveling, my hours and routine were actually much more stable and predictable than they'd been in the Senate. Our adaptable children even found the up side of some of the awkward protections that surrounded them. Tucker actually *liked* the bulletproof windows: on rainy days he and Ben could toss their lacrosse ball back and forth inside the house without worrying about breaking them. Our children were very concerned that their friends like them for themselves, not because their father was Vice President. Corinne didn't like my going to her school games, because the visiting team and their parents would ask me for autographs. Our children never thought of themselves as celebrities, and never showed that much interest in the real celebrities they had a chance to meet. On days when the White House would be buzzing with excitement because the Queen of England, Michael Jackson or one of any number of sports champions or Hollywood stars was due to drop by, the kids would often decline the chance to come to the office with me, pleading school or even homework as their excuse. When we were all together on a weekend, we lived as normally as possible. Tucker, Ben, and Corinne would rent videos at the local Blockbuster, and we'd relax as we used to. We were a close family before moving into the VP residence, and four years later, after some terrible pressures, we left it even closer.

From 1989 to 1993 I spent most of my time in Washington in an office in the White House, only feet away from the Oval Office. My loyal secretary, Cynthia Ferneau, who had worked for me since I came to Congress, now joined me there. Cynthia had worked for many years on the Hill while raising her two sons, and she was always a warm mother figure to my staff, the one who kept in touch with them even after they'd moved on to other positions. She was always proud to be called a secretary (instead of an "administrative assistant"), and she loved helping out the Quayle family when we needed her. In a pinch she'd pick up Corinne at school. She kept me on schedule for sixteen years and was a friendly presence through happy and stressful times. Cynthia remains a special member of our family.

The rest of my staff settled into quarters in the Old Executive Office Building next door. The OEOB is a great, cavernous, overdecorated nineteenth-century landmark—a monstrosity to some and a masterpiece to others—that seemed an unlikely head-quarters for a modern-day operation with faxes and cellular phones. The OEOB is where we had photo ops. I also had two offices on Capitol Hill. As President of the Senate, I had one just off the Senate floor and another in the Dirksen Senate Office Building. I used the Capitol office when I pushed the President's legislative program, and I hung portraits of the four Hoosier for-mer Vice Presidents there. (The most famous of these four men was probably Thomas Marshall, number two to Woodrow Wilson, who pronounced that what this country needs is a good five-cent cigar.)

In the ornate old OEOB, I couldn't forget history and tradition, and that was not a bad thing. My desk there was the one Harry Truman had once used in the Oval Office, and thinking about his situation was instructive. Back in April 1945, when Truman hur-riedly assumed the presidency, he didn't even know that the United States was developing an atomic bomb; a few months later he would have to make the decision to drop it over Japan. By the time Nelson Rockefeller and George Bush held the vice-presi-dency, the office had evolved, from sheer necessity in the nuclear age, to a point where the Vice President's awareness of national security matters was kept on a par with the President's.

It's easy to succumb to the powers and perks of an office that supplies people to do whatever you want done, and whose status ensures that everyone takes your phone calls. Fourteen years ear-lier, I was a young lawyer and newspaper publisher in a small town, and now I was Vice President. It was important to remem-ber that I was the same person I'd been in Huntington.

The power of the presidency and vice-presidency attracts staffers with unusual talent and ambition. One such person was Bill Kristol. Bill is a Harvard Ph.D. in government and political science, son of the distinguished historians Irving Kristol and

Gertrude Himmelfarb. He had been in Washington since 1985, when Secretary of Education Bill Bennett made him his chief of staff. It was Ken Adelman who first brought Bill to my attention during the transition. Bill had interviewed for the job of domestic affairs adviser to the President, but for one reason or another John Sununu wasn't going to give it to him. When I heard that, I told Sununu I'd be interested in having Bill Kristol for that job on my own staff, and that's the position he held until he replaced the departing Bob Guttman as my chief of staff in May.

Bill is an intellectual with good political skills, somebody not content to be a theorist but eager to turn his ideas into action. Despite Sununu's reluctance to have him in the White House itself, Bill developed strong ties to the West Wing operation, and that contributed greatly to his effectiveness for us. From the beginning he was aggressive, and even before he took over from Guttman, he worked long hours and dominated staff meetings.

I would rather have to hold somebody back than push him forward, and Bill Kristol certainly belongs in the first category. He had many ideas—some of them were excellent, and some of them would be discarded soon after they were advanced. But he was passionate about all of them. He'd come into government, in his own words, to change the world—"not to hum quietly." From the time I came to Congress I always attracted smart, competent people. I knew I had good political instincts and a feeling for the big picture. I depended on the staff to challenge me with ideas and information.

Nobody was more challenging than Bill Kristol, but the office I put together was full of talented people. Al Hubbard, a good friend from Indiana, who served as deputy chief of staff, was a Harvard Business School grad, a hard charger with a passion for ideas who, like me, relished the opportunity to slay dragons in the federal bureaucracy. He directed the Competitiveness Council, breaking china and making news. Carnes Lord—who had *two* Ph.D.'s, one in government and another in classics—had been a senior analyst for the National Institute for Public Policy and came recommended by Jeane Kirkpatrick and my Wyoming Senate colleague, Malcolm Wallop. Each morning Lord and I would share a 7:45 CIA briefing before meeting with the President and

Brent Scowcroft. Lord had some excellent, almost philosophical, ideas, but he worked in a rather solitary way on a staff that required give and take, and eventually I needed somebody in the job who was better built for the political rough and tumble. So about halfway through the administration I brought over Karl Jackson from the President's national security staff. Karl is a terrific combination of intellectual *gravitas* and common sense. He and I became close personal friends. We're still working together at the Hudson Institute and have formed a consulting firm. Karl is a former professor—from Berkeley, no less.

Dave Beckwith was my press secretary and Mark Albrecht directed the Space Council. Bill Gribbin came aboard as special assistant for legislative affairs. A consummate Hill rat who'd worked most recently for the Senate Republican Policy Committee, Gribbin was a natural fit; he is a great speech writer and was extremely loyal. Dave Ryder, our deputy chief of staff, was still in his early thirties. He was a good friend of Bush's vice-presidential chief of staff Craig Fuller and had worked as an advance man in the Bush campaign. My experience with Spencer and Canzeri had made me leery of putting anyone on staff just to please another office, but I did select Dave largely as a goodwill gesture to the President's staff. Greg Zoeller (the one who could "just smell it" that morning in New Orleans) came over from my Senate staff and assumed responsibility for public affairs. Cece Kremer and Anne Hathaway, who had both worked for Jim Baker at Treasury and for Marilyn and me in the campaign, now became my scheduler and assistant, respectively. Anne later became director and today is a trusted political confidante who is with us in Indianapolis.

As with any office, there were frictions and disappointments. Diane Weinstein, my legal counsel, departed in less than a year. In the beginning the coordination of my various staff units did not go as smoothly as it should have. Bob Guttman had set things up in a way that did not really include Marilyn's staff, trying to avoid more of those silly press stories about her running my office. Some of the tension that did exist was a creation of the press, and perhaps I did not pay as much attention to it as I should have. Denise Balzano did a wonderful job setting up Marilyn's office and getting her established in the areas of disaster preparedness and cancer awareness and prevention. However, things seemed to work better under Bill Kristol and Marguerite Sullivan, who became Marilyn's chief of staff halfway through the four years.

Marilyn did not like being a "potted plant" with the "adoring Nancy Reagan gaze." She had excellent political instincts and made no secret of her opinions. Even so, she's much softer than the public perception of her. The harshness that the press kept referring to was really a defense mechanism—her way of protecting me and her children more than herself.

On the whole I was pleased with the way the office ran, and with the loyalty that people showed me. Whatever my shortcomings, I hope that most of the staff would say they had a good boss. I certainly had one.

10 | President George Bush

George Bush was well aware of the frustrations of the vice-presidency. He had had eight years in which to feel them, after all—and to feel them with a greater intensity than I could have. When he assumed that office in 1981, he had already been a national figure for a decade, the man they used to say had "the best résumé in American politics." Aside from serving in the Congress, he had been our UN Ambassador, CIA director, envoy to China, and chairman of the Republican National Committee. By 1981 he was used to the kind of executive responsibility that the vice-presidency simply doesn't permit. He had also made a credible run for the presidency itself against Ronald Reagan. Being selected for the second spot by a man who's defeated you has its own awkwardness: the Democrats never tired of mentioning how, during the 1980 primary season, Bush had referred to Reagan's proposed program as "voodoo economics." In fact, though he did say the job had had its rewards, and despite Ronald Reagan's giving him plenty to do, I think George Bush's frustrations in the vice-presidency must have resembled those of his fellow Texan Lyndon Johnson, who had wielded enormous power in Washington before becoming number two and, like Bush, was picked for the job by a man who defeated him for the presidential nomination. In such a situation, if the President doesn't keep his Vice President busy and informed, the office can feel like a demotion, the kind of job it was in the nineteenth century, when Daniel Webster declined it by saying, "I do not propose to be buried until I am dead."

The President and I talked about this curious institution on a number of occasions. He knew how rudely the West Wing of the White House tends to treat the vice-presidency, and he urged me to put my own stamp on the office: "You ought to go ahead and establish the Quayle model," he said. I told him that I felt very comfortable with the Bush model—the combination of loyalty and preparedness he had always exhibited during Reagan's two terms in office. He agreed that those were the two most important elements of the job—stick up for the boss and be ready to take over at a moment's notice—but he thought I would develop my own ideas about it and that in due course a "Quayle model" would emerge whether I consciously molded one or not. He emphasized the need to "be prepared" by telling me that he wanted regular meetings together. What's more, he urged me to attend absolutely any Oval Office meeting, on domestic or foreign policy, that I wanted to. In fact, he was offering an astonishing amount of access—unprecedented. This is the way it should be. The other chief requirement of the job—loyalty—was never much discussed. He just assumed it on my part, as he had a right to.

What I had no right to assume at the start—what I had to earn, and what was his to give (or not) as he saw fit—was his confidence. His political instincts, and what he knew of me from the Senate, had made him pick me for the ticket, but after the battering I'd taken from the media and others, he needed to see that his instincts had been correct. He believed that Vice Presidents should stay in the background, which was fine with me; I'd have a chance to prove myself. I never once went to him with any strategy to improve my image, though many friends of the President's and mine suggested it. Vice Presidents aren't supposed to worry about their own political fortunes, and it would have been a sure sign of weakness for me to do that in front of him. I gained his confidence the old-fashioned way: by earning it. From time to time I'd be told by mutual friends that Bush had gone out of his way to mention my name and let it be known that he was pleased with me.

I'm sure that there were times when he became irritated with me, such as the one in 1990, when I took a harder public line on Soviet policy than the administration wanted to put out, or those occasions when he believed Bill Kristol was leaking more to the press than he should have been. He never expressed any disappointment with me directly. I could see it on his face and he could communicate it very directly through body language. He might send me a friendly, oblique message, through Sununu or, later, Sam Skinner, but he never really chewed me out, not even when I asked him to. When I sensed that I had gone too far on the Soviet question, I brought it up myself, volunteering to be taken to the woodshed. He just dismissed it. I suppose he figured that if I was bothered enough to mention it, then his message, however indirectly it had been sent, had gotten through. When the President got angry, he didn't get loud; he got quiet.

He could not stay mad at anyone for long, but a few things drove him crazy. He despised leaks, and he felt contempt for Ed Rollins and other Republicans who would try to grab headlines by trashing him. When he was upset over something, he was likely to ignore it: that's how you knew he was bothered. He always wanted people to be comfortable. During a meeting he'd pour cream in people's coffee or offer them Velamints.

George Bush wanted to avoid friction. He didn't mind debate within his administration, but he was very bothered by any report of people not getting along. Brady and Baker, who considered themselves friends, had some interesting fights over territory. Each had a long-standing personal relationship with the President, and since each knew he could go directly to Bush, neither would give in to the other. I remember how during one turf battle between the two of them, Bush told Scowcroft: "I shouldn't have to be their referee. They owe it to me to work this out." I myself don't have much stomach for dressing people down, even when they haven't performed as I would like them to, and I wouldn't describe myself as a confrontational person. But I didn't mind the fights within the administration nearly so much as the President did. My feeling was: that's the way things get hashed out. The strong will survive and the weak will disappear. I didn't like it when things got personal, but I had a fairly high tolerance for the infighting that comes with any administration. He did not.

Sometimes the President was too courteous, too forgiving. Along with moments of strong leadership and an absolutely inspiring display of skill as commander in chief, there came moments when the President let himself down with his own kind-ness.

He enjoyed the job. He was better prepared for the office than any of this century's Presidents. He knew what the position entailed, and he worked hard at it. He was excellent at the cere-monial work required of the President as head of state. Ronald Reagan was the toughest possible act to follow in that regard, but George Bush looked and acted every inch a President. On the basis of the record—presiding over our victory in the Gulf War; low interest rates and low inflation; a 4 percent economic growth rate at the time of the 1992 election—he may even have been a great one. But he sometimes got distracted from what he himself had called "the vision thing." It wasn't that George Bush lacked a vision—he had a clear vision of a strong internationalist America that got her strength from her people. He had a clear understand-ing of markets and how they created wealth. He was skeptical of government solutions to domestic problems and antagonistic toward government regulations. What his administration never had in four years was a credible communication strategy. His staff would get bogged down in detail and forget about the big picture. Bush was a problem solver. Everyone would bring their problems, large and small, for him to resolve. Very seldom would there be a long strategy session focused on what direction the President wanted the country to take. Unfortunately, we turned into a reac-tive administration, and once the Gulf War was won and our poll ratings were sky-high, we kidded ourselves. There is more than enough blame to go around here, and I'm willing to take my share of it. But I do think I was one of the people who tried to give the administration more ideological edge than it had, even after it was too late.

The presidency can be, according to Teddy Roosevelt, a bully pulpit, and while George Bush did a splendid job of rallying the country at some very crucial moments, he was Reagan's opposite in that he didn't enjoy giving speeches. To him they were just a requirement of the job. He tended to prepare for them very quickly, to give his notes a once-over and then go out and get them over with. As a result, the White House lost the chance to define itself through clear, focused rhetoric. To go back to Lee

Atwater's term, the presidency (unlike the vice-presidency) *does* provide defining moments, but only if you're willing to grab them. President Bush liked to do his duty in a quiet, unflashy way. He knew how to go about the job, and he simply wanted to do it. There were times, however, when I think his staff let him get bogged down in busywork. In fact, on a couple of occasions I learned that they had scheduled him to do events that my own office had turned down. I think he realized these events were not very important, but he figured they would let the public see him going about what the press played up as the business of being President, while he knew the real work was conducted quietly, back at the office. I can remember seeing him one time after he had returned from a not-very-important trip to California and asking him what he had been doing out there. "Looking busy," he replied.

I developed a true affection for George Bush. He was a completely genuine, decent man. What's more, he went into and out of the office as absolutely the *same* man, and I think that says it all about the solidity of his character. He knew who he was. He didn't need power to tell him that. Sometimes before our weekly lunches the White House would schedule photo opportunities, during which the President would quickly pose with a parade of visitors and pass out what we called "chum," presidential souvenirs like key chains and cuff links. At one of these photo ops I remember the President being introduced to a little girl who was terminally ill. He put his arm around her, walked her over to a chair, and sat down to talk. He must have kept on talking with her for ten minutes. Her parents were standing over to the side in disbelief, as they watched the President of the United States forget about his schedule and just allow himself to be touched by the tragedy and strength of this child and her family. I will never forget this moment. I looked at George Bush and realized that while he was with this little girl he was absolutely unmindful of all his power and all the trappings of his office. He was relating to her not as the President but as a father—one who many years before had lost a little girl of his own.

George Bush is the kind of man I would aspire to be myself, and would want my own sons to emulate. In our personal conversations we frequently related as father to father, sharing news and anxieties about our children or grandchildren. My son Ben was the same age as George P. Bush, the President's grandson, and my daughter, Corinne, was about the same as George P.'s sister, Noelle. The two boys and the two girls became good friends and spent time at Camp David, the White House and our own house together.

Comedians used to caricature the President as a kind of goofy, overgrown schoolboy who sometimes fractured his syntax (imagine that!). Sometimes these depictions were affectionate and sometimes they were cheap, but every single day in my four years as Vice President I was proud to have George Bush's confidence and was honored to serve him.

11 | Face Time

When histories of the Bush administration are written from some dispassionate distance, without undue emphasis on its flaps and feuds, I think that its chief of staff, John Sununu, will come out very well. My own relations with John were good from the start, and I counted him as an ally and friend. He came out to our house in McLean one day during the transition, and we talked a little about my dismal experience in the campaign just past. John had been supportive of my selection—he'd wanted to see an ideological soulmate on the ticket—and sympathetic to my struggle with the press. In hindsight he said, "We should have sent you up to Harvard to have a debate on arms control with somebody like Sam Nunn. Let the two of you go at it for three hours, talking nothing but arms control, and the press would see that you'd mastered the most complex issue of all. If we'd done that, all this stuff about your being unable to hack it would have just gone away."

Intrigued, I asked, "Did you ever suggest that?"

"Yeah, I mentioned it," he said, "but the campaign just wasn't interested in it."

As Governor of New Hampshire, Sununu had helped rescue the Bush campaign, engineering Bush's victory in the New Hampshire primary, after Bob Dole had won the Iowa caucuses. Being chosen chief of staff a year later by Bush was generally seen as his reward. In some ways George Bush acted as his own chief of staff, solving whatever problems he was brought, but Sununu was exceptionally, almost blindly, loyal to the President. It's true that he could have used a few more diplomatic skills, but he preferred being around people like himself, ones who had edge. He had no taste for press-friendly moderates like Rich Bond, the RNC chairman, and Bob Teeter; he preferred combative guys like Lee Atwater and Roger Ailes who played the political game hard and weren't afraid of throwing an elbow once in a while. By 1992 none of these people, including Sununu, would still be around, and I think the President realized, too late, that he couldn't win without them.

The American public probably knows Sununu better from his later appearances on "Crossfire" than from his White House days. John has a brilliant, quick mind, and he could be as stubborn as all get-out. He has a dry sense of humor and was always cracking jokes. He was a strong family man, and you could see him warm up when his wife, Nancy, on whom he was quite dependent, was around. During the 1988 transition he was still busy as Governor of New Hampshire, and as a result he failed to get some of the people he wanted into key White House jobs. Baker, Darman, and Teeter, who were always on the scene, managed to get those slots for their own people. Sununu liked to do things himself. He would not delegate, and the staff he had never tried to assume much authority. They let John do it all, because that's what he wanted. And that, eventually, would contribute to his undoing. He never made any real friends in the press. Reporters didn't like him because he had an edge and refused to leak. He didn't care for them either. (He didn't suffer fools gladly.) He felt that the *Washington Post* had been out to get him from the start. He once told me that during a meeting with two *Post* reporters, they strongly implied that if he didn't supply them with a certain amount of inside information, he couldn't expect them to write favorable stories.

When he ran into trouble about his personal travel on government aircraft, this notorious nonleaker, with no friends in the press, found himself without any defenders. In fact—and this shows how desperate he was at the end—he called Bob Dole and asked him for help. But Bob has a long memory, and it certainly extended as far back as the New Hampshire primary of 1988.

I learned my own lesson about leaking early on—in fact, before the administration even took office. During the transition, ABC

News's White House correspondent, Brit Hume, asked me if Jack Kemp was going to be named HUD secretary. I didn't say he was or he wasn't, but I let him read between the lines. "Well, don't you think he'd be pretty good?" I asked. And Brit said yes; so I said something like, "Well, stay tuned." That night on the ABC news, Peter Jennings told viewers that he had just learned from a White House correspondent that Congressman Kemp would be the new head of the Department of Housing and Urban Development. Maybe Brit had multiple sources. But I knew he *could* have gotten it just from me, and that taught me a lesson about hinting at things during off-the-record meetings, which is what my encounter with Brit supposedly was. I realized that you had to strike a balance between trying to curry favor with the press through leaks and stiffing them, the way Sununu often did.

Leaking is a dangerous but critical part of government. When information is leaked, it usually has enhanced credibility, because the press thinks it is getting something special. Some leaks are planned and coordinated, but most are not and some do a great deal of damage to an administration. Some people become leakers to show they are in the loop, something more important in Washington than one's salary and title. Other leakers do it—even if national security is involved—because they're not getting their way with the President. In the Bush administration, national security matters were handled in the Oval Office among a very small circle: myself, Scowcroft, Gates, Cheney, Powell, Baker, and the chief of staff. As a result, not once during the Bush administration was there a serious unauthorized leak involving national security.

Sununu wound up with almost as few friends in the Cabinet as he had in the press. As time went on its members began to complain that he wasn't conveying their messages and arguments to the President. Everything had to flow through John, and some of it was getting stuck. Why, you might ask, couldn't each department secretary make his points during the freewheeling give-and-take of a Cabinet meeting? That may be the popular idea of those meetings, but it was far from the truth in our administration—and in most modern presidencies.

Cabinet meetings in the Bush White House were stilted, boring affairs. Instead of creative ferment and the clash of ideas, there were droning reports—Carla Hills would give one about trade, and then Baker would give one, and Darman another, and so on. The truth is, Cabinet meetings are an anachronism. Generations ago the Cabinet was small, a handful of key individuals who would meet and quietly hammer out policy. Now it has swollen to the point where it can barely fit around its enormous table. (From time to time, Darman and I would kick around the idea of consolidating the federal government into fewer larger departments.) Over the decades, the White House press corps has swollen, too, and the way the two groups use each other ensures that nothing much is going to get done at Cabinet meetings. They are notoriously leaky, so the more substantive work is done in smaller meetings where there is a greater assurance of confidentiality.

When George Bush was selecting his Cabinet, John Sununu and I made a strong pitch for Jack Kemp. Jack had been a friend of mine since I was elected to Congress in 1976. I had urged him to run for the Senate from New York in 1980, the same year I ran in Indiana. If he had run, I'm convinced he would have won and become an even more influential voice in our party than he is today. Marilyn and Jack's wife, Joanne, are close friends. We all attended the Fourth Presbyterian Church in Bethesda, Maryland, and we sometimes played tennis together. I have always enjoyed being around Jack and Joanne. They are good people who want their country to succeed.

During the transition I argued that Jack was the type of person we needed for the Cabinet: a man full of ideas, mainly conservative, a bundle of energy and talent to help push the Bush agenda. Though some view us as potential rivals, on most issues Jack and I have the same viewpoint. Sadly, he disappointed me during the Bush administration. I know he was frustrated. He confided to me that he would have preferred to be Secretary of the Treasury or Defense, where he would have real power. Even so, he garnered more positive press attention as HUD secretary than any of his predecessors. But many times the attention came when he was criticizing the President or letting it be known that he was unhappy. Many questioned Jack's loyalty to Bush, and there were times when the President would have been justified in letting him go.

During Cabinet meetings Jack would sometimes squirm in his chair, and cough that nervous cough of his as he signaled that he couldn't wait to speak. (Baker called this Kemp's "High School Harry" mode.) The President—invariably with trepidation—would call on him, knowing that he would sometimes go off on tangents and not make any discernible point. Jack was constantly at war with Darman and Brady, and meetings where the three of them were present (without the President) turned into a mudfight of words.

The Bush Cabinet contained talented individuals, among them Dick Cheney. An ambitious insider, sometimes taciturn and apt to be cautious, he knew how to keep ahead of the politics involved in almost any situation. He was good at compromise, but in tricky circumstances he was much more willing than Jim Baker to risk losing. Lamar Alexander was good at Education, Sam Skinner did well with Transportation, and Bob Mosbacher performed ably at Commerce.

For all my disappointments with him, I saw, on occasion, how impressive Jim Baker could be. He was a skilled negotiator. The longtime Bush–Baker relationship was misunderstood by many. Bush always had the upper hand in it. It was the President who, years before, had taken Baker under his wing: George and Barbara Bush helped console Jim Baker after the death of his first wife. During all their years in politics, it was Bush who brought Baker along, not vice versa. That's why so many Bush loyalists were hurt in 1992, when the President was depicted as being so needy of Baker.

In fact, Baker's frequent invoking his "thirty-five-year friendship" with Bush was taken as a sign of weakness by some. As I mentioned, his negotiating skills are first-rate (if you tell him to go in and get a good deal, he will), but during the four years of the administration he lost most of his turf battles with Brent Scowcroft. When you meet Baker, you want to like him—he's quick and congenial and he enjoys jokes—but he socializes with only a select few. On almost every matter that came before him, he'd want to know what was in it for Jim Baker.

Taken as a whole, though, the Bush Cabinet was a more competent than creative group. Former members of Congress, retired or defeated, didn't always make the best Cabinet choices, since they found it hard to switch to an executive mentality. Among the most innovative and underrated members was Jim Watkins, the Secretary of Energy, who had a plethora of plans for getting his department more involved in high-tech research. A former admiral, Jim would speak up on military affairs and arms control matters, which exasperated Cheney. Meetings of the Cabinet ought to be natural occasions for the sharing of turf, for a little cross-fertilization, but whenever the group actually assembles, turf ends up getting more sharply staked out by the individual secretaries.

Meetings of the NSC were a completely different matter: specific, substantive issues would be crisply debated, and the President would either decide something immediately or indicate that he would wait—which usually meant that Brent Scowcroft was going to get his way, and you could pretty much count on whatever position you'd just heard him argue being the one that would prevail. Another big difference between the NSC and Cabinet meetings was that, except on rare occasions, the NSC didn't leak.

Scowcroft himself was a tenacious infighter, very turf-conscious, and as the years went on he became closer than anyone else in the administration to the President. In fact, they eventually developed the best working relationship I've seen between any two people in all my years in politics. They saw each other constantly, and the advice that Scowcroft gave to the President was unvarnished. Scowcroft knew how to win his battles with Jim Baker. He kept them from breaking out into the open, and he used his time with the President in a subtle way, moving Bush toward his own position and away from Baker's.

Access is what's craved beyond anything else in Washington, and Cabinet meetings provided only a diluted form of it. Without access you were simply out of the loop and a nonplayer. Fortunately, though my vice-presidency would present many challenges, having access to the President was not one of them.

12 | Thurs., 12:00 Noon, Lunch with Pres.

The centerpiece of my contact with the President was our Thursday lunch. Sometimes we'd put it on a Tuesday or Wednesday, if he or I had travel plans on the regular day. We fell off a bit when the 1992 campaign picked up steam, but throughout the four years we were remarkably consistent. The President had a little hideaway right off the Oval Office, and a steward would lay the meal out there. Sometimes on warm days we'd eat out by the pool, and a couple of times Marilyn and I had the President and Barbara out to the Vice President's residence, the house they'd lived in for eight years.

The lunches between the two of us were very informal. The President was always interested in political gossip, from the Hill or anywhere else around town, so I tried to keep him supplied with that. He also liked good jokes. He might not have been in Ronald Reagan's league when it came to telling them, but he wasn't bad either, and I always tried to have a couple to pass on to him. I'm one of those people who tend to forget jokes as soon as they hear them (no small blessing during these four years of my life), so rounding up jokes for the President became a line-item responsibility of my press secretary, Dave Beckwith. He'd call up some of his old buddies in the press and get me one or two that I could tell Bush.

The President and I would talk about our foreign travels, and then about whatever was going on in a given week. Sometimes, when there was something particularly important happening in one of my domains, like the Space or Competitiveness councils, I would go in with a slightly more formal agenda, a little sheet of paper on which I'd listed points to go over. The lunches became such an institution that other members of the administration learned to get in touch with me on Thursday mornings to request that I pass something on to the President. Nick Brady, the Treasury secretary, a Bush loyalist and confidant who had his battles with Darman, would ask me to be his messenger, just as Bob Mosbacher from Commerce might tell me to remind the President of a promise he had made to make a decision on something. Lou Sullivan of HHS, as well as Jim Watkins, also caught on to this opportunity, and Rich Bond, the head of the Republican National Committee, got into the act as well: "Could you tell the boss . . . ?" I was usually happy to oblige. After the lunch I would call back and tell whoever had made the request what the President's response was. But it was a little tricky, in that they were doing an end run around John Sununu—or later, Sam Skinner, when he took over as chief of staff. With that dislike of friction I've mentioned, the President would let the apparent contradiction persist: he didn't get mad at any Cabinet secretary who tried to speak through me, but I don't think he ever told Sununu or Skinner to unclog the pipeline either. He saved his anger for leaks.

Eventually some other members of the Cabinet, like Brady, had their own weekly meetings with the President. And that's where things got done—either there or at small group meetings in the Oval Office. Each morning at 8:15, Scowcroft, Bob Gates, Sununu, and I would meet with the President. The first order of business was national security. When that was concluded, Scowcroft and Gates would leave, but Sununu and I would stay. We'd talk about Congress, politics, the domestic agenda, the media, and whatever issue was on the front burner. For example, about a month into the administration, Congress began pushing for an increase in the minimum wage. It was a bad idea, something that would only trigger inflation and end up hurting the very people it was designed to help. But that's a complicated point to make to the voters, whereas coming out and calling for the increase is an easy way to look compassionate and score political points. In the face of this pressure from the Democrats in Congress, the administration needed a response that made both economic and political sense. It was not enough for us to say that an increase was a bad idea; we had to put forth an idea of our own. I suggested we propose an earned-income-tax credit for people at the lower end of the wage scale. It's not as simple and immediately attractive a notion as an increase in the minimum wage, but it was a better idea, and proposing it would keep us from appearing to be hard-hearted obstructionists.

On this matter I was disagreeing with the President. He was inclined to support an increase in the minimum wage if Congress would also create a "subminimum" or "training" wage for young people holding first-time jobs in places like fast-food restaurants. I still thought the tax credit made more sense, and I said so. Then and at other times, I had no trouble taking a position different from the President's. What he wanted me to do in meetings like this was to say exactly what I thought.

This time my argument did not carry the day. It was listened to carefully, but finally rejected on the theory that the earned-income credit would decrease the amount of revenue we needed to combat the deficit. So I had to accept that, and the next time a microphone was put in front of my face, my job was to say that an increase in the minimum wage tied to a subminimum training wage was a top-flight idea.

The distinction between private disagreement and public loyalty is clear and necessary, and both George Bush and I understood it. Anyone who thinks cheerleading for a policy you don't believe in amounts to hypocrisy doesn't really understand the way government has to work. If a Vice President or Cabinet official publicly undermines his President, then he's going to lose all effectiveness as an adviser, and he won't get a second chance to fight for what he *does* believe in—in private, where such fights ought to take place. Kemp periodically opposed the President publicly—only to meekly claim that he'd been misquoted. This didn't do the President or Kemp any good. The famous 1990 budget agreement would be the most severe test of loyalty I'd experience during the administration—a time when I really had to grit my teeth and smile and speak up for a deal I had grave questions about. But if I hadn't, I would have been no use to the President and, eventually, of no use to the country.

My arguments around the minimum-wage issue didn't go completely unheeded. I lost the central one, but once the administration had its position, I argued—successfully this time—that the President should present his offer to Congress on a take-it-or-leave-it basis. We didn't want to get caught up in protracted negotiations over a figure and end up looking as if we were trying to nickel-and-dime poor people. And we didn't want to set a precedent for that kind of haggling with the House and Senate.

On most domestic policy matters, including this one, I found myself in agreement with Sununu. About the only thing John and I disagreed on was our judgment of what would fly on Capitol Hill. The situation up there was always very fast-moving and fluid, and Sununu and I didn't always read it the same way. But we respected each other's analyses, because we knew they were based on experience: mine on my twelve years in both houses of Congress, and John's on both his dealings with the New Hampshire legislature and the advice he was now getting from Bob Dole and the rest of the leadership.

The old rule that knowledge is power is probably truer in Washington than anywhere else. And no one in the capital had more knowledge than Dick Darman, the President's OMB director. He was one of the key figures in the administration because he had more inside stuff—and more insights—than just about anybody. He loved to overwhelm you with facts. Darman was a Machiavellian, somebody who was always looking for the catch, the hidden trap. He liked power, and he liked being able to dominate others, but only if he'd beaten them in a fair, intellectual fight. He was a control freak who usually arrived at a meeting with written "talking points" that he'd pass around. He was always able to cite precedents from the Ford and Reagan years, and he had no awe of elected politicians. Running for office (i.e., shaking hands at factory gates at 6:00 A.M.) would seem beneath him. He could be very brusque with people who didn't prepare cogent arguments to buttress their positions. He used to come into my office and complain about the lightweights he was surrounded with on the White House staff. Those lightweights did not, he and I would hasten to add, include Sununu, who was Darman's equal in intellect and ambition. At first I thought the two of them were *too* much alike and would not get along. I wasn't sure their egos would be able to fit into the same room. But they wound up developing a surprisingly good relationship, though Darman usually got the upper hand because of his insider knowledge. As time went on, Sununu wound up being almost deferential to him—a posture one didn't see the chief of staff assuming often.

The President relied on Darman, and never more so than when he was getting ready for a press conference, because Dick could take a complicated question and give Bush a clear answer in two sentences. He had a hand in the President's speeches, too. There were many times when you would ask George Bush something and be told by him to "ask Dick." That's how much he depended on him. Darman gathered power to himself, and there was no going around him. When Sam Skinner replaced Sununu as chief of staff, he tried to cut Darman out—an absolutely impossible thing to do. Like anyone else, Darman could have been fired, but he could not be cut out; if he was in the White House at all, he was going to be heard, because he's been around so long and because he's so darned smart.

Darman and Sununu were the two most forceful personalities and, along with Brent Scowcroft and Jim Baker in foreign affairs, the most powerful players in the Bush administration. Over the four years I watched them and worked with them and tangled with them, never forgetting how formidable they could be. But in all the time we were in office I never got rid of the feeling that there was somebody else, just as strong and sharp as Darman and Sununu, missing from those discussions in the Oval Office, somebody who was absent from his rightful place at the table during Cabinet meetings, but who haunted them like Banquo's ghost. I'm talking about John Tower.

13 | The Man Who Wasn't There

John Tower was a tough man and a good Senator—maybe even a great one. He was also my friend. He could be rough on people. I can remember catching it from him during my very first meeting as a member of the Senate Armed Services Committee. Cap Weinberger, President Reagan's Defense secretary, was testifying, and I went beyond my allotted ten minutes of questioning. I think I even asked for a second round. When the meeting was over, John stopped me on my way out and suggested I have a seat. He took a cigarette out of his gold case and started tapping it (a gesture I would get to know well over the years), and then he told me: "I notice that you like to ask a lot of questions. Now, I want your help, but I served on this committee for six years before I ever spoke. I just wanted you to know that." I got the message: John wanted me to follow his lead and play by his rules. (I later found out that one of my parents had inadvertently made matters worse by sitting in Tower's wife's usual seat when they came to watch that hearing.)

During my years in the Senate, John and I developed a very good relationship; in fact, I know that in 1988 he told George Bush I would be a good choice for Vice President. John and I had such respect for each other that when the going got rough in the 1988 campaign, he was one of the Republican Senators who stood by me, traveled with me, and gave me much needed wise counsel. He was a true friend. Following his lead on the Armed Services Committee was never a problem, because his ideas about national defense contributed mightily to the revitalization of our forces during the Reagan years. That's why I pushed hard for his nomination to be Secretary of Defense. There were some on the Bush team who had their doubts—Brent Scowcroft and Bob Teeter among them. During the transition, somebody even leaked to the *Washington Post* that I was the one pushing Tower hardest, because they thought that would hurt his chances of being picked—an indication of my weak standing in the polls just after the election. But I kept pushing, and I was delighted when the President made the nomination.

I did not expect the trouble (certainly not the *kind* of trouble) that the nomination ran into in the Senate. In all the time I served with him there, I never saw John Tower even a little bit tipsy—not on the Senate floor, not during a meeting, and not when we traveled together. He was a very conscientious, dedicated legislator. But certain rumors about the way he conducted his private life (and I'm not claiming John was any kind of saint) got to Sam Nunn, and that got the whole ferocious ball rolling.

Once it was going, I was surprised at how friendless John turned out to be. I'll never forget a brown-bag lunch I had in Fred McClure's office at the White House during this period. Fred was Bush's chief congressional lobbyist, and we were trying to come up with a strategy for the nomination. John was there too, and I said to him, "This is not that difficult. The only thing you need to do is find two Democrats who are your friends to go get the five Democratic votes you'll need." It turned out that John really couldn't go to anyone, not even Fritz Hollings, whom he thought he could trust but who wound up violently opposing him; he couldn't even go to John Glenn, who had promised his vote but finally turned against him. It was an extraordinary betrayal, after twenty-three years of distinguished service in that body. Lloyd Bentsen ended up voting for him, but that was because John was from Texas and Bentsen had introduced him during the confirmation hearings; if the vote had been closer, even he would have come down against John.

One Democrat who stuck with him was Chris Dodd of Connecticut, because John had been a defender of his father, Senator Tom Dodd, when the Senate conducted censure proceedings against him twenty years earlier. That's the kind of collegiality one used to be able to count on in the Senate, and I think John might have gotten through if more of the older, forceful personalities like Russell Long, Richard Russell or Scoop Jackson had still been around. But the Senate was a different place in 1989. The Republicans were in the White House for the ninth straight year, and a great load of partisan frustration had built up since 1981. The courtesies the Senate once granted to its own—even to an irascible loner like John Tower—could no longer be counted on.

It was a depressing several weeks, during which even some people who should have been John's natural allies wound up making things much worse. My friend John Warner, by then the ranking Republican on the Armed Services Committee, let people know he hadn't made up his mind. That's all the Democrats needed to start smelling blood. Ken Adelman (an especially good friend of mine who lent me plenty of support in the dark days of 1988 and beyond) wrote a piece in the *Washington Times* maintaining that John's "lack of discretion" with women and liquor, during arms control negotiations in Geneva a few years before, now "raise[d] questions about his overall judgment and probity." Ken genuinely believed that, after all the controversy surrounding the confirmation, John would never be able to function effectively in the job: how, for example, would he be an inspiration to the troops? I thought this whole notion of John as some sort of drunken sailor who couldn't keep anything straight was a lot of nonsense, and I called Ken up to tell him so.

But the one who really put the screws to John Tower was Sam Nunn. Some say that his opposition had to do with the way John had mistreated him on the Senate Armed Services Committee. Heck, John Tower mistreated everyone. He was aggressive, determined, and he usually got his way. Others say that Sam was beginning to position himself to run for President in 1992 and felt that he could score points with the liberals in his party if he could be seen standing up to the hawkish Tower. There were other instances of his political behavior that gave credence to this analysis: changing his position on abortion (from pro-life to moderately pro-choice), resigning from the all-male Burning Tree golf club, and eventually going against the administration in the debate on the Persian Gulf War (a fatal mistake as it turned out).

Sam Nunn is a mystery even to his friends. When I was in the Senate, I felt reasonably close to him. We golfed together (he is a ferocious competitor on the links), and Marilyn was good friends with Sam's wife, Colleen. For a while we all went to the same church. Sam and I both regularly attended the Senate's Wednesday morning prayer breakfasts, and on most major issues we weren't really that far apart. The real motive for Sam's opposition to John's nomination still escapes me. The supposed womanizing and drinking were excuses. Sam Nunn genuinely feared John Tower's becoming Secretary of Defense, but to this day I don't really understand why.

Some of the more aggressive lobbying on John's behalf was left to me. Encouraged by the President and Sununu, I eagerly became the administration's point man on the issue. One somewhat unlikely arena I chose for making the case was the Economic Club of Indianapolis. They'd heard me speak many times, usually in a lighthearted way, without notes and followed by a lot of give-and-take, but this time I made it a formal thing with a podium and prepared text. I can remember, about five minutes before I went on, hearing someone say, "Oh, I hope he doesn't talk about the Tower nomination." I meant for them to hear a great deal about it. I opened with a constitutional argument against what the Democrats, frustrated over being so long shut out of the White House, were trying to do. "Simply put," I said, "Senate Democrats are escalating their attack on the powers of the President. And when they cite the 'advise and consent' powers granted them by the Constitution, they undoubtedly assume that Americans do not know that the prevailing view among the framers of the Constitution was that the Senate's role in the appointment process would be largely reactive and, for the most part, passive. As Alexander Hamilton put it in *Federalist* paper number 76, 'it is not likely that [the Senate's] sanction would often be refused, where there were not special and strong reasons for the refusal.'" I didn't—and still don't—believe there was anything in John Tower's record or character to justify that refusal; his personal problems, much exaggerated by his opponents, just provided a convenient opportunity for the kind of confrontation that had been brewing in any case.

The part of the speech that got the most notice was my reference to a quotation by *New York Times* liberal columnist Anthony Lewis—not someone I often cite in an argument. About the confirmation controversy, Lewis had written: "Reliance on untested accusations evokes one of the nastiest periods in our national life, the McCarthy era." I followed up by asking the audience: "Is Mr. Lewis the only commentator who hears echoes of McCarthyism in the wave of untested accusations being made against John Tower? Not at all. Indeed, I think virtually every objective observer of Senate proceedings in this matter has been deeply troubled by the 'raw sewage,' as one Republican Senator has termed it, that has spilled into the Senate Chamber in the form of excerpts read from FBI reports and unsubstantiated anecdotes repeated for public consumption."

Right after that speech, Sam Nunn called me to ask what was going on. I said, "Sam, I didn't use your name," and he replied, "I know that, but I sure feel it." He had heard only a portion of the speech, out of context, so I sent him the whole thing. In fact, I also sent him an earlier draft—the one I had toned down. Even there I had been careful not to step over the line and attack Sam personally, but I was plenty disappointed in him.

The President was in a peculiar position. He and John had been longtime allies: together they had more or less created the Republican Party in Texas. Not many people remember that John Tower, thought of by some as the ultimate Reaganite, had been a supporter of George Bush during the 1980 primaries. (In fact, he was enough of a believer in party loyalty to support the incumbent, Jerry Ford, when he battled Ronald Reagan for the 1976 nomination.) But even while George Bush had full faith in John's ability, and reason to be grateful for his loyalty, he couldn't succeed in turning around any of the Senators he lobbied on John's behalf. To some extent, the President may have been a victim of his own gentlemanly good nature. To give you an example: Paul Weyrich, the conservative activist and fundraiser, let us down with what I thought was his shortsighted opposition to John's supposed drinking; he even testified against him on the Hill. Afterwards, Weyrich wrote the President a conciliatory letter, and the President wrote back saying that he hoped they could let bygones be bygones. As for me, I'm still disappointed in Paul Weyrich for the way he opposed John Tower, even though he is a crusader for the same principles as I am, as well as a friend. It frustrates me to think of how it's so often members of one's own party (look at Warner, Adelman, and Weyrich) who hurt you the most. As I write this, a year into the new administration, Bill Clinton is already finding out the same thing: when Democrats go against his programs— take NAFTA for an example—they get more publicity and inflict more damage than his Republican critics.

When it was clear John's nomination was going down in flames, there was a big discussion in the White House about whether we ought to go through with the scheduled vote. I can remember talking to John two days beforehand and telling him: "John, I hope you're not going to let these Senators off the hook by forgoing a vote—even though we know we're going to lose." He replied, "Don't worry, you know me. I'm going to make 'em vote." He wouldn't make it easy on them—that's the way he was. A lot of them were going to vote against him only because Sam Nunn was pressuring them, so John decided, and I agreed, that they should be made to go on the record and walk the plank.

Not long after it was over, I ran into Sununu, who was on his way up to the Hill, and we got to talking about who would be the next Defense nominee. We had both been asking ourselves, "What about Dick Cheney?" I told John I couldn't think of any problem with that. Since I was about to have lunch with the President, I decided to mention Cheney to him. I told him that both Sununu and I thought Cheney was not only up to the job but easily confirmable. The President liked the suggestion, and nobody else ever really got into the running. Ironically enough, once he took up his new job, Cheney didn't get along very well with Sununu. Dick had served Gerald Ford as White House chief of staff, and he knew too much about how the White House operates. He liked dealing with Scowcroft but would withhold information from Sununu, who would try—and often fail—to pry it out of him.

I experienced a bit of lingering bitterness over the Tower battle. A week after the nomination was defeated, I spoke at the forty-fifth annual Radio & Television Correspondents Association dinner. "Sitting up here and witnessing your conduct throughout the evening," I said, "I realized that most of you do not aspire to be Secretary of Defense." Plenty of boos came back at me, including "a lusty one," according to the *Washington Post*, from my old friend Ted Kennedy. But I regretted nothing about how I'd carried the fight, and the administration learned one important lesson from it: Sam Nunn was not going to be our friend. I remember that Brent Scowcroft didn't quite want to believe this, and he found out the hard way later on, during the Gulf War.

A couple of years after the confirmation fight, John Tower died in a plane crash. I was honored to speak at a memorial service for him at Arlington National Cemetery, where I told the story of how one time, around three in the morning, John was holding forth at a conference committee on the National Guard. He was really working over Congressman Sonny Montgomery, coming at him again and again. Finally, he tapped his cigarette on that gold cigarette case of his and said, "Okay, Sonny, this is my last, best, and final offer. I can't do any more." Basically, he was offering Sonny the same thing he'd been offering for four hours. Strom Thurmond, who was sitting next to John, was tired, and I remember him saying, in that high-pitched Southern accent, "Take it, Sonny, take it. It's the best you're gonna *git*." So Sonny threw in the towel and took it, because Tower wasn't going to give an inch. He couldn't. That's just the way he was.

John Tower lived his life in service to the United States, and if at its end there were heartaches, they could not lessen what he gave America.

▲ Tucker *(far left)*,
Marilyn, Benjamin, and
Corinne endured a brutal
1988 campaign. What was
already a close family
became even closer.

◄ Marilyn's favorite
picture of us en route
to the inaugural balls.

◄ During 1974, we moved from Indianapolis to Huntington, where I began my political career. I am holding our first child, Tucker.

▼ With Tucker and Ben in 1977 in our home in McLean, Virginia, as I read them "Twas the Night Before Christmas."

▼ In July 1982, when I was still in the Senate, Marilyn and our children visited with Second Lady Barbara Bush at what one day would be our home.

▲ A normal family breakfast at the Vice President's house on the grounds of the Naval Observatory. We did extensive restoration and made the sprawling, high-security quarters feel like home.

▲ Everybody takes care of Dad. Here my real handlers are preparing me for a holiday television appearance.

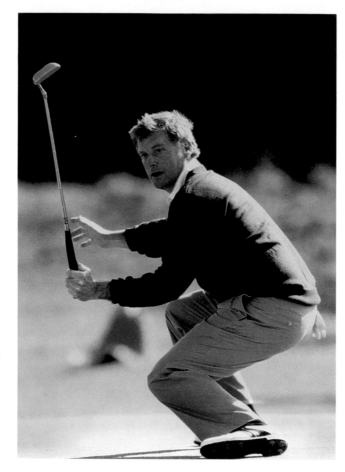

► My passion for golf is well documented.

▼ George Bush and I were as close as any President and Vice President in American history.

White House

▲ White-water rafting on the Colorado River. Spending time with my family is a priority.

▲ Skiing is another favorite Quayle activity. Our children beat me down the hill every time.

White House

▲ Gulf War debriefing—
Rose Garden—April 23,
1991.

Tom Sullivan

◀ April 1991. I threw
out the first ball at an
Orioles-White Sox game
in which the Orioles paid
tribute to the brave men
and women who fought
in Desert Storm.

▲ Reintroducing myself at the Republican Convention in 1992.

▲ Campaigning with a great President and true gentleman.

▲ I don't know if my children will follow me into politics. Right now they're pleased to be out of it, and I'm pleased I can make time for them more easily than I did in the past.

White House

14 | Meeting the Media

During the first year of the administration, the stories about my supposed "education" often made grudging acknowledgment of the fact that I was a player within the administration, an insider who wasn't afraid to speak up on policy issues and who was in no danger of disappearing. I was generally not subjected to the kind of stories about Vice Presidents that typically appear after a few months: "Where's Fritz [or Spiro, or George, or Al]?" I wasn't being hidden. Nor was I being turned into an attack dog, somebody trotted out to be the "point man" on especially controversial issues.

I owed recognition of my insider status to the same man who had given me my job: George Bush. He went out of his way to emphasize the role I was playing, stressing any contributions he thought I was making to his presidency. I never had to worry about him making the sort of remark Eisenhower uttered about Nixon in 1960 when a reporter asked if he could name one important thing Nixon had done for his administration. Ike said he probably could, if he were given a week to think about it. Eisenhower didn't mean it the way it sounded, but the question itself would never have come up with George Bush: from the start he took too many pains to paint an accurate and favorable picture of the role I played within his presidency.

Still, a President can't be expected to spend time worrying about his Vice President's image, and if I was going to undo the caricature of the campaign, I had to make my own impression on the press. I liked to think that all I had to do was a good job and they would notice, but I wasn't naive enough to entertain such a fantasy for very long. There are essentially five things the media will cover when it comes to politicians: polls, attacks, scandals, flip-flops, and gaffes. A deliberate press strategy was required, and in the first weeks after taking office I began to hammer one out with Dave Beckwith, my press secretary, and others.

Beckwith had been one of my first appointments, and I'd thought carefully about it. Dave Prosperi had done a good job as a press spokesman for our campaign, but he'd been totally under the thumb of Spencer and Canzeri, and I didn't want someone who would continually remind the media of 1988. I would have liked having Mark Goodin, who'd been assistant press secretary for the Bush campaign, but Lee Atwater snatched him away to the RNC. Then Goodin recommended Beckwith. Dave was a lawyer who had gone into journalism and become a respected correspondent for *Time*. I heard reports that he'd been fairly sympathetic to us during the campaign, when he was covering George Bush. An affable redhead in his mid-forties, Dave would be very good with journalists, I figured; I would be putting one of their own in the position of working for me. Maybe I could co-opt them from the inside out.

Beckwith urged me to spend some of my time schmoozing the media. "Right now they don't really know you. Once they get to, they won't write these horrendous stories," he would say. It sounded logical, and I relished the opportunity. But exactly how we would pursue this strategy was a matter of some question. Would we work from the top down or the bottom up? Court the national media directly, or try to get good local coverage that would percolate up and force national reporters to take a new look?

We finally tried a combination of the two, putting special emphasis on the latter. Vice Presidents don't get a chance to make much news except when they're traveling, so we decided to be very generous with local media access in our trips around the country. And we did get some very good coverage in the places we went. In the end, though, it didn't make much difference on the national level: the star reporters of the networks, newsmagazines, and dailies like the *New York Times* and *Washington Post* are a little too proud to pay much attention to what's written in Lubbock and Laramie. Political press coverage operates the way the liberal press always said Reagan–Bush economic policy did: trickle down. You can't really get around the national media. During the 1992 campaign, Perot and Clinton would have some success going over their heads, when candidates would go on programs like "Larry King Live" and bypass the big-time correspondents accustomed to setting the agenda. But the first months of the Clinton administration would prove that such a strategy can only take you so far. Clinton's press relations were a disaster, and his polls plummeted. George Stephanopoulos was reassigned, and David Gergen, that Republican spin-master, was summoned to the rescue.

The media had its obvious Quayle haters, like the *Wall Street Journal's* Al Hunt, *Newsweek's* Eleanor Clift, cartoonist Garry Trudeau, and writer Garry Wills. But there were a number of individuals who were usually objective. Among these I'd include Ann Compton (ABC), Karen Dewitt (*New York Times*), David Lauter (*Los Angeles Times*), and Helen Thomas (UPI). I hesitate to put more names on the fairness list, for fear that any accolades from me may damage their good standing with their peers. But in fact there were many. Actually, Beckwith would remind me that in many ways my press was better than what George Bush had had as Vice President in the early years of the Reagan administration. Bush himself didn't go quite that far, but I do remember being bucked up the time he suggested I take every awful story about myself and substitute his name for mine to have an accurate picture of what *he'd* been through as number two.

There was a great deal of truth to this, but there was also no pretending that my situation wasn't, shall we say, special. As Vice President, George Bush may have been called a lot of names, but whatever "wimp" imagery surrounded him, he never had to contend with being labeled just plain dumb. That is what I was up against.

During the first few months of our administration the Quayle jokes became a national institution. Comedians could rely on them the way politicians call on patriotism and the flag: they were guaranteed to work. I didn't go out of my way to listen to them, but from the ones Tucker passed on (he continued to be the family's monitor) and those that filtered into my press clippings, I thought Johnny Carson and Jay Leno remained this side of tolerable. Letterman was usually another story.

Was there any way for this stuff to be turned to my advantage? I thought about that, but the situation only reminded me of one that occurred in Indiana back in 1986, when Mayor Winfield Moses of Fort Wayne, a popular, aggressive Democrat considered a potential challenger to my Senate reelection, was indicted. Moses told the press that the indictment was going to *help* him run against me, because it would make him look like a victim and boomerang back as sympathy. Right. The Quayle jokes were the same. I don't begrudge any honest laughter they gave people watching TV at the end of a hard day, but when it came to my career they were totally destructive. Do you know how many favorable stories it takes to overcome one zinger by Johnny Carson?

I'm not talking about local stories either; I'm talking about national ones, the kind that are very hard for any Vice President to get. There is almost nothing in the way of day-to-day coverage—certainly not enough to change first impressions. Every few months national editors will say, "Gee, maybe it's time to do a story on the Veep. Let's get somebody to write about how he's doing." And the story will be accompanied by a poll whose respondents are asked to comment on a man they've heard nothing about (or, in my case, heard nothing about since the last poll was taken, except a few more months' worth of Quayle jokes). I've mentioned what Lee Atwater used to call "defining moments," and a Vice President's lack of them. Unfortunately, in my case the jokes were the defining moments.

At least most of them were. The Vice President sometimes gets national attention when he travels outside the country, and my first foreign trip came just two weeks into the administration. With the encouragement of Fred Fielding, who had been helpful during the transition, I pushed to represent the United States in Caracas at the inauguration of Venezuelan president Carlos Andrés Pérez. (I'd met "Cap" in Washington the previous December, and we'd gotten along very well.) From Caracas I wanted to go to El Salvador, where I could make a strong case that the

Duarte government should not postpone its plan for March elections. I also wanted to take the opportunity to give the Salvadoran military a stern warning against abuses of human rights, a matter that had given us some recent cause for concern. Coming from a conservative, such a lecture to the generals would make a lasting impression. (As a matter of fact, the Bush administration's tough stand against human rights abuses led to the peace accord I would witness in January 1992.) Also, the media would not expect this tough, unsolicited lecture from me, and—as often comes with doing the unexpected—that would yield political dividends.

The President enthusiastically approved of this trip, not only because he thought I could be useful down there but also because I had gone through the proper channels in getting the trip set up. Foreign travel is one matter in which a Vice President must work from the bottom up. Once the President knew that I'd gone through Jim Baker at State and Brent Scowcroft at the NSC, and that they had no problem with my going, he was eager to bless the trip himself. So I began to prepare for it, calling Richard Nixon and former Secretary of State George Shultz, among others, for advice.

Typically, I would be briefed before foreign travel by the State and Defense departments, the NSC, and the CIA. Before I even got out, an official from State or my own foreign affairs adviser could contact the American ambassador in the country I was visiting and tell him my agenda with that country's leader. Then the ambassador would tell the leader, so that he wouldn't be surprised. The hope is for these trips to be successes, and the best way to ensure that is to know what the news will be before you even leave home.

The press greeted the announcement of this first trip with considerable interest. Dan Quayle abroad! Now here was a story. Was he up to it? Would he embarrass the country? Or would he surprise us? Let's go see. This is what the *fair-minded* ones were thinking. I could almost hear the others cupping their ears for a gaffe, the kind of thing that would make a good story next to an editorial cartoon of me in an oversized sombrero.

Things did not get off to a good start. In fact, they were sour even before we took off from Washington. When we realized we didn't have enough Secret Service and staff to justify a second plane, Dave Beckwith canceled it. Economy was the reason, but some of the press who would have ridden on it—and who then had to make their own arrangements to get to Caracas—thought we were getting cold feet about having so many reporters along. They then complained that the ones getting to ride the main plane (or *Air Force Two*, as any plane carrying the Vice President is dubbed) were chosen for the friendliness we might expect from their coverage. It was pointed out that the *Indianapolis News* (one of my grandfather's newspapers) was one of them. The Indianapolis papers were always accommodated, because of home-state interest in me, but once the press has its hackles up, anything can turn into a flap.

Take our background session with them the day before we left. We were going to have a "senior official" give them an off-the-record briefing. This is standard practice before and during official trips, except that this time we decided I would be the unnamed "senior official" to answer their questions. Beckwith and I thought that this would look bold and friendly, but it didn't work: the *Washington Post* ignored the off-the-record agreement and reported that I had done the briefing myself. They also noted that, in a slip of the tongue, I'd said we "condoned" violence in El Salvador. I immediately corrected myself to say that I, of course, meant "condemned." Now, if this really had been just a "senior official," no reporter would even have noted it. But it was Dan Quayle—and another gaffe was born! Needless to say, we never again employed this particular technique as part of our "meet the media" strategy.

The real business of the trip went very well. While meeting with the regional leaders gathered for the inauguration in Caracas, which was crowded, exciting, and under heavy security, I promoted free markets, trade, and democracy—as I would on six other trips to Latin America over the next four years. I talked with Colombian president Virgilio Barco Vargas about drug traffic between his country and ours. And, I argued once more against the idea that nations in the region might get together in a "debtors' cartel," as some had proposed they do to solve their problem of delinquent loans to the United States. I deliberately did not meet with Fidel Castro, who sat several seats away from me during Pérez's swearing-in and was the reason for a lot of the security in the Venezuelan capital, but I did talk to leaders of the democratic opposition in Panama and Nicaragua.

When we got to San Salvador, I followed through on my intention to talk to the right-wing military about respect for human rights. Aside from being the right thing to do, it was smart politics. The press was not expecting this sort of utterance from me— as a conservative I was expected to care only about threats to democracy that came from the left. "Democracy means human rights and decency," I told the press just before I saw the army commanders. "When I emerge, there definitely will be no doubt in their minds about the seriousness of our commitment to human rights and justice."

When they listened to my speech, those army commanders sat on their hands, and this convinced me that we provided a necessary dose of reality for them. They got the message that the Salvadoran government could not expect the American Congress to keep voting them aid unless they adhered to American democratic values; and I am convinced the speech had an impact on events that unfolded after the Salvadoran elections were held. When the right-wing Arena Party, preferred by the military, came to power, defeating Duarte's Christian Democrats, there was considerable fear that Colonel Roberto D'Aubuisson, with his unsavory reputation, would be running the show. But having heard my warning, the army didn't press its luck. President Alfredo Cristiani ran his own government, and we were eventually able to get a peace agreement that respected the rights of the defeated rebels.

Later in 1989 I met with D'Aubuisson himself, which gave fits to liberal commentators, but I didn't care. He had influence, and if we were going to keep him in line, then we had to talk to him. The situation had its parallels to the one that developed in China that year: one might not be in the mood to talk with that country's leaders after Tiananmen Square, but if you really wanted to move them in the direction of democracy, and get them to restore the very rights they had trampled on, you were better off talking to them than driving them into hard-headed isolation. If you want to have leverage, if you want to see progress, then you've got to engage.

Refusing to talk may make you feel self-righteous and pure, but in the end it doesn't accomplish much for the people you claim you're trying to help.

I returned to Washington from that first foreign trip feeling good. I had had substantive discussions in each country I visited, and had had a real effect on the Salvadoran situation. By any rational, proportionate measure, the trip was a success. But that's the problem: the press doesn't always deal in rationality and proportion. The so-called gaffes got about as much ink and airtime as the substance. A few examples: I joked to Ann Compton about President Bush's laryngitis problem, saying, "Reagan used to use it to not have press conferences. But it won't be that way in this administration." That became: Quayle attacks Reagan! When I ate an unwashed guava at a Caracas fruit stand, my lack of hygienic caution was reported. (If I'd asked the vendor to rinse it off, would I have been scolded for ugly Americanism?) As I've said before, you've got to accept that you can't win on some issues.

If those were "gaffes," there was one "flap," involving former President Jimmy Carter, a media favorite after eight years of Ronald Reagan. Carter was also in Venezuela for the Pérez inauguration, and while he was there, he had a three-way meeting with the new president and Nicaragua's Daniel Ortega. A reporter told me (incorrectly, it turned out) that Carter had come out for a tougher line against Salvadoran human rights violations than we had, to which I responded: "I don't think it is particularly helpful to have former Presidents make these kinds of statements." I added that "when you have former Presidents meeting with heads of state that we don't meet with, it has a chance of complicating matters." I said this, unfortunately, after the reporter told me that Carter and Ortega had met one-on-one, which they hadn't. So suddenly I found myself in a little dust-up with Jimmy Carter, because I'd been misinformed by a reporter. I learned a lesson: never believe the premise of a reporter's question unless you have evidence it is correct.

Despite the mixup on this occasion, I would still level some criticism against Carter as former President. In many ways his years out of office have been praiseworthy—his work for Habitat for Humanity and so forth. But when he travels overseas, he stays much too close to the microphone. He often criticizes the sitting President, and he winds up being distinctly unhelpful at times. Bill Clinton is already finding out: Carter's 1993 discussions with the Somali warlord General Aidid only complicated matters for the current President. Nixon is of much better service to his country on trips abroad. He travels quietly, has high-level meetings in a very low-key way, and then comes back and reports useful, confidential information to the President. I once heard him brief George Bush after he returned from a trip to China: he was so intent on what he was doing that he never touched his lunch. He's been helpful to every American President, Republican and Democrat, since he left office—and that's why you'll see George Bush following the Nixon model. Carter goes abroad and holds press conferences.

So we were on our way back to Andrews Air Force Base after just three days abroad, having done, I thought, a pretty good job. On the plane home, I celebrated my forty-second birthday, and along with a cake, the press gave me an inscribed Venezuelan bank note: FIRST FOREIGN TRIP: QUAYLE FAILS TO SCREW UP! That wouldn't have been so bad, but it wasn't only their point of view. It was Dave Beckwith's, too. When reporters asked him to evaluate the trip, he said it was a great success. Why? No mistakes. This was the benchmark being set not only by the press but by my own press secretary! Pretty sad. I just cringed when I heard it, and I called him on it. But not as hard as I should have. We were new to each other, and I wanted his loyalty. Also, I have trouble blowing my stack—a trait that earns me other people's affection but sometimes lets them sell me short.

Selling me was the essence of Dave Beckwith's job, and I would constantly remind him not to buy into the press line of the day. In many ways, as time went on, Dave would do his job quite well, except when he let his temper get the best of him. But as I look back on the four years, I wonder if it really was such a good idea to have one of the media's own in the job of press secretary. It's hard for a member of the press to make the switch. Those who plan to return to the media after their temporary stay in government are careful not to offend their once-and-future colleagues.

It's an almost impossible balancing act. (We'll see how David Gergen turns out.) Instead of co-opting the press, as we'd hoped, we too often wound up letting them cover us the way they wanted to. There were times when we would have been better off just stiffing them. In fact, a willingness to let the media set the agenda would prove to be one of the things that killed us in the 1992 election.

But that was a long way off. Two weeks into the new administration, coming back from my first foreign trip, I was just pushing ahead, practicing the Woody Hayes approach to football: three yards and a cloud of dust. I was still determined to "meet the media." That willingness would last another three months, until one interview would convince me, once and for all, that getting a fair shake from the media was hopeless.

15 | Flaps, Gaffes— and Serious Diplomacy

The only real duty the Constitution requires of the Vice President is that he preside over the U.S. Senate. In practice, it's usually a junior Senator who's wielding the gavel; during my first months in office I sat in the presiding officer's chair only once, during the Tower vote, when I hoped I might have to break a tie. That was something, by the way, that I never got to do in the four years I held the office. (Al Gore got to be the deciding vote just a few months into his term, a duty he probably relished but which showed everybody that Bill Clinton's budget couldn't muster a majority of votes in a Democratic-controlled Senate! And Gore's tie-breaking vote for higher taxes may come back to haunt him.)

Since Franklin Roosevelt, a President's first hundred days have been a much used, if artificial, benchmark. About the only newspaper to take note of my first vice-presidential hundred was, not surprisingly, the *Indianapolis News*. Their article on May 19, 1989, noted that, in addition to my one time presiding over the Senate, and on top of the trip to Latin America, I had had discussions with President Bush on average three or more times a day; met with sixty foreign leaders in Washington; spent seventeen days traveling to nine states outside the capital (actually, it was more than that); and made fifty public appearances and a dozen major speeches.

But as I've said, not much of this gets covered. I didn't really come back into the news until April, when I once more took the office on the road, this time for an eleven-day tour of Australia and Asia, during which I was scheduled to visit Indonesia and

Singapore, as well as a Catholic Relief Services camp for Cambodian refugees on the Thailand–Cambodia border. If it sounds overscheduled, it was. I was between chiefs of staff at this point (Bob Guttman was getting ready to depart, but Bill Kristol had not yet moved over), and Dave Beckwith, whose wife is Australian, was involved with putting together some of the itinerary. The two of us were determined to highlight my energy, to show the press just how much I could do, and as a result we overdid it.

Flying to Asia, against the winds and the time zones, leaves you more tired than going in the opposite direction, and I was pretty beat before I got there. I didn't even go straight from Washington: on my way west I stopped in Chicago to visit a high school and speak to the American Newspaper Publishers Association; then it was on to a fundraiser at the Reagan Library in California and an evening awards dinner. After that I was immediately back in the air, flying across the Pacific, briefly touching down in Hawaii and then making a quick refueling stopover in American Samoa.

I stepped off the plane there bone tired. The crowd that came out to greet us contained a lot of kids. Because of my visit the Governor had declared the day a holiday. The children were ebullient, so I said the crowd looked like "happy campers" to me. I don't know whether to classify this as a flap or a gaffe; let's settle for a tempest in a teapot, which is what it was. But that didn't matter—I had just done a couple of days' work for the late-night comics' scriptwriters. And I would soon be receiving a written complaint from American Samoa's nonvoting delegate to the House of Representatives, Eni F. H. Faleomavaega: "The use of this term, with which I am not personally familiar," he wrote, "has created quite a stir. It appears that some individuals have even drawn the conclusion that you were implying that the people of Samoa are simple, illiterate natives happily camped out in the jungle." This delegate was not even there, but Samoa's Governor Coleman, who was with me, came to my defense and could not understand why there was such a fuss.

As I explained to Mr. Faleomavaega, the crowd that greeted me was full of children, and in trying to give them a friendly hello, I picked a term that I'd used for years when referring to my own kids. Case closed? Nope. More like a federal case. When I got back to Washington two weeks later, it was all that some of my colleagues in the administration could remember from the trip. (Perhaps needless to say, the explanation I've just given you never became much of a follow-up press story.) I can remember Dick Darman, downstairs in the White House, welcoming me back and saying he'd heard I'd had a good trip, "though we could have done without 'happy campers.'" A little exasperated, I told him about all the kids who were at the Pago Pago airport, and my use of that term at home. All he could add was, "Well, that's not the way it came out." Which in the end was all that mattered to the talk-show comedians.

As I think I've made clear by now, I was a special case when it came to press coverage, but on this Asia trip I experienced one frustration from print journalism that I believe a lot of other politicians, whatever their political stripe, are also running into when they travel these days. I'm talking about a kind of "snapshot" reporting—cute and colorful vignettes, as opposed to longer, serious stories on the real business of the trip. Maureen Dowd of the *New York Times* was with us on this trip, and she filed a lot of these little squibs that would be collected under the heading "Reporter's Notebook." In one batch she'd note that a round of golf I had in Singapore (five holes, played at the insistence of the American ambassador) may have made me a few minutes late for a meeting with Prime Minister Lee Kuan Yew, and that in my speech to the American Business Council there, I had pronounced the name of the French writer de Tocqueville as "TOCK-a-vil," instead of "TOKE-veel." Earth-shattering stuff like this, often without any other coverage on the day it appeared.

Maureen Dowd—who's earned a reputation as the Princess of Creative Journalism—may be at the top of her profession, but she doesn't let the facts get in her way. Once, at an off-the-record lunch in my office, which Maureen attended with the *Times*'s Washington bureau chief at the time, Howell Raines, Maureen dropped a pen—with which she'd been secretly scribbling notes. There was a clatter. Dave Beckwith picked it up and handed it to her. Nothing was said. Who, after all, is going to start a fight with the *New York Times*?

We were in Australia to talk trade and to make the unpopular

point that American subsidies to our wheat farmers—under the
Export Enhancement Program—were designed to help our farmers in the European markets. They were not intended to hurt Australian farmers also hoping to export, and we didn't think they
were doing that in any case. But I got into a public tussle with
Australian Prime Minister Bob Hawke, a friend of George Bush
(who in early 1992, alas, convinced the President to make his ill-
fated visit to Japan). Hawke countered my position by saying, "If
a bullet hits you in the head, it hurts as much if it was not aimed
at you as if it was aimed." I stuck to my guns in public and private. President Bush was concerned that this scuffle would turn
into a bigger disagreement than it needed to be, and while I was
over there he sent word asking whether I wanted him to weigh in
on the issue himself. I cabled back that I did not see the need,
because I was certain Hawke was making all the noise for political reasons. He had an election to face within the following year,
and he wanted to act tough in front of me, because that's how the
game is played. Of course, I knew how it was played too—what
might anger the wheat farmers in Australia was sure to bring a
smile to the ones in Kansas.

When we got to Indonesia, I talked up trade and American
business, as I did on virtually all my foreign trips. What sometimes caused criticism was my willingness to make a pitch for
individual companies seeking new markets, whether it was a
giant like AT&T or a relatively small glass-maker from Michigan.
If it were a case of American companies bidding against one
another for those markets, then of course we would stay out of
things entirely. But when there was just one American company
that was seeking a little leverage, I had no problem with it—just
as Margaret Thatcher had no problem doing the same for British
firms. I would leave it to the editorialists and the cheap-shot
artists to distort whatever efforts we made as attempts to do political favors. A Vice President is always in the position of being a
salesman, whether it's for the President's program on Capitol Hill
and out in the country, American democratic values abroad, or, as
I've said, American firms and products.

Sometimes helping democratic values and particular companies even went hand in hand. On one trip to Singapore I got into

a little scrap with B. G. Lee, the son of Prime Minister Lee Kuan Yew. Now Lee Kuan Yew is an impressive public figure, a true geopolitical thinker, but his son acted like a hothead when I made a pitch for the *Asian Wall Street Journal*, a subsidiary of the American paper that had gotten on the wrong side of his father's government and had its privileges pulled. We were instrumental in getting things straightened out, but not until after B. G. Lee tried to shout down our delegation during a meeting with the Prime Minister. I held my ground, but B.G. almost came out of his seat. One of the ironies of my life, as I've indicated before, is that, being from a newspaper family and having worked for a newspaper, I consider myself a special defender of press freedoms.

One delicate bit of business I had in Jakarta was a meeting with Cambodian Prince Norodom Sihanouk, whose relations with the United States have been an up-and-down affair for decades. The legacy of Pol Pot's reign of terror during the 1970s still tormented Cambodia. The country remained torn by warring factions, and in 1989 (before the UN-sponsored peace plan that eventually led to elections) the United States was thinking seriously about arming Sihanouk's faction, which was fighting both Pol Pot's Khmer Rouge guerrillas and a government that was kept in power in Phnom Penh only by the support of Hanoi.

Sihanouk has a hold over his people that is part sentimental and part mystical. In 1989 he was "our man" in Cambodia, insofar as we had one, and throughout the trip I expressed the American desire to see him at the head of a democratic coalition government. But he was, to say the least, not my type. There he was in Jakarta, away from the homes he maintained in Beijing and North Korea, talking to me in his peculiar pipsqueaky voice and striking me as an operator, someone always ready to make a deal.

I couldn't get into Cambodia itself, but our next stop after Indonesia was a refugee camp ("Site B") near the Thai border. It was a terrible place, despite everything that Catholic Relief Services was trying to do there. Marilyn and I approached it from a dirt road, and we felt overwhelmed by the flies and the odor. The place was full of small children, and as I walked around the huts and hospital, I realized that most of them had been born in this place. They might be seven or eight years old, getting what schooling they could here but living out a wretched existence with little prospect of escape. The Catholic Relief Services was training their mothers to weave, and that was something, but their lives remained an awful, bare subsistence. The children's fathers, if they hadn't been killed, were off on guerrilla patrols across the border. The camp held about sixty thousand people and was led by Sihanouk's son, but the portraits looking serenely down on all this misery were of Sihanouk himself—who was nowhere to be seen. There was something sickening about it. We were given a touching welcome—complete with a beautiful, delicate dance performance—but I went away dispirited, and mindful of all the blessings my own children had. There was never enough time for Marilyn and me to reflect on an experience like this. As soon as I'd walked through it, I'd be thrown into a noisy helicopter for the next stop—in this case, Bangkok. But even a quick look reminded me of how religious relief services help mitigate the world's suffering. Thinking of Sihanouk and of our own country's involvement in this land, I am surprised by what God can do through His people that doesn't happen through rulers and kings.

Back home, it was soon summertime, and the beginning of the political silly season.

Spencer and Canzeri were back! In book form. They resurfaced in the interviews they gave to Jack Germond and Jules Witcover for their account of the 1988 campaign, *Whose Broad Stripes and Bright Stars?* It was what I expected: they stressed how childlike I was, how much I was in need of their wisdom to program my every move. Well, I've had my say about them already, and I'm not going to do it twice. As unpleasant as it was to relive any part of 1988, I was heartened by the way the President came to my defense. He blew his stack, letting reporters know just how "ugly" and "personally offensive" he found this kind of disloyalty and these untruthful comments. Sununu weighed in, too: "Canzeri is persona non grata in the White House," he said. "He's history." Having this kind of support was great, but the overall effect of the episode was to bring back the image of me as bumbler, someone who *needed* defending.

Throughout these months the media Gaffe Patrol was out in

full force. Partly it was my own doing. Yes, I did mangle the United Negro College Fund's slogan ("A mind is a terrible thing to waste") during a quick stop-by at a reception attended by around fifteen people in the Dirksen Senate Office Building. I was there just to say hello, not, as was reported, to give a speech. There were no cameras, and I was told it was off the record, but somebody got what I said on tape. I'll admit it: "mangled" isn't enough. I fractured, scrambled, and puréed the slogan. But I suffered far less from my own tongue than from the media's incessant repetition of trivia—even untrue trivia. I wouldn't be surprised if many still think I'm the fellow who said my Latin American travels made me regret not having studied Latin harder in school. Of course I never did say it, but in political terms, maybe even historical ones, it almost doesn't matter whether I did or not. One of the first rules for a politician is to realize that perception equals reality, and in the summer of 1989, tens of millions of Americans were shaking their heads over the Latin remark. The truth is that it was a Quayle joke made by Claudine Schneider, a Rhode Island congresswoman—a Republican, too! She told it to some people at the Belgian embassy one day, and before long it was being repeated as a true story by the newsmagazines, major newspapers and, needless to say, the talk shows. The *Washington Post,* to its credit, wound up doing an editorial on the subject, laying out in detail just how this little joke had ballooned. But I wasn't laughing. (Be honest: would you have been?) Schneider called up to say she was sorry, and I couldn't even bring myself to return her phone call. (Not long after, she lost her race for the Senate.) About a week after that *Post* editorial supposedly laying the thing to rest, Marilyn and I went to a reciprocal dinner for Prime Minister Benazir Bhutto of Pakistan and had to listen to *her* repeat the Latin story in some of her official remarks! I guess one of her old Harvard friends had thought this would be a funny addition to the government-to-government toasts.

I was always fair game. Even my friends in the media would step up to the free lunch if they could get some entertaining copy from it. When asked about my magazine-reading habits by a *Wall Street Journal* interviewer, I casually described the conservative *American Spectator* as being somewhat "hard to get through," whereas it was easier to read the more liberal *New Republic*. Come June I found myself cartooned on the *Spectator*'s cover, wearing a propeller beanie. The lead story was "Why Danny Can't Read." This from a magazine that counted Bill Kristol among its contributors (though not after this issue) and had started out in Bloomington, Indiana, in the 1960s, before relocating to Washington during the Reagan years. That's what can happen even to some Hoosiers when they move inside the Beltway.

If I had any lingering illusions that I could turn my image around, they were dispelled once and for all in the middle of August, when I did an interview with Sam Donaldson and Diane Sawyer on "PrimeTime Live." The setup to it consisted largely of Quayle jokes; in fact, the whole purpose of the thing seemed to be to give them a chance to entertain their viewers with them. This was in the days when that program actually was live, and some friendly observers pointed out that both Donaldson and Sawyer made their own slips of the tongue that night. Diane—who at that time reportedly made $1.6 million a year—also asked me about my "easy" life. The pampered rich boy image was once again reinforced. I tried to be as pleasant as I could, and I joked about all the work I was providing for comedians, but I was fuming. I had worked hard in my first half year in office, and I think I had accomplished as much, both at home and abroad, as the office of Vice President permits any of its occupants to. Almost none of it was getting through. I had to resign myself to the possibility that it never would. The media had put too much of their own credibility into creating the caricature to abandon it now. I was resigned to the fact that I would never get an opportunity to climb out of this hole until the 1992 convention, when a new "defining moment" would present itself. For now, there was nothing for me to do but keep going.

Only four months after my first trip to Asia, I was back there again, partly at the request of the State Department. This time I was off to Korea, Japan, and the Philippines. In Tokyo I had the so-called trade war on my agenda, and I sought to calm fears that one was breaking out between Japan and the United States. The administration was engaged in a bit of a good-cop/bad-cop strategy here. Our trade representative, Carla Hills, had recently been over with Commerce secretary Bob Mosbacher, and they had done some tough talking. Now that the point was made, I was there to do a bit of soothing.

It was not trade war, but real war, or at least the ever-present threat of it, that was on my mind once I got to Korea. In Seoul, shortly before I visited the Demilitarized Zone between North and South Korea, I told my hosts that the Bush administration was opposed to any unilateral reduction in American troops that the Congress might try to bring about. If there is any place on the globe that demonstrates the importance of maintaining a military deterrent, it's the Korean peninsula. While at the 38th parallel, I was shown a massive secret tunnel that the North Koreans had dug with the intent of launching an invasion against South Korea. It was nearly complete before it was discovered. The situation in 1994 is probably even more worrisome than it was in 1989. The North Korean leadership is aging and its succession uncertain, and they've shown a reckless willingness to go ahead with developing nuclear weapons. Our administration kept its commitments there, and the Clinton people have no reasonable choice but to do the same. I hope they understand the gravity of the situation.

In the Philippines, the leftist threat was internal: the communist guerrilla movement known as the New People's Army. My chief business in Manila was to urge President Corazon Aquino to begin negotiations for a renewal of the American lease on Clark Air Base and the Subic Bay naval station, as well as some smaller facilities. All these installations remained vital to U.S. interests— and freedom—in the region, but the leases were due to expire in 1991. The guerrillas, needless to say, wanted us out, and they had a tragic welcoming present for me. The day before my arrival they killed two American civilians working near Clark.

Marilyn and I changed our itineraries so that we could pay our respects to the families of these men, and I also stopped in at the wake for a murdered member of President Aquino's personal security staff. This gesture was much appreciated. One staple of jokes about Vice Presidents (a genre that existed long before the Quayle jokes came along) is the number of funerals they are dispatched to. But I can tell you that the national presence signified by their being there is of great value. My cultural perspectives and my own faith were broadened by the chance to observe other peoples performing one of the most basic human rituals. At the Hindu rites for Rajiv Gandhi, for example, I sat for three hours in the hot sun, not far from the pistol-toting PLO leader Yasir Arafat, on whom the Secret Service kept a vigilant eye. I watched the ritualistic crushing of Gandhi's skull with a stick—so his spirit could escape his body. In 1991, when I attended a memorial for Japanese Foreign Minister Abe, I was surprised at the appreciative response this generated—some of it more useful to American–Japanese relations than any speech or formal meeting. I thought of my own extended family. There are people you never see except at weddings and funerals, but even on the latter occasions, sad ones, family bonds are renewed and strengthened. The wake for Cory Aquino's security guard was not a state occasion, but my being there helped President Aquino and me become better, and more personally, acquainted.

Just nine weeks later, without warning, we'd have a reason to be glad we'd gotten to know each other.

16 | Saving Aquino

I spent the first Veterans Day of my vice-presidency with President Aquino, who had by then survived three years in office since the nonviolent People Power revolution against Ferdinand Marcos. I say "survived" because for all her popularity with Philippine citizens, and her status as a folk heroine in the United States, Cory Aquino had had to tough out a number of coup attempts by elements in the military who would not accept the will of their countrymen and did not believe that she was up to dealing with the Philippines' formidable problems, which ranged from terrible poverty to the communist guerrilla movement.

President Aquino was in Washington on a state visit. Marilyn and I had helped welcome her to the White House on Thursday, November 9, and that night we were among the guests at the dinner hosted by President and Mrs. Bush. On Friday morning, after breakfast together at the VP residence, President Aquino and I drove out to Arlington National Cemetery for a wreath-laying ceremony. As I watched her, I admired the dignity and spirit with which she paid tribute to those American soldiers of World War II who had rescued the Philippines from Japanese aggression and set the islands on the road to democracy. During this trip, and our earlier one to Manila, her manner fluctuated, maybe because her position was so insecure. She could be warm, as she was when we talked about our children, but I could tell she didn't have a strong grip. She was always quick to blame her Senate for a lack of support, and at one point she more or less confided to me that she would not run for a second term as President (information I reported back to George Bush and which eventually proved accurate).

What I didn't know on that Veterans Day was that three weeks later, President Aquino and I, sitting in war rooms half a world apart from each other, would be partners in another struggle, however brief, to maintain freedom in the Philippines.

Thursday, November 30, started out as a fairly routine day. I'd had my early-morning CIA and NSC briefings, followed by a Cabinet meeting and my usual Thursday lunch with the President. My afternoon appointments included talks with a delegation from the Supreme Soviet and another with the interim government of Afghanistan. After an appearance at the American Foreign Service Association and a number of photo sessions, I went home to the VP residence for an evening with my family.

At about 8:30 I was in my study working on a speech I thought I'd be delivering the next day in Florida, when the phone rang. It was Bob Gates, deputy national security adviser, and he had some bad news. Another coup attempt was under way in the Philippines. The situation might become critical and I should keep myself available. The President (as well as Jim Baker and Brent Scowcroft, Gates's boss) was somewhere over the Atlantic in *Air Force One*, en route to a summit in Malta with Mikhail Gorbachev.

A half hour later Gates called again and recommended that I get over to the White House Situation Room. The coup attempt looked serious. The rebels controlled the air and were bombing the presidential palace. I put down my speech, got hold of Bill Kristol, and told him to meet me at the White House. I arrived around 9:30 P.M. and convened a meeting to determine what needed to be done.

The White House Situation Room has a futuristic look. It's dominated by big TV screens on which officials at the State Department, Pentagon, JCS, and CIA can, in times like these, be patched together into a video conference. On the screens that night were General Colin Powell, from the Joint Chiefs of Staff office; Larry Eagleburger and Bob Kimmitt from State; Harry Rowen from the Pentagon; and Bill Webster (followed by Richard Kerr) from the CIA. Dick Cheney was home in bed with the flu. Around the enormous table with me were Kristol; Bob Gates;

Attorney General Dick Thornburgh; White House counsel Boyden Gray; my future national security adviser, Karl Jackson; and a couple of White House staff people.

General Powell, over at his headquarters, spoke to us from one of the big screens, and the news he had was not good. Government forces had lost control of whole sections of Manila. President Aquino's own defense minister, General Fidel Ramos, had requested American intervention. Our first task was to determine if this represented a direct request from President Aquino herself. The difficulty we faced was that firing on Filipinos to put down the coup would open us to charges of interfering in the internal affairs of our former colony. Nonetheless, from the start of the meeting, it was clear we had to do something. Larry Eagleburger (a foreign service professional with credibility and clout, the Kissinger protégé Baker had made deputy Secretary of State) made a strong case for our responsibility to ensure the survival of Aquino's democratic government, which the United States had helped to power back in 1986, by persuading Ferdinand Marcos to leave the Philippines.

Our first priority was to prevent further attacks on Malacanang Palace in Manila, which had already been strafed and where President Aquino was holding out against the coup. But even after I got a direct request from her to provide whatever military assistance was necessary, which could include bombing, there was disagreement in the Situation Room about how we should procced. I questioned those around the table and those up on the screens about how we could best neutralize the rebel airplanes. I also made the first of a series of phone calls to *Air Force One*, bringing Brent Scowcroft and John Sununu up to speed on the situation and telling them that before the night was out we might be asking the President to approve a recommendation for U.S. military action.

As the four years of the Bush administration went on, I would share many hours of crisis and strategic planning with Colin Powell, but that night of November 30—which soon turned into the early hours of December 1—we were both going to be pushed to make a quick decision and recommendation. Time was of the essence. I'd first encountered Powell when he served Ronald Reagan as national security adviser. The two of us clashed over the details and results of the INF treaty, about which I had serious concerns. Despite that, we had a close and collegial relationship. At first, several participants in the meeting recommended that our F-4s bomb the rebels or shoot down their aircraft to bring this rebellion to an end. Colin then proposed that we fly a "cap" over the Philippine Air Force and let the rebels know that if they attempted to fly, they would be shot down. I agreed with Colin that the "cap" option was preferable to bombing the rebels and recommended that to the President, who was on *Air Force One*. Once we had his approval, the American F-4s took off from Clark Air Force Base in the Philippines.

That night I was on the phone with President Aquino three different times. I could sense the tension in her voice. She was for more aggressive action than I could recommend. I didn't blame her, under the circumstances. I convinced her that our limited action would be effective. "Just stop the coup," she said. I made it clear that our assistance was predicated on her publicly issuing a statement asking for our help. Without such a statement, our military actions could be misinterpreted as unilateral.

I instructed Larry Eagleburger to make sure our ambassador pressed Aquino. The next day, however, she would talk of her request for help only privately; her public statements did not reflect her commitment to me.

By the middle of the night it seemed clear that the cap was working, but I remained in the Situation Room until 5:30 before going home for a few hours of sleep. I was back at the White House by mid-morning. (Marilyn went down to Florida and gave my speech for me.)

I think everyone who was in the Situation Room that night would agree that they have rarely done more concentrated and effective work. Because I had been well briefed on the Philippines and knew Aquino, I was prepared for the crisis. I was the one asking the questions, seeking the options, and pushing for a consensus. I can remember Larry Eagleburger saying afterward that if I hadn't been there, we might not have stopped the coup in the Philippines. It was a great hour in the relations between our two countries, and a great moment for me personally. We saved democracy without firing a shot.

It was also a moment that I couldn't talk about! This looked like a dream come true to Dave Beckwith: Dan Quayle in charge, competent, making a difference. He wanted to get out as much of the story as national security would permit, but I had to slow him down. "Dave," I said, "this is *not* a press opportunity. Maybe the story will get out eventually, but we can't play it up. The important thing is not for me to try to turn my image around in one story, but to look as if I'm being a good Vice President. That means being loyal and quiet. If you go out and try to spin this thing, we're going to get ourselves in trouble." For one thing, I knew how much George Bush disliked bragging; his mother detested it with a special passion, and she had constantly schooled her children against it.

But I can't pretend that I wasn't almost as frustrated as Beckwith. I was proud of what we'd accomplished in the Situation Room, and pleased with my role in it. Even though Dave and some of the Bush press people did spin it just a little, and a small spate of welcome stories got out, for the most part I had to suffer the usual stuff in silence. Strobe Talbott of *Time* made a point of noting how frightening it was to think that Dan Quayle was in charge at such a critical moment. (At five years' remove it's nice to be able to note how Talbott, now Bill Clinton's deputy Secretary of State, was wrong about nearly every important strategic issue involving the former Soviet Union. *National Review*'s John O'Sullivan captured the hypocrisy of guys like Talbott, all of whom spent years opposing the Reagan defense build-up: "In the 1980s," O'Sullivan notes, "Mr. Talbott judged the Soviet Union too strong to challenge; in the 1990s he looks back and considers it too weak to have been a threat." Almost one third of the Senate would vote against his confirmation as deputy Secretary of State.)

By Friday night, December 1, having been up the whole night before, I was tired, and even happier than usual to welcome Marilyn home. She told me that "my" speech in Florida had gone well. I was ready for a quiet weekend with my family, which we'd be spending at Camp David. The Bushes had suggested we make ourselves at home at the presidential retreat while they were in Malta. The two nights we spent in the Maryland mountains, after the one spent presiding in the White House Situation Room, gave the week a peculiarly "presidential" feel for me, but I had no doubt about who was the real boss. In my cabin I spent part of the weekend watching George Bush on television, at the Malta summit, as he helped construct the basis of what he would call the "new world order," just weeks after the fall of the Berlin Wall.

17 | Nailing Noriega

It's hard to remember that George Bush, who would become the greatest wartime commander in chief since Franklin Roosevelt, once suffered from what political journalists called The Wimp Factor. Some of it had to do with his natural caution ("wouldn't be *prudent*" was the signature line of Dana Carvey's impression), and some of it had to do with the two long terms he spent in Ronald Reagan's shadow. The vice-presidency is not a natural stature-builder. *I* got used to hearing about myself portrayed as a small boy sitting on Dana Carvey's knee.

Late in the first year of the administration, there was a specific, nagging issue driving The Wimp Factor: the continuing outrageous behavior of Manuel Noriega, the Panamanian dictator. The President's perceived failure to do anything about him looked like a broken campaign promise. Throughout the fall of 1988 we had both talked about how we would deal with this embarrassment, a strongman who had received CIA support for many years but was now trafficking in drugs. Noriega was probably an unsavory character from the start, but the American assistance he received over many years and through several administrations, Republican and Democratic, was a matter of realpolitik. In holding the line against communism in Central America, and in protecting vital American interests (in this case, the Panama Canal), we couldn't always be as choosy as we liked. Still, by the late 1980s there was no question that Noriega's behavior had overstepped any acceptable limits, and when we took office, things only got worse.

In May 1989, after suffering a clear defeat at the ballot box, Noriega voided the election results and unleashed his goon squads against the election's winners. Americans were sickened by the sight of Guillermo Endara, the legitimate winner, and one of his duly elected Vice Presidents, Guillermo "Billy" Ford, beaten about the head and dripping blood. President Bush was so revolted by the pictures and reports, and so concerned about the violence Noriega might soon direct against American citizens in Panama, that he took the extraordinary step of saying he would welcome Noriega's overthrow by the Panamanian people.

If that didn't happen, we were ready to seize an opportunity to help overthrow him ourselves. But as the months went by and one didn't materialize, the administration began to look weak. The Wimp Factor, created by the media, was in the air (or should I say the airwaves?). In October, we decided not to support an impending military coup we'd gotten wind of (the army major leading it was not reliable), and when it failed, the administration took flak from just about everyone. Even Jesse Helms called us "Keystone Kops."

President Bush wanted nothing more than the chance to get Noriega out of there, and the administration, which often paid too much attention to the press, was rattled by the criticism. He never really talked about any personal dealings he had had in the past with Noriega; he just tried to concentrate on the honorable alternative to him that we now had in Guillermo Endara. But before we could help him toward the power that was rightly his, we needed a pretext for moving against the dictator who had robbed him of victory. During the next two months, tensions worsened, and most U.S. dependents were ordered home from Panama. But it wasn't until a week before Christmas that two incidents made taking action imperative: Noriega's forces shot and killed an off-duty American Marine, Lieutenant Robert Paz, and then proceeded to detain and mistreat an American married couple who had witnessed the shooting. President Bush was especially enraged by reports that Noriega's thugs had threatened the woman with sexual abuse while she and her husband were held in the general's own headquarters, the "Comandancia," in Panama City. Noriega had clearly gone over the edge:

that same week he had declared Panama to be at war with the United States.

The Pentagon's contingency plan for an invasion of Panama was called Blue Spoon, later to be changed to the more inspiring Operation Just Cause. Dick Cheney and Colin Powell presented it to President Bush in the White House, just after a weekend Christmas party, on December 17. The military operation they outlined did not seem unduly difficult; everyone was sure that most of its objectives could be met decisively.

But there were potential problems. One of the invasion's key goals was the capture of Noriega himself, so that we might bring him to trial on drug-trafficking charges in the United States. Our intelligence operations assumed he would head for the hills once American troops landed in Panama, and while they had a good idea where his hideouts were, there was always the chance he might slip through their grasp.

In our planning of the invasion, there was less concern with our ability to do it than anxiety that we might overdo it. We had no doubts about the legitimacy of what we were attempting, but any display of American military power in Latin America is bound to revive bad memories for some in the hemisphere. One of my chief responsibilities, while the operation was under way and after it reached a successful conclusion, was to reassure our friends in the region. Others in the administration would go about the business of making sure we had at least tacit support from our allies in other areas of the world.

Shortly after midnight on Wednesday, December 20, the F-117As roared into Panamanian air space—with great combat success—and our troops began to secure their objectives. Secrecy was of the utmost importance, and it held, partly because Dick Cheney focused almost as hard on handling the press as he did on troop deployments and targets. The Christmas holidays worked to our advantage, since Congress was out of town and wouldn't be back for another two weeks. (It's much more difficult for congressional opposition to coalesce if reporters seeking reactions from the leadership have to chase down Speaker Foley in Barbados.) As it was, because of the emergency, short-term nature of the operation, the President had only limited obligations to consult with Congress.

Still, the administration was eager to see the Panamanian matter under control before the Senators and Representatives came back to town with the New Year.

Once the bombs began dropping, I started calling all the Latin leaders I knew, from Cristiani in El Salvador to Menem in Argentina, to tell them what was going on. I heard the most misgivings from our friend Carlos Andrés Pérez, the Venezuelan President. "Cap" told me that the invasion posed real political problems for him, and I gathered that he, like a number of the leaders in the region, just didn't put much stock in Endara, who had a somewhat buffoonish image (unjustified, in my opinion, but probably enhanced by his enormous girth). I made a case for his legitimacy and reminded Cap and the other Latin leaders of the two very competent Vice Presidents who had been elected with Endara in May. Perhaps more important than any doubts they had about the new men was their absolute distaste for Noriega. I detected no support for him whatsoever, so I tried to appreciate the delicacy of the position of these Latin leaders. They knew how bad Noriega was, and they were relieved, if only privately, that the United States had finally undertaken to get rid of him. We would just have to accept that there were certain things they'd be saying, for domestic political consumption, on the question of American intervention.

The military operation met with great, quick success—except when it came to finding Noriega. "Well, where is he?" I can remember the President asking Colin, who during those first few days had to admit that we didn't really know. I worried that once Noriega got into the hills, he might lead a guerrilla force, and that we'd have to expend quite a lot of effort on capturing him, but Colin insisted that, once we located him, it wouldn't be that difficult. After all, most of his own countrymen wanted to be rid of him. The invasion had been received with great enthusiasm among ordinary Panamanians, who, in all of the TV pictures, were waving their white handkerchiefs (not in surrender but to celebrate the swearing-in of Endara, whose political party's color was white).

On Christmas Eve, Noriega delivered himself to the Papal Nuncio in Panama City—thereby creating a tricky situation, given the nature of embassy sovereignty and the special diplomatic standing of the Vatican. It brought to mind all the years that Cardinal Mindszenty spent in the American mission in Budapest after the Soviet invasion of Hungary. We didn't want that kind of protracted situation to develop. So we put the ball into the Vatican's court, keeping up polite diplomatic pressure (and getting our European friends to join in), so that a deal might be arranged that would turn Noriega over to American authorities. There was also some pressure that wasn't so subtle: American forces blasted the nuncio's residence with loud, heavy-metal rock music, partly so no one could intercept conversations between our military and the Vatican envoy, and partly (or so it was widely reported) to wear down Noriega. President Bush, with his usual sense of dignity, did not like this tactic at all, and he was relieved when the standoff ended in our favor. The President also regretted the ransacking of the Nicaraguan ambassador's residence in Panama by U.S. troops, though he wondered just what the ambassador was doing with all the Uzis, semiautomatic rifles, and rocket-propelled grenade-launchers that were inside his home. In my comments I refused to be apologetic—I didn't see how the principle of diplomatic immunity could apply to an ambassador's residence that had been turned into an arsenal.

Still, my main work in the weeks after the invasion continued to be diplomatic in nature. As January came I prepared for a tour of Central America and the Caribbean, where I would attempt to smooth any feathers that had been ruffled (at least publicly) by the invasion. In some ways, the trip was actually a substitute for one I didn't get to take to Eastern Europe. During late 1989 and early 1990, the communist regimes there were falling like dominoes (if I can borrow a term from another era). The Berlin Wall had literally disappeared, and the excitement and opportunities in the region were enormous. I was eager to go there and have a look for myself, so my staff and I tried to put together a trip. We had support from the NSC, but the State Department and Jim Baker put the kibosh on the idea. Baker wanted to be the first American official to visit that newly free part of the world, and the President, who rarely got involved in these kinds of squabbles, came down on Baker's side. So that was that—and if I'd been in Baker's position, I would have done the same thing.

In matters like these, my way was to work the bureaucracy from the bottom up and to deal first with NSC, where my initiatives were more likely to meet with enthusiasm than they were at State. So when the Eastern European trip was no longer a possibility, my office worked with the NSC to put together a Latin American itinerary that would include Panama itself. We already had a reason to visit the region in the near future: the upcoming inauguration of Honduran President Rafael Callejas. Adding a stop in Panama seemed like a good idea—though not to everybody. Certain bureaucrats within the administration thought it would be best for the President himself to be the first American official visiting that country after the invasion, but we convinced them that I could act as a kind of lightning rod: if there were any displays of popular discontent, I would be the one to catch them, not the President.

Actually, most of the flak came before I left Washington. Those putting together a schedule for me had asked Mexico and Venezuela if they wanted to be included on my list of destinations, and both countries declined. Whether these stops were "canceled" or never really scheduled doesn't matter much now, but the coolness came across in press reports as a more serious matter than it really was. We knew, as I've said, that the invasion posed some political problems for the friends we had in Latin America. If they thought a visit by a high administration official so soon afterward would exacerbate those problems, we just had to accept that. Mexico, in particular, follows a very left-leaning foreign policy, and its president, Carlos Salinas de Gortari, had to take the line that any interference in the region from the United States was a thing to be resented. This didn't change the fact that he, like Carlos Andrés Pérez in Venezuela, remained privately glad to be rid of Noriega.

I was happy to be going in any case. The trip provided me with a chance to keep developing into the administration's most active man for Latin American affairs, a role Jon Glassman, who would eventually be our ambassador to Paraguay, had been urging me to seek. There were three reasons I made Latin America a priority. First, the region was extremely important to the United States; second, Jim Baker had no special interest in the area; and third, the current crop of Latin leaders were mostly people of my own generation.

When I got to Honduras, there was a bit of an obligatory chill: I heard talk in Tegucigalpa about the need for the United States to bring its troops home as soon as possible. But the inaugural luncheon I shared with six Latin leaders there convinced me that the invasion was not going to hurt our relations in any serious way. I did not bring up Panama, waiting instead to see whether they did. And I found that what they wanted to discuss most was trade. That was fine with me, since an approach that involved "trade, not aid" was the cornerstone of our policy for improving not only the economic lot of the Latin nations but our relations with them as well.

My second stop was Panama, and it was a thrill. I got a wild reception from the crowds in the capital city, thousands of them waving their white handkerchiefs and shouting, some in English and some in Spanish, how much they loved both George Bush and the United States. The real heroes deserving their cheers were the American troops still patrolling the streets. We went to Endara's own church, which was packed with a hot, happy crowd, a number of them carrying signs that were a delightful variation on the YANQUI GO HOME refrain from the bad old days of American–Latin relations. THANK YOU FOR JUST CAUSE, said one of them. KEEP U.S. TROOPS HERE FOR NOW. It was a gratifying sentiment, but for practical purposes I was more impressed by the advice I got during a meeting with Deane Hinton, our ambassador to Panama and a veteran of other Latin American postings. Fearing guerrilla attacks against them, he wanted us to get our troops out as soon as possible. If a couple of our soldiers got killed, then the withdrawal we had intended all along would begin looking like a retreat. The Panamanians wanted us there, but we couldn't become a crutch. That wouldn't be in their best interests or ours.

My last stop before returning home was Jamaica, where Michael Manley, a handsome old protégé of Fidel Castro's, had returned to power. During his first period in office, he had tried the socialist route, and it hadn't succeeded in making his people prosperous. Now he seemed willing to veer away from the leftist line and try free markets. There were those in the administration who had their doubts about the sincerity of his conversion, but I had met with him in my office in Washington the summer before this current visit, and I was inclined to accept his change of outlook as genuine. The extent to which he criticized us over Panama would be regarded by many in the press, as well as some in the White House, as a test of just how much he had evolved, and how great our chances were to do useful business with him.

Before we went out to face reporters together, I told him, "Look. The press thinks that you're just going to be all over us on Panama, and they really want to write that story. If that's going to be the case, tell me now, so that I'll be prepared to respond." And he told me that he wasn't going to do that. He would make some mild criticism, but that would be it.

He kept his word. In very temperate, carefully chosen language he condemned the invasion, but only after acknowledging what a "menace" Noriega had been. "We exchanged views on Panama and we are friends," he said, "but friends do not always agree." Frankly, I was delighted by the statement, and those aware of our past relations with Manley and Jamaica should have been, too. But we didn't "spin" things as well as we might have, and press accounts of our meeting were more negative than they ought to have been. "Quayle ends a three-day mission on a sour note" said a *New York Times* story. I didn't feel that way at all. Manley and I had, in fact, spent most of our time talking about narcotics trafficking, including his efforts to combat drug cultivation in Jamaica, as well as his concern about how our Drug Enforcement Agency was monitoring air traffic in and out of his country. As far as Panama went, I figured that if this was the toughest criticism we were going to get, then the administration was diplomatically home free.

I made an encouraging report to President Bush, who was very pleased with the outcome of the trip. He agreed with Ambassador Hinton's advice about an early troop withdrawal. In fact, he seized on it, for its strategic and political sense. You cannot imagine the extent to which Vietnam was on everyone's mind during the planning and execution of Operation Just Cause. The possibility of getting bogged down in Panama was everyone's worst nightmare. It would mean not only the failure of this one operation but also the perpetuation of "post-Vietnam syndrome," the reluctance ever to employ American military power on a large scale. When such reluctance becomes paralysis, then a nation's ability to act as a true world leader is gone. By late January 1990 it looked as if the operation in Panama might enter history as an end to the post-Vietnam syndrome. What those of us in the Bush White House could not know was that, when the history of our administration was written, Panama would be not so much a postscript as a precedent. A just cause, precisely defined objectives, no stinting on whatever military might the job required, secrecy, aggressive diplomacy, timely withdrawal—all of these were elements in Panama, and every one of them would prove applicable to another, much larger war, in a place far away and coming much sooner than we knew.

PART THREE

Beyond the Cold War

1990

18 | Latin America: An Inaugural Quartet

As we entered our second year in office, democracy was flowering throughout Latin America. In the first several months of 1990, I represented President Bush at no fewer than four inaugural ceremonies in Central and South America, where I had a chance not only to celebrate democratic successes but to witness and influence the whole range of forces, left and right, that continued to threaten elected governments in the hemisphere.

Being booed from the right (and cheered from the left) was a new experience, but it's what happened to me in Chile in March 1990. After more than sixteen years, General Augusto Pinochet was at last giving up power, and on the morning his elected successor, Patricio Aylwin, was to take the oath of office, I paid a courtesy call on the general at his Santiago residence. A crowd of his supporters was nearby, chanting against me and the United States; they were angry about the sanctions we had placed on the Chilean regime to pressure it into holding free elections. The day before, these supporters had given a few kicks to my limousine, and mindful of Vice President Nixon's Caracas experience in 1958, I didn't linger in their presence. These demonstrators simply weren't ready to see the general, who in 1973 had seized power from the Marxist Salvador Allende, leave office. One purpose of my visit was to make sure he knew we wanted him not only to step down but to keep his hands off the new government once it was in place.

The general put on a good show. He seemed confident, not particularly anxious about the turn of events that was removing him from office. If he had any real bitterness, he didn't show it to me—although he did make sure I'd noticed all the demonstrators cheering for him. He justified the coup he'd staged against Allende and made a fairly preposterous analogy between it and the fall of the Berlin Wall. I let this pass. We were willing to concede certain of his economic achievements, but his self-image as a defender of democracy was a fantasy. We just wanted to soothe his feelings as he went off to the sidelines—where we hoped he would stay. He did remark that Chile was a violent country, and mentioned how he would be keeping an eye on certain persons who were likely to get out of control. Even so, I left feeling that Aylwin would be secure in governing on his own.

Pinochet talked about all the fishing he planned to do during his retirement. I asked him if one of these contemplated fishing trips might be part of a visit to the United States. I wasn't extending him an invitation, just trying to see whether he was willing to risk leaving Chile. No, he said, he would do all of his fishing at home. I'm sure he realized he might not be allowed back into his own country if he ever left.

Ted Kennedy, my old friend from JTPA days, was part of the U.S. delegation to the Aylwin swearing in. In fact, I'd invited him to come. He chose to call on some of Pinochet's old opponents rather than the general, which was all right with me, but before we left Washington, I'd told him that we had to have an understanding. I said, "You cannot criticize me, the President, or our policy when you're down in Chile." He told me that he understood and that this was exactly the kind of condition his brother Jack would have laid down in such circumstances. In a private meeting with Aylwin, Ted intended to discuss the notorious Letelier case, the 1970s murder of a Chilean diplomat in Washington. I told him that that was fine, because I too would mention this. (The perpetrators would be eventually extradited to the United States and prosecuted.) But I was adamant that while Ted was on foreign soil there be no public criticism of administration policy. He gave me his word, and he kept it, and the trip became a pleasant chapter in our unlikely friendship. (On the plane ride down, he gave me a New England Patriots jersey, number 96, with QUAYLE on the back.)

Over the past year we had developed another thing in common besides our work on the jobs act—namely, our rough press. I remain grateful to Ted for sticking up for me in 1988. Kennedy, much to the chagrin of the Dukakis campaign, said that the media had not only been unfair to me but never accurately covered my Senate career. As chairman of the Senate Labor and Human Resources Committee, he invited me to participate as Vice President in a meeting the committee was holding to discuss changes to JTPA. In the time-honored mode of vice-presidential self-mockery, I thanked him for the opportunity, as "someone who used to have an important job around this town." Throughout my four years as Vice President, Ted was one of several Democratic Senators who would drop by my office to chat. He would always talk enthusiastically about his family, especially his mother. He speaks quickly, many times without completing sentences, just rushing on. He's not an organized man—like many of us in public life—but he's got other people around to do the organizing for him. He's a guy's guy, loud and fun-loving, but he also loves children and is very attentive to them. He enjoys being a Senator and the point man for the liberal agenda.

Nicaragua's Daniel Ortega was also at the Aylwin inauguration, and ironically enough, he was in a position similar to Pinochet's, though the two of them could not have been more different politically. Ortega's military government was also giving way to an elected one: Violeta Chamorro had won the Nicaraguan presidency on February 25. The United States wanted to do what it could to keep Ortega on the sidelines, too, so that the government voted in by the people would actually have the chance to rule. (Having taken a swing at Jimmy Carter a bit earlier, I must give him his due here. The pressure he applied to Ortega was useful in getting him to hold the election at all.)

Venezuelan President Carlos Andrés Pérez gave Ortega a ride to Santiago on his plane. The globetrotting "Cap" loved playing diplomatic matchmaker, and since I had cleared a meeting with Ortega through the White House and State (it would be the highest-level encounter we'd had with the Sandinistas since they ousted Anastasio Somoza), he was eager to act as my conduit. Cap arrived in Santiago around midnight and called me to ask if

I'd like to meet with Ortega right away. During my four years of working with them, I found that the Latin leaders and I worked to different rhythms. They generally got up late and worked late; I was just the opposite, early to bed and early to rise. I decided to put off my encounter with Ortega until lunchtime of the next day, when I would spend an hour and a half talking with him at the luncheon and reception for President Aylwin and the visiting leaders. (Cap and Ortega, along with some of the other foreign officials, actually put off coming to Santiago until after the swearing in, to avoid having to greet Pinochet.)

Ortega had a steely gaze and an appearance of being ready to explode in anger. Even so, I found him willing to talk and listen, and I did not underestimate him, remembering the hard, shaping years he had spent locked in Somoza's Nicaraguan jails.

The linkage I was offering was simple. If he allowed Mrs. Chamorro to take office and appoint her own ministers, then he would find Nicaragua eligible for the $300 million in American aid he wanted. I complained about the Sandinistas' harassment of President Chamorro's supporters since the election, and he asked me to undo the economic sanctions that were still in place against Nicaragua because of his regime. I left with Ortega's promise that President Chamorro would be permitted to govern as she wished. Ortega also pledged to take control of an ominous situation that we had heard was developing: Sandinistas were passing out weapons to their supporters, who intended to hoard them in rural areas until they got the chance to resume fighting. When I got back to Washington four days later, the first thing I did (after stopping to watch a school play Corinne was in) was meet with contra leaders. I briefed them about my conversations with Ortega and the other Latin chiefs, and thanked them for all the pressure they had put on the Sandinistas. It was their sacrifices that had led to the elections. But now it was time to get on with peacemaking and to prepare for a new day under Mrs. Chamorro's moderate leadership.

Before coming back home, however, I had a second inauguration to attend. On Thursday, March 15, four days after President Aylwin was sworn in in Santiago, Brazil's Fernando Collor de Mello took the oath of office in Brasília. He, too, was coming to power democratically after a long spell (almost thirty years) of authoritarian rule. An ambitious free market reformer, Collor looked very promising. He was two years younger than I, and such an all-around athletic daredevil that President Bush compared him with Indiana Jones. In the end—very quickly, in fact— he turned out to be a huge, corrupt disappointment, and the Brazilian congress impeached him.

On that inaugural day in 1990, the Latin American leaders who had come to Brasília included many of Monday's cast from Santiago, among them the old nemesis of the United States and the region's great destabilizer, Fidel Castro. The Latin leaders had a curious way of behaving toward him. In private, they had no qualms about expressing their antipathy toward Castro. Argentina's able Carlos Menem, for example, was very outspoken when he criticized the Cuban dictator to other South American leaders. Nearly all of these leaders would tell me how awful and out of step Castro was these days, going on to suggest that we soften our stand against him, try co-opting him with a little kindness. The Bush administration, like the six before it, never bought this strategy, but it was heartening to note that the Latin leaders now felt they had more in common with us than Castro.

Still, I learned that there was no disregarding Castro's charisma. Even George Bush was a longtime Castro watcher and always eager for me to report my glimpses of Fidel. Castro is an imposing figure, someone who for thirty years has managed to loom much larger than he ever should have in the region's history. When Latin leaders gather in a room with him, they will, one by one, succumb to his presence. They will each go up to him and pay their respects. With all the progress the region has made in the direction of democracy, this deference to him saddened me. At the receptions where I noted it, I would challenge the Latin leaders as soon as they came back over to me. "I just saw you go over and talk to Castro," I'd say. "Yeah, it's too bad," they'd respond. "He shouldn't even be here."

I had my own plan to avoid him. Castro is a dictator who has spread revolution and hate throughout our hemisphere, and he, like North Korea's leaders, refuses to move toward democratic rule. If, at one of these inaugural receptions, he decided to come up to me with an extended hand, I'd tell him, "I'll be happy to shake your hand *after* you agree to hold free elections in Cuba."

We did have a small victory over him in Brasília. He arrived for the Collor inauguration with two planes, the second of them full of weapons and an outrageously large security operation. Afterwards, the front page of the Brazilian newspaper showed him getting off his own plane in full uniform, looking just like the old military dictator he was; right next to him on that same front page I was pictured playing a game of basketball with a bunch of Brazilian kids. It wasn't my own image I was thinking about here; it was America's. And that pair of photos scored two diplomatic points for our side.

The American media's coverage of the trip focused more on irrelevant matters—a pair of jaguars and a Chilean doll—than on the substantive policy that was being made.

Upon arriving at the American Embassy in Paraguay, Marilyn and I were surprised with a gift from the country's president—two adorable jaguar cubs. The traveling press corps felt we shouldn't have accepted the gift, criticizing us even after we asked that the animals be returned to their natural habitat. At no point did anyone in the media make the more relevant point: that the real mistake would have been to sanctimoniously refuse a gift from a head of state.

But this "flap," if you can call it that, paled in comparison to the fuss kicked up when, in a lighthearted moment, I had one of my advance men purchase an "anatomically correct Chilean doll." As I learned then, and as President Bill Clinton would learn a few years later when he compared Chancellor Kohl's girth to that of a sumo wrestler, a President or Vice President exhibits a sense of humor at his own peril.

Fortunately, all this couldn't undo the good work I'd done with Ortega: President Chamorro was sworn in in Managua on April 25, 1990, a little more than a month after I had met with Ortega in Chile. She is a wonderful, gracious woman and a special favorite of George Bush. Like President Aquino, she would have preferred to live the quiet, genteel life she was born to, but when her husband, the editor of *La Prensa*, was murdered by Somoza's men in 1978, she was propelled into politics—first on the side of the Sandinistas and then, when they betrayed their own revolution, on the side of their democratic opponents. Slowed down by trouble with her knee, she waged her successful campaign for the presidency on crutches. A few months before that, when Cory Aquino came to breakfast at the VP residence, I arranged for candidate Violeta Chamorro to be there, too. I thought she and Aquino—both of whom had lost husbands to assassination and then taken up the cause of democracy themselves—had much in common. I also hoped that Aquino's popularity might lend legitimacy to Violeta's campaign against Ortega. But some of Cory's leftist friends persuaded her that being photographed with Chamorro was not a good idea—a disappointment to me and Democratic Congressman Steve Solarz (whom I used to call "Mr. Secretary of State" because he was always giving us unsolicited foreign policy advice and traveled more widely than anyone else in Congress).

On April 25, President Chamorro sounded a note of reconciliation when she gave her inaugural address. The Sandinistas did not give Marilyn and me a very pleasant reception, however. Some of their demonstrators screamed *"Asesino!"* (Murderer) as we sat down for the ceremony next to Carlos Andrés Pérez. Ortega's speech personally attacked me. He spoke in Spanish, but I always took note when he said "Dan Quayle." When I asked what he was saying, Cap had the interpreter tell me: "You don't want to know."

Ortega did not entirely live up to the promises he had made in Santiago. His brother Humberto remained in charge of the country's armed forces, and we had reason to be concerned about continued Sandinista influence. The revolutionary FMLN was allowed to maintain offices in Managua, a dismaying development that I mentioned to President Chamorro's son-in-law, Antonio Lacayo Oyanguren. But he was afraid that the FMLN would turn violent if they were kicked out. Chamorro had good will and a sincere desire to bring peace to her tormented country, but she allowed her new government to be compromised by antidemocratic forces. That is why the full demobilization of the contras needed to be delayed. We wanted them to maintain some cohesion as a military force and provide Chamorro with some back-up muscle. But she didn't want any part of them. "Violeta," I would tell her, "the contras are not your problem. The Sandinistas and Humberto Ortega are." She kept promising that she was going to get rid of him, but to this day she hasn't. She continued to buy the appeasement prescription of her son-in-law, and the results have been unfortunate. Because of continuing Sandinista influence, Chamorro hasn't been able to implement the reforms she promised.

That summer, *Air Force Two* headed south yet again, for the inauguration of César Gaviria Trujillo as President of Colombia. He had promised to continue his government's strong stand against drug traffickers, and I was there at his swearing in to demonstrate American support for him against the Medellín drug cartel. The security precautions were tremendous. We were surrounded by bulletproof glass and tanks. The cartel had killed three candidates for President during the campaign.

With democracy able to function even under conditions like those, two Latin American countries still under dictatorial rule were by now conspicuously out of step. One, of course, was Castro's Cuba, and on our way home from Bogotá we stopped in the other, Haiti, where I gave some of the military officers running the country my message: "No coup, no murders, no threats, and instead, free and fair elections that will bring honor to the brave people of Haiti." They nodded, a bit like the Salvadoran generals a year before. They had enough confidence in themselves to remain indifferent. The military in Haiti had maintained control for so long that the ambitious and talented in that country gravitate toward it, not politics, as the surest path to advancement. I tried to send a strong signal that we wanted things to change.

The generals were the real power behind Mme Ertha Pascal-Trouillot, a former Haitian Supreme Court justice who had been installed as interim President when one military regime threw out another. She was very shy, talking to me about how they had spent three days cleaning the presidential palace to get it ready for me. This was sad, amid all the poverty that I had witnessed. The next few years remained a terrible trial for Haiti, which spilled forth refugees to the United States. These desperate people were further exploited in the 1992 campaign by Bill Clinton, who unrealistically pledged to reverse the Bush administration's refusal to grant asylum to those who were economic and not political refugees; then, as soon as he took office, he had to reverse himself. It was naive of him to think he could get the Haitian generals to step aside for Father Jean-Bertrand Aristide— for that matter, he put too much faith in Aristide himself. Aristide is not truly devoted to democracy and has a tendency to believe justice derives from street demonstrations instead of the legal system. His people have practiced violence against the country's elite, and on the two occasions when I met him I was struck by his almost weird intensity.

I'd spent a large part of my youth in Arizona, which has a growing Hispanic population, and in the Senate I'd become interested in Nicaragua and El Salvador from an anticommunist perspective, but before becoming Vice President, I had never been any deeper into Latin America than Mexico. In fact, I had declined an opportunity to go there in 1978, when the late Congressman Leo Ryan, a Democratic friend and a colleague on the Government Operations Committee, asked if I'd accompany him to Guyana, where he wanted to investigate the abuses of cult leader Jim Jones, who had gotten his start as a preacher, years before, in Indiana. In the fall of 1978 Tucker and Ben were very small and Corinne was on the way. I took as few trips away from home as possible, so I begged off this one, even though Leo asked me two or three times. He lost his life on that trip—a victim of the Jonestown Massacre.

But it made sense that Latin America ended up being the chief focus of my foreign travels a dozen years later. By 1993 I had made seven trips to the region, including one in 1991 on which I was accompanied by a number of high-powered American CEOs, who talked trade with the business and political figures they met. This economic effort was an essential part of our strategy to help achieve a stable, democratic Latin America whose capacity for growth, if markets and free trade develop, rivals that of Asia. I believe that by 1993 I had helped the Bush administration make a real contribution to the region, and I had reason to be grateful to Jon Glassman, who early on had urged me to make Latin America a special area of interest. Jon himself is now our ambassador to

Paraguay, helping that country in its first years of democracy after decades of military dictatorship, a more satisfying experience than one he had had as America's chargé d'affaires in Afghanistan. Jon was the last one out of our embassy in Kabul, the man who brought the American flag home (a flag I gave to Ronald Reagan) after the Soviets took over. Neither he nor I could have predicted that the Soviets would soon be lowering their own flag, not from an embassy in a distant land but from the flagpole over the Kremlin.

19 | The Former Soviet Union

When I was in the Senate, Marilyn and I took a helicopter tour of Berlin. We flew along the Wall, and the contrast between the two halves of the divided city was visible from the air. On one side of Checkpoint Charlie there was a bustling, prosperous, and friendly city; on the other, the communist, side was a grim, empty-looking area dominated by a huge military presence and almost devoid of ordinary pedestrians. My finally seeing the Wall, after more than twenty years of picturing it in my mind, had a great emotional impact on me. Here was the way the Soviet empire kept itself alive: it imprisoned its citizens.

I was a teenager when the Wall was erected—just like Peter Fechter, the German boy shot to death by Soviet police as he tried to flee from East Berlin to the West in 1962. Daring stories of escape—by tunnel or rope, successful or doomed—were a feature of my growing up, and they helped shape my lifelong belief in anticommunism. The Wall was not just a brutal fact but a mythic symbol, and in November 1989, in disbelief I watched its fall on television. Our children didn't seem terribly impressed. In their youth the Wall had become more of a landmark, like the Great Wall of China, rather than a massive symbol of oppression and enslavement. So I talked to them about it, told them they needed to realize what a huge historic event this was.

The Wall came down, and communism collapsed with it. The transformation of Eastern Europe was swift and staggering. The governments of the satellite states fell to freedom as if a great army were overrunning them. But the advancing forces were coming from within: forty years of pent-up desires for liberty and democracy, the yearnings of tens of millions of people who had been cheated of the peace and freedom that should have been theirs at the end of World War II. The great peaceful movements that had begun a decade and more earlier in Poland and Czechoslovakia reached a sudden triumph there and soon spread down the Danube and into the Balkans.

The changes that had been taking place within the Soviet Union itself were bound to accelerate as its captive nations cut themselves loose. Within the Bush administration there were differing points of view on how to accelerate and manage those changes. Secretary of State Baker, who had formed a fast friendship with his counterpart, Eduard Shevardnadze, favored a Gorbachev-only policy: Baker thought the Soviet leader should have all the support he needed in bringing glasnost and perestroika to fruition. The United States had to do all it could to support Gorbachev against his hard-line communist foes, even if that meant not encouraging the more radically democratic opposition of Boris Yeltsin and his supporters.

The President was more skeptical of Gorbachev's intentions, and of his ability to carry the day. I would place Scowcroft somewhere between Bush and Baker. That left me a little to the right of all of them. I had real doubts about Gorbachev's commitment to democracy; I still believe that most of his reforms were simply concessions to political reality at home and abroad. I made little secret of my reservations, and commentators wondered whether Baker and I were in serious conflict, or perhaps coordinating some good-cop/bad-cop strategy toward Gorbachev. A month before the Wall fell, as Baker hailed the Soviet Union's apparent new peacefulness, I was stressing its continuing support for outlaw regimes in countries like Afghanistan and North Korea. Pressed to account for the seeming contradiction, Marlin Fitzwater, the White House press secretary, said, "We all sing from the same song sheet, but there are several verses."

This sounds like Marlin at his best, spinning like a down-home smoothie, but what he said was basically true. Everyone in the administration wanted democracy to spread within and outside the Soviets' borders. If Jim Baker was speaking softly while I rattled the big stick, one had to remember that those simultaneous approaches have been vital to American foreign policy ever since Teddy Roosevelt. After his Malta summit with Gorbachev, the President stressed the Soviet leader's "new thinking," while I reminded audiences that the Soviet Union remained a totalitarian state. The President did not try to muzzle me, because I don't think he felt my "verse" in the administration's song was completely off-key. He could see my point. He didn't enforce a rigid consistency, and, despite what some have said, he wasn't using me as part of some deliberate plan he had for keeping the pressure on Gorbachev.

Nor had I been ordered to placate conservative Republicans at home, though a number of the press saw it that way. Liberal *Washington Post* columnist Mary McGrory said that the President wanted me to talk to a constituency of "flat-earthers." "If Quayle wants to dissent on Malta," she reasoned, "it's okay because someone has to persuade conservatives that life is worth living without the Soviets to kick around." Actually, it was writers like McGrory who were wondering how they could explain themselves now that the kind of anticommunism they so disliked—the uncompromising, muscular variety practiced by American conservatives from Taft through Goldwater to Reagan—stood triumphant. Her immediate point, which the *New York Times* shared, that I was being asked to "say things that Mr. Bush or Secretary of State James A. Baker 3d believed but would feel uncomfortable articulating," was just plain wrong. Obviously I had conservative credentials that could be useful on certain matters, and it's true that Sununu always liked the idea that I could protect the President's right flank. But far from telling me to give the conservatives what they wanted, the President, every once in a while, would give me a reminder: "You've got to realize this party is broader than just the conservatives. Don't get carried away." He would say the same thing to Sununu, who was, in the abortion debate, for example, more unyielding than the President. When it came to Soviet policy, George Bush didn't want to "muzzle" me, and he didn't want to "unleash" me; what he wanted was for me, within political reason, to be myself.

As the Soviet bloc began to dissolve, the new enemy became, at least from Brent Scowcroft's point of view, instability. Unless we managed the massive changes that were under way, made them gradual and steady, things might get out of hand, and the Soviet Union might overreact, in panic. Was there a case to be made for prudence? Of course, so long as we didn't forget that the real enemy was the form of government that had tyrannized the Eastern European nations for two generations. At one point Baker seemed to be inviting the Soviets to stabilize the situation in Romania, almost giving them a signal that we expected them to intervene, and that was carrying prudence too far.

Few people remember that when he proclaimed the Soviet Union an "evil empire," Ronald Reagan also predicted its imminent demise. He described communism, in 1983, as a bizarre episode in human history whose final chapters were then being written. Oh, how Reagan's liberal opponents scoffed at his cockeyed optimism, the reckless assumptions that, they felt, were so typical of him. The liberals knew better, knew that communism might be contained but never defeated, knew for sure that it was an eternal fact of life, not a monstrously clumsy system that just might, if given the right push, topple over from its own weight.

It was Ronald Reagan who knew better. He knew that while the rest of the world was growing richer, the Soviet empire was getting more miserable and poor. He knew that the only way to get Soviet missiles out of Eastern Europe wasn't to "freeze" them in place but to have the western nations deploy intermediate-range weapons of their own. He knew that, if we rebuilt our military and pressed ahead with SDI, we would force the Soviets to keep up and to spend themselves toward their own demise. During his first term he simply stiffed the Soviets. It wasn't just that he wouldn't hold a summit with their leader; so long as they were in Afghanistan he wouldn't even let their ambassador walk in the front door of our State Department. The Soviet craving for respectability, for acceptance within the world community, was as strong as it had always been, and when Gorbachev came to power after four years of the Reagan treatment, and was faced with four more years of the same, the Soviets had no choice but to start giving in. Reagan had never wanted coexistence; he wanted the mighty USSR, just like the puny Sandinistas, to cry "uncle." If you listened closely as the Berlin Wall's pieces hit the ground, that was the word you could hear.

There's no question about Gorbachev's charm. He had it in abundance along with humor and tactical brilliance. But for all the accolades and prizes he's received, he will end up being regarded by Russian historians as a monumental screw-up. He appeared to be an innovator, someone rushing to freedom's side, but his perestroika was a ramshackle mess, and he had little choice but to grant the liberties of glasnost. The truth is that he was almost always reactive, not the grand strategic thinker he fancied himself. He was desperately trying to keep up with events, and in the end he wound up presiding over the death of communism and the Soviet Union—neither of which he wanted. (Why the National Republican Senatorial Committee, chaired by Phil Gramm, should now want to pay him $70,000 to hear his views on foreign policy is beyond me.)

To hang on as long as he did, he needed to travel abroad in search of international prestige and foreign aid. He was just as dazzled by Western wealth as his less cosmopolitan predecessors had been. When he helicoptered to Camp David with President Bush, he leaned over to the window and pointed to the homes below, and asked the President: "What are they, those things down there?"

"Well, they're homes," answered Bush.

"Homes?" asked Gorbachev. "Well, who owns them?"

"Americans own them," said Bush.

Gorbachev was surprised that ordinary citizens could actually have title to these houses he was seeing.

He came to Washington in the spring of 1990, desperate for a trade agreement. He could talk of nothing else, not even when the President gave him a little tour of the White House grounds, strolling with him past the pool and the horseshoe pit. During a large bilateral meeting in the Cabinet room, the President passed me a note saying that he just didn't think he could give Gorbachev his trade agreement. But as the meeting wore on and Gorbachev's relentlessness became clear, you could see the tide turning. He was wearing us down. Still, when I met with him later, in the

Soviet embassy, I pointed out that it would be difficult to sell the American people on any sort of trade agreement unless there were serious economic reforms. I also criticized the USSR for subsidizing Castro's regime in Cuba. What was the point of our giving money to Castro's banker?

In the end a compromise was reached. Gorbachev got the trade agreement and we got his firm commitment to economic reforms, which were desperately needed.

Gorbachev's winning personality was a good match even for Reagan's. When the two of them finally sat down in Reykjavík in 1986, Reagan nearly got suckered into accepting a surprise proposal from Gorbachev that would have come close to eliminating nuclear weapons altogether. It appealed to the visionary side of Reagan, the part of him that was always able to think big, but it was finally blocked by another side of his character, the stubborn one, as well as his unwavering support of SDI.

Gorbachev was a good salesman. In public, and at press conferences, he was very sure of himself and almost verbose, but in private he was less talkative and less confident. By the time the Russians hosted a reciprocal state dinner at their embassy in June 1990, Gorbachev had come to identify me with both SDI and the space program. He noticed Marilyn's star-shaped earrings, and as we sat down to the evening's entertainment, he told her, through the translator, that the two of us must really be obsessed by space for her to be wearing them.

His charm was such that by the time both Reagan and Bush met with him on Ellis Island, during the transition toward our administration, I think that Reagan was actually less skeptical of Gorbachev than Bush was. As our administration went on, the main obstacle to Gorbachev's salesmanship was that he was left with very little to sell.

I'm afraid that whatever charm Gorbachev's wife, Raisa, possessed was pretty much lost on me. At that reciprocal state dinner she lectured me on how misunderstood Lenin was; if Stalin hadn't stolen the revolution, she said, the USSR would be in much better shape today. She expressed to me her contempt for the American Civil War as opposed to the Russian one: *there*, she said, they had been fighting to overthrow a despot, whereas over here it was simply brother fighting brother. She also said that she could not understand why Napoleon, who had attempted to conquer her country, was held in such high esteem here, while no room was made to admire Lenin. I said something about how I wasn't sure Napoleon was much on American minds. Then we got into a spirited discussion of SDI, during which she turned to me and said accusingly, "You sound like Margaret Thatcher." I took this as a compliment. Up at Camp David a couple of days later, I got to sit next to her again, by which time I'd wearied of her pronouncements but continued to be impressed by the confidence with which she claimed to express her husband's views: "Yes, absolutely," she assured me, "I am speaking for him."

In November 1990, when Marilyn's work in the field of disaster preparedness and response took her to the Soviet Union, she went to have tea at the Kremlin, at Raisa's invitation. Marilyn was expecting the usual formal diplomatic tea, where everyone strains for conversation, but to her surprise, at Raisa's request, the only people present in the elegant Kremlin room were Raisa's interpreter, her husband's chief of staff, and Raisa and Marilyn. They sat at a small table for four, with Marilyn and Raisa facing each other. What was to be a fifteen-minute meeting lasted almost two hours. Raisa was obviously in great distress. She talked of how her happiest days had been those at the university, where she believed totally in what she was taught. Everything had been wonderful, a perfect world. Now it was falling apart around her. The ideals of her youth were proving false.

She became very emotional but continued talking. She spoke at length about the psychological, political, and economic condition of her country. Marilyn remembered every detail of the conversation. Afterwards, she went back to the ambassador's residence and dictated a nearly verbatim account of it to Jon Glassman, who was traveling with her. Jon immediately cabled the State Department and the Situation Room at the White House with this detailed report.

The next day, at my early morning meeting with the President, Brent Scowcroft, and Larry Eagleburger, Larry reported on the cable and said it was the first true indication of the gravity of the situation in the USSR, and that it was my wife who had made the breakthrough. It was a double pleasure to call Marilyn on our anniversary, November 18, to tell her I loved her and to congratulate her on a job well done. (I also managed to send her eighteen roses—no mean feat in the USSR.)

If Raisa's apparent equality with her husband didn't seem to fit the Russian stereotype, there was someone rising to the top who did. I first met Boris Yeltsin in Brent Scowcroft's office back in 1990. At this point the administration was walking a fine line, trying to build friendly relations with the Moscow deputy without looking as if it were beginning to favor him over Gorbachev. For that reason the President wouldn't receive Yeltsin in the Oval Office itself. I had to go down to Scowcroft's office to get my first glimpse of this burly man with the thatch of white hair.

People in the White House, and especially those over at State, were skeptical of him. He had terrible image problems: there were plenty of reports that he was a drunk and incompetent, a great uncouth bear in the Khrushchev manner. "Very Russian" was Brent Scowcroft's assessment of him, and it wasn't meant as a compliment. But I liked Yeltsin from the start. He may not have had Gorbachev's polish, but I could immediately see how confident he was. During that short encounter in Scowcroft's office, he joked about the bad press we shared, and I was impressed at how well briefed he must have been in order to know this. (Actually, my feeling was mixed with a bit of annoyance: was my press *so* bad that it made its way to *everyone's* attention?)

We needed to get out in front of the Soviet situation. I worried that, by clinging to a Gorbachev-only policy, we were losing the chance to deal with someone who was beginning to look like the future. Mrs. Thatcher was ahead of us on this. When we talked in London in 1991, I asked for her impressions of Yeltsin. She told me she thought he was legitimate, someone we should be prepared to support. Several years earlier, she had startled people by describing Gorbachev as someone she could "do business" with; now she saw Gorbachev receding and this new man coming to the fore.

This new man, it's important to remember, was a kind of Soviet leader we had never dealt with before: a freely elected one. The people of Moscow had voted him into the position he held, just as the Russians would soon vote to make him their President. He had assumed that position by the time of our next meeting, which came, fittingly enough, at a dinner hosted by the Center for Democracy, in June 1991. Before the proceedings, complimenting him on his fine-looking Russian tie, I joked that it was an American custom for acquaintances to exchange neckties. He then told me he'd bought the tie the day before in New York City, and asked if I still wanted it. We both laughed.

When we gave our after-dinner speeches, I praised his commitment to democracy and reform and listed a half dozen things I thought were important to America's relationship with the changing Soviet Union. The Soviets must continue to democratize, I said, to privatize, and to reduce nuclear weapons. Moreover, they needed to get out of the Baltic states and quit funding Cuba. Also, they had to consider giving the Kuril Islands, taken at the end of World War II, back to Japan.

I could see Yeltsin listening carefully before he got up to offer an on-the-spot response. He went straight down my list, item by item. He was for democratization, for privatization, and for arms control. If he got his way, the USSR would be getting out of the Baltics. Cuba? We were right: it didn't make sense for the USSR to go on funding Castro. But as for the Kuril Islands, no, he would never support returning them.

I was struck by his boldness and apparent sincerity. He was very impatient to keep driving the extraordinary developments taking place in his country. In fact, when he finished responding to my speech and began to deliver his own, he got only about two minutes into it before announcing: "In order to save time, ladies and gentlemen, I'm just going to let my interpreter give my speech in English." This cut the delivery time in half, and when it was over the crowd responded with a standing, cheering ovation.

Just two weeks earlier, I had finally gotten my chance to visit Eastern Europe and see the fallen Soviet dominoes. It was an extraordinary experience to be representing America, which embodied the democratic future these nations sought. The leaders I sat down with, among them Lech Walesa in Poland and Václav Havel in Czechoslovakia, were men of a new generation and outlook, men who had already suffered through long, hard years when they were jailed and their efforts for freedom driven underground. Walesa and his wife were both very warm and witty. He is a consummate pol, a glad-handing guy who would have had a great career in the local wards of Chicago or Milwaukee if he'd been one of the millions of Poles who sought their dreams in America. Havel, by contrast, was less talkative, more philosophical. At this point he was trying to keep the Czech and Slovak republics together, so we went to the latter, where his position was weaker and where he could use some good press. We planted a tree in the seven-hundred-year-old town of Bardejov on what had been the perimeter of the Roman Empire. Now, thanks in part to him, Bardejov had been set free from the Soviet empire as well.

The energies and ideals that these men had nurtured were bursting forth across half a continent. Thirty thousand people came out to see us in Sofia, Bulgaria, and by their deafening cries I knew what they had really come to glimpse and cheer: the United States of America. That I, at that moment, should be its symbol was a humbling, thrilling experience for Marilyn and me, and also for Ben and Corinne, whom we'd brought with us to see history in the making. The crowd stood there in the rain, which was drenching Alexander Nevsky Square, and shouted, "Down with Communism!" along with "USA! USA!" During the rally, the rain stopped and the sun came out—a moment so perfect no movie director could have gotten away with it. "See," I said, "the sun is shining upon freedom in Bulgaria." The crowd went crazy.

Officially I was there to sign an agreement with the new Bulgarian President, one that would send two hundred thousand tons of American corn to Bulgaria, whose reformed economy was struggling to get on its feet. But my chief purpose was to nourish democracy itself, which had so little history in this part of the world. In Poland just a day earlier, Marilyn, Ben, Corinne, and I had been taken on a tour of Auschwitz, guided by one of the camp's survivors, Miles Lerman. We were given ten suitcases to take home, ones that a half century before had been snatched from terrified arrivals; now we would be bringing them to Washington, to the U.S. Holocaust Memorial Museum, which was then under construction. This visit shook all of us. I remember Corinne being particularly upset by the piles of baby shoes and socks, all of them stripped from murdered children; Ben was horrified by blankets made out of human hair. This was a very hard, indelible experience. I didn't like watching their distress, but I wanted my children to have this terrible, permanent lesson of man's inhumanity to man.

To be standing in Bulgaria's Nevsky Square a day later, amidst such joy and hope, was a contrast almost too vast for the mind and heart to absorb. For fifty years Americans had contributed their blood and treasure and vigilance to defeat the two murderous tyrannies that had darkened Eastern Europe. Finally, a new generation, many of whose members were there in the square, might get to experience something like true freedom and peace.

How we could best help them along was not always clear, particularly when it came to the Soviets themselves. In the summer of 1991 the USSR and the Gorbachev-only thinkers back home were proposing enormous infusions of U.S. financial assistance. "Please do not think there is going to be massive direct aid going to the Soviet Union," I had to tell reporters in Budapest that month. "That really is a nonstarter." Even on Capitol Hill it was highly unpopular. Such aid would have been poured into a dying system, eaten up by a corrupt bureaucracy before it ever got to the people and industries it was intended to reach. It was one thing to give aid to the "enterprise funds" being set up inside the fledgling economies of Eastern Europe, but government-to-government aid to the faltering Soviet Union made no sense at all. If I had known, that summer, just how quickly the USSR's demise was coming, I would have been even more adamant in my opposition.

As it was, in the second half of 1991 the course of events was hard to predict. In August I was vacationing at my parents' home in Arizona, with Marilyn and our children, when word came of the attempted military coup against Gorbachev. For a while it appeared as if the USSR might be headed back toward a hardline communist regime that would be even more belligerent and paranoid now that its satellite states had been lost. I immediately flew back to Washington, where the administration was in a holding pattern. The information we were getting from our own embassy in Moscow was not that encouraging, and we remained very uncertain about the outcome. The degree of optimism and pessimism varied among the other world leaders with whom the

President was talking. I particularly remember hearing that François Mitterrand had said, "Not all coups succeed." My own feelings were relatively gloomy. The administration's official line was that it continued to recognize Gorbachev, and no one ever suggested, even in private, that we make plans to recognize the coup leaders. But there were those, Brent Scowcroft among them, who urged us to be measured in our condemnation of those who had seized power, because if they held onto it we would be forced to deal with them. A world in which the nuclear superpowers would not even talk to each other was not an attractive option.

Yeltsin, of course, saved the day. The sight of him standing atop that tank in Moscow and rallying his supporters remains as vivid for me as any image from our four years. By the time Gorbachev returned to Moscow from his house arrest in the Crimea, it was clear that he owed his survival to Yeltsin. Gorbachev was already a part of the past. Yeltsin, as he's proved in difficult times, was the future—and the Clinton administration has been right to stick with him.

August 1991 was a very nervous time, and the following month, in a speech to the Baltimore Council on Foreign Affairs, I stressed what a close call the coup had been: "The coup plotters sent special troops to arrest President Yeltsin at his home at the very beginning of the coup. They missed him by twelve minutes. That is how close it was. Twelve minutes that potentially were the difference between freedom and oppression, democracy and dictatorship." The role of the West was not to break out the champagne but to remain vigilant. Within the Soviet Union itself, the instability Scowcroft feared was indeed an enemy. The USSR was imploding, collapsing into a black hole like a giant, dying star. Havoc would soon be wrought by the unleashing of long-repressed nationalistic feelings within the republics. Nonetheless, the all-encompassing tyranny of communism was ending, and I had faith that the people it had held captive would in time work through their rivalries and fears, and rise to the occasion of freedom. On Christmas Day, just four months after the attempted coup, we watched them lower the hammer-and-sickle flag that had flown above the Kremlin for three-quarters of a century.

From that moment on, commentators began referring to "the former Soviet Union," a phrase that still astonishes me.

Within a matter of weeks more than a dozen new nations were formed, each one cut loose from the old empire and requiring a new American ambassador. In the case of the Baltic countries, it was a matter of reopening American embassies that had been shut for a half century. Jim Baker continued to insist, with some reason, that the President or Secretary of State be the first American official to visit most of the nations in Eastern Europe that had gone through the recent upheaval. But he and George Bush couldn't be everywhere, and so in February 1992 it fell to me to go to Estonia, Latvia, and Lithuania—the "captive nations" that Stalin had swallowed up at the beginning of World War II. These three small countries had always had a special place in the hearts of American cold warriors, and I was delighted at the chance to see them in their early days of freedom.

It was a very quick trip (I visited all three countries in the space of two days), but Marilyn and I were going with important cargo: large quantities of medical aid from America and a message for the future. We would stand with these countries as they struggled to create or return to democratic values. I realized how difficult that achievement would be when I talked with a cab driver in Riga, the Latvian capital. I asked him how old the city was, and he said about eight hundred years. I then asked him to estimate how many years out of those eight hundred it had been democratically governed. He guessed about thirty.

In Vilnius, Marilyn and I laid a wreath at the television tower, where, a year earlier, Lithuanian patriots had lost their lives in a violent struggle with Soviet troops. After performing that somber duty, we went to Independence Square, where I was greeted by a crowd of ten thousand Lithuanians who were as delirious with freedom as the Bulgarians I'd seen in Sofia eight months before. "USA! USA!" was what I heard, along with cries of "Thank you! Thank you!" I knew what those thanks were for: the half century during which Americans had not flinched from what President Kennedy called the "long twilight struggle" of the cold war. Faith in their God, despite all repression of religion, as well as faith in America, had kept alive a dream of freedom. I told the Lithuanians, as I told their President, Vytautas Landsbergis, that we supported the complete withdrawal of all Soviet troops, a matter that they would now have to negotiate with the new Russian republic. Recalling Boris Yeltsin's response to the six points I had made at the Washington dinner in June 1991, I was confident that this goal would be reached.

I was also confident that the economic changes taking place across what had been the USSR were irreversible, no matter how many obstacles—from sheer bewilderment to black-market corruption—might block the path toward a market economy. What worried me most were the bitter ethnic and national feelings that now had a chance to boil over. Everywhere we went in the Baltics we heard horror stories about friends and loved ones who over the years had been snatched to Siberia, to be brutalized and killed at the hands of those who held these small countries captive. The hatred of Russians was vividly expressed, and the Russians left behind in these countries now had reason to fear for their future. What's more, the new Russian republic, if it fell back into the expansionist ways it had had even before communism came along, might use the predicament of its nationals to justify another lunge at the Baltics. But as I made some stops in Western Europe on my way home, I still marveled at having been able to tell that cheering crowd in Vilnius the incontrovertible and glorious truth: "The great question of our time is settled: Freedom lives. Communism is dead."

20 | Rockets and Red Tape

Our oldest son, Tucker, is now a sophomore in college. That's hard enough for me to believe, but even harder to believe is that he was born two years *after* the last men who were sent to the Moon returned to Earth. When I was growing up, the idea that people from this planet would travel to, and even settle, other ones, was becoming a common assumption. With good reason, too: the United States was making the first bold strides in that direction. I can remember watching television with my parents, at home in Huntington, when Neil Armstrong took his first steps across the surface of the Moon in 1969. My dad and mom watched with a certain disbelief, but the whole thing, exciting as it was, didn't seem impossible to me. It was the logical culmination of the Mercury flights that had begun when I was in the eighth grade. To my parents, manned space exploration was the future; to me it was the present. It is unfortunate that, to my children, the whole idea of Americans walking on other globes belongs to the past, a part of American history that sometimes seems as fully finished as the Civil War.

Even so, millions of Americans of different generations retain the dream of manned space exploration—something more than space flight, which has continued through the shuttle launches but no longer seems headed beyond Earth orbit. One such unlikely enthusiast is Dick Darman: despite his image as a budget cruncher and political arm-twister, Darman has his visionary side, and he was a cheerleader for a manned mission to Mars.

In fact, the Bush White House was a natural for the space program. Space exploration and research not only satisfy our pioneering spirit but also have important practical applications—especially in medicine. The President, who hailed from Houston where the Johnson Space Center is located, certainly believed that. Another supporter was John Sununu, whose engineering background gave him a strong interest in science and technology. In his inaugural address the President stated that we had "more will than wallet"—words that had to be kept in mind when any initiative was contemplated—but I still hoped that during his time in office we would be able to bring the space program out of the doldrums. I didn't expect that the greatest hindrance to doing this would be NASA itself.

By 1989 the White House Space Council had been made the statutory responsibility of the Vice President. This was, in fact, something of a reversion to earlier custom. President Kennedy had given his Vice President, Lyndon Johnson, a big role in the space program, but the last time the council had been run by a Veep was during the Nixon administration, when Spiro Agnew headed it up. In the fifteen years since he'd left office it had been dormant. So here I was with a mandate to revive it, right at the time the space program itself was getting up off its knees: the first shuttle launch since the 1986 *Challenger* accident had taken place only a month or so before we were elected.

Some friends and staffers actually wondered if I shouldn't try to find a way out of running the council. Sure, there were potential political dividends—being involved with the space program could be glamorous and could identify me with what is most important for any national leader: the future. On the other hand, there was a distinct downside. "Dan," they told me, "think of your, er . . . , image problems. Do you really want to be known as Mr. Space?" They were envisioning all the potential space cadet jokes and lost-in-space cartoons.

Point taken. But I was going to do it anyway. I was too interested in the field to walk away from the opportunity, and too convinced that the space program—not just manned exploration but every scientific and technological aspect of it—was vital to maintaining American leadership in the world. I didn't want to see us surrender our history of accomplishment in this area to any other people—not the Soviets, not the Europeans, not the Japanese. Throughout the eighties, I had fought hard for the Reagan defense buildup, because it was vital to restoring America to its prime position in the world. All during that period I had been concerned that our investment in defense was not being accompanied by a corresponding push for the space program. Here, I thought in 1989, was our chance to correct that.

This tendency to think of space and defense together was what made NASA suspicious of me from the start. When they looked at me, they saw Star Wars, since during my years in the Senate I had been such a strong advocate of SDI. Indeed, I remained one as Vice President, but the essential connection I saw between space and defense was not so much SDI as this whole question of American leadership. We should be second to none in all aspects of space science and exploration. NASA's suspicions weren't eased, however, when I selected Mark Albrecht to serve as the Space Council's executive secretary. I had gotten to know Mark when he was Senator Pete Wilson's legislative assistant, in which job, it's true, he was heavily involved with defense issues and a big supporter of a space-based defense system. So it's understandable that the NASA guys were a bit nervous: they thought Mark and I were going to turn the council into a mini Star Wars lab.

That was not my intention, nor his. Mark understood my vision and was tuned into that bigger picture. Still in his late thirties, a tough infighter with a political mind, Mark was interested in winning—and he was willing to play the political game in order to get things accomplished. He was eager to move my agenda forward. He was like many of the people on my staff: young, ambitious, conservative, and smart.

NASA was, to a great extent, still living off the glory it had earned in the 1960s, and I thought Mark Albrecht was just the sort of guy who could shake it up. I wanted the Space Council to work *with* the agency. After all, I assumed that NASA had been pleased to see the council revived. In fact, the revival had been Congress's idea; NASA had just been unable to find any good arguments against having a small group concerned with the space program inside the White House. Those on the outside who wanted vigorous space exploration knew the benefits of having the Vice President take the lead. A Vice President can end-run the Cabinet. He has direct access to the President, and he has what counts in the Washington tug of war: clout. The problem for NASA bureaucrats, a very pampered bunch, was that space policy would be run by the White House. That's why they feared the revival of the council and ended up hating the one run by me. They wanted to keep making space policy themselves, even if it was obvious to outsiders that the projects they had going were too unimaginative, too expensive, too big, and too slow.

NASA didn't mind having us help fight its budget battles with OMB and on the Hill, but they wanted to make up those budgets themselves. I can remember one meeting I had in my West Wing office that included Albrecht and Dick Darman; Admiral Richard Truly, the head of NASA; and William Lenoir, associate administrator for Space Flight. We were discussing ideas for a new unmanned launch system to aid in assembling the space station. Up to that point all plans for the station's construction had involved the shuttle. One of the plans for a new unmanned system came from the Defense Department, and it promised an Initial Operating Capability (IOC) in 2003. The other plan was NASA's, and it had an IOC of 1999. This was never a realistic date, and Lenoir knew it, but he had a scheme for getting Congress's okay and then stringing out the funding. "Well, we could *tell* Congress 1999 but really plan to launch in 2003. After all, we might blow up an engine. In fact, we *could* blow up an engine." That way they'd have an excuse to ask for the extra four years they'd known they needed all along. Everyone's jaw hit the ground, and there was an enormous pause; then I said that what he was suggesting was outrageous. Don Atwood, deputy Secretary of Defense, emphatically disassociated himself from Lenoir's remark, and Darman jumped in to agree with me. Truly and Lenoir said nothing. The arrogance was unbelievable. They were just used to throwing around figures and estimates and counting on the old NASA glamour to dazzle whoever was listening. After the meeting Darman told Albrecht that this made Watergate look small.

NASA and the Space Council had different ideas about who would be running the space program. "What the Vice President is doing," said Dr. John M. Logsdon of George Washington University, "is calling for a new voice and new ideas rather than continuing the monopoly by a single agency and its contractors." That was true, and if anything was going to get done, we needed somebody heading up the agency who was sympathetic to the council's goals. It was unfortunate that we didn't have such a person. Dick Truly, a former astronaut, had done very well with the shuttle program in the difficult days after *Challenger*; he had helped it get off the ground, literally, once more. But he was not the kind of new broom the agency needed, and looking back, I think I made a mistake in not trying to block his appointment to head up NASA in 1989. Dick Truly was a friend of Sununu and became his candidate; I didn't have a good candidate of my own, and so I went along with Truly's selection. As often happens in Washington, Truly got the job by default: he didn't have the sort of negatives that might make news and sink the nomination. As our four years went on, I realized that, dedicated though he may have been, Dick Truly was functioning as a caretaker when NASA needed a bull in its china shop. Not surprisingly, Truly never got along with Mark Albrecht.

Within months of taking office, the administration had a great opportunity to take advantage of those past achievements on which NASA was still coasting. July 20, 1989, would mark the twentieth anniversary of the first Moon landing, and the President wanted to use the occasion to make a major address on the space program, a speech that didn't just look back toward former glory but ahead to bold new achievement. He was heartily in favor of space exploration—and not unmindful that this was a chance to cut into the Democrats' turf. After all, it was Democratic Presidents, Kennedy and Johnson, who remained principally identified with a visionary approach to space. Here was an occasion for George Bush to lay out his own vision of America's future as an exploring nation.

Two weeks before the anniversary, Albrecht and I and the rest of the Space Council met with people from business, academia, and the science community to talk about an agenda we envisaged for the next twenty years of manned space exploration. This included a permanent base on the Moon, one that might even be used as a staging area for a trip to Mars. All of this was to be accomplished by the year 2019—the fiftieth anniversary of the first lunar landing. We were dealing with numbers that were both astronomical and soft. What we had in mind might take $400 billion or $500 billion, and the date itself was somewhat fanciful. Sununu had picked it, more for its historical resonance than because of any strict technological rationale. But the space community was enthusiastic, and the Space Council staff began pitching its ideas to Senators and Congressmen who had a special interest in space—among them, of course, Ohio's John Glenn, who had been the first American to orbit the Earth.

If this sounds like a somewhat ad hoc, improvisational way to think about going to Mars, you're right. But what was important right then was to think big, to put a bit of "the vision thing" back into the program, to get people excited about it once again, even if that meant getting ahead of ourselves. (At least we weren't trying to fake specific IOCs in order to stay *behind* ourselves.) The only time people had gotten excited about our space program in the last fifteen years came when seven *Challenger* astronauts died; for most of that period NASA was simply boring the public, when it could have been challenging it to dream, and lifting America's whole sense of itself. We don't know what scientific and medical dividends a Mars mission might eventually pay, but the point of going is the same one John F. Kennedy recognized about the Moon program: we should do it not because it is easy but because it is hard.

George Bush understood this, and when the July 20 anniversary came around, the speech he gave at the National Air and Space Museum in Washington, in front of the *Apollo 11* crew, had been essentially written by the Space Council staff. "Back to the Moon and on to Mars" was its bold message, one that was challenged, immediately and predictably, by some. "You can't go to Mars on a credit card," said Leon Panetta, the head of the House Budget Committee and now Bill Clinton's OMB director, who never seemed to mind doing much else on a credit card and who tried to kill the space station after we left office. It was pie in the sky, said the Democrats, who really meant that it was Republican pie in the sky. (Forget about Republican support for the enormous space appropriations that Kennedy and Johnson had requested a quarter century before.)

Even if it was a little half-baked, the fact remained that the space program *needed* a bit of pie in the sky, something big that it could aim for once again. I was not averse to unmanned space exploration, and when I spoke to the 175th national meeting of the American Astronomical Society in Washington the following January, I assured them that the administration was committed to a balanced space program, one that also reserved plenty of room for unmanned missions carrying purely scientific payloads. But I knew the only thing that would again excite the American public—to the point where they would back more space appropriations for all kinds of activity, manned and unmanned—was a revival of wonder in the idea of sending people to *explore* space, not just orbit around and around in it.

The politics of space exploration are as complicated, perhaps more so, than those surrounding any other issue. For one thing, they quickly get you into international politics. When I met with Gorbachev in May 1990, nothing set his eyes alight like my mention of joint U.S.–Soviet activity in space. There were any number of possibilities: we could put cosmonauts on the shuttle; they could send an American astronaut up to their Mir space station; and we could even cooperate in the lunar and Martian ventures that the President had talked about.

Later on, such joint possibilities created turf problems between me and Jim Baker, who believed in giving Gorbachev pretty much everything he wanted. I did not like the idea of American satellites being launched on Soviet rockets: we were trying to help develop some commercial launch capability in our own country, and these Soviet rockets would only provide unfair competition. Nonetheless, the idea appealed to Baker. "Who is Mark Albrecht?" he asked me one day, with pursed lips. So now Mark had the Secretary of State on his case. "Congratulations," I told Mark the next time I saw him. "You have really arrived in life. Jim Baker knows your name." Toward the end of the administration, we were preparing a space treaty with Russia, and Baker didn't want anyone negotiating it but himself. I said fine, you'll negotiate, but the Space Council will set the administration's space policy. Sometimes I had to remind Jim that I worked for the President, too.

Where space was concerned, I had enough problems on my

hands—bureaucratic and otherwise—without Jim Baker and State confusing the issues. Right around the time of my mid-1990 meeting with Gorbachev, NASA was hit with a wave of bad publicity. The shuttle seemed to be grounded all the time with fuel leaks; the mirror on the Hubble telescope couldn't focus; and the agency was pushing a space station design that was so overblown it looked as if we were asking to launch a big white elephant.

The mood at the Space Council was grim, but events were about to turn rather suddenly, along the peculiar, almost accidental, lines they sometimes follow. Flying home from the Houston "economic summit" on Wednesday, July 11, I talked space with Sununu and, among others, former astronaut Gene Cernan; Dr. Bruce Murray of Caltech; and Tom Paine, who had run NASA during its glory years and remained a strong advocate of innovative ways to do manned space exploration. I was searching for a solution for NASA. Unfortunately, over the weekend, CBS went with a rumor that I was calling Admiral Truly in to fire him.

George Bush wasn't pleased with this CBS story, and neither was I. On Monday in the Oval Office, I told the President that I didn't know where it had come from. I did confess some of my frustration with Truly, but I didn't suggest a change. I knew how protective the President was of those he had appointed. Bush told me that he'd informed Truly of his support, regardless of what CBS was saying.

Much later, when I *did* want Truly replaced, the memory of this incident gave him the false impression that I would not have George Bush's approval for the change. This underscores how leaked stories can complicate governing, the way they create lasting frictions that never quite get smoothed over. On the other hand, leaks and rumors have their uses, and in July 1990 this CBS story did some good, even as it irritated me and the President.

The reports floating around over the weekend had really dramatized my dissatisfaction, and when we met on Monday I found that Truly was ready to accept the appointment of an outside commission that would evaluate U.S. space policy. Another thing helped make it a little easier: when I asked Truly to come up with names of potential members, one that he mentioned jibed with one on a list of my own. That was Norman R. Augustine, the chairman of Martin Marietta, who would now head up the Committee on the Future of the U.S. Space Program—the Augustine Commission, as it came to be known. Some in the media objected to Augustine's being from inside the aerospace industry; they made the argument that the fox was coming to guard the chicken coop. Despite the skepticism no one could deny his skills or stature. In fact, George Bush had considered Augustine for Secretary of Defense before he selected John Tower. He had had an impressive career and is one of those men who speaks very softly, almost matter-of-factly, and still manages to get a hush to fall over the room. For all Truly's reluctance to have the commission, he wound up developing a good rapport with its head.

I was determined that the commission's report, which it was asked to produce by the end of the year, would not become one more blue-ribboned dust catcher. I wanted it to bust the clog and get NASA moving again. If that was going to happen, then the commission had to have the authority to look into every aspect of the space agency. The result was a long negotiation about the commission's scope. Truly's original position was that it should look only at the future management structure of NASA—that is, what would come after the space station was built. "No," I said, "it will look at the current management situation." Truly next tried to exempt programs from review, and I said, "No, programs will be reviewed as well." He asked that the space station be "off the table" and said that we would all be better served if both it and the Moon–Mars missions were off limits to the commission. In other words, the commission shouldn't pay attention to all the most important things we were trying to do during the next couple of decades. "I'm sorry," I said to Truly, "but everything is on the table, and let the chips fall where they may." This was certainly the kind of top-to-bottom review Augustine himself wanted to undertake. I tried to soothe Truly's feelings by making the commission report through him to me, but everyone understood that this was my baby. When they came back with their work, people would have to listen, if only because of the stature of the man Albrecht sometimes referred to as St. Augustine.

The report the commission submitted in December was, no matter how politely phrased and presented, devastating. "Among the concerns that have most often been heard," it noted, "has been the suggestion that the civil space program has gradually become afflicted with some of the same ailments that are found in many other large, mature institutions, particularly those institutions which have no direct and immediate competition to stimulate change." The Space Council was now the competition, at least when it came to making policy, and we wanted the programs to be cheaper, smaller, and faster. The Augustine report told NASA that it had too many people in charge with too little accountability, that it needed to think beyond the shuttle, and that it should not expect the government to build any more orbiters for it. The space station had to be completely rethought on a smaller scale, and while we were willing to back the huge Earth Observation Satellite (what Dick Darman once called the "$34-billion thermometer"), we wanted the next generation of satellites to be less expensive and faster and to be put into space as a series of components, to reduce the risk of losing everything at once in a faulty launch.

On December 4, 1990, shortly before its report was scheduled for release, I invited the commission—along with Truly, Albrecht, and Darman—to have dinner at the vice-presidential residence. Our intended celebration of the commission's work turned into a discussion of how the report would present its "priorities" for space. And here's where the members ran into some trouble. The draft of their report endorsed the space station and the missions to the Moon and Mars, but it put all of the manned exploration last—after scientific research, technological development, space-based environmental studies, and a plan for a new launcher to replace the shuttle.

As he listened to a summary of the report, Darman, the manned-space-flight visionary and political realist, was quietly dismayed, but he played it in his usual way. He let everyone else finish talking, since he knew the importance of having the last word. He waited, and waited, and then pounced, telling us we were all wet about these "priorities." "If you put manned exploration as number five, you might as well not support it at all," he said. Given the way politics is practiced and budgets are passed, those looking at the report would just lop off the last priority or two and fund the rest.

He was right. The report was rewritten. Science was still put ahead of everything else, but we found a way to avoid any numerical ordering. Before he even left the residence, Darman knew he had gotten his way. "I think I saved your space station," he told me, in his usual modest way.

There's no question it was useful having Darman on our side. Six months later we would be in an uphill battle with Congress over funding for that station. On May 15, 1991, by a vote of 6–3, the House appropriations subcommittee that oversees NASA voted, in effect, to kill it. Over the next three weeks, as the appropriations bill made its way to the House floor, I did considerable lobbying up on the Hill, among both Republicans and Democrats, arguing to the latter that they were throwing away a proud party tradition and would end up handing us Republicans an issue—we would be sure to talk about ourselves as the party of the high-tech future when the presidential election came around next year. I kept at it even after I'd left for my trip to Eastern Europe. On the day of the full House vote, I was calling members from Poland, where I was getting ready for a state dinner with Lech Walesa. I'd have individual House members paged in the cloakroom, and word would get around that the Vice President, all the way from Eastern Europe, was trying to reach members. It was a nice bit of flattery for the people whose arms I was trying to twist.

One call I made from Poland was to Michigan's Bill Broomfield. Bill's fellow Michigander, Bob Traxler, a baron on the appropriations committee, was playing power politics, threatening Bill and the whole Michigan delegation if they didn't vote against the station. Bill Broomfield knew that Traxler could be vindictive, but I was able to bring him around with an argument I knew he'd be sensitive to. Bill was the ranking Republican on the House Foreign Affairs Committee, and I told him that the space station was, in effect, a foreign policy issue. Canada, Japan, and seven European countries were involved in building it along with the United States. If we pulled the plug now, we might never again be able to assemble a coalition like this.

In the end, we put together a good bipartisan coalition, and on June 6 the space station came back to life when the House voted 240 to 173 to fund $1.9 billion for it for the next fiscal year. Every year the space station finds itself in peril, but as of this writing it is still alive, and I still believe that it is important to American prestige, to America's technological future, and to whatever chance we have of getting to Mars by any date even close to the one we picked in 1989.

Overall, how important was the Augustine report? Did the commission escape the fate of irrelevance suffered by so many other ones the government sets up? Let's run down a partial list of its key recommendations:

- Split space operations—the shuttle—from space development—the station. (This was done, very reluctantly.)

- Reduce duplication at space centers; allow them to grow and shrink with circumstances. (This was never done.)

- Get exemptions from civil service employment regulations or start converting centers to contractors, like the successful Jet Propulsion Lab in Pasadena. (This was never done.)

- Rely on more contractors, not fewer, and reduce the size of the NASA organization. (This was never done.)

- Don't buy more shuttle orbiters. (This I managed to block despite NASA's continued push for them.)

- Don't fly more than eight shuttles a year. (This was done.)

- Phase out the shuttle over the next decade. (No follow-through yet.)

- Start a new evolutionary launch system to complement the shuttle and provide the basis for its eventual replacement. (Killed by Congress with the active urging of NASA.)

- Completely redesign Space Station Freedom. Make it cheaper; have its construction require fewer launches and less maintenance. (What NASA did instead of a redesign was a downgrade of the original configuration. The General Accounting Office and NASA itself now estimate the station will cost as much as was estimated for the original design.)

- Keep the Earth Observation Satellite but look for cheaper, faster satellites; offload from big platforms and reduce risks. (Done over NASA's strenuous objections.)

I count four and a half followed through out of ten. Sound atrocious? As follow-through from government commission reports goes, such a ratio is actually outstanding. You can see from the list how much opposition we had from NASA itself, even though it should have been our ally in revitalizing the program. Late in 1991 it was clear to me that the agency required a new head, and I finally found a qualified candidate—Dan Goldin, the general manager of the TRW Space & Technology Group in California.

Shortly before Christmas I went in to talk to the President. He agreed to the change. So I called Dick Truly in and, with regret, told him what we were planning. I hoped, of course, that he would agree to resign and that it would not look like a messy firing. I thanked him for his service and told him that we wanted to find an ambassadorship for him. He said he wasn't interested, and I understood. But then he tried to go around me. He talked to Andy Card, the deputy White House chief of staff to Sam Skinner, who came back to me and asked what was all this about my trying to get rid of Truly? Then Skinner called up Mark Albrecht and asked what was going on—even though he'd been with me and the President when the President agreed to the change. So suddenly the thing was coming unraveled and we had to do it all over again. It went back up to the President, who agreed to the change once more. Skinner then told Albrecht to line up a lot of people, space experts, who would be ready to make statements that the firing was essential. Albrecht hesitated, but the next morning Skinner was immensely relieved to find that he had: in the meantime the President had told him he wanted everything done in as friendly a way as possible. What a mess.

By the middle of February 1992 Truly was finally on his way out—though only after his wife wrote President Bush an indignant letter asking how he could do this. And the President, gentleman that he is, felt bad about it. He should not have had to go through that. I respected Admiral Truly, but the administration had the right to appoint whoever it thought was needed to carry out its space policy, and I was annoyed that Truly's leaving had been so needlessly complicated. He told the press that the departure was not his idea, and it was not surprising that in the 1992 election he came out for Clinton. I regret the unpleasantness but not the change. Dan Goldin was just the person we needed, and after he went to NASA he started breaking some china. He was the highest Bush administration official to be retained by Clinton.

The long-range implications of the Augustine commission are still hard to detect at this point, but I do think it brought about the beginning of the end of the status quo at NASA. My successor, Al Gore, talks a lot about reinventing government and seems to think that he can accomplish that with a lot of town meetings and touchy-feely retreats for administrators. But that is not how government will be reinvented. That will only happen when it's reclaimed from entrenched, indifferent, and powerful bureaucrats who fight dirty and have the kind of lifetime civil service job security to wait out changes in administration. We did change NASA, though not as much as I would have liked. And I still hope that Americans are walking on Mars by the time my grandchildren go off to college.

21 | The Pre-Plummet Summit

I certainly don't regard the Bush presidency as a failed one, but when any administration ends up not getting itself reelected and receiving only 37 percent of the vote, historians look for the moment when things went off track: the wrong turn, the fatal mistake. For Jimmy Carter it may have been that "malaise" speech in 1979, where he blamed the American people for the country's ills. For LBJ perhaps it was the Tonkin Gulf resolution in the very first year of his presidency. If you're looking for the beginning of the end of the Bush administration, I'm convinced you've actually got to go further back than the President's own inauguration. To say things were over before they began is a little melodramatic, but I believe that you can find the wrong turn, the one that led to the fatal mistake, in a meeting that was held during the Reagan–Bush transition.

It was at this time that deficit consciousness was really taking hold among the electorate and, to some extent, politicians. In fact, Bob Strauss, that longtime Democratic power broker, had joined Drew Lewis, Reagan's former Transportation secretary, at the head of a bipartisan commission on the subject, and there were some people in the incoming administration who were advising George Bush to make a commitment to receive the report with an "open mind"—that is, be willing to think about raising taxes. That way he could look as if he were rising above partisan politics and truly seeking a way to tame the deficit monster.

One day in December 1988 we met at the vice-presidential residence (which was still George Bush's home, not mine) for a discussion of the commission's work. Darman wasn't there, but Jim Baker, Nick Brady, and Bob Teeter, the President's pollster, were. Before the meeting really got under way, and while the President-elect was on the phone, Baker whispered to me, "Watch these guys [meaning Brady and Teeter]. They're going to try to get him to raise taxes." And sure enough, I remember Teeter saying, once we began to discuss the challenges the new President would face: "Well, he doesn't have any choice; he's probably going to have to raise taxes."

Whoa! I thought. This was an administration that had gotten itself elected on the "read my lips, no new taxes" pledge made in New Orleans, and here its own people were, even before the swearing in, talking about George Bush breaking this central promise. Baker, to his credit, said, "Well, we're not going to do it this year," and I wouldn't say that anyone, Teeter and Brady included, made any special push to do it. But I could see from the beginning—before the beginning—that eventually they were going to try to convince George Bush to raise taxes.

The President-elect, wisely, rejected such counsel for the near term, but the transition meeting showed that there were those around him who never intended that he keep his promise—or at least didn't think he needed to keep it for very long. I had expected such pressures from Democrat members of Congress and the *New York Times* editorial board. I wasn't prepared for it from our own team. But by the spring of 1990, the tax raisers got their way.

On June 26, with the congressional elections just months off and the prospect of prolonged budgetary bloodletting in between, the President called for a "budget summit" with the Democrats, and he bought the argument that for the deficit to come down taxes would have to go up. I was out in California on a fundraising trip for Republican candidates when I got the news. I was in the shower, actually, when my personal aide Dan Murphy came running in to say: "It's on CNN. The President just agreed to a tax increase!" I probably should have looked at the drain, because that's where the Republican Party's best issue—the one that had gotten us elected in 1980, 1984, and 1988; the one that had, more than any other, made the Reagan revolution possible—was headed (and maybe, along with it, some of those Republican candidates I was out here to help). But I couldn't yet believe what Murphy was telling me. "You're kidding," I said. "No," he replied. "It really happened. They reached an agreement with the leadership on the Hill." My traveling staff confirmed what Murphy told me.

I called Marilyn. She had already heard and was very upset with the decision. "Do you know what you're doing?" she asked. "Do you know how much this is going to hurt you guys?" I got into my defense-of-the-administration mode and tried to make the best case for what had been done, but Marilyn would have none of it.

When I got back to Washington, I asked Darman what in the world had transpired, and he said, "I'm the fall guy, but it wasn't my fault." He put the blame on Nick Brady, the Treasury secretary, who had attended the meeting between the President and the congressional leadership. Brady had said, "You know, Mr. President, to get these budget negotiations moving, we're going to have to agree to put revenues on the table," which would mean raising taxes. The President, on his own, according to Darman, agreed to do it.

"Oh, come on," I said, when I heard this version of the event.

"No," Darman insisted, "that's the way it happened."

The Democrats were as full of disbelief as I was, but their disbelief was mixed with glee. Here we were at the beginning of negotiations, and the President had given away his trump card, receiving nothing in return. He breaks his pledge, swallows taxes, and all they say is they're willing to negotiate. Sununu couldn't see the storm ahead of him. He would publicly say that the President hadn't really put taxes on the table, that he just wanted the process to go forward. But the fact is the President had put them there.

While I continued to disagree with what the President had done, I felt throughout the summer that there might be a way to salvage the situation. Maybe along with the tax increase we could get massive reductions in spending and a cut in the capital gains tax. In July, at a meeting of the Republican National Committee in Chicago, I insisted on "a good deal, or no deal at all." I wanted the President to reserve the right to back out of what he'd promised in June—or, to put it another way, I wanted him to have the option of returning to his promise from the summer of 1988. We were already taking terrible heat from conservatives in the party. The Conservative Victory Committee, L. Brent Bozell's outfit, had sent Lee Atwater a letter, saying: "If the Republican Party compromises the basic tenets of the 1988 platform, it will spell disaster for its candidates in the upcoming Congressional elections." I was in the difficult position of having to defend the President's tax initiative and rally the party troops around him, when my heart was really with those conservative opponents. I knew we were buying into bad politics and bad economics. The President was going to lose political capital from breaking the pledge, and the economy was going to slide—because that's what happens when taxes are raised.

For all my talk of "a good deal, or no deal at all," I knew there would be one. The system works that way. But Darman and Sununu were dealing from a weak hand, and as a result the Democrats got to do their favorite fiscal routine: raising taxes without cutting spending in any meaningful way. Our people couldn't even get them to throw in a decent cut in the capital gains tax, which we'd constantly pushed as the kind of tax relief most necessary to expand the economy. All the President got was four months of agony and a broken promise that would haunt him for the rest of his presidency. By the time of the 1992 reelection campaign, there would be a few bright spots in the economic picture (including low interest and inflation rates), but the budget deal, plus a regulation-induced recession, which made financial institutions clamp down on lending as part of the S&L bailout, would keep the economy sluggish and the public perception of it even worse.

In these negotiations Congress always has the upper hand. Tax and spending bills originate in Congress; the President can only force Congress to cooperate with him through his veto. All too often administrations crack under congressional pressure. The White House rarely likes to fight. It compromises much too quickly, and the Clinton White House, even with a Democratic Congress, is proving no different.

In the early days of October, a number of people, myself included, were urging the President to back out of the deal. "You shouldn't do it," I argued. "You got a bad deal, and you should walk away." Dick Darman may have done good work when he helped save the space station, but when he worked out the final budget deal, he doomed the President politically. Of course, he wouldn't see it that way. At the time, Dick pointed out that Ronald Reagan, even though he was known as the great tax cutter, had in fact raised taxes a number of times as Governor of California and in his two terms as President without any lasting political damage. The President tried to take some comfort in this, but he knew that his situation and Reagan's (that is, the amount of political capital each had, even within their own party) were not comparable. And Reagan had always been able to make it seem as if he had been left with no choice. When he was Governor of California, he said he was standing so firmly against a tax increase that his feet were in cement. When he finally had to accept one, he disarmed a press conference by asking the reporters if they could "hear the cement breaking" around his feet, as he tapped the microphone for sound effects.

Now George Bush tried to convince himself that there were laudable reasons to stay in the corner he'd painted himself into; he listened to people like Alan Greenspan, the head of the Federal Reserve, who argued, "Look, I know it's tough, raising taxes. But in the long run this will help the economy to grow." You know how that prediction turned out. The budget deal put the economy into the tank, and by the time it started growing again, in 1992, it wasn't coming back fast enough for people to realize it.

I would be a good soldier and make a public sales pitch for the package. I told the media that the President had agreed to abide by what came out of the budget summit because he couldn't afford a domestic crisis while he had so much to cope with abroad: between the June 26 announcement and the late-summer summit, Saddam Hussein had invaded Kuwait and the President was preoccupied with the Desert Shield buildup. There was an element of truth to this, but of course the essential concession on raising taxes had been made more than a month before Kuwait, so the argument was hardly compelling. I think Mark Shields awarded it his Outrage of the Week accolade on "The Capital Gang," and I probably deserved it.

The selling job I had to do on the Hill was awkward. Many of the House Republicans revolted as soon as the deal was announced, but the fact that I was being a good soldier, lobbying for a plan my heart wasn't in, actually gained me a more sympathetic ear than I might have gotten otherwise. My fellow Republicans knew I wasn't gung-ho about asking them to raise taxes a matter of weeks before they faced their constituents in the midterm elections. They knew I was being a loyal Vice President.

"I hear what you're saying," I told them. "But the decision's been made, and we've got to support the President. If what we agreed to was a mistake, it would still be a bigger mistake to desert the President on this. He's out there, he wants it, and he can't bail."

"He *should* bail," someone would respond. "It's going to be bad for the economy."

"He *can't* bail," I would argue back, trying to ignore the point that had been made about the economy. How could I argue against it? I agreed with it! I retreated into the Persian Gulf argument, which here had some real merit. "Look," I said. "What sort of message is this going to send Saddam Hussein? What's he going to think when he sees the President can't depend on his own party? I appreciate your difficulties, and I know you want to stand up for principle on the tax issue, but the most important principle to keep in mind right now is that your President needs to have a *success*." Bush genuinely thought he was doing the right thing. He knew he'd take heat for breaking his promise, but he was more upset with attacks by his own GOP colleagues than he was angry at the Democrats.

It was Newt Gingrich, the House minority whip from Georgia, who had been howling the loudest. He was in a very tough race to hold onto his own House seat that year (I wouldn't be the only one surprised by how close he came to losing it), but instead of arguing on grounds of self-interest, he made the loftier case for what he called a "congressional shield." Basically the argument went like this: "I cannot go along with the President because I have a constitutional and moral obligation to my constituents to represent their views." Newt is the most ferocious foe the House Democrats have, and he's spent most of his career trying to break the hammerlock majority they've held in the lower body since 1954. He is tough, shrewd, and partisan, and figures to be the new House Republican leader after Bob Michel retires. In this position he will exasperate the Democrats even more. Politics per se drives him much more than ideology. He made waves from the moment he arrived in the House. I can remember how years ago Bob Michel, who was running for minority leader when Newt was new to Congress, groused to me that he had to "go to another Newt meeting"—one of those at which this newcomer would be plotting his parliamentary guerrilla war against the Democratic leadership. Newt has been known to be equally vehement arguing against members of his own party and even his own President.

There has been an ironic element in the relationship between Republican Presidents and GOP Representatives during the forty years that the latter have been in the minority. What these Republican Congressmen want most is somehow, after four long decades, to achieve a majority—not just in order to prevail on the issues before the country but also to come out from under the petty tyrannies the House Democrats, arrogantly secure in their majority, have imposed upon them for years. As I've said, nobody has been as fearless as Newt in trying to test the rules, even when that means taking on the Speaker, but these frustrated Republicans know that the only way they are ever going to build toward a majority of seats is to have a long stretch—at least two terms—of Democrats in the White House. That's something they haven't often had in the last forty years, when Republicans have been much more successful at winning the presidency than at winning House seats. The truth is that minority parties pick up most of their seats during midterm elections that occur while the opposing party holds the other end of Pennsylvania Avenue. The Republicans made huge gains in the elections of 1966, halfway through LBJ's increasingly unpopular tenure. Republican presidential victories help give GOP Senate candidates a couple of percentage points, but the coattails don't have much effect when it comes to the House. The Republicans' best hope there lies in chipping away at the Democrats' majority during a series of off-year elections, during which they can run against the White House. By contrast, when a Republican occupies 1600 Pennsylvania Avenue, he can become a burden to the reelection hopes of GOP House members. The electorate always has gripes against even a popular President, and during off-year elections they take out their frustrations on the Congressmen in his party.

I talked about this theory with George Bush, and he didn't really buy it—perhaps because it was too appalling to contemplate. He seemed willing to concede that it might be true of a handful of House Republicans, but he didn't want to believe that scores of them were gripped by this subliminal mind-set. I did, however, make Sununu a believer in the theory, and I continue to hold to it myself. Look at 1982, 1986, and, sure enough, 1990: during all of those years a Republican was in the White House, and the Republicans lost seats in the House. Their day of liberation from the Speaker's tyranny was put even further off.

Although Newt was aware of how I felt, I never advanced this theory before large groups. I was not going to get up before a caucus of Congressmen from my own party and urge them to fight their own subconscious, because one of the worst things to do in a political argument—especially with your allies—is to challenge someone's motives. It only gets you into trouble. If I'd said, "You guys aren't being loyal to the President, because you don't really want a Republican in the White House," they would have gotten their dander up something awful. A caucus of your own party ought to be a place where you can get away with some Dutch uncle talk, but I would have been creamed by a great wave of piety: "Are you attacking my motives? How *dare* you attack my motives!" I didn't want a spectacle like this, but I wasn't afraid to make the argument to individuals and very small groups.

The House rejected the budget deal—254 to 179—less than a week after it was announced. The Democrats had wanted plenty of company in voting for the President's tax increase. If Republicans were deserting their President, the Democrats would be delighted to participate in the bashing. That's how bad the situation became: the summit hadn't just led to an unwise compromise; the supposedly bipartisan deal that came out of it became so identified with the President that voting against it was a way to hand George Bush a defeat. I cannot think of a better example of extending one's hand only to have it bitten off—or a better example of my cardinal political rule: set your own agenda, and don't buy into your opponent's.

Since there was no budget, House members wound up being trapped in Washington throughout much of October, when most of them wanted dearly to be back home in their districts campaigning for reelection. The public's esteem for Congress—never very high, though voters continue to reelect their own individual Representatives almost ad infinitum—fell even further. Sununu and Darman, the principal negotiators at the summit, came out of the whole experience with bruised egos and a lame agreement tied to them like a tin can. The Congress finally passed it on October 27.

Oddly enough, I came out of the debacle somewhat enhanced, within the party and the West Wing. For one thing, the House Republicans much preferred my being sent to twist their arms instead of Darman and Sununu, who on visits to the Hill would often get impatient and talk down to them. Congressmen want to be treated with respect, if not kid gloves. I at least had been one of them, and I let them know I was making an effort to see their point of view (not only to see it, but to pass it on to the President). Newt would ask me, "Does the President know this?" before launching into one of his arguments against the deal. Whatever the point was, I would write it down and pass it on to the President. I took care to follow through and report back, whether it was to Newt or anyone else who asked me to convey something to Bush. They knew the trouble I was having with the tax increase myself, and that made it easier for me to come to them with the arguments I've summarized above about the need for sticking with the President. *National Review* quoted one House Republican as saying: "The reason for Dan Quayle's popularity down here is only partly related to the way he handled the summit. Members respect him because for the last 18 months he's been down here listening to our concerns and helping us out. You see the rest of those guys (i.e., Darman, Brady, Sununu) only when they want something from us. People remember that."

In public, all I could do was blame the congressional Democrats, so it's not surprising that I didn't reap much benefit with the voters.

My poll numbers remained low: An NBC–*Wall Street Journal* poll from around this time had me with 27 percent approving, 38 percent against, and the rest in between. Not very impressive, but I had resigned myself to low numbers at least a year earlier—when I realized that the press coverage was never going to change. But at the White House there was talk of making more use of me up on the Hill, and among conservatives there was more of a sense than ever that I was their man within the administration. One editorial cartoon showed a guy on the bus reading a newspaper with the headline BUSH TAX HIKE. "You know," the man was saying as he read, "the idea of President Quayle doesn't scare me like it used to."

Actually, among the faithful I was always a successful fundraiser. In fact, during the four years I was Vice President I helped raise over $15 million for the Republican party. I traveled around the country addressing local GOP groups as often as my duties would permit. By the middle of 1990 one newspaper was calling me The Quayle Cash Machine in an article accompanied by a chart that showed how in one thirty-two-hour period (during which I lunched, photo-op'd, spoke, and mixed and mingled in Raleigh, Austin, San Antonio, and Houston) I raised $465,000 for the party.

People came out to see me for a couple of reasons. For one thing, conservative activists, who supplied so much of the party's energy at the local level, could count on me to serve up redder meat than they would get from other members of the administration. Sununu was always trying to protect Bush's right flank, to convince the Reaganites, some of whom never stopped being suspicious, that George Bush really was true blue. For this reason he, too, was always eager to have me out before conservative audiences, just as he was always bringing them to the White House. Another reason I did well on the road was pure curiosity: What is this guy really like? Is he as helpless as they say? How has he managed to stand the pounding? I generally got a terrific reception, and all of the flesh-pressing and "Hang in theres!" bucked me up. Nothing was ever as bad as 1988, but this kind of up-close contact with supporters helped me in the same way the crowds along the campaign trail had two years earlier. By 1990 I was enduring the media trashing with equanimity, but I still enjoyed some personal strokes from time to time.

I traveled with my own agenda as well as the White House's. I did not have any serious doubts that I would be George Bush's running mate in 1992, but I also knew that if we were in trouble in the polls shortly before the next election, there would be pressure from some in the party to "dump Quayle." Changing the number two man is, after all, a perpetual matter for speculation when an incumbent is in trouble. (The summer of 1992, as I'll show, would turn out to be no exception.) So I kept in mind all the IOUs that Nixon had assembled in his first term as Vice President, none of which hurt him when it came to riding out a brief "dump Nixon" movement in 1956. Later on, in the sixties, when he was out of office, Nixon continued to campaign tirelessly for Republican candidates at the local level, amassing a huge pile of chits (some of which might just buy neutrality later on) that helped get him the presidential nomination when 1968 rolled around. So was I thinking about 1996 as well? Why not?

Spence Abraham, the Michigan state party chairman and my deputy chief of staff, devised much of our campaigning strategy for the midterm elections in 1990. In Michigan itself, we went in for John Engler five times, and he scored an upset win in the Governor's race. Like Lee Atwater, who at this point was already showing the effects of the cancer that would eventually kill him, Spence was a party builder. I had a little trouble over Spence with the President and some Bush loyalists, who had not quite forgiven him for sitting out the Bush campaign during the Michigan caucuses in 1988. Nonetheless, once he was hired, he did terrific work for me. A great believer in Tip O'Neill's all-politics-is-local school of thought, he had us campaigning for candidates way down the ticket, ones who several years later would be moving up and running for Governor or Senator. We needed to strengthen the local bench for the bigger games they'd be in later—around 1996 or 2000. So, for example, when we went into Florida, we campaigned not only for Bob Martinez for Governor but also for state legislative candidates.

I enjoyed being out on the campaign trail—even if I had to wear the budget albatross around my neck. The 1988 race had almost made me forget that I *liked* campaigning and was good at it. Unlike some of my Republican friends, I even like early morning hand shaking at factory gates. Barnstorming in 1990 felt much more like the good old days when I was running for the House and Senate myself. I went to Texas to help out Clayton Williams, a down-home, Stetson-wearing rancher who was running for Governor. One night we were set to appear together at a big fundraiser, and I made us late by dragging the two of us to a bowling alley—along with a lot of press. I'd always campaigned in bowling alleys when I was running for the House and Senate, and I felt right at home. Claytie and I had a great time, but when we got to the fundraiser, the folks running it were not amused. "We saw you on television, at the bowling alley," they said with a frown. Exactly. And so had hundreds of thousands of others. If the rubber chicken got a little cold, it was because I was doing what any successful politician does—meeting and greeting as many people as I could.

In the end the Republicans didn't do too badly in 1990. We lost some House seats (enough to make my theory of nonsupport for the President hold up) but probably not as many as we might have, given how bad a taste the budget mess had left with the voters. They should have been blaming the Democrats, but it just doesn't work that way. The party that holds the White House is the one that catches it. The Democrats know this and they've been very successful in making voters think that Ronald Reagan single-handedly created all those budget deficits in the 1980s. You'd never know, to hear them tell it, that every one of those spendthrift, pork-filled budgets was really created by House Democrats who treated Reagan's budgets as "dead on arrival."

Republicans paid the real price not in 1990 but in 1992, when the President had to deal with the credibility he'd lost by breaking the read-my-lips pledge. Clinton hammered away and hammered away, and by the end of the campaign succeeded in making the electorate think he was more trustworthy than George Bush—something that even now boggles my mind. Of course, within months of being elected, Clinton would break his own promise of a middle-class tax cut, delivering instead an enormous tax increase to the people who'd voted for him. And there would be all the other broken promises on everything from Haitian refugees to gays in the military. But in the fall of 1992 the

Democrats could hardly be blamed for replaying that read-my-lips clip over and over and over. All the President could say was that he had made a mistake. I hoped he would blame the Democrats in Congress and say that they had made him do it—which was the essential truth—but he followed a Baker strategy: give the media the answer it wants and the question will go away. There's something to that, but in the process we gave the Democrats an enormous gift-wrapped present.

If you want to look for the place where things first went wrong, I'd pick the "budget summit" of 1990. In October of that year, Congressman Dick Armey, a Texas Republican, proved himself a prophet. "The historians will look back," he said, "and call this the pre-plummet summit." When it comes to both the economy and the President's political fortunes, Dick was on the money. Voters have a longer memory than they're given credit for, and 1990 would come back to haunt us, even if in the intervening two years George Bush would have higher poll ratings than any President in the history of polling. In fact, the 1990 elections would have been worse for the Republicans if some voters hadn't rallied to the President's party over tensions that were brewing, not in the chambers of Congress but on the floor of a desert half a world away.

22 | A Line in the Sand

At the end of 1990 *Time* magazine would select George Bush as Man of the Year. Actually, what they chose to do on their cover was merge two photographs of the President and call him Men of the Year. One of the pictures was supposed to represent the administration's domestic drift: indeed, the budget deal showed how rudderless we could be when it came to setting social and economic policy here at home. But the other photograph was meant to stand for the resolute George Bush, the superb manager of foreign policy who, as the year ended, had assembled the greatest military coalition since World War II. Looking back, it seems impossible to believe that both of these images were fixing themselves for history at the same time—those last months of 1990. As the budget fiasco dragged on, the President was managing the first real crisis of the New World Order and playing his role as commander in chief with a kind of awesome calm.

During the first week of August we scheduled our lunch for a Wednesday, the first of the month, since I had some travel planned for the next day. Earlier in the week intelligence reports had filtered into the press that Iraq was massing troops near its border with Kuwait. On Wednesday morning, Carnes Lord, my national security adviser, told me that people in the Pentagon were saying an invasion was imminent. Obviously this was one of the things that came up over lunch with the President. He had, of course, been getting the same reports, but he professed not to be concerned. King Fahd of Saudi Arabia and President Mubarak of Egypt (especially the latter) had both told him that Saddam Hussein was bluffing. The President considered what they said to be the best intelligence he had, and they were telling him that Saddam Hussein would never cross the border into Kuwait.

By that evening he had. I was at home when, at about 9:00, Bob Gates called with the news. The first thing I did was call Brent Scowcroft to ask if it was necessary to convene the National Security Council that night. Brent was opposed to it and suggested we wait until morning.

That meeting, which was held at 8:00 A.M, seemed routine. The President did allow some reporters in before we got started ("We're not discussing intervention," he said), but once they were gone and we got down to business, there wasn't an overpowering atmosphere of crisis. The various implications of what Saddam had done were calmly assessed, and the normal machinery of government went to work. CIA director Bill Webster said he thought there were now over one hundred thousand Iraqi troops inside Kuwait, and Bob Kimmitt, who was substituting for Jim Baker while the Secretary of State was in the Soviet Union, brought us up to date on what the UN and other diplomatic organizations were doing to condemn the invasion. In terms of punishing Saddam, the only measure really discussed was economic sanctions that would keep his own oil (and now the oil he had captured in Kuwait) off the world markets. The President did not underestimate the seriousness of the situation, and he did say that aggression could not be tolerated, but there was no sudden brainstorming about how we could achieve the military liberation of Kuwait—or even any agreement that that was our objective.

At this point our discussions did not involve pushing Saddam back but rather keeping him from going any further. The real catastrophe everyone feared was an invasion of Saudi Arabia by Iraq, and that's what our military planning was concerned with on that first day. Throughout the 1980s, the United States had wanted Iraq to be strong enough to counter Iran. In doing so, we now realized, we had created a far more dangerous monster.

Just what it might take to protect the Saudis from a move by Saddam was outlined by a general I'd never really noticed before, a man who even that morning seemed like just another briefer from the Pentagon. His name was H. Norman Schwarzkopf, and as he gave us his report he seemed very matter-of-fact and, like all the military brass we saw, very deferential to Colin Powell. By the time the Gulf War was over I would recognize him not just as a good soldier but, like his commanding officer General Powell, a master of the press.

Early Saturday morning I helicoptered from the vice-presidential residence to Camp David, where President Bush wanted his team to gather in the big conference room located in Laurel cabin. This turned out to be the crucial meeting, the one that launched Desert Shield, but as we sat down at the table, two and a half days after the invasion, the essential premise for a response had yet to be decided. What was our goal beyond preventing aggression against the Saudis? To get Saddam out of Kuwait? This most basic question remained unanswered.

I sat between the President and Sununu. Jim Baker, back from the Soviet Union, was across from me. His side of the table included Colin Powell, Scowcroft, and General Schwarzkopf; Cheney was across from the general, on Bush's right. Bill Webster, the CIA director, was also present; a judicious, competent man, he was forced, like other CIA directors, to be overly solicitous of Congress, because of all the oversight legislation that existed. He told us just how vulnerable the Saudis were at the moment, how Saddam had positioned himself to overrun their very small defense force at any moment he wanted to. General Schwarzkopf gave us a rundown on the state of the Iraqi army: formidable but not invincible. He outlined two phases of a massive, still hypothetical, military operation. One phase would involve the deployment of up to a quarter of a million troops on the Arabian peninsula. This would be about half the maximum number the United States had at any given time in Vietnam; combined with American air and naval power, Schwarzkopf thought it ought to be enough to repel any move Saddam might make against the Saudis. But dislodging him from Kuwait would require even more in the way of troops, money, and time—it could take a year before everything was in place for a fight that would include a very bloody ground war. An even worse thing to contemplate: Iraq's known possession—and willingness to use—chemical weapons.

By the end of the meeting we were still far from committed to a war that would force Saddam back across his own borders. Although there was general agreement about the need to protect the Saudis, there was no certainty that even the first part of the military scenario Schwarzkopf had outlined could actually be implemented. Would the Saudis, threatened not only by Saddam's army next door but by the convulsions of Islamic fundamentalism throughout the region, really allow a quarter of a million American troops to base themselves in a country that contained the Moslem world's holiest sites? Could they afford the hostility that American protectors might excite among zealots in the region? Would the Saudi royal family be thinking of the price Anwar Sadat had paid for his closeness to the United States, and therefore decide to appease Saddam, letting him content himself with the meal he had just made of Kuwait? By the time the Camp David meeting broke up, the only thing definitely decided was that President Bush would call King Fahd and ask him if the Saudis would be willing to talk about the idea of having American troops on their soil. The King agreed to receive American representatives to discuss the matter, and so the following day, Sunday, Cheney and Powell were on their way to Jidda, seeking permission to lay a massive American shield across the Arabian desert.

I was not optimistic that the Saudis would go along, but the President and Scowcroft were inclined to believe they would. I was soon relieved to have misjudged the Saudis' willingness for an unprecedented American presence. I thought that standing up to Saddam was absolutely crucial, and as the first week of the crisis passed, with the Saudis giving their permission for the start of Operation Desert Shield, I saw the President's own feelings begin to harden, very calmly, into an unshakable resolve.

By the end of August the Saudi desert was filling up with American GIs, and I was out on the road in my salesman's role, explaining the rationale for our involvement in the Arabian peninsula. On the 29th, at the annual American Legion convention in Indianapolis, I told the assembled Legionnaires about all the changes that had taken place in the world since we'd taken office a year and a half before—most of them, like the ones in Eastern

Europe, astoundingly hopeful. But in the midst of the post–cold war era, we had "a man who rules through terror and slaughter; who has used poison gas against his own countrymen; who invaded Iran in a war that cost the lives of over half a million people; who plunders tiny Kuwait and threatens Saudi Arabia; who aspires to gain control of the oil resources on which the entire world depends for economic well-being; who threatens his neighbors with weapons of mass destruction; and who poses a growing threat to the peace and stability of the region." Was it any wonder that the President was insisting that Saddam's aggression "will not stand"? The uncertainties about our ultimate objectives in the Middle East were gone. We wanted Saddam Hussein back where he had been before August 1.

The Persian Gulf War would eventually be such a triumph for America—and its principles—that we now have a tendency to look back on it as something that was easy or inevitable. We forget just how much uncertainty there was (during that first weekend meeting at Camp David there was hope Saddam might even withdraw on his own) and how intricate the military, diplomatic, and political preparations, the ones that would make success possible, really were. I recall one conversation I had with Jim Baker. It was after one of the Saturday meetings the President conducted at Camp David throughout the fall. It was a cold rainy day and we were riding back to the helicopter pad in a golf cart. We had unusual privacy, since at Camp David the Secret Service never rode the golf cart I was in; they just followed behind in another one. I said, "Jim, what do you really think about it?" "I don't know," he answered. "It's a big gamble." Then I looked at him and, thinking about the next election, asked, "Would you put your presidency on the line for this?" Neither one of us had an answer to that.

Throughout Desert Shield and Desert Storm, we had surprisingly little valuable intelligence. Even the Israelis' much vaunted intelligence agency, Mossad, could not penetrate Saddam's inner circle. No one knew for sure what was motivating him, and it is hard in any case to predict what a terrorist and totalitarian will do. I think part of Saddam wanted to be an Arab hero like Nasser—taking on the infidels. There was also the appeal of martyrdom. But he had simpler political motives, too: invading Kuwait was a way of shifting his population's attention from the grave problems they had at home. We could not be sure which motive was paramount.

I was convinced that the President was making the right decision, the only decision, but neither Baker nor I, nor anyone else in the "inner circle," could predict the outcome. Cheney and Powell were out in front of the issue during those weeks when everything was doubtful. At times, Cheney acted like both Secretary of Defense and Secretary of State. If the whole operation went south, we knew the President would never be reelected. People were worried about getting bogged down in the Middle East, and there were always the nagging questions. Should we be committing American lives and prestige in order to save a sheikhdom ruled by a rich oil family that didn't share our democratic values? This was, some pointed out, not Europe, but Kuwait, and Saddam was a bully but not much else. Was it really worth it? Might we do more harm than good by fanning the fires of radical Islamic fundamentalism?

But the principle of self-determination was at stake. When Margaret Thatcher went to war for the Falkland Islands in 1982, she knew that these little dots of land in the South Atlantic were not themselves essential to the well-being of Great Britain. What was essential—to the peace of the world—was maintaining the principle that a country cannot simply reach out and gobble up whatever landmass it chooses when the whim strikes. The Falklands War was not fought for land; it was fought for justice. The Gulf War had far more at stake in the strategic and material sense— keeping oil flowing to the industrialized world was part of the serious business we were faced with—but in the end, it was fought more than anything else for principle. The President knew that the entire new world being born, the one taking shape as the Soviet Union shrunk back to its own borders and began to wither within them, depended on respect for the idea of self-determination. All nations have to recognize that when this principle is under attack anywhere on the globe, a failure to respond will only leave them vulnerable, too. It is not an overstatement: in Kuwait we were getting ready to fight for the future of the whole world.

In the end—to answer the question Jim Baker and I asked ourselves—domestic political considerations had to be put aside, and
George Bush knew that. He wound up doing what was right with
spectacular success, and he was still not reelected. But he left
office knowing he had made a lasting contribution to world
peace.

As the months before the fighting passed, some managed to
hold onto their optimism that a peaceful solution would be
reached. Some would keep believing in that possibility through
the very last days leading up to the bombing of Baghdad, when
Jim Baker was negotiating with the Iraqi foreign minister, Tariq
Aziz. My friend Ken Adelman, who is as hawkish as I am, continued to feel that Saddam could be brought around by pressure and
negotiation. My own optimism was pretty much shot by the end
of the summer.

And yet, even if all the diplomacy we were engaged in failed to
avert this particular conflict, it still had its long-run uses. The UN
approved economic sanctions against Iraq, and on August 25,
because of the incessant diplomacy of the President, it followed
up with a resolution giving countries the right to use force to keep
Iraq from trading with the rest of the world. I may not have had
much faith in economic sanctions (Dick Darman, from the very
first week, had also expressed doubts about their ability to bring
Saddam around), but our victory at the UN was an astonishing
one that boded well for the future. No longer was that body
locked in bilateral paralysis, seeing everything in terms of the
U.S.–Soviet equation and unable to take any meaningful action.
In the end, sanctions did not do the job, but the August 25 vote
left even this skeptic—who had always taken a dim view of the
UN—willing to admit that in the world that was emerging the UN
would have its uses.

About a month after the UN resolution, the President's own
optimism for a peaceful settlement was fading, but he never got
distracted from his goals. He remained clear-eyed and calm in the
face of all kinds of emotional pressure. Saddam was holding civilian hostages, and while the President cared deeply about their
fate, he was not going to see all he was trying to achieve, along
with his presidency, become tied to their situation. Like all of us,

he had seen the Carter presidency destroyed and the Reagan White House pushed dangerously off course, when the lives of a handful of people—individuals with faces and names and relatives who could not be blamed for working on presidential emotions—diverted the chief executive from making policy that was crucial to millions of people. George Bush was not going to let that happen, and he didn't. Saddam Hussein thought he had a card to play with the hostages, but he was wrong. When he released them, in part through the efforts of King Hussein of Jordan (someone who was of absolutely no help to the United States later on in the crisis), Saddam thought this might be enough to appease President Bush. Not a chance.

The diplomatic efforts that went into assembling the coalition were almost unbelievable. By the end of August, when I gave my speech to the Legion, we had not only gotten the UN to pass its resolutions and succeeded in getting the Soviets to condemn what Saddam Hussein was doing, but had persuaded eleven nations, including nine from the Islamic world, to send their troops to the Gulf. The efforts were tireless. The degree to which things worked was extraordinary, but there were disappointments. The President had high hopes, for example, for support from Yemeni President Saleh, whom he had met with in 1986 and counted as a friend. Early in the administration we even had a state dinner for him. But as the crisis went on, Saleh turned out to be completely unreliable and in bed with Saddam Hussein—partly because the Yemenis don't like the Saudis. Personal diplomacy can only go so far in undoing resentments that have festered for hundreds of years. But we left nothing untried.

Some of our traditional allies were showing a reluctance that required special handling. The French couldn't seem to make up their minds. They were hoping they wouldn't have to participate, but if there was any action they wanted to be part of it. The Germans were only a small factor, though they did provide money—as did the Japanese. In November I made a trip to Tokyo, principally to represent the United States at the enthronement of Crown Prince Akihito as Emperor, but also to talk to the Japanese government and the array of world leaders who would be gathered there—everyone from President Aquino to Prime Minister Ozal of

Turkey, whose support in Desert Storm was absolutely essential because of his country's common border with Iraq. (In the diplomatic opportunities, coronations surpass even funerals and inaugurations.) When I met with Japan's Prime Minister Kaifu after the ceremonies, I urged him not only to support the growing allied coalition with money, but also to send some military equipment and some of Japan's Special Forces to the Gulf. Kaifu was a good friend but a quasi-pacifist. He kept citing constitutional prohibitions that kept Japan from joining in with troops—ones that our experts did not believe actually forbade the Japanese to take part in an effort like this. In the end, the Japanese did provide financial support, but they sent no more than a single minesweeper to the Gulf.

The British government changed hands in the middle of the crisis. Around Thanksgiving, Mrs. Thatcher was brought down by a revolt within her own party. She and her successor, John Major, were rock solid in their support of Desert Shield and later, when the actual war got under way, Desert Storm, but it was George Bush who did the leading. During the first days of the crisis, Thatcher met with the President in Aspen and gave a tough statement at their joint press conference. But back in Washington in the Oval Office, her tone changed slightly. The President, Brent Scowcroft, the British ambassador, and I were meeting with her when Dick Cheney called from Saudi Arabia with the news that King Fahd had agreed to the deployment of troops. The President told Cheney to take steps to accomplish that right away. Turning to Mrs. Thatcher, the President said, "Okay, now we've done it and we need your help." She was a bit tentative in the amount of British support she could guarantee. "I'll need to go home and talk to my people." She's been portrayed as urging Bush to be resolute (as when she told him not to "go wobbly" when it came time to turn back an Iraqi ship defying the blockade), but the truth is that Bush was always out in front of her, and everyone else, on the Gulf crisis.

Meetings between Bush and Thatcher may have looked to many like "listening sessions" for the President. Margaret, as he called her, tended to dominate the conversation. But this wasn't unusual with Bush. He was always solicitous of his guest's opinion, whether it was Thatcher's, Gorbachev's, or Salinas's. That was his style. He gave the guest an impression that the United States cared deeply, even as he was taking a detailed measure of that head of state. George Bush was a master at letting people feel they were getting their way, but he always knew exactly what he would—and would not—agree to before he went into a meeting. He knew the questions his guest would raise, and he knew the answers. Nothing in his foreign policy was done on the spur of the moment. This was in striking contrast to domestic issues.

My admiration for Mrs. Thatcher is extremely high. She is imposing and articulate, an ideological politician instead of a compromiser. She was a great Prime Minister and her influence was felt around the world. But she has undermined her successor John Major with steady complaining. She will always get publicity with her second-guessing, because she is fascinating and quotable. But her criticism is ironic, given how she used to complain about the way Edward Heath, whom she ousted as Conservative Party leader, never stopped carping at her from the sidelines.

Margaret Thatcher was not everybody's cup of tea. She and Germany's Helmut Kohl, for example, never got along. She thought he was weak, and he projected an attitude of indifference toward her. Even when she was well disposed toward people, she could act like a governess. In the spring of 1990, Bob Gates and Larry Eagleburger went over to see her to discuss plans for troop reductions in NATO, an idea she had not been keen on when they made a similar trip with a similar message the year before. This time, they walked into her office and she said, "All right, gentlemen, assume your customary seats." She referred to them as Tweedledum and Tweedledee and lectured them on why she didn't want to hear any more about these troop withdrawals—before they could even tell her why they were there. Back in Washington, they made the mistake of telling the story to some of us, who ever after called them by their new nicknames. To this day we aren't sure which one was Tweedledum.

On Thursday, November 29, 1990, the UN Security Council was approaching a vote on a resolution giving Saddam Hussein until

January 15 to get out of Kuwait. If he didn't withdraw by then, the allied coalition that had been assembled had the blessing of the United Nations to go to war against him.

At noon on the day the UN was supposed to vote, I made what I consider the most important speech of my four years as Vice President. The remarks I made at Seton Hall University in South Orange, New Jersey, were intended to be not just an outline of the administration's aims in the Gulf but also a moral justification for pursuing them through war. The speech was cleared by the White House, but it was made at my initiative because I thought there had been a gap in the administration's otherwise forceful explanation of why Saddam was a threat that had to be squashed. What was missing from these months of extraordinary diplomacy and military buildup was a clear statement of why we would be right to go ahead and use that military force if diplomacy failed. I've talked before about the Vietnam syndrome, the terrible emotional hangover it left America with, and part of that was a sense that all war was necessarily despicable. The nation's uneasiness about Vietnam had clouded its historical memory of wars that were unambiguously just, that were in fact moral crusades, such as the Civil War and World War II. I felt that if war came to the Gulf it would be one of these crusades, and I thought that the moral case for force had to be made.

In the days before my scheduled appearance at Seton Hall, I sat down with Joe Shattan, one of my speech writers, and talked to him about what I wanted to say and why. A Brooklyn native, a family man about Bill Kristol's age, Joe had done some excellent speech writing for George Shultz at State. I gave him a conceptual outline, and he did a first draft. After that we went back and forth on it. I worked on this speech as much as any I gave during my years in office. I wanted to address a much larger audience than the students who would be in front of me. I wanted these points to be heard by the Senate Armed Services Committee, which was then holding hearings on our Gulf policy and which I was afraid might not support any action beyond economic sanctions. I wanted them to be heard by as much of the American public, and as many of our allies and adversaries, as possible. And I wanted them to reach the men and women who were now camped out in the Arabian desert and might, come January 15, be called upon to give their lives for a policy I had helped devise.

At Seton Hall I talked about political reality—the need to keep oil flowing through the Gulf and the need for regional stability— but the heart of my remarks went to what I saw as "the first crisis of the post–cold war world," the "new world order" the President had spoken of. While our situation was new, parallels and precedents and the long historical view were now more important than ever. "In 1936," I said, "the world faced a rather similar challenge when Adolf Hitler, who had only recently come to power, moved German troops into the Rhineland, in open defiance of the treaties of Versailles and Locarno. British and French leaders faced a major dilemma. To confront Hitler militarily could mean war. Not to confront him means acquiescing in a cynical breach of international law. What to do?" The answer—which would be tragically ignored—came from Winston Churchill, who looked to the League of Nations and declared, "The constabulary of the world is at hand. On every side of Geneva stand great nations, armed and ready, whose interests as well as whose obligations bind them to uphold, and in the last resort enforce, the public law. This may never come to pass again. The fateful moment has arrived for choice between the New Age and the Old." The failure to heed what he said led to so much death and slaughter just three years later, when what Churchill called "the unnecessary war"—World War II—got under way. It was unnecessary because resoluteness at the right hour would have prevented it.

On the day I spoke, November 29, 1990, the United Nations— against all odds and against nearly forty years of its own disappointing history—rose to meet a challenge that the League of Nations had failed to rise to a half century before. It passed the resolution authorizing any means necessary to expel Saddam Hussein from Kuwait. He had forty-seven days left to leave on his own.

Campuses are still not the favorite locations for conservative Republican politicians to speak of military action—one more part of the Vietnam hangover. But I do enjoy student audiences, and the reception from these students at Seton Hall that afternoon was very encouraging. They had known I was going to talk about Iraq, and there were some protests outside. Even though I was warned

I would be heckled, I was not. I came away feeling that America was reaching the point when it could put Vietnam behind it and again contemplate the massive and sustained use of force—beyond anything that had been employed in Panama—for the enforcement of just foreign policy objectives.

After my speech I had lunch in New York with some CBS executives and correspondents, including Dan Rather and Mike Wallace. The Seton Hall speech had gotten a lot of press attention, as I'd hoped, and they were all eager to talk about the situation in the Middle East. We got into a long discussion of Saddam Hussein. I admit that I went into this lunch with a fairly low opinion of Dan Rather (based in part on the President's unpleasant experiences with him during the campaign and his annoying tendency to refer to me as J. Danforth Quayle III), but I was impressed by his grasp of issues and intensity. He kept offering very focused hypothetical questions anticipating one contingency or another in the Gulf. "What if Saddam says that he will get out and is willing to take only a bit of Kuwaiti territory in the north?" Rather threw all of his political acumen into this conversation, raising possibility after possibility, and I left glad that Saddam Hussein hadn't been able to overhear it, because if he had followed Rather's line of thinking he might have come closer to outfoxing us.

Mike Wallace was more surprising than impressive. "Why don't you guys just use covert operations?" he asked. He was suggesting that we just go in there with some CIA operatives and kill Saddam Hussein. "Are you serious?" I said. "For one thing, it's illegal—in part because of the way CBS used to take such pride in blowing the whistle on covert operations!" I don't know if he was pulling my leg or not. This was an off-the-record lunch, and he may have been trying to see how far I would go in front of all his colleagues. Even so, I was incredulous, and I turned to the others at the table and asked, "How many people here really think that we ought to go in and knock off Saddam?" Of course there was dead silence. I couldn't have said it at that lunch, but the truth is that I believe the executive order prohibiting assassination of foreign leaders (put through in anticipation of Congress's passing a law to that effect) should be rescinded, so that the President would have one more option in extraordinary circumstances.

By the end of December the military alliance against Saddam had swelled to twenty-eight nations, but the President was still willing to try diplomacy. There was a standing offer to send Jim Baker to Baghdad to talk with Saddam Hussein. But in the meantime, war preparations had to proceed on every front, and one of those was Capitol Hill. Could the President succeed in getting Congress to endorse military means to dislodge Saddam if he allowed the January 15 deadline to pass without getting out of Kuwait? Just as the President had wanted the international authority for war making that the UN resolution provided, so, too, did he want a resolution from our own Congress approving the use of force. Once more, the object was to avoid the mistakes of Vietnam. What the President wanted was clear approval—in effect, a declaration of war—nothing ambiguous or fragile, like the Gulf of Tonkin resolution, which wound up being used to justify much more than it actually involved.

We weren't sure we had the votes. In fact, Cheney felt we did not, and he argued against seeking congressional approval. "Don't do it," were his words of advice. I myself didn't believe military action required congressional approval, but I thought that it would be politically much more feasible—and much better for the country—if the President went to war with the authorization of Congress. I also thought we could get a resolution through, though I knew it would be difficult. I argued for an early vote: hold Congress's feet to the fire before the Christmas vacation. I did not want to wait for the new Congress, though I knew that either one—the departing 101st or the incoming 102nd—would try to duck responsibility, to look for the opportunity to have it both ways. Politicians always want a win-win situation. Whatever the outcome, they want to be on the winning side. In the end, a decision was reached to put the resolution before the new Congress—just before the January 15 deadline arrived.

During these months, the degree of cooperation between the United States and the USSR—at the UN and even behind the scenes—was astonishing. But some of the old cold war jousting remained. Gorbachev wanted to be more of a player in what was going on than he was, and even after Desert Shield turned into Desert Storm, he kept proposing peace plans. CNN was one means we used to keep ahead of him. Media critics have talked about how that network really came into its own as an institution once the Gulf War got going: people remember the vivid pictures of the antiaircraft guns in Baghdad sending up their green-colored tracers, and they remember the controversial reports from Peter Arnett. But CNN's influence was enormous even before the fighting got under way. In the administration we had learned to watch Gorbachev's press conferences, as well as his spokesman's press briefings, on CNN. We'd learn that he'd be speaking in a few hours (the middle of the night, U.S. time). We would then monitor what he said and prepare a quick response. The time zones worked in our favor with American audiences: by the time most people would be getting up to hear or read what Gorbachev had said, we would already have a reply out there. This considerably undercut whatever impact he might have had at a time when we didn't need any more complicating factors.

It was a nervous Christmas. Marilyn, our children, and I spent it in Vail. The January 15 deadline approached and the war preparations we were making inside the White House and at the Pentagon continued. Most of my time was spent on the phone in contact with the NSC (the slopes saw much more of Marilyn and our children than they did of me). Just before New Year's I flew to the Middle East to talk to our allies and our most important asset— the American troops who were preparing to go into combat against Saddam Hussein.

The Saudis had already put up $9 billion to pay for our Desert Shield, and one of the things I did while in Riyadh was to ask for more. King Fahd appeared to be totally committed to the war; his resoluteness both surprised and pleased me. I knew the President was fond of the diminutive King. He seemed clearly in control after facing down opposition within the royal family and amongst the mullahs (religious leaders). Crown Prince Abdullah seemed somewhat less resolute and said he thought that Saddam might actually withdraw before the deadline. Whether this was wishful thinking, I couldn't tell. I met with—and requested more funds from—the exiled Emir of Kuwait ("a quiet pathetic figure," I noted in the diary I began to keep). He talked about the atrocities that Saddam's forces were perpetrating in his country, and he became emotional, as he had during his Washington encounter with George Bush, a meeting that had affected the President profoundly.

It was between my meetings with the Emir and King Fahd that I visited with the troops. This was my idea. The President and Mrs. Bush had been over at Thanksgiving and gotten a rousing reception, and during December some reporters began asking me whether I was planning a trip myself. In fact, why hadn't I gone already? Going over before the President would have been out of the question, but after his visit there was nothing to prevent me.

I talked to the President about it, and he said he was comfortable with my going or not going. It was up to me to decide. Obviously, I was concerned about the way the press would play it. If I didn't go, I would be criticized for ignoring our fighting forces—and the administration would be attacked for being "afraid to send Quayle to the Gulf." If I did go, they would have a field day reviving the old National Guard issue from the 1988 campaign. The strongest supporter of my going—and this surprised me a bit, because he hadn't been a conspicuous ally in the past—was Brent Scowcroft. When I told him that I thought I had to do it, Brent, a retired Air Force general, agreed heartily and said, "You know, you've got to lance this boil sometime. You might as well do it now." The fact is I *had* to do it. The essence of the vice-presidency is preparedness, and if I ever had to take over from President Bush—especially at a time like this—I would not be able to function if I felt I couldn't comfortably visit the troops who would be under my own command.

Besides, no matter what the press said, I felt I had plenty in common with some of the troops over there. In fact, some of my old Guard buddies were in Saudi Arabia. Sam Graves, a lieutenant colonel in the reserves, had arrived there just three weeks before. He's only a year older than I am, but he'd been my commanding officer in the 120th Public Information Detachment at Stout Field almost twenty years earlier. The Guard, as usual, was at the front, ready to do the job.

Lieutenant General Calvin Waller, deputy commander of U.S. forces in the region, was my official guide. I ate a spaghetti dinner with the troops, played a little basketball and volleyball with them, and told them: "You have been patient enough and so has President Bush. So our message is simple: Saddam Hussein, either get out of Kuwait peacefully, or leave by force." But as far as I was concerned the most important part of the message, the one they most wanted to hear, was that this will "not be another Vietnam." They would be permitted to use all the force that was necessary to accomplish what, just two weeks from now, we might be asking them to do. A day later I went aboard the carrier *John F. Kennedy* and repeated the message. In fact, one of the sailors told me they'd already heard my remarks piped through the P.A. system the day before! But it was a message that could bear a little repeating. The people aboard this awesome ship—a miniature city—had just spent Christmas without their families. They were ready to do the job they had been trained to do, and they were ready to get it over with. Their morale, as I wrote in my diary, was "skyhigh," but everywhere I heard the same concern: "Let's make sure we get the job done so we don't have to come back."

That was the constant theme, and that's what I reported to President Bush at our lunch on January 2, the day after he ordered the NSC to prepare the National Security Directive that would turn Operation Desert Shield into Operation Desert Storm.

PART FOUR

Daring and Drift

1991

23 | Desert Storm Diary: Part One

Swore in the members of the Senate. Almost all showed up for photos, except Gore. Harkin surprised Mitchell in demanding immediate debate on Persian Gulf. I continued to call on Harkin, as he is good fodder for us.

—January 3, 1991

The new Senate took up its business just after New Year's, and over the next week, as debate proceeded on the resolution authorizing force in the Gulf, I did everything I could to help the President get the votes he needed. Iowa's Tom Harkin tended to be so far out of the mainstream, and to use such extreme rhetoric, that I was happy to let him pop off for the opposition as I presided in the chamber. Majority Leader George Mitchell knew exactly what I was doing, and I could tell it exasperated him.

Over the next several days, I'd speak at congressional caucuses, turn up at luncheons, make phone calls. The Republicans were basically united, and I tried working on moderate Democrats like Connecticut's Joe Lieberman and Virginia's Chuck Robb, as John Sununu managed to bring both of Nevada's Democrats, Harry Reid and Dick Bryan, over to the "yes" column.

Baker-Aziz meeting. Went as planned. Baker failed. Aziz was obdurate and refused Pres.'s letter. This should help us w/ Congress. Cong. delegation: Solarz, Torricelli, Murtha, Levine; McCurdy, others, including Aspin. Told

>*that Foley threw a fit in Demo. caucus. Threatened Torri-*
>*celli & Solarz. Cheney says Foley almost a pacifist. . . .*
>*Dark day for peace.*

Foley is a gifted individual in a tough job, and this episode doesn't seem especially characteristic. Today, the Speaker of the House has nothing like the power of a Sam Rayburn. Within the House there are too many special-interest caucuses that will cast him out if he decides to rock their boats. But insofar as possible, Foley likes to rise above partisan politics and get the job done. He started out as a pro-defense Scoop Jackson Democrat but became much more dovish, probably because of left-wing pressures within his party.

The resolution authorizing the use of force would pass the House by a wide margin, thanks to the help of moderate Democrats like New Jersey's Bob Torricelli, Wisconsin's Les Aspin (Bill Clinton's first Secretary of Defense), and New York's Steve Solarz, who is strongly pro-Israel. The fact that we had gone the last mile for peace—allowing Jim Baker to be rebuffed by Iraq's foreign minister at the final moment—proved to these moderates that we were doing everything we could to achieve a settlement. Still, the Senate promised to be a tough hurdle. We had the whole Democratic leadership against us—Mitchell, Byrd, and Sam Nunn, who was usually much more hawkish than his Democratic colleagues and worried us the most. He wasn't as passionately against this war as he had been against the nomination of John Tower, but there wasn't much prospect of turning him around, either. Former Defense secretary Jim Schlesinger surprisingly was quite critical of us, and I think Schlesinger's opposition to the war in the Gulf may have influenced Nunn's own thinking.

>*Pres. still firm. Not changing. I advised he go to Camp*
>*David instead of waiting the weekend out [here].*

>*—Thurs., Jan. 10, 1991*

As the week went on, the atmosphere became more and more charged. Our short-term thinking was focused on the Senate debate, but we knew that, even if we won there, we then faced some extremely suspenseful days before American air power was launched against Iraq. But the President remained rock solid, almost serene.

> *Gorby calls early a.m. with peace offer. Amb (USSR)*
> *briefs Pres., but nothing much. . . . Lunch with boys, who*
> *are out of school. Tucker throws olive in Ben's milk. . . .*
> *Went to Hill. Met with Kuwaiti hostages. Great advocates*
> *for Pres. Presided over Senate. We now have votes.*

> *—Fri., Jan. 11, 1991*

A reader of my diary might find it odd that, in the midst of this crisis, I would have recorded little details like this bit of horseplay between the boys. But it was at times like these, I found, that the simple, ordinary things I loved about my life became more important. Throughout the diary, mention of things like Ben's basketball games and my Valentine's Day present for Marilyn are just a line or two away from the most gripping events of my career. Upon rereading the journal, I realize that's the way it should be, since that's how those months were lived—my attention shifting back and forth between the things I cherished and a war that was half a world away. As always, my faith and my family kept me centered, and if they were missing from this diary, then only half of the story would be told.

On Saturday, January 12, I went to the Hill to preside over the Senate's vote on the war. After all these months I was anxious to get this vote behind us. I was prepared to break a tie if necessary, but by now we were confident we had the votes. The atmosphere in the chamber was quiet, very solemn. The speeches were impassioned, much more eloquent than the rhetoric of more ordinary debates. Every Senator knew that the country was watching.

I was told that we could expect Senator Gore, whose vote we did not need, to be among the Democrats joining the administration's side. As I listened carefully to the speech he made before announcing his vote, he offered so many arguments *against* the administration's position that I thought he had changed his mind at the last minute. In fact, he was trying to have it both ways. I didn't know that several months later I would have reason to point to his tortured remarks as the kind of irresolution we can ill afford when it comes to conducting the foreign policy of the United States.

Maybe he's a product of his era, but George Mitchell is regarded by many as one of the most partisan majority leaders the Senate has ever had. When he's not performing his role, he's pleasant and easy to be with. But when the cameras are on, he's a different person. I don't think he could ever do what Howard Baker did when it came to the Panama Canal treaty. Baker helped President Carter get it through the Senate—even though his support of the treaty damaged his presidential ambitions.

In Mitchell's closing speech during the debate over the Gulf War resolution, he put all the blame, should things go wrong, on those who were supporting the President. He was dead right. Those voting for the resolution would be held accountable for their votes, but he should have added that those who voted against the President would also be held accountable for theirs. Mitchell surprised the political world by recently announcing his retirement. (Actually this is just one more sign of the immense frustration of Senators who are tiring of the "gotcha" politics played these days.)

Ordinarily, during a vote, Senators mill about, but on this day everyone stayed at their desks, waiting for the tallies. The first resolution to be voted on was actually Sam Nunn's—a watered-down alternative to the firm deadline and authorization of force that the administration was proposing. Once it failed, our own resolution, sponsored by John Warner and Bob Dole, was brought to the floor:

> *Vote ag. Nunn 53-46. For Warner-Dole 52-47. Hatfield voted ag. both. Grassley didn't return my phone call and voted ag. us. Nunn came up afterward to say if conflict comes he will then support the President. I told the Pres. but discouraged Nunn from calling directly. . . . Many Rep. Senators don't want bombs starting Jan. 15th. I asked what difference 15th or 17th. They said politics & perceptions.*

In the end, Sam Nunn's position may have kept him from trying for his party's 1992 presidential nomination. The war's eventual popularity required candidates who wanted to get very far to have taken a position that was, if not in favor of the resolution, at least muddled. (Bill Clinton's statement certainly fit that description. "I guess I would have voted with the majority if it was a close vote," he said. "But I agree with the arguments of the people in the minority.") Even the Republicans were, to some extent, trying to have it both ways: they were afraid that if we took military action at the first moment the resolution gave us permission to do so, we would look overeager. The resolution did not itself authorize bombing; it just declared that, from the 15th on, the United States could use whatever means were necessary.

The resolution's passage made prosecution of the war much easier. Witnessing the debate on it made one realize how the lack of a similar discussion and vote by Congress had made the Vietnam War even harder for the Presidents who had to conduct it and more distasteful to those citizens who opposed it. They could always point out that it had never been declared by Congress. Call the 1991 resolution what you will—to everyone's mind it was a declaration of war.

Although he was glad that the resolution had passed, President Bush, I am convinced, would still have made war against Saddam Hussein without it. Though not a direct response to the War Powers act that Congress had passed in the 1970s, the resolution was a symbolic compliance with what the President had never felt was a good piece of legislation. On that point I strongly agree with him as do many others. Howard Baker, to this day, speaks out against the act as unwarranted interference with presidential prerogatives. But there's no question that congressional approval— once we had it—was helpful.

> *Coalition intact. Cong. pacified and Pres. calm.*

> *Corinne senses something about to happen. She hasn't slept for 2 nights. . . . I pray all goes well, but it will be massive, hopefully decisive.*
> —*Mon., Jan. 14, 1991*

I was bringing the tension home with me. Marilyn and the children could see that I was totally preoccupied. On Sunday I had met with the President, Cheney, Powell, Sununu, and Gates to discuss the targets we would be hitting in Iraq. By Tuesday, Marilyn and Ben saw me writing in the diary and could sense what was approaching:

> *Meeting in Oval before lunch. Baker, Scowcroft, Gates, Sununu, Cheney. Signed off on final plan. . . . Pres. gave me draft of nationwide speech. I suggested some changes. Mention peace upfront; talk of UN; Pres.'s service in war; time on Saddam's side; and don't mention the word WAR. . . . Tomorrow it all begins.*

Before we went to bed, I told Marilyn when the bombing would start. The potential consequences of our decision weighed heavily on me. We knew the justness of the cause, but any time you put American soldiers in harm's way you take the nation's anxiety on yourself. We relied on God's understanding for what we were about to do.

The following morning was quiet. As we passed the last checkpoints in the plan—at any one of which the action could be canceled—the President tried to throw the press off. He called a meeting about educational policy and was partly successful in diverting their attention. For the rest of the day I nervously went back and forth between home and the office.

> *I come home for lunch wt the boys. Start to watch TV at 2 p.m. Can't believe it has held. We've known since Sunday. I go home around 4. Can't wait any longer. Tell them to watch TV at 7 p.m. Things will happen. MTQ sad as we all are. Return 5:30. Pres. on phone to leaders. Major [is] called at H-12 [12 hours before commencement of the operation]. Mitterrand and others H-2; Cong. and Gorby H-1. 15 min. after Cong. hears about it, leak to press. Marlin tells Pres. we'll remember this. ABC breaks it by accident. Defensive shooting starts at 6:40. Still not sure why. Bombs drop right at H-hour 7 p.m. EST. . . . Have*

hamburger in office as Pres. prepares for nationwide
speech at 9 p.m. Teeter, Kristol & Abraham join me. Pres.
gives great speech. Everyone winds it up by 10 p.m.

—Wed., Jan. 16, 1991

Before the speech, I watched CNN in the office. My concern for the pilots carrying out the air operation was mixed with personal worry for news anchor Bernie Shaw. His son was attending Gonzaga College High School with Ben and Tucker. Now Bernie and his CNN colleague John Holliman were broadcasting from a hotel in downtown Baghdad as bombs fell all around them. I knew that the hotel was not a target, but I kept wondering whether these two guys were going to make it out. Even if they weren't hurt by a stray bomb, I thought Saddam might take both of them hostage. On Wednesday evening the White House kept getting calls from CNN's Tom Johnson, asking if he should get his people out of there. We kept telling him yes, get all of them out. In one conversation, while searching for some hint of what might happen next, he asked: "Well, are you trying to tell me something?" I just told him the truth: "We're not saying anything other than what the policy is. That we'd like to have all people out of there." That included Peter Arnett, whose continued broadcasts from Baghdad throughout the war were an irritant to the administration. We felt that Saddam was using these reports, with their emphasis on bomb damage by American planes, to his own advantage.

On Thursday night, Iraq's Scud missiles began to fall on Israel. The President and Eagleburger talked to Israeli Prime Minister Shamir, urging him not to retaliate. An Israeli response would only create support for Saddam in the Arab world. For the moment, the Israelis were coy about their exact intentions, but I was glad that Larry Eagleburger, who was among those with me at a White House meeting, weighed in against condemning Israel if she chose to fight back on her own. The next day (after the polite rejection of another Gorbachev peace plan) the President and I sat down for lunch. Shamir called at the end of our meal, and the President pleaded with him for no retaliation. We were convinced that that would have very negative consequences.

Shamir remained noncommittal, and the next day, Saturday, the discussion at Camp David still focused on Israel:

> *Pres. more understanding than others on Israel's need to retaliate. Cheney and I are only ones sympathetic toward Israel. Baker totally opposed. Fears Jordan will get involved because of overflights. . . . Eagleburger dispatched to Israel. Considered a friend. . . . Pres. called Shamir to thank for restraint.*

Within the administration there was a real division over Israel. There were strong supporters, such as Cheney, Eagleburger, and me, but the more "even-handed" approach favored by Baker and the State Department was usually what dominated policy. Some of that policy reflected the thinking of Democrat Bob Strauss, who would tell his fellow Texans, Bush and Baker, that the American Jewish community was more moderate and divided about American policy toward Israel than some American Jewish leaders would admit.

The President's record on Israel was, in fact, excellent. He supported the Israeli government's position on everything except loan guarantees, which he did not want to offer until there was a resolution of the West Bank dispute. He appreciated Israel's strategic importance, as well as its status as the only democracy in the region. His personal relations with Shamir were never good, but relations with Israel would improve toward the end of the administration, when Rabin's Labor government came to power. George Bush did much behind the scenes to move the peace process forward, and history will give him credit for that, even if, by the time Rabin and Arafat finally shook hands, it was Bill Clinton standing with them on the White House lawn. George Bush was there only as a guest.

During the Gulf War, it took great patience for the Israelis to hold back. One of the decisive factors was our promise to send them Patriot missiles, which were already proving themselves an invaluable part of the military success we were achieving. By Saturday evening there was good news on the battlefront.

> *Patriots down 8 missiles out of nine. . . . A big boost for*
> *SDI.*

I had been a big supporter of the Patriot missile when I served on the Senate Armed Services Committee, working to make sure that the missile and its upgrade survived congressional attempts to kill it. The Patriot was originally designed as an antiaircraft weapon, but it was later modified to make it effective against incoming missiles, too. I had pushed it for defensive use in the European theater, but it proved a lifesaver for the Israelis in the opening days of the Gulf War. Not only was it more militarily effective than the media would later report, it also gave a tremendous psychological boost to both Israel and Saudi Arabia. On a visit to Fort Bliss, Texas, in February, I went jogging with some enlisted men and proudly wore a "Scud-buster" T-shirt depicting the Patriot.

Suddenly, the critics who had argued that all the new high-tech weaponry developed during the Reagan defense buildup was too expensive and would never work in combat were forced to re-evaluate their analysis. Every night, on television, Americans were seeing these weapons blast enemy missiles out of the sky. To all those who for years had contended that ballistic missile defense was wishful thinking, I now said: watch CNN and see the irrefutable evidence. The same arguments that had been used against the Patriot were the ones being used against SDI. The Gulf War gave renewed life to SDI supporters, and for a time I thought we would really see the program make great strides. But it finally died in the Clinton administration, a victim of the worst kind of short-term thinking. It's impossible to predict the new threats that will emerge in the volatile postcommunist world. Indeed, just three years after the Gulf War, we are beginning to realize that radical Islamic fundamentalism may represent the same kind of expansionist threat that Soviet communism once did. Ballistic missile proliferation is one of the most pressing dangers in the world today. By the year 2000 at least twenty nations are likely to have ballistic missiles. If they develop a nuclear warhead capability, the geopolitical situation will change drastically. To date, negotiations on these matters have not been especially productive, and if terrorist nations like North Korea, Iraq, and Libya develop nuclear capacities, the international community may even have to consider preemptive strikes against these outlaws. We are lulling ourselves into a false sense of security if we think we don't still need to keep American defenses on the technological cutting edge. North Korea, according to some reports, has already developed nuclear weapons. Furthermore, it doesn't take much to extend the range of a theater ballistic missile, which North Korea already has, to make it intercontinental, bringing the United States within range. Attempts to denigrate the Patriot and SDI don't square with the facts accumulated during Desert Storm; they also ignore how Japan, with plenty of potential foes in its region, has expressed interest to us in acquiring the technology to develop a theater ballistic missile defense, which could become a sophisticated Patriot-style system or a mini-version of SDI. I believe the time will come when we regret abandoning SDI, whose practicality the Gulf War allowed us to glimpse with our own eyes.

24 | Desert Storm Diary: Part Two

From time to time during the weeks of the Gulf War, something Winston Churchill had said in 1941 would cross my mind: "Never, never, never believe any war will be smooth and easy." The air war over Iraq seemed to go so spectacularly well that one could become too confident about the ground conflict ahead. We had no idea, once it got under way, how long it might actually take or how many casualties we might finally suffer. Even in the air war, American pilots were being killed and taken prisoner, and one of my duties in January and February was to visit the families of military personnel throughout the country, from Virginia's Norfolk Naval Air Station to Camp Pendleton in California. The media would frequently ask those who came to see me: "Gee, doesn't it feel a little strange having Dan Quayle here, when he didn't serve in the last big war, in Vietnam?" Those being asked had more important things on their mind than this. I always found them glad to see me and hear me repeat the administration's policy that we would do absolutely everything it took to win the war and get their family members home.

These trips were very difficult emotionally. At Mayport Naval Station in Jacksonville, Florida, I met with Joanne Speicher, whose husband, Michael, was one of the first Americans killed in Desert Storm. I also met with spouses and children who had begun the agonizing wait for their loved ones—some now being held prisoners of war in Iraq. (We were not just concerned about husbands and fathers but wives and mothers too. We had reason to believe at the time, and it sadly proved true, that the Iraqis would reserve especially horrifying treatment for the female POWs.) These meetings were kept out of the press's view, as they should have been. There were tears on both sides—the emotions were intense—and I came away with immense admiration for the courage of these families, whose loved ones were helping us secure victory. Most of the military families I met were spiritual people, and I felt bound to them by our common faith. I would always let them know that they were in my family's prayers. Almost always I heard these soldiers' loved ones tell me: "This is what he [or she] wanted to do." The POW families were always hoping I might have more information for them, but I didn't. However, I was able to tell them that from the beginning there had been one point on which there was no debate within the administration: Saddam Hussein would not be free from American military pounding until every one of our POWs had been safely released.

George Bush had gone to military funerals and consoled bereaved families when he was Vice President. From time to time during our weekly lunches, we'd talk about how hard it was to think of the children involved and about how the families we saw, in the midst of their grief, seemed stronger than we did. We discussed the difficulty of looking at the big policy picture when you'd just been around suffering families. But it is impractical to pursue policies in the national interest that completely eliminate individual risk of suffering. Governing by emotion is shortsighted and, in the long run, potentially disastrous.

When I visited Camp Pendleton I spoke at the Rev. Robert Schuller's Crystal Cathedral in Garden Grove, California. I talked about the concept of a just war, expanding on some of the ideas in the previous November's Seton Hall speech. "God listens, God understands, and God answers," I said, reflecting that it was less important to worry about whether God was on our side than to make sure we were on His. Over the past two years I had played the vice-presidential role of cheerleader many times, for everything from missions to Mars to local candidates to dubious budget deals. But I knew I would never do anything more important than my part in keeping the country united around what we were trying to achieve in the Gulf.

Met with more families. Tough part of job. Plane home: press didn't like criticism: Devroy led charge. They are so sensitive. Any criticism they feel unjustified. Think I'll keep it up.

—Wed., Jan. 23, 1991

I would not allow myself to think that victory would come quickly. During these weeks I was watching videos of PBS's acclaimed series on the Civil War. Like Churchill's warning against believing any war will be short or easy, the series kept me mindful of the possibility that this conflict would be a long one. If that happened, I worried, a peace movement might begin to grow, undermining our military efforts just as surely as the one from the Vietnam era had. There were a few signs of it from the beginning. A small group in Lafayette Park, across from the White House, beat a bass drum—morning, noon, and night—knowing that the President could hear it all day. (His bedroom was on the opposite side of the mansion, so he got some relief when he went to sleep.)

On January 23, at Fort Bragg, I told the Desert Storm families who had come out to hear me that, "as expected, there have been some demonstrations against our policy in the Gulf, and some American flags have been burned. Unfortunately, the media seem compelled to devote much more attention to these protests than they deserve." As my diary shows, I was quickly taken to task for this observation by reporters like the *Washington Post*'s Ann Devroy, a driven, plugged-in reporter whose articles about White House decision making drove people inside the administration crazy. But her complaint about my criticism of the protesters didn't faze me. I knew the media could be counted on to cover whatever protests there were all out of proportion to their numbers or influence, and I decided I would play along and mention the protesters myself. Though few in number, they were highly unpopular, and they became a useful foil in keeping the great majority of the population at our side. Referring to them in my speeches was a bit like calling on Harkin in the Senate: give them a little rope.

Leave for Norway one minute after State of Union.

—Tues., Jan. 29, 1991

Norway's King Olav died at the end of January, and the President asked Marilyn and me to represent him in Oslo. The trip provided a critical opportunity for me to consult with foreign leaders and to find out what their concerns were now that we were two weeks into Operation Desert Storm. I had the chance to thank Turkish Prime Minister Akbulut for his country's support and to listen to the USSR's Vice President, Gennadi Yanayev, tell me that the Soviets were worried about any escalation of the war, as well as the possible involvement of Israel and Turkey. Our conversation soon switched to the situation in the Baltics, and even though Yanayev didn't give any clues to Soviet thinking, I was very direct. I told him the whole world was watching and that it expected to see the Baltic states given their independence. It was a question of how and when, not if. He did not reply. (Several months later, Yanayev—whom I would meet again in the spring at Rajiv Gandhi's funeral—would be among the Soviet coup leaders trying to topple Gorbachev.)

France's Prime Minister Michel Rocard began our conversation by asking what the American opinion of France was these days. I was diplomatic and told him it was good. Obviously he knew that some Americans still resented France's fair-weather friendship a few years before, when that country refused to allow American planes to fly through French air space on their way to bomb Libya. Since Rocard didn't have foreign policy responsibilities, we did not go into much detail on the Gulf. I concentrated most of the discussion on getting France's cooperation on the GATT trade talks.

From Oslo, Marilyn and I went on to England, first to visit American and British Air Force families at the Lakenheath RAF Base in Suffolk, and then to London for meetings with British Prime Minister John Major and Foreign Secretary Sir Douglas Hurd. John Major and I had met when he'd visited my office as Chancellor of the Exchequer, and we'd liked each other immediately. He's a committed conservative but casual in his manner, without the forcefulness of his predecessor, Mrs. Thatcher. There's an attractive soft-spokenness to him that appeals to a wide range of people. (My mother was quite taken with him when they met at the VP residence in Washington.) The President and Major got on so well that each would be accused of violating the normal taboo against trying to give an ally a boost in his domestic election campaign. There's no question that we were for Major, and he for us, in 1992.

> *Did Newsmakers. CNN did story on us "not ruling out" nuclear weapons. I tilted more against it in interview. So CNN said I ruled them out, which I didn't. You can't win.*
>
> *—Sat., Feb. 2, 1991*

Here we go again! While in Britain, I'd been asked if the United States would ever contemplate using atomic weapons in Desert Storm. I'd answered truthfully that we didn't rule anything in or out. We had no intention or expectation of using them, but we were hardly going to say anything that would make Saddam Hussein comfortable. There was nothing extraordinary about my remark, but it generated a small, panicky flap. Others, including President Bush, would have gotten away with saying the same thing, but my "image" made people see the comment as a bit fast and loose. In any case, this was a fairly pointless distraction. All our attention was on the impending ground war. Massive American air power had been "softening up" Saddam for weeks, and the time was approaching when American ground forces would have to go in and actually push him out of Kuwait.

> *Ground war next Wed. But problem wt Queen Margrethe and state dinner.*
>
> *—Thurs., Feb. 14, 1991*

We were ready for the troops on the ground to go in on February 20, but we were faced with a dilemma. The President was hosting a formal dinner for the Queen of Denmark on the 20th. To cancel the dinner would have tipped the Iraqis off to our invasion plans. In the end, Gorbachev gave us our out. The ground war was postponed, and the dinner went on, because he kept throwing out peace plans. The last of them was presented as Dick Cheney and I were getting ready for a reciprocal dinner Queen Margrethe gave at the Danish embassy on the 21st. The President was going to Ford's Theatre, and we agreed to meet with him, late that evening at the White House, to prepare a response. As we were driving to the Danish embassy, Cheney said to me, "You know, I'm very concerned. Gorbachev's liable to deep-six this whole operation if we're not careful." At the White House we joined the usual cast (Baker, Scowcroft, Eagleburger, Powell, Gates, and Sununu) in the President's living quarters. Bush declared that the only way to keep ahead of Gorbachev was to put out a peace plan ourselves. We talked about the risks of getting into a "bidding war" of competing peace plans, or of having Saddam pretend to accept one of them. But in the end we went ahead and outflanked Gorbachev.

> *GB gets briefing for final [plan] then takes off for C[amp] D[avid] to divert media.*

> *—Fri., Feb. 22, 1991*

The ground war was now scheduled for Saturday, and I spent the day as calmly as I could, finishing Robert Heilbroner's classic book, *The Worldly Philosophers*, about the great economists from Adam Smith to John Maynard Keynes. That night Marilyn and I went to an annual dinner in honor of Father Dooley of Gonzaga College High School, which our sons attended. At 8:45 I was called away from the event, and though I left as casually as possible, most of those in attendance could guess what my early departure meant. I went immediately to the White House and waited on the South Lawn with Scowcroft, Sununu, and others for the President's helicopter, which was bringing him back from Camp David. All the early reports indicated that things were proceeding exceptionally well.

The following morning at St. John's Church in Lafayette Square Marilyn and I and the Bushes gave our thanks for how well things were going. Some of our opponents, including Ted Kennedy and Ross Perot, had conjured up a vision of thousands of Americans returning from the ground war in body bags. It's true that the hospital facilities set up at an American installation in Germany could have handled thousands of casualties, but we didn't expect them, and using the possibility as a rhetorical chip in the debate over the war had been, I felt, gruesomely irresponsible. I'd thought of calling up Ted to protest but decided that we were so far apart on this matter that it would be a waste of time.

Throughout Sunday and Monday, reports from the front indicated that all predictions of ferocious resistance by Saddam Hussein's elite Republican Guard had been grossly overblown. Saddam's army was in full flight, heading back across the border into Iraq, where it had always belonged. We had never doubted that the allied forces would accomplish their mission, but nobody expected that mission to become known as the Hundred-Hour War either. The coalition victory that was unfolding seemed reminiscent of the battle of Agincourt, which American audiences, including Marilyn and me, saw depicted that season in Kenneth Branagh's film *Henry V.* In that battle, the English killed ten thousand French troops, while losing only twenty-nine men themselves. In Desert Storm, we destroyed an Iraqi army of over half a million troops, while suffering slightly more than a hundred fatalities.

> *Things going too well. GB wants to get out ahead of curve before people say too much. Decides to make speech at 9pm to tell the world. Schwarzkopf oks plan. All will be done by midnight.*

> —Wed., Feb. 27, 1991

The ground war had achieved such swift, complete success that our gratitude was mixed with apprehension. America, now the only world superpower, seemed so utterly invincible, so capable of anything, that people were liable to forget that the objectives we had set out to accomplish were limited. We had fought the war to get Saddam Hussein out of Kuwait, and we had done that. We had *not* fought it to dislodge Saddam from power. If that had been our stated objective, we would never have been able to assemble the military and diplomatic coalition we did—and we would probably never have been able to get Congress to agree to the January resolution. Of course, none of this stopped the very same people who opposed even our limited objectives from spending the next two years complaining that the President had not "finished the job" they never wanted him to start in the first place.

In the Oval Office with the First Lady and John Sununu, I watched the President announce the end of the war. Afterward we gathered upstairs in the family quarters. Cheney and Powell joined us. The President took a few calls, including one from his son George, but there was no real euphoria. We were proud of what had been accomplished, but it was sobering to think of the suffering Saddam Hussein had unleashed by his pointless invasion: the loss of life (mostly of his own countrymen); the prolonged terror inflicted on occupied Kuwait; the astonishing ecological damage that resulted from his destruction of the Kuwaiti oil fields.

The war had taught us many lessons, about everything from missile technology to the need to get away from "micromanagement" of the military by the White House. The President set the war's broad objectives, and having done that he allowed the military to carry out his policy. He treated our servicemen and women like professionals, not like instruments of the federal bureaucracy; he let them use as much force as they needed to accomplish their mission. Like any President, he agonized over casualties. I can remember him saying, just before the decision to begin the war, how lonely his job felt. But throughout Desert Storm, his World War II experience allowed him to make life-and-death decisions confidently, perhaps more so than men of a later generation could. The memory of World War II's nobility gave the men who fought it a certain strength, a feeling of legitimacy. Bush was always the calmest man in the room.

With victory achieved, we now had to go about the business of stabilizing the situation, reestablishing the legitimate government of Kuwait, and bringing America's troops home. The day before the ground war ended I had gone to Fort Dix, New Jersey, to tell 263 Kuwaitis, who were completing a combat-training program, that they now had the responsibility of going home to make Kuwait a more democratic place than it had been before the war. Opponents of the war had made much of the fact that Americans were being asked to restore to power a regime that severely limited the rights of its citizens, particularly its women. That was true enough, though in the short run it had to be beside the point. What we did in the Gulf War was punish aggression, uphold the principle that one nation cannot simply swallow up another. Having done that, we could now help make Kuwait itself a freer place. I told those graduating soldiers: "Where Saddam Hussein has made a mockery of human rights, you must be the champions of human rights and freedom." I hoped that, as a hardliner on the war, I would have the same credibility I had had when I lectured the Salvadoran military.

As the war ended, the most painful human rights situation involved not the Kuwaitis but the Kurds. It had been our hope—a vain one, as it turned out—that the Iraqi army might, after their defeat, turn Saddam Hussein out of power. Certainly that had been the wish of the Kurdish population in northern Iraq, who now, after years of abuse at his hands, were in open revolt against the dictator. The extent to which the United States should support them presented the cruelest dilemma of the war. At a March 26 meeting in the Oval Office I was one of those who spoke up for more aggressive aid to the Kurds, but those in the military and at State were opposed to much involvement. American assistance was eventually restricted to humanitarian aid and the enforcement of a "no-fly zone": Saddam's planes were not permitted to enter air space above the 36th parallel. This took some pressure off the rebelling Kurds, but it did not get them out from under his tyranny.

There were great pressures on the President not to intervene further than he did. For one thing, the Turks had given us loyal support during the war, and they would now feel betrayed if we intervened on behalf of the Kurds, who make up a sizable minority population in Turkey as well as in Iraq. To do anything that might lead to the creation of an independent Kurdish state would risk alienating not only the government in Ankara but also the region's Arab countries. These countries had gone along with Desert Shield and Desert Storm precisely because the limited objectives were so clearly defined. So, even while I felt there was more we could manage to do, I was sympathetic to the President's dilemma, and in public I defended him against the "newly hatched hawks" (Sam Nunn and Joe Biden among them) who now said he was too timid in deploying the American military might they hadn't wanted him to use against Saddam to begin with.

Bush no longer viewed as phlegmatic.

—Fri., March 1, 1991

I was part of what the media called the Big Eight of Desert Shield and Desert Storm, operations which dramatically changed the President's image. The Wimp Factor had been buried. The President had proved himself a great wartime leader, and our polls were sky high. The administration had passed its halfway point, and on February 28, I noted in my diary:

> Met with Ron Kaufman, Spence [Abraham], MTQ, Kristol & Hubbard to begin '92 planning.

How could we lose?

▼ My parents, Corinne and Jim, were always involved in politics. They worked the precincts and helped form the new Republican Party in Arizona in the 1950s. They met and were married at Depauw University which I would attend two decades later.

◄ My grandmother Nana, the family matriarch, once told me that I could do anything I wanted if I just set my mind to it. My mentioning those words in the 1988 debate drew derisive howls from many in the national media.

▲ The stair-step Quayle children starting from the top: Me (I'm the oldest), Chris, and twins Mike and Martha.

▲ I loved my childhood home, though it was hardly the palace people imagined. My dog, Wimps, loved it, too.

▲ My father and my grandfather, Eugene Pulliam, at my graduation from Depauw. Grampa, a self-made man, was an inspiration to me.

▲ The media often mocked my full name, James Danforth Quayle, offering it as proof of my supposedly elitist background. In fact, I was named after James Danforth, my father's close college friend, who served as a captain in the U.S. Army and was killed in World War II.

▲ In 1968, I went to the Republican National Convention and was captivated by the charisma of Governor Ronald Reagan.

▶ Marilyn and I at our wedding. We were married in a small ceremony at her home in Indianapolis, with only our families attending.

Dan Quayle Museum

▲ At the Tidewater Conference in 1980 George Will, et al., listen as I talk to Republican National Chairman Bill Brock.

▶ My first Senate campaign was an uphill struggle. I challenged three-term incumbent and past presidential candidate Birch Bayh who was considered a political giant. We had seven tough debates, and on election night the networks called me the winner even before some of the polls in Indiana had closed.

Wide World

▶ An unlikely alliance with Ted Kennedy produced the Job Training Partnership Act, which I sponsored. With Kennedy as my primary cosponsor, the Senate could find little room for argument and passed the legislation unanimously.

Wide World

JoLene Hum

▲ The 1988 campaign began with my delivering a friendly punch to Vice President Bush. Many thought I came across as too hot. Others felt I exhibited the kind of energy the campaign needed.

Jeff Atteberry

▲ ▶ The Battle of Huntington: When I was besieged by the press at a hometown campaign stop, twelve thousand friends came to my defense.

▲ One of the few happy moments on the 1988 campaign plane was celebrating our son Ben's twelfth birthday.

▲ There were times in 1992 when I wished Lee Atwater were still alive to help guide us to another inaugural ball where he might jam once again with President George Bush.

▲ I strongly pushed the President to name Jack Kemp as Secretary of Housing and Urban Development. He received more favorable publicity than any HUD secretary in history, but unfortunately it was usually at the expense of the President.

▲ Admiral Jim Watkins, Energy secretary, was one of the more creative people in the cabinet. His strong ideas sometimes strayed from the consensus, but like all good military men, once the decision at the top was made he was the loyal soldier.

◀ Budget Director Richard Darman *(left)* won congressional approval for a new budget that raised taxes, but in doing so, helped destroy the President politically. Treasury Secretary Nicholas Brady *(right)* was the fall guy when the President gave away his trump card for nothing in return.

▶ I fought hard for John Tower's nomination for Secretary of Defense. John's ordeal was much like that of Robert Bork and Clarence Thomas, who were also unfairly subjected to fierce partisan attacks.

▲ Thursday. 12:00 noon. Lunch with the President. It became an institution. The other members of the administration learned to get in touch with me if they had something they wanted to pass on to "the Boss." I was usually happy to oblige.

▶ My personal relationship with President Corazon Aquino and decisive, effective work during the night of the coup attempt helped save democracy in the Philippines.

White House

Wide World

▲ On this Latin American trip I met with Daniel Ortega *(center)* to negotiate the transfer of power in Nicaragua. Costa Rica's Oscar Arias was helpful.

▲ Operation Just Cause: the Panamanians wanted us there, but we couldn't become a crutch. That wouldn't have been in their best interest or ours. Panama was not so much a postscript as a precedent for our administration.

▲ I had real doubts about the genuineness of Gorbachev's commitment to democracy and wondered if Baker and I were in serious conflict on this point. It wouldn't have been the first time, nor would it prove to be the last.

▲ At the demilitarized zone in Korea, observing the deployment of North Korean troops. This area remains one of the world's flash points.

DESERT STORM

▶ The press called this the Meeting of the Big Eight. Gates, Sununu, Cheney, the President, Baker, Scowcroft, Powell, and I assembled in our customary seating arrangement for national security meetings. I can't think of one time anything from these meetings ever leaked to the press.

▼ National Military Command Center: a Pentagon briefing by General Colin Powell.

▲▼   The Persian
Gulf War would even-
tually be such a tri-
umph for America—
and its principles—
that we now have a
tendency to look back
on it as something
that was easy or
inevitable. In fact,
we were in a struggle
for the future of the
world.

▲ Boris Yeltsin and I developed a good relationship.
He was the kind of Soviet leader we had never met
before—a democratically elected one.

I WISH A GOOD
HEALTH TO THE
FUTURE US PRESIDENT

▲ As the highest ranking U.S. official to visit the Baltic states since their
independence, I was moved by the chant I heard as I walked through the
crowd: "USA . . . USA."

▲ Clarence Thomas: the long knives of "political correctness" were being sharpened against this strong independent man. He suffered an even worse assault on his character than I did.

▲ Candice Bergen of "Murphy Brown" fame: my speech, which contained a reference to the show and discussed family values, created the real ideological firestorm of my vice-presidency.

▲ Marilyn and I watch an always impressive space shuttle launch. As chairman of the Space Council, I fought continuously with NASA's bureaucrats who were unwilling to implement reforms.

Wide World

◄ A little "photo op" in Trenton, New Jersey, created a "defining moment" of the worst kind imaginable. The card prepared by the school read "potatoe." I can't remember if the spelling struck me as odd or not. It does now.

▼ Once I took the national stage there were no more Battles of Huntington with their welcome reinforcements. I had to go it alone with the media—and play on their turf.

White House

▲ Pat Buchanan hurt us in New Hampshire—he drew first blood.

▶ Marilyn's 1992 convention speech was eloquent and philosophical, yet the liberals panned it. They couldn't tolerate an intelligent, conservative woman championing the contributions of all women.

▼ In the 1992 campaign I had my own staff. There were no destructive handlers—only people who shared my vision for America.

White House

◄ The day after losing the election we waited for the President and Mrs. Bush to arrive so they could say thank-you to a White House staff that truly loved them. It was a heartbreaking moment for us all.

▼ How you exit is important—especially if you're thinking of coming back.

White House

25 | Domestic Drift

It is understandable that domestic affairs play a minor role in the diary I kept during Desert Storm. But, going back to it now, I find one entry that seems telltale. On February 13, I noted:

> *Brady, Darman et al. tell GB recession over by May. Also indicate no interest in any tax bill. This may be wishful thinking.*

Among many high-level people in the administration there was a feeling that the domestic affairs of the country would take care of themselves. If the economy would just revive, then everything would be all right. The President's budget compromise would be forgotten, and the electorate he faced in 1992 would focus on his deserved reputation as a wartime leader.

There was ample historical precedent for avoiding this kind of complacency. The British, impatient for peacetime prosperity, had no problem turning Winston Churchill out of office the same year he brought them victory in World War II. A half century later, Americans were delighted by the end of the cold war and proud of what they had achieved in the Middle East, but their pleasure in the nation's foreign successes did not leave them willing to put up with domestic ills. In fact, it was the opposite. After so many years of sacrifice abroad, the country was beginning to feel it had earned the right to concentrate on its own pressing needs.

This created political dangers for the administration, which, even before the Gulf War, had begun to suffer from a perception that it was intellectually out of gas, that it was bored and disengaged when it came to imagining solutions for our more intractable problems here at home. After the two highly ideological Reagan terms, during which the country truly changed course, our administration looked less like Bush I than a watered-down Reagan III. Back in 1988 I had ridiculed Michael Dukakis for saying that the election was about competence instead of ideology, but midway through what we still thought would be only George Bush's first term, his administration had begun to appear merely competent, without any driving creed. We were, in some minds, turning into the caretakers of the Reagan revolution, appearing unable to keep up with changes in the country's circumstances.

Parallels to earlier administrations came easily to mind: George Bush had become a world leader on the order of Eisenhower, who at home was a moderately successful President with a much younger, more ideological Vice President. One could also make a comparison with the Nixon years, presided over by a man much more interested in rearranging the international scene than in tinkering with domestic affairs. In fact, the problem for the Bush administration was that it was always being seen in terms of *other* presidencies rather than as something original, in and of itself.

As the second anniversary of the President's inauguration approached, *U.S. News & World Report* ran a big story on a White House it characterized as "George Bush's idea-free zone." In that article the President was quoted as taking exception to the charge (he cited the Clean Air Act and sweeping legislation he had signed to grant new rights to disabled Americans), but from the very beginning of his term—during his inaugural address, in fact, when he pointed out how the country had "more will than wallet"—he knew his chances for pushing bold domestic initiatives were limited. The deficit, which the recent budget deal would do nothing to alleviate, was an absolute bar to going ahead with the kind of new appropriations requested by the administration's more innovative thinkers. Over at HUD, Jack Kemp would complain that his budget always lost out to NASA funding in the same appropriations bill. Whenever Kemp came up with proposals for new spending, we would ask him: okay, how are you going to finance this? His answer was always: cut taxes. He believed, as I do, that slashing taxes would expand the economy and eventually lead to more revenue, thereby reducing the deficit. But another way to reduce the deficit was to cut spending—something Jack was never willing to do.

There was always some sentiment in the administration for cutting the capital gains tax as a means of unleashing entrepreneurship, though some, like Nick Brady, thought it made the White House appear to favor the rich. Whether it did or not, this approach ignored political reality (Congress had just forced us to *raise* taxes).

I can remember Dick Darman's flirting with the idea of a Domestic Desert Storm, a series of bold proposals that would put the President's reputation as a domestic leader on a par with his stature as commander in chief. But, sadly, it never amounted to very much. Even Jim Pinkerton, a young policy planner who was a big advocate of individual "empowerment" and had a cluster of relatively inexpensive new proposals known as the New Paradigm, never succeeded in getting people to share his agenda. In fact, Darman used to mock it as "Brother, Can You Paradigm?" The administration fell victim to its own short-term, reactive thinking.

George Bush wanted to be "the education President," and at the heart of that desire lay the concept of school choice—a fundamental change that was not simply a matter of big new appropriations. But we never pushed it hard enough. In many areas—including education, health care, and the environment—we were reluctant to advocate much, since Congress probably wouldn't pass the legislation anyway; if it did, it would load it up with so much additional spending, going so far beyond what we had intended, that we would have been better off doing nothing. Enterprise zones for the inner city were a case in point. We would push for them, and then Congress would turn the bill into a Christmas tree festooned with all sorts of additional appropriations that we not only didn't want, but that went against the very theory behind enterprise zones: helping individuals generate wealth for themselves instead of addicting them to more government aid.

During my years in Washington, I became more and more certain that some of the most pressing problems of urban life, ones that seemed resistant to any solution, were really the result of family breakdown and the reduced role of spirituality in our lives. These social crises can't be treated with simple government programs. Whether I was visiting a parochial grammar school in Boston's Mission Hill neighborhood or residents in a drug-plagued neighborhood right in southeastern Washington, D.C., I met people who knew that they were going to find their way to the American dream only by depending on themselves, on their own discipline and creativity. I paid a visit to Jacqueline Mitchell's house in Washington when the President was attending the international drug summit in Colombia. The timing was deliberate: while he was at one end of the drug pipeline, I would be at the other. Jacqueline Mitchell and the other women on her block had gotten together, on their own initiative, to form a neighborhood crime watch. They would patrol their own streets, letting the dealers who brought their guns and drugs into the neighborhood know that they were not going to be passive victims. They achieved some success in reducing drugs and criminal behavior in their neighborhood. These women had had the help of the Rev. Russell Dillard of St. Martin's Church, but they were for the most part on their own. Most of their men were no longer around, and they knew they had to take matters into their own hands. I admired their commitment and courage.

I spent part of the same morning at the Greater Southeast Community Hospital, visiting "boarder babies"—ones who are too weak from inherited drug addiction to leave the hospital and who, when they are well enough to go home, have no home to go to: their mothers have abandoned them, leaving them in legal limbo. Everything I saw that day left me more convinced than ever that government programs in the old Great Society manner can never be more than a drop of balm into this ocean of misery. A reawakening of the values imparted through faith and family is what's needed to give these people hope, to give them a chance. If the administration was short on wallet, then it could at least display some willingness to use the bully pulpit of the White House on behalf of law and order and family values.

In Indiana, when I was starting out in politics, family values were hardly under the sort of siege they faced in southeastern Washington. Even so, as I looked at every issue affecting my constituents, I became aware of the family as the basic unit of society: the family farm, the family business, you name it. Without the family, any kind of true social coherence is impossible to attain. In our inner cities, intact two-parent families have become almost extinct, and the price paid by those neighborhoods and the individual lives within them is enough to make the angels weep.

This need for families is what the Republican Party should embrace as its cause. By 1990 its liberal foes had taken to joking about how much Republicans must be missing all those communists who had now folded their tents. Who would be our enemy now? What great cause was there for us to champion? The enemy was ourselves: the spiritual decay we'd allowed to rot us, the poverty of values we were too afraid to challenge for fear of appearing "unsophisticated."

The war on drugs was a good example of how futile it is to try to combat a great social evil without first trying to repair the chief social unit, the family. In his inaugural address, George Bush declared that "this scourge [of drugs] will stop," and he named Bill Bennett, Ronald Reagan's Secretary of Education, to lead the effort. The President could not have found a more zealous "czar," but despite a few successes (such as a notable reduction in cocaine use), the drug war in the inner cities was, and is, being lost. The law enforcement funds required are so massive that there is little left for treatment and education. (The Clinton administration thought it was going to be able to change the proportions of budgeting, but when they came into office, reality forced them to keep the appropriations very similar to ours.) Bennett's job was made all the harder by his lack of Cabinet-level status. He got caught up in turf wars, like the one he provoked at a meeting of the National Security Council, when he suggested sending American troops down to Peru to go after the drug producers. I had some sympathy for unconventional approaches like this one, but the State Department crushed the idea right away. In the end, Bennett just felt stymied and tried to salvage what political capital he could: he declared victory and went home. But no amount of money—for enforcement or treatment or education—

was going to make up for what was missing in the neighborhoods hardest hit by drugs, and that was the family unit.

As the second half of the administration got under way, I found myself getting more and more uncomfortable with our approach. I traveled extensively throughout the country and became more convinced than ever that the social deterioration I kept seeing was a direct result of the decay of the nuclear family and a general dismissing of the values that make a society civilized: integrity, responsibility, industry, and duty. But not everyone shared this concern. Flush with victory in the Gulf and with staggeringly high poll numbers (one survey put the President at 91 percent approval), most of the men and women in the administration lacked any fire for domestic initiatives, much less a "Domestic Desert Storm." We continued to send up legislation to Congress— including health care—but the Democratic leadership played hardball politics. They refused to hold hearings on our new initiatives. They didn't want the Republican White House to have any more victories.

A month or so after the war ended, David Broder wrote a piece in the *Washington Post* titled "Bush Could Take the Hill, Too . . . ," suggesting ways in which the President's personal popularity might result not only in his reelection the following year but in a Republican Congress, too. Broder outlined the competing proposals for domestic action within the administration—from the "empowerment" agenda of "school choice, housing vouchers, and enterprise zones" to the beginnings of a move to cut entitlements. He quoted Kate Walsh O'Beirne, the Heritage Foundation's Vice President, as saying: "The generals are all in place; all Bush has to do is give the marching orders." Broder himself argued that the President would "have to lay out a real domestic agenda if he wants to provide coattails for Republican congressional candidates. If he does, the 1992 election could yet be of great importance. It might even—miracle of miracles—produce a government, not another four years of stalemate."

George Bush was not so optimistic. For one thing, he never put much stock in his own poll numbers. I can remember being there when Sununu gave him a glowing set of them. The President just said, "You know, this may not be such good news, because they're going to come down, and then the press will love writing stories about 'how far he's fallen.'" Which is exactly what happened, of course. The President was never smug about his achievements in the Persian Gulf or his standing among the voters. In a sense, his entire life had been a preparation for Desert Storm, and when the moment came to meet this supreme test of leadership, he met it spectacularly. But now the country was asking him to dedicate his energies to the domestic front, and this was an arena in which he felt less confident.

The 1992 campaign people were having their first meetings around this time, and they were sorely missing one man whose untimely death had been the cause of real personal grief for both George Bush and myself. Lee Atwater died from brain cancer late in March 1991. I had first met him ten years earlier, when we both received the U.S. Jaycees Outstanding Young Men of America award. I knew Lee's reputation, and our first meeting showed me the kind of hard charger he was. My speech to the group was on the family as the basic unit of civilization. Henry Cisneros, then mayor of San Antonio and now President Clinton's HUD secretary, was in the same group of honorees, and as we listened to his speech, Atwater turned to me and said: "You know, that guy's going to give us problems some day. He's good, but there's a way I can knock him off." He was already strategizing for some statewide Texas race that might be years away. Lee had as much edge and high spirits as anyone. He spent years as a Reagan man, but he became genuinely devoted to George Bush, not just a holdover. The two of them developed a father–son relationship.

Lee gave me a great deal of personal support during the 1988 campaign, and during the first part of the administration he and his able RNC associate, Mary Matalin, would sometimes drop by the office. (Mary would be one of the few in the 1992 campaign who fought and was loyal to the bitter end.) His illness was a deep shock to everyone in the White House, especially the President. Together we visited Lee in the hospital, finding him in good spirits, still talking politics, still talking about "defining moments." He bore his illness with great courage, even when it had rendered him almost physically unrecognizable to his old friends. I will never forget how touched I was by his coming to my forty-fourth birthday party, less than two months before he died. In his last months, he became more serious about his religious faith (he was holding a rosary in his hands when I visited him in the hospital), and I know his faith gave him the courage to face his death. Much has been made (too much, in my opinion) of the apology he made, not long before his death, for some of the sharp elbows he threw during the 1988 campaign. But that was a rough-and-tumble race, and Lee was absolutely committed to the victory of Bush over Dukakis, an outcome I can assure you he never regretted seeing. I am sure that, if he had lived, his renewed faith would have made him a great advocate for having the Republican Party speak out on moral and cultural issues, not just the free market and strong defense issues of the 1980s.

I spoke at his funeral in South Carolina, and it wasn't easy to remain somber while I tried to evoke Lee's personality. I talked about the husband, the father, the blues player, and the pol. He was a true friend.

How we missed him in those last two years! There's no one whose advice the President listened to more closely, and if Lee had been around the West Wing, energizing everyone (and cracking them up), we may not have become the reactive administration that we did. There's no way of knowing, but I think 1992 might have turned out differently. There are times when I like to imagine a healthy, happy Lee Atwater once more on the stage of an inaugural ball, jamming with George Bush, who's on air guitar, the two of them having a high time celebrating the reelection of the President of the United States.

26 | A Heartbeat Away

For many years before he became Gerald Ford's Vice President, Nelson Rockefeller dismissed any possibility that he would take the second spot on a GOP ticket by arguing that an active man like himself wasn't cut out to be "standby equipment." However much the office's functions have expanded in modern times, there's no denying that that remains the Vice President's chief constitutional duty. Rockefeller, oddly enough, became part of the minority of postwar Vice Presidents who have not either succeeded to the office (by the President's natural death, assassination, or resignation) or faced, during a tense few weeks, the possibility that they soon might have to take over. Into this category one can put Richard Nixon (after President Eisenhower's 1955 heart attack) and George Bush (following the March 1981 attempt on Ronald Reagan's life).

The hours after John Hinckley wounded Reagan had a chaotic aspect, made worse by Secretary of State Al Haig's telling reporters that he was "in control" at the White House. When George Bush became President, he was determined, in the event anything happened to him, that the country be spared the kind of confusion it experienced on March 30, 1981. That's why, on a Tuesday afternoon in April 1989, he called a meeting to discuss how power might be transferred to me if he were ever incapacitated. Present with us in the Oval Office were the President's personal physician, Dr. Burton Lee II; his White House counsel, C. Boyden Gray; John Sununu; and the First Lady. (Marilyn was not at this meeting, though the *Washington Post* would report that she had been there and tried to dominate the discussion. So much for *Post* sources.)

Mrs. Bush said she wished we didn't have to think of these things, but she knew that her participation was crucial. If the President were ever in a situation where he could not make his own medical decisions—for example, whether to perform surgery—those decisions would fall to her, just as Jacqueline Kennedy's wishes would have been paramount in 1963 had her husband survived his gunshot wounds for even a little longer than he did.

Boyden Gray took us through various scenarios in which the President might be rendered mentally or physically incapable of performing his duties and of how, in such situations, power would be transferred under the 25th Amendment, either temporarily or for the rest of the term, to the Vice President. The amendment had been adopted in 1967, when the public was still mindful of the way Lyndon Johnson's succession had left the vice-presidency vacant, and the elderly Speaker John McCormack and Senate President pro tem Carl Hayden next in line for the presidency. The amendment provides for presidential appointment (and congressional confirmation) of a new Vice President and outlines procedures by which the President himself, or a majority of the Cabinet, will inform Congress that the President is unable to perform the duties of his office. The main sponsor of the amendment was my 1980 Senate opponent Birch Bayh, who in 1989, after word of the Oval Office meeting got out, commended President Bush and me for holding it.

Anyone who has ever made up a will or taken out a life insurance policy can imagine the awkwardness of that discussion. At one appearance I made before a group of Washington political reporters during this period, a journalist remarked: "We read in the papers where you and the President were sitting around talking about succession. That's a great concern to some of us." My response to the questioner was that he should be more concerned if we *hadn't* talked about it.

For the next two years the country and I had little reason to think much about the possible incapacitation of George Bush, a man so fit and energetic it was hard to believe he was in his mid-sixties. He jogged and drove his boat *Fidelity* and played tennis and pitched horseshoes with the restlessness of a teenager. But then came the late Saturday afternoon of May 4, 1991. I was at the VP's residence, getting ready to host a reception for the National Space Society, when one of the Secret Service agents came up to me and asked, "Can we have a moment?" I could tell that it wasn't good news, and my first thought was that something had happened to Marilyn, who was down in Florida; just a day or so before, a hotel maid had found a rifle on a table beneath a window in a room directly facing Marilyn's. But as soon as the agent and I were where we could speak privately, he told me: "We just want you to know that the President has taken ill." He'd been out running when his heart began to beat irregularly. I immediately thought back to the time when Jimmy Carter had collapsed while jogging, and I hoped that this would turn out to be no more serious than that. The agent said the President had been taken to a hospital and was comfortable.

I called the White House for more information, but within minutes the Secret Service were back with an update: the problem with the President's heart was apparently not serious, but he would be staying at the hospital overnight. I was relieved, but also determined to be ready for anything. Since it was Saturday, all three of our children were at home, and I immediately summoned them to the same room where I'd gotten the news. I said, "I need to talk to you about something. The President has gotten sick. It looks like a heart problem, and while it may not be serious, I think you ought to know this." I could see their eyes widening, especially Corinne's, as I talked. This was the last thing in the world they wanted to contemplate. I didn't like the idea of alarming them, but I thought things would be even worse if something happened and they had no preparation.

We all went into the National Space Society reception, which they'd been looking forward to, since some of the cast of *Star Trek* had been invited. Knowing that rumors might soon rush through this Washington party, I came into the room as casually as I could and announced that I'd received word the President was resting comfortably in the hospital after having taken ill this afternoon. I knew we all wished him well, and that I was sure he would not want us to change our plans on his account.

So we went ahead with this party full of scientists and space buffs, but my mind was never far from the responsibilities of my office and the condition of my friend, for that's what George Bush had become over the past three years. That night, even though Marilyn and I were hundreds of miles apart, our prayers to God for George Bush and his family drew us together. My own certainty that I could ably perform the duties of the presidency, if things came to that, was a comfort.

I talked to Mrs. Bush on Saturday night and to the President on Sunday morning. I was cheered by both conversations and by medical reports that his "atrial fibrillation" (caused, it seemed, by an overactive thyroid) could be expected to stabilize through drug therapy.

After talking to the President, I headed for church, where a small army of reporters was waiting. I strove to appear upbeat and nonchalant, and I went back to the residence for a deliberately normal Sunday. Jack Kemp came over to play tennis, and I played catch with Ben. Marilyn was still away, and we decided she should follow her planned schedule so as not to alarm anyone. The kids and I did what we do every Sunday evening—order pizza.

All in all, a very pleasant day, unless you turned on the Sunday political talk shows. On "Meet the Press," a long-shot possibility for next year's Democratic nomination, Governor Bill Clinton of Arkansas, was suggesting I would be a campaign issue in 1992 if President Bush chose to run with me a second time. That was predictable enough, but I was surprised by the tone of some of the "analysis" being given by reporters. On ABC, Cokie Roberts, who sometimes betrays the partisanship of her Democratic parents (the late Congressman Hale Boggs and former Congresswoman Lindy Boggs) but usually seems pleasant and level-headed enough, was talking about the "moment of terror" people were supposedly experiencing when forced to deal with the thought of my becoming President. This was, I thought, over the limit for mainstream political discourse, and I actually had Beckwith call ABC to complain.

On Monday morning the President's doctors came close to treating his heart with an application of shock, which requires a general anesthetic. That would have incapacitated the President for a brief period and necessitated invoking the 25th Amendment. At 5:30 A.M. the Secret Service and some White House staffers began arriving at the VP residence for the transfer of power, but around 6:00 I got a call saying that the electroshock procedure wouldn't be necessary. Fortunately, there was very little press on the subject—proof that when matters are kept to a small group leaks can be avoided.

I knew that, even if the President's recovery was as robust and complete as it appeared it would be, I was in for some rough times. "Feeding Frenzy: The Sequel" had just begun. As Marilyn would remark after about ten days of it, at least "nobody was sitting in front of our mailbox. There are advantages to being in the Vice President's house." Even so, once the President was back at work, some reporters found time for a new version of the old "death watch" outside the gates of the VP residence. Bill Kristol told the press he welcomed the new scrutiny if it replaced the existing caricature of me with a fairer evaluation. We didn't have much alternative to saying that. The locomotive was coming at us whether we liked it or not, so we just smiled and said, "Oh, we're so glad this train's coming our way." In truth, I wanted none of it, because I had no faith in the media since that "PrimeTime Live" interview in 1989. They had invested too much of themselves in the caricature; to change it now would have called into question *their* credibility. I was still the chief target for the late-night comics (the Center for Media and Public Affairs actually indexed 3,025 jokes and found I was the subject of 162 of them), and my poll numbers hadn't gone up much. I still thought my best shot lay in waiting for 1992, when I could use my convention speech to reintroduce myself to the American people—my way.

Even without the atrial fibrillation episode, some additional scrutiny would probably have been coming. When the Gulf War got started, a strong set of personalities—Dick Cheney, Colin Powell, and Jim Baker—began making an impression on the public as never before, and each one of them was now mentioned as a possible new running mate for the unbeatable-looking George Bush. Still, I didn't really worry; the President's own poll numbers seemed my best insurance. I can remember, too, that my most glamorous potential replacement, General Powell, called me up to say he was embarrassed by all the speculation his name was generating. "I think you're doing a commendable job and always have," he said. "I've known you since your Senate days, and I think you've gotten a bum rap from the press. I just want you to know that I haven't done anything to encourage this."

"I know that, Colin," I replied. "It all just comes with the territory."

In the weeks after the heart episode, that territory was pretty rough. Both major newsmagazines did cover stories on me— *Time*'s suggesting five different vice-presidential replacements; *Newsweek*'s showing me taking a golf swing near the title: THE QUAYLE HANDICAP. The *New York Times*'s Maureen Dowd, objective as always, came into the White House press room wearing a T-shirt depicting Edvard Munch's famous painting "The Scream" (that eerie figure with the open mouth and hands over his ears) above the caption: PRESIDENT QUAYLE? The reaction of the rest of the media? Blasé. I wonder if it would be the same for a reporter who wore a SLICK WILLIE T-shirt into that room. Every editorial page and columnist seemed newly motivated to discuss me: "As long as [the President] was the picture of health," declared the *Miami Herald*, "his choice of Mr. Quayle didn't make much difference. Now it does." Some prominent Democratic senators, like Illinois's Alan Dixon, Arizona's Dennis DeConcini, and Vermont's Patrick Leahy, came to my defense, the latter with a dose of human perspective that's rare in Washington. "I wish everybody would just lay off Dan Quayle," Leahy said. "He works hard. He has the President's confidence. . . . This is a man who's got a family. He's got a wife and children and it's a rough thing." Speaker Tom Foley also resisted the chance to make cheap political hay: "I don't have the slightest concern about Vice President Quayle's ability to carry on the duties of his office." I'm sure his own situation had created a new empathy. On Monday morning, when the electroshock procedure was being considered and there was thought of invoking the 25th Amendment, the Speaker was briefly given Secret Service protection, since in such a situation he would be next in line for the presidency.

As always, the President displayed confidence in me. Back at work in the White House, he answered a question about whether I would be on the 1992 ticket by asking another: "You want that by hand or do you want it by word?" (an allusion to what the *Washington Post* called the "digital reply" Vice President Rockefeller once offered a heckler).

After a few weeks things seemed to be calming down. We made a trip to Asia and then, in June, to the newly free countries in Eastern Europe. Bob Woodward, the *Post*'s star political investigative reporter of Watergate fame, came along, supplying a level of coverage we weren't used to. The *Post* was planning an extensive series about me, a whole new look, to be written by Woodward and the paper's other heavy hitter, David S. Broder. For a series that would run to forty thousand words and eventually be published as a book (*The Man Who Would Be President*), they intended to cover me for months, in Washington and out on my travels. They also wanted to do lengthy taped interviews. Len Downie, the *Post*'s managing editor, later told me that he felt the paper had let its readers down with inadequate coverage of Bush as Vice President. People in his newsroom and elsewhere had told him they were sure Bush would never be President, and might not even get the nomination in 1988. As a result, the paper never paid enough attention to him, and Downie didn't want that to happen with another Vice President.

To say I wasn't looking forward to this is putting it mildly. I got some of the people in the office together and said: "Okay, make the best of this sow's ear, but it is *not* a good sign. The last thing I want is Bob Woodward going over every single thing I've ever said or done." I told Dave Beckwith that nothing good would come of this and that he shouldn't go promising them lots of interview cooperation. When the *Post*'s Ann Devroy called to ask him, "What do you think of Bob Woodward going after you?" he responded, "Oh, this is good news. They'll really find out what the Vice President is all about." He appeared to be spinning for all he was worth, and Devroy just laughed: "Oh, yeah, I'm supposed to believe that? Boy, if I were you, I don't think I'd welcome this at all." That was certainly the buzz in journalism circles: this was the beginning of the end of Dan Quayle. Some anonymous source in the administration was quoted as warning me to beware of these "two rabid skunks" (David Broder, always a complete gentleman and with a sense of humor, soon gave me a "Rabid Skunk" T-shirt).

The funny thing is that Beckwith wasn't just spinning Ann Devroy. Part of him really did believe I had a great opportunity here. While I kept resisting, he kept pushing me to give Woodward and Broder all the access they wanted. As the summer and fall passed, I felt myself getting sucked in, agreeing to more and more interviews—aboard *Air Force Two*, in the office, and at the residence.

Woodward is an immensely talented guy, and as time went on I enjoyed being around him. His style is to get into the heart and mind of the interviewee without him knowing it. But he is a journalist, and he is not going to let friendship get in the way of a story. Ask Dick Darman, who viewed Woodward as a friend until Woodward wrote some absolutely devastating stuff on Darman and the rest of Bush's economic team a few weeks before the 1992 election. Darman was crushed by it and furious with Woodward, who Darman was convinced wouldn't run the articles until after November 3. The episode reminds me of the David Stockman interview with William Greider, the one that forced Reagan to take Stockman to the "woodshed." Stockman had been convinced that friendship was thicker than journalism. Wrong. A good journalist will have political friends, but he'll put friendship and emotion aside when a story is at stake.

Woodward is smart, very quick and endlessly curious. You forget he isn't some kid fresh out of college working his heart out on his first job. He affects a laid-back Midwestern niceness that charms people into giving him what he's come for. He pretends to be naive, and he flatters people no end. He'll zero in on anybody when they've got their guard down—whether it's Bill Clinton's mother at the track or Colin Powell at home in his Jacuzzi. Most journalists I've known save their biggest question for last; when you hear "I have one more question," brace yourself for the kill. But Woodward is so sharp, and his mind functions in so many different directions at once, that he may go in for the kill with some innocuous-sounding question in the middle of the interview: he's gotten in and gotten out before the subject even realizes it. The book he wrote called *The Commanders*, which followed military decision making in the Pentagon and Bush White House right through Desert Shield, is about 80 percent on target—not bad for instant history. It came out shortly after the war. I turned down requests to be interviewed by him for it, but Dick Cheney granted them, and in the summer of 1991 he gave me a warning: "You're going to like Woodward," he said. "He's a likable guy, but don't be fooled by him. He's not on your side."

I told Dick I was sure he was right, and I knew from experience and my own newspaper background that Woodward and Broder were not "on my side." But the series of articles they wrote were very helpful—if only by being so much better than what everyone had expected from these two stars of the *Washington Post*. Their bottom-line purpose was to find out if Dan Quayle was qualified to be President, and they answered that question with a firm yes. They portrayed me as hardworking and well informed, and they devoted a lot of copy to the political skills I'd used to bring myself to George Bush's attention in 1988. The book was hardly a rave review (there was plenty of criticism of what they saw as my limitations), but no one could read it and think I wasn't a player within the administration or that in my special areas of responsibility, particularly the Space and Competitiveness Councils, I wasn't having an impact. They asked the tough question to both friends and foes: Does Quayle have the moral authority to be President? The answers were vague and not especially flattering, but moral authority is something you gain by experience. There are only a few Presidents who had moral authority when elected. Washington and Eisenhower come to mind. But Lincoln didn't; nor did FDR. Certainly Bill Clinton didn't have it when he was elected. They also went back to, and shot down, the worst rumors from the summer of 1988, providing the kind of substantive coverage that had been lacking then. Three years later I was glad to set a few matters straight. Beckwith was entitled to an "I told you so."

And I wound up, as Cheney predicted, liking Woodward. He's a fascinating, quixotic person. I'd already liked and respected David Broder—with whom, I suspect, Woodward teamed up in an effort to bolster his credibility with me. In the end, my biggest complaint about their book involves its harsh chapter on Marilyn, who is portrayed (via a couple of ridiculous anecdotes) as a kind of angry manipulator.

She feels, and she's right, that she's been burned too many times not to be combative, or at least wary. In 1990 she gave a speech to the National Press Club and talked about the 1988 ordeal, which she agreed had left her overly protective of her family and inclined to freeze out the press. She proposed that they now meet each other halfway, and she then took far more steps in that direction than they did. But while there was a slight, temporary softening of their coverage, cruel stories soon again became just as frequent, and the mistrust persisted. The press earned it. This is typical media treatment for smart conservative women. The press wants to say that they are mean and rude, when more often than not it's the liberals who treat people with disdain.

Because of this, some of Marilyn's most important contributions didn't always get the attention they should have. She made a real impact in the area of breast cancer. Betty Ford, when she was First Lady, valiantly led the way for women to talk about this disease. Marilyn was determined to build on Betty Ford's work and make breast cancer a priority in the health care debate. With the help of her friend Nancy Brinker, who founded the Komen Foundation, an organization dedicated to finding a cure for breast cancer, Marilyn convinced me that the fight against breast cancer would move forward only if men started talking about it. I remembered all too vividly Marilyn's mother's battle with the disease, so I joined the fight.

In the summer of 1990 Marilyn received some disquieting medical news of her own. She was diagnosed as having severe cervical dysplasia (a precancerous condition). As a family we were hopeful, and our prayers focused on Marilyn as we awaited pathology reports. Throughout the ordeal, which included a successful operation, I was touched as I watched our children give their mother the emotional support she needed during this difficult time. This scare made us even more committed to raising the public awareness of early detection of cancer.

Marilyn and I did a series of breast cancer awareness commercials, and I added breast cancer centers and mammography van tours to my travel itinerary. We talked members of Congress into publicly backing our work. Marilyn and I established the Race for the Cure in Washington, D.C., to raise money for research and to sponsor awareness programs and low-cost screening projects in the D.C. area. In the last year we were in Washington, nearly twenty thousand people "raced for the cure." Breast cancer became a much more discussed illness than ever before. President Bush increased the funding for research, and we created a women's health section at the National Institutes of Health. Many more women began taking charge of their lives, having regular mammograms and doing monthly self-examinations, while more husbands started urging their wives to take care of themselves.

Perhaps Marilyn's greatest contribution came in the area of disaster preparedness and relief, work she began as a specialist with the Agency for International Development's U.S. Office of Foreign Disaster Assistance (OFDA). It was important to her not to be just a ribbon cutter but to have a real impact on the policies of our government. When we traveled to other countries, Marilyn would meet with their disaster specialists and interior ministries to learn more, to trade knowledge, and to discuss mutually beneficial cross-border treaties. If the country was a recipient of U.S. foreign aid, Marilyn would highlight the projects that we had funded, and if we were having trouble getting cooperation within the country, it was Marilyn who would meet with the relevant official there and try to iron out the problem. In addition, if there was a disaster in any part of the world, Marilyn was notified immediately. If her services were needed at the crisis headquarters in OFDA, she was trained to lend a hand. If she was needed in the field, she was prepared to go, as she did to Bangladesh after the devastating cyclone of 1991.

Word travels fast in Washington. It wasn't long after Marilyn began her work at OFDA that the director of the Federal Emergency Management Agency (FEMA), Colonel Julius Becton, called her to ask if she would like to extend her expertise and knowledge to FEMA. She then added extensive training in domestic disaster response to her schedule, and over the next few years aided with relief efforts that followed the San Francisco earthquake and Hurricanes Hugo, Andrew, and Iniki, and floods, fires, and tornados around the country.

The press was never kind or accurate where Marilyn was concerned, and the outrageous stuff about me never completely died out either. The story of Brett Kimberlin (the convicted Speedway bomber who claimed to have sold me marijuana years before) was revived for a time. He was suing federal prison officials for supposedly harsh treatment and for interfering with the press conference he'd planned to hold just before the 1988 election. To my genuine amazement, the *New York Times* put the Kimberlin story—a tale concocted by a convicted felon who never met me and whose vicious crime permanently maimed an innocent man—on its front page. The "Today" show gave Kimberlin extensive national air time, and Bryant Gumbel fell all over himself trying to put a positive spin on the story. Most egregious of all, Jane Pauley's husband, Garry Trudeau, turned all this into a cartoon vendetta in his *Doonesbury* strip, playing with scenarios and allegations so outrageous and unsubstantiated that some of the newspapers refused to run the installments. As I've said before, "60 Minutes" spent two years looking into Kimberlin's tale before deciding it had absolutely nothing credible they could put on the air. Woodward even mentioned to me that Don Hewitt of "60 Minutes" told Trudeau, "Look, you're just wrong on this thing. There's nothing there." Even the media have their limits, and for a while (I was enjoying this) Trudeau was getting worse press over this thing than I was.

More than two years into my vice-presidency, I was less preoccupied with the day-to-day progress of my public image than I'd been at the beginning. But around this time, I did an interview with Barbara Walters that, without any real intention on my part, disclosed an important aspect of my life: my faith in Christ. She asked me, rather casually, the sort of question she often asks her guests, be they politicians or movie stars. "What was the most significant day of your life?" she wanted to know. And I found myself talking about the day I personally accepted Christ as my savior. I have never spoken very publicly about my religious convictions, and I've never tried to exploit them for political gain. I rarely insert them into speeches, other than to talk about the general importance of faith and Judeo-Christian values. When Barbara asked her question, I just tried to answer it as straightforwardly as I could. People in my office argued over the political wisdom of my speaking about my spiritual experience more frankly than before, but I wasn't much concerned about it either way. Faith in Christ is not something you "spin." I shouldn't have been surprised at the enormous amount of mail we received from people who were pleased to hear me talk about Christ and who were happy they could identify with my experience. The same thing happened some months later when David Frost asked me to talk about it a bit more.

Although I had been raised a Presbyterian, my personal acceptance of Christ occurred in a Methodist church on a Sunday afternoon in 1964, when I was seventeen years old. With about fifteen or twenty other young people, I'd gone through an ecumenical Bible study course, one that alternated between the local Methodist and Presbyterian churches. We talked a good deal about the importance of accepting Christ openly as our personal savior, and about His having died for our sins. On this particular Sunday afternoon, our group leader urged each of us to make a personal, open statement, there in the house of God, about accepting Christ. And in a quiet, peaceful way most of us did. Almost as much as that moment itself, I can still remember how the next day at school we nodded to one another as brother and sister Christians who had publicly professed our faith. Had we been "born again"? Those words mean different things to different people. I had already been baptized and brought up in a Christian home, but I had never openly expressed my allegiance to Christ—or felt filled with Him as I did that afternoon. That Sunday remains an unforgettable part of my life.

In the thirty years since, I have practiced my faith as best I know how, and I am all too aware of how many times I've fallen out of grace with the Lord. But if my life has any meaning, and if I have been able to endure the hardships that have come along with great showers of blessings, it is because I tried to walk with Him. Politics is one of the more brutal careers one can choose, and I have seen people who came to Washington without faith, only to find themselves with nothing that sustains them in their most troubling hours.

I have also seen those whose steady Christian beliefs allowed them to survive even worse assaults on their intellect and character than I ever suffered. It was such a man that President Bush, in the summer of 1991, nominated to the United States Supreme Court.

27 | A High-Tech Lynching?

In July 1989 I addressed the NAACP's annual convention in
Detroit. I came with two messages: one contrite and the other
combative. I admitted that, during the civil rights revolution of
the 1960s, lack of Republican participation earned us "a perception that we did not care about civil rights." Back then the party
made a political, social, and moral mistake. In the end, most
Republicans supported the legislation that made the civil rights
movement a fact, but we should have been out in front of it,
instead of bringing up the rear. By 1989 the judicial part of that
revolution had been achieved: no one could seriously argue that
in our country the races were still unequal before the law. The
problems being faced by large numbers of black Americans—
those who had not joined the burgeoning black middle class—
were now more social and spiritual than they were legal in
nature.

Drugs, fatherless families, teenage pregnancies, street crime,
dropouts—this list of woes, not unique to black Americans but
disproportionately suffered by them, will not respond to so-called
civil rights legislation or, as all the evidence clearly shows, to
heavy federal spending. What is needed to fight these scourges is
a new kind of empowerment for the people they attack. These
evils need to be repelled from within, by self-help and self-respect,
not by federal money. By 1989 the Republican Party was ahead of
the Democrats in recognizing what the situation required from
government. Enterprise zones, school choice, toughness on crime,
and above all a refusal to pretend that the devastation of our

urban ghettos could be reversed by appropriating more funds for the same old tired programs. For this revolution, I wanted the party of Lincoln out in front, offering a complete change in approach and attitude.

It's true we had a credibility problem, but I still believe that it's best for American minorities in urban areas to look skeptically at the Democratic Party, which has fostered a mind-set that breeds economic servility and social decay. The Democrats are still offering quota-ridden legal tinkering to combat massive social dislocation.

That's what happened in 1990, when they put forth a bill mandating racial quotas in certain areas of hiring. They never used the word *quota*, and they swore up and down that the bill didn't involve quotas, but that's exactly what it amounted to, in all its pointlessness. It wouldn't expand the economy, wouldn't give a single job to anyone who didn't already have one. It would, in fact, kill off some jobs by hampering small business with yet more regulation and paperwork. What would the bill do to strengthen families? What would it do to help single mothers on crime-ridden streets? What would it do to help the pregnant, unwed teenager? Absolutely nothing.

If anything can show us the futility of quotas, it is the performance of our armed forces over the past several years, from Panama to the Persian Gulf to Somalia. The military has maintained a strictly enforced policy of color-blindness. It is a true meritocracy. In today's Army, you don't get ahead because you're white, and you don't get ahead because you're black. There are no quotas. You get ahead because you're good and willing to work hard. And far from causing racial friction, this policy has promoted racial harmony and self-respect.

Even so, the civil rights leadership and the Democratic Party, as if on automatic pilot, persist in offering legal solutions to social problems. In 1990 President Bush refused to go along with its quota bill and was roundly criticized for being the first President to "veto a civil rights bill." He was right. But the criticism stuck, and although his veto was sustained, a year later he wound up signing a milder version of the same useless bill.

The Democrats and civil rights leaders may be short on vision, but Republicans remain guilty of faint-heartedness. We allow the liberal establishment to get away with calling a piece of legislation like the 1990 one a "civil rights bill" when it was nothing of the kind. And then we get defensive and sullen and don't follow through on truly beneficial approaches like enterprise zones and school choice, because we decide we're never going to have any real constituency in the black community, no matter what we offer.

Our best hope as a party is to have the nerve to keep pushing initiatives that rely on the free market and personal responsibility—like proposals to turn public-housing tenants into owners of their own apartments. Our other real hope is to try to attract a new generation of black Republicans who are as tired of the Democrats' "civil rights" sloganeering as earlier activists were of waiting for segregationists to change their minds. The small, brave corps of black conservatives—which includes the economist Thomas Sowell and the only Republican member of the House Black Caucus, Gary Franks—is offering fresh ideas and leadership.

In the Senate I got to know one of these young black conservatives when he came before the Labor and Human Resources Committee for confirmation hearings on his nomination to head the Equal Employment Opportunity Commission in 1983. Clarence Thomas favored zealous enforcement of antidiscrimination laws, but he was just as firm in his belief that real advancement for any minority can come only from hard work and personal merit, not favoritism and quotas. His own life was the best testimony he could offer. He had grown up poor in Pin Point, Georgia, a little town in the segregated South. But the nuns at his school taught him to believe in himself and to claim a piece of the American dream as his own. Eventually, he would distinguish himself at Yale Law School and rise to a seat on America's second-highest court, the U.S. Court of Appeals for the District of Columbia circuit. The Senate confirmed him for that position, almost unanimously, in 1990. In fact, by July 1, 1991, when President Bush nominated him to replace Thurgood Marshall on the U.S. Supreme Court, Clarence Thomas had been confirmed for federal positions *four times* by the U.S. Senate.

Thomas was an ideal replacement for Thurgood Marshall: one symbol of black advancement would give way to another with a whole new outlook. But we weren't so naive as to believe reason and fairness would prevail. As soon as the President announced the nomination from his summer home in Kennebunkport and Clarence Thomas had thanked him (and those Georgia nuns) in an emotional speech, we knew that the long knives of "political correctness" were being sharpened for use against this strong, independent man who did not fit the liberals' idea of what a black jurist—in fact, any black man—should stand for. When George Bush said flat out that Clarence Thomas was the most qualified man for the court, the press worked itself into a frenzy. But if one considered Thomas's credentials, the President's desire to maintain diversity on the court, and the way Thomas generally reflected the President's judicial philosophy, then Thomas was not only eminently qualified—he was arguably the *most* qualified.

A few days later, back home in Huntington for a Fourth of July parade, I made a speech from the courthouse steps, noting that Clarence Thomas fit right in with the triumphant story of America. I knew a real fight would be necessary to get his nomination through the same body that had confirmed him four times previously. Ever since Ronald Reagan had nominated Judge Robert Bork to the court four years before, confirmation hearings had become political circuses instead of sober examinations of a nominee's credentials.

Before the nomination was made, I called Senator Jack Danforth, a pillar of integrity for whom Clarence Thomas had once worked (in both the Senate and the Missouri attorney general's office), and asked him how strongly he supported the nomination. I could detect his enthusiasm from the moment he began to answer, so then I asked him, point blank: "Will you do for Clarence Thomas what Warren Rudman did for David Souter?" I was asking him to take charge of steering the nomination through the Senate, where Danforth's colleagues were about to be inundated with mail, phone calls, and visits from a host of ideological lobbyists seeking to destroy Clarence Thomas. Jack was absolutely committed to the fight, and this was important to both the President and Boyden Gray.

But the forces lining up against Thomas were considerable, and the nature and rhetoric of their opposition was sometimes almost sickening. Columnist Carl Rowan said that "if you gave Thomas a little flour on his face, you'd think you had [KKK leader] David Duke talking." A leader from the National Organization for Women said, "We're going to 'Bork' him. We need to kill him politically," while one black Congressman declared that "a black conservative is a contradiction in terms." All of them refused to accept that black men and women could make a rational decision, for the good of their race and the good of their country, to leave what some have called "the liberal plantation." Even so, the administration was surprised by the number of civil rights groups, including the NAACP, who wound up opposing the nomination. I had hoped it would split the black community right down the middle and inject some freshness into the national debate. But the black civil rights leadership, bent on maintaining political correctness and their own political clout, became some of Thomas's strongest opponents.

Within a week the attacks on him were full throated. His opponents sought to portray him as "unqualified" for the court, claiming it wasn't his ideology, but his lack of experience and credentials, that bothered them. The hypocrisy of this argument was blatant. There was no one in America with more distinguished credentials and experience than Robert Bork, but that hadn't stopped the liberals from savaging him a few years earlier, entirely on the basis of ideology. And the fact remained, even if the much younger Clarence Thomas hadn't yet had a long enough career to produce as voluminous a record as Bork's, that he was a superbly qualified jurist—as his most recent Senate confirmation attested.

That July we began a full-court press for the nomination. Key Senators like Danforth and Orrin Hatch made speeches on Thomas's behalf. I began approaching Democratic Senators, such as Illinois's Alan Dixon and Virginia's Chuck Robb, who might be persuadable. I also talked to some of the weaker Republicans, to make sure they stayed on our side. Danforth would tell me who could use a call, from me or the President, and we'd make sure that that Senator got it. Meanwhile, Judge Thomas was making the rounds of Capitol Hill, visiting Senators one by one and demonstrating to them his intellect, his independence, and his passionate commitment to judicial restraint.

Early on I thought the nomination might turn on the abortion issue. Justice Souter, when he appeared before the Judiciary Committee, had quite properly refused to take a stand on *Roe v. Wade*, the 1973 court decision legalizing abortion. The committee was, after all, charged with examining his overall judicial philosophy and temperament, not his opinions on particular matters that might come before the court. This had been the accepted practice for many years, but it was clear that for the Thomas nomination the rule book would be thrown to the winds. Ohio's Howard Metzenbaum declared his intention to force the nominee to declare himself on the abortion issue: "I'm through reading tea leaves and voting in the dark. . . . I will not support yet another Reagan–Bush Supreme Court nominee who remains silent."

Did Judge Thomas's previous writings contain hints of his position on abortion? His opponents made much of a 1987 speech in which he praised an antiabortion article in *The American Spectator* as a "splendid example of applying natural law" to a judicial question; but that single sentence in Thomas's speech could easily have been meant to praise the writer's skills in debate and logic, not endorse every piece of his argument. Certainly it gave no firm indication of whether the judge would actually vote to overturn *Roe* if it came before the Supreme Court. I myself never discussed the abortion question with Judge Thomas because I knew that doing so would only undermine his independence once he became an associate justice. It's important to remember that the Democrats, not the Republicans, were imposing an ideological litmus test on the nominee—and that is how it has been with the abortion question for some time.

With the appointment of Ruth Bader Ginsburg in 1993, the politics of abortion would change. The court lost Byron White's pro-life vote and gained another one that's pro-choice. The court is now at least 6–3 in favor of legal abortion, and so debate over the issue will inevitably shift to its secondary aspects, such as federal funding and parental consent. Because the American people tend to favor Republican positions on these matters, the media will pay less attention to them.

The pro-life movement must overcome its feelings of frustration. It must work to regain the moral high ground, convincing Americans not only that abortion is wrong but also that there are wonderful alternatives such as adoption. The movement must be sophisticated and disciplined, and it must absolutely renounce violence, remembering that it will always be in the media's interest to make the pro-life crusade as extremist as possible. And when they can, the men should leave debate of this issue to the women, who speak better on it and who are pro-life in larger numbers.

Few people recall Clarence Thomas's disciplined, thoughtful performance during his confirmation hearings before the Senate Judiciary Committee. It was what happened after the main hearings, when the committee reconvened to take up the charges leveled by Anita Hill, that burned itself into the American political memory. Just before the story broke, a lobbyist friend of mine, Tom Korologos, picked up word of what was about to happen. He did not mention Anita Hill's name to me, but he asked if I'd heard about some sexual harassment charges against the judge. In fact, our side had earlier heard some rumors of this, but as I told Tom, they had found there was nothing to them. Tom told me that we might want to be a bit more concerned: there was a woman ready to talk.

I don't know where he was getting his information—as a lobbyist he has to play both sides of the political aisle—but the next time I was in the Oval Office I thought it was important enough to mention to John Sununu and the President. Both of them told me they'd been hearing rumors, too, but that Boyden Gray, the White House counsel, assured them there was nothing to worry about. So I didn't consider the issue again until the Anita Hill story leaked.

Once it did, I wanted to push ahead as before. The Judiciary Committee had had its hearings, and it was time for them to vote. To me the leak looked like deliberate sabotage, an eleventh-hour attempt to throw the proceedings into chaos by opponents of the judge who realized they were short of the votes needed to block his nomination. But I had to trust Jack Danforth, who had done long, hard work on Thomas's behalf and who believed that not allowing the committee to schedule a special hearing to discuss Professor Hill's charges might, in the end, lead to more political trouble than holding it would. It's hard to say, more than two years later, whether he was right or wrong. But at the time he had some important Democrats (among them Sam Nunn and Wyche Fowler from Clarence Thomas's home state of Georgia) telling him that, while they wanted to vote for the judge, they would have a hard time doing so if we tried to ram this through. The Senate prides itself on being unhurried and deliberate, even while the introduction of television has made it less so. In this case, both sides wanted to delay because neither was sure it had the votes.

And so the hearings were held, consuming the country's attention as much as any since Watergate. Professor Hill testified first, and I thought she came across as very credible. By the time she was through, it appeared that Judge Thomas might have been mortally wounded. But in his rebuttal he was equally impressive—full of passion and pain. When it was over, the American people, according to polls, believed him two to one. (A year later, the public seemed to have changed its mind, but by that time the media had transformed Anita Hill into a symbol of victimized woman-hood, and Clarence Thomas's principal defender—himself—was not being heard from. He was quietly going about the business of making himself a distinguished Supreme Court Justice.)

I followed the hearings very closely and since then have read and thought a great deal about the matter. I have no absolutely firm opinion of what happened between Judge Thomas and Professor Hill, but my instincts and the weight of the evidence lead me to believe that he told the truth. On the other hand, I think that Professor Hill *believed* she was telling the truth herself, even if she was misremembering or misconstruing the long-ago events she described. Whether she felt "spurned" by Clarence Thomas, as some have said, is something we will never know. I do feel that her background and career somehow never added up: she moved from job to job and ended up at a not terribly distinguished law school, even though, one would have thought, as a black female graduate of Yale Law School, she was in a position to write her own ticket.

It was a sad, lurid spectacle, one that Clarence Thomas called "a high-tech lynching." I certainly don't believe the people who dragged the reluctant Professor Hill out to testify against him were pure in their motives. They were using her to get him, and they didn't especially care if her story was true or not. What's most ironic, and sad, about the whole situation is that Clarence Thomas, in his fight to save his good name, played the "victim card." By using that phrase—"a high-tech lynching"—he was appealing to the kind of race-consciousness he'd spent most of his professional life trying to move people away from. As a politician I cannot blame him. By stealing a trick from his opponents' book, he was able to regain some of the ground he lost during Professor Hill's impassioned testimony. He held onto Nunn and Fowler, his Georgia votes, and a couple of other key ones, like Alan Dixon's. Alan and I talked during this period, and he told me, "Look, I gave my word to you and to the President and to Judge Thomas. I'm going to vote for him, but please don't let it out. I'm under unbelievable pressure from people in the Senate and people back home." I told him we would not tell anyone we knew we had his vote, and we both kept our word. Alan, a man of honor, voted for Clarence Thomas—and the following year lost renomination to a primary opponent, Carol Moseley-Braun, who went on to become the first black woman elected to the U.S. Senate.

I very nearly had to cast a tie-breaking vote to get the nomination through—a high-profile task I would have relished, but it was a prospect that George Mitchell, the Democratic leader, must just as ardently have loathed. I am convinced that if, at the last minute, it appeared to be coming to that, he would have put fierce partisan pressure on a few wavering Democrats to deny me that opportunity. In the end, Clarence Thomas was confirmed by a vote of 52–48.

The televised sight of fourteen white males strenuously questioning a single black female was not one that appealed to anyone's sense of demographic reality or fair play. The committee's chairman, Joe Biden, must now be relieved that the group looks considerably different, with the addition of Senators Dianne Feinstein and Carol Moseley-Braun. One interesting footnote to all this is that the committee might have looked a little less homogeneous back in 1991 if Governor Pete Wilson of California had taken my advice a year before that. His own election to the state house in Sacramento had created a Senate vacancy, and as Governor, he had to appoint his own replacement. His choice of John Seymour (who in 1992 would be beaten by Feinstein) was solid, but it wasn't the one I'd urged him to make. I had suggested he consider one of President Bush's top foreign policy advisers, Condoleezza Rice. Had he chosen her, it's possible that one of Anita Hill's questioners would have been a very talented black woman.

In any event, the Senate dealt itself a blow from which it will be a long time recovering. The Anita Hill hearings were chaotic and crude, and they only cheapened the reputation of the world's greatest deliberative body. I still believe they shouldn't have been held at all, even if they did prompt a national discussion of sexual harassment. Certainly, sexual harassment is an important issue. As a law student, Marilyn had been a victim of a professor's unwelcome attentions (her response to him is not printable) and we have been sensitive to the issue ever since. It is full of gray areas and legal complications, and every segment of society is now grappling with it. But those hearings were not the best way to bring the issue to the fore. Clarence Thomas paid a terrible price. His reputation was trashed, and his pride was devastated. Given his strong faith in Christ, the latter will probably recover, but no matter how well he performs on the court, he will never get back his reputation. Justice Thomas and his wife, Virginia, have avoided much of Washington social life. After the confirmation battle, Marilyn and I saw them only two more times at the vice-presidential residence, one of them the night before Bill Clinton's inauguration. I know something about caricatures, and it is sad that the one of Clarence Thomas may be fixed for all time. By our getting sidetracked into the Anita Hill fiasco, black America lost the chance to highlight the talent, integrity, and wisdom of one of its own. America lost a chance to shift its social debates to the proven civilizing influence of personal responsibility and empowerment.

28 | Too Many Laws

Each year politicians treat voters to a great deal of talk about "regulation" (or, if Republicans are doing the talking, "deregulation"), without making it clear what regulations really are. They might best be defined as the fine print of legislation: Congress passes laws, and then the different departments and agencies of the executive branch write the detailed rules that specify how those laws will actually be applied. Regulations are the letter of the law, and as such they amount to laws themselves. In fact, the real power is often not so much in the statute itself as in the regulations that accompany it.

Democrats are enamored of regulation because they believe that the more involved government is with anything, the better it will be. What some have called the "iron triangle" of lobbyists, federal agency bureaucrats, and congressional staffers has for decades permitted regulations to grow, like layer after layer of barnacles, over the legislation passed by Congress and signed by the President.

Republicans generally want to scrape those barnacles away, because they understand the human cost of too much government regulation. Workers pay with their jobs, when small businesses have to reduce their work force because of regulatory costs. Consumers pay higher prices, when businesses pass on the cost of implementing regulations. Small businesspeople pay, when they can't compete with foreign manufacturers who aren't burdened by the same regulations. Taxpayers pay, when cities and towns have to spend huge sums to comply with pointless federal mandates.

During the Reagan years, the President's Task Force on Regulatory Relief (headed by Vice President George Bush) started the barnacle-scraping. When Bush assumed the presidency, he worried about the "regulatory creep" that would undo the task force's work, unless his own administration committed itself to the same sort of effort. That's why Boyden Gray, the incoming White House counsel who had done much of the task force's work, talked to me during the 1988–89 transition about the need for someone who would review the work of the various regulation-writing departments and agencies, and referee any disputes among them without the President's having to intervene. I was interested, but wanted to broaden the old task force's operation and give it a new name, one that identified the ultimate aim of its mission. That's how the White House Council on Competitiveness came into being.

I checked with Dick Darman to see whether he would be comfortable with the arrangement Gray and I were discussing, since the Office of Information and Regulatory Affairs (OIRA), which oversees all the rules and regulations of the federal bureaucracy, was under the jurisdiction of the OMB director. John Glenn, chairman of the Senate's Government Affairs Committee, was refusing to confirm any Bush appointment to head OIRA until the administration agreed to cede some of the post's powers to Congress. This we were unwilling to do. Darman felt that the Competitiveness Council could fill the resulting void. He thought that in certain cases, when he might get caught in an argument with a Cabinet official, the Council's presence might work to his advantage.

Dick became one of the council's permanent members, along with John Sununu (and later Sam Skinner), Treasury Secretary Brady, Commerce Secretary Bob Mosbacher, Attorney General Dick Thornburgh (and later William Barr), EPA Administrator Bill Reilly, and economics adviser Mike Boskin. We filled out the council with other members of the White House staff to make sure the Bush team stayed behind it, and several people from my own office did its day-to-day work, preparing policy recommendations and trying to resolve regulatory conflicts before they worked their way up to higher levels. Al Hubbard, an Indiana businessman and good friend whose wife, Kathy, had been my campaign finance director in 1980, was the absolutely committed guy I brought in to serve as executive director. The President liked Hubbard because of his friendship with his son George. David McIntosh, a young lawyer who had previously been with the Justice Department, became his deputy. Once the team had been assembled, we went looking for dragons to slay. Over the next few years we managed to put our sword into a few of them, and at other times we got scorched by their breath. But the battles were always worth fighting.

Take our struggles with the Food and Drug Administration. We announced the ambitious goal of radically reducing the period it takes to approve new drugs for treating serious diseases. We wanted to cut the average time of their getting to market by 45 percent, from nine and a half to five and a half years. Toward this end we recommended using private universities to review some of the testing data, allowing drugs approved in other industrialized nations to be sold in the United States, and redirecting the FDA's efforts toward testing for safety and away from determining whether a drug actually works.

We had some success in getting the agency to implement accelerated approval for AIDS drugs. In battling the FDA, we got some unlikely support from the late Congressman Ted Weiss, a Manhattan liberal whose district had been especially hard hit by the disease. In fact, though they might not like to admit it, the radical group of AIDS activists, ACT UP, had a powerful Washington ally in the Council on Competitiveness.

Unfortunately, the FDA let many of our recommendations die a slow death, even though it assured us of its cooperation in implementing them. The FDA cannot resist the impulse to overregulate. In the area of food labeling, it succeeded, over our objections, in greatly restricting the type of information that can be placed on labels unless it is precleared by the agency. They're now even starting to regulate restaurant menus—something we once managed to stop them from doing.

Some of the Competitiveness Council's most celebrated battles involved Bill Reilly, chief of the Environmental Protection Agency. I had a good personal relationship with Bill, who was friendly and dedicated to his work. But his concern with maintaining his own credibility in the environmental community sometimes overwhelmed his loyalty to the President. I would talk to Bill about this conflict. He would always counter that maintaining credibility with the environmentalists *was* being loyal to the President, since George Bush had expressed a determination to be the environmental President as well as the educational one. But in practical politics things aren't that simple, and our fight over implementing the Clean Air Act showed that. The council did not believe that the EPA and the state environmental bodies could require notice to environmental groups, and preclearance from the agencies, every time a manufacturer changed its operation. EPA argued that it needed this power to enforce the Clean Air Act—which, it claimed, we were trying to gut. We countered that this was bureaucratic overreach and would only help kill off manufacturing in the United States. In the end, we won, although Bill Clinton has sought to reverse the decision.

This was one instance where President Bush sat through an immense amount of testimony and statements and discussion and got personally involved in hashing out regulatory decisions. When Reilly pushed, he usually got his way—since the President remained conscious of his environmental campaign pledges. Like all of us, Bush hoped to be on the politically popular side of this issue, even though many of the regulations put into the Clean Air bill ended up costing industry billions and billions of dollars for only marginal improvements to air quality. There were moments during these discussions where the way Congress was taking advantage of both Reilly and the President was apparent, and at a number of points I just urged him to veto the whole Clean Air Act. If it was going to be loaded with a plethora of provisions we didn't want, then it would be better to have no bill at all. But the President hadn't liked being the first President to veto a "civil rights bill," and he wasn't going to veto an environmental one on top of that.

In the end, the EPA prevailed and got most of its regulations. It successfully resisted the council's efforts to expand "pollution trading" arrangements that would have reduced the costs of clean air by allowing companies that can clean up their emissions cheaply to "overcomply" and sell credits to other companies, whose compliance costs are higher.

Wetlands became another battleground. During the campaign, George Bush promised that there would be "no net loss" of them during his administration, a pledge that Reilly and the EPA went way overboard trying to fulfill. Along with the Department of Agriculture and the Fish and Wildlife Service, the EPA went about rewriting the federal government's wetlands manual, subjecting huge new tracts of land to federal control. This effort created a tremendous backlash among farmers, developers, and homeowners who suddenly could not use their own property. A battle was joined between pro-environmental appointees who wanted an expansive definition of wetland and pro-property-rights appointees who wanted to restrain the federal government. In July 1991 I was astonished to discover that thousands of acres of Indiana farmland that I'd seen with my own eyes and walked over with my own dry feet were, by the EPA's standards, wetlands. The council came down on the side of property rights. EPA published the new rule our way but then worked with environmental lobbyists to create public opposition. Farm groups and developers supported us, but Congress passed an appropriations rider prohibiting enforcement of the old, more realistic, manual. Eventually the administration compromised on a version somewhere between the council's and EPA's.

Perhaps our most successful battle against Bill Reilly involved the biodiversity (or Rio) treaty. As it was written, this agreement would have killed U.S. innovations in biotechnology, a cutting-edge realm of research and manufacturing where, if we're going to remain competitive with the rest of the industrialized world, American success is absolutely crucial. We kept Reilly from agreeing to the treaty, even though the sympathetic media uproar he generated put pressure on the United States to sign. Since coming into office, President Clinton has gone ahead and signed it, but only after the treaty language was changed to ensure that patents and other intellectual property rights were protected, thus vindicating the council's position.

The Competitiveness Council became a power center, a place in Washington where things actually got done. It drove Democratic

Congressmen and their staffs crazy, because they wanted to be the ones dictating regulations to the agency bureaucrats. They didn't like the idea that the White House was telling its own Cabinet members what those regulations should be. They saw this little council increasing in power and stature, having much to say about what the government was doing or not doing, and they didn't like that one bit. Congressman Henry Waxman called it a "shadow government," while Congressman George Miller, chairman of the House Interior Committee, went sound-bite crazy with his description of it as "a polluter Star Chamber."

It drove them crazy that they couldn't haul Al Hubbard up to testify on Capitol Hill, but that was their own fault. If they'd really needed someone to go up and testify about regulation, they could have confirmed our OIRA appointees. I was willing to have Al go up to the Hill and brief Congress, but only if he did not have to waive his executive privilege and give formal testimony. This offer was spurned; Waxman and company preferred whining to the cameras to any real give and take. At one point the council was being investigated by seven different congressional committees, and there were calls for Hubbard's head. Senator Gore insisted that Al's part ownership of World Wide Chemicals, in Indianapolis, put him in violation of conflict-of-interest laws while he was reviewing regulations for the Clean Air Act. There was, in fact, no conflict. Hubbard recused himself from any decision making that might directly affect his company. Gore never followed up on this; Al Hubbard is originally from Memphis, and some mutual friends of Hubbard and Gore quietly got the Senator to back off. But the investigating committees did go on elaborate fishing expeditions for the council's records, and I refused to cooperate on grounds of executive privilege. We were perfectly within our constitutional rights, so the liberals in Congress then tried another tactic: they attempted to cut our funding. But this only galvanized our supporters in the business and farm communities, as well as many conservatives on the Hill. We were able to stop them in the Senate. Even so, the fierceness with which they went after us shows why the lifer bureaucrats in federal agencies are always more scared of congressional staffers than the White House. Bill Clinton is currently finding out the same thing: it doesn't change much from Republican to Democrat.

We were making things happen, and the more we were attacked by the liberal special interest groups and their congressional allies and the bureaucrats, the harder we pushed. If they hadn't cried foul, we wouldn't have been doing our job. Ralph Nader's group charged that the "Quayle Council" showed a pattern of intervention on behalf of businesses that had given "a torrent of contributions to the Bush-Quayle campaign." It's only obvious that businesspeople seeking regulatory relief would feel more comfortable coming to the council than to, say, Ralph Nader. Did some campaign contributors benefit? Probably. Just as all the liberal political action committees (PACs) supporting the Waxmans and Millers and Metzenbaums in Congress benefited by having their agendas pushed. I told the council's staff that they were to maintain an open-door policy—we'd even listen to Ralph Nader. They were to give a hearing to anyone legitimately seeking relief from government regulation. But since I had to be the final decision maker, I myself would never hear a direct plea from any business or interest group. The staff was very sensitive about protecting me from any such contact. I preserved what powers the council did have by avoiding turf battles we couldn't win. If I'd overplayed my hand and forced the President to take the side of a Cabinet secretary against the council, word of that defeat would spread quickly, leaving us with that much less clout for the next fight.

By 1991 the council was often in the news. The press loved the story, either because it agreed with the council's opponents (we were the "back door for business") or because the council's activities gave the press a chance to write about infighting within the administration. (The council was one of the reasons Woodward and Broder did their series.) In many ways the attention was helpful. It was impossible for the council to review all regulations and stifle all the bad ideas generated by the agencies, and the press coverage (especially those articles claiming we had more power than we did) sent a signal to those agencies to keep regulation in check.

On a personal level, the coverage had a few drawbacks. I developed an antienvironmental image, which was not in line with the truth. When I was in the Senate, I wrote legislation to protect the Indiana Dunes and to add territory to the Hoosier National Forest. I was always in favor of aiding industry in the development of new technology that would not only clean up the environment but prove to be exportable as well. One reason I'm pro-competition is that without a robust economy we won't have the wealth to undertake the legitimate environmental cleanups and protections we all support.

Competition beats regulation every time, whether you're trying to repair the environment or mainstream the disabled. After the 1988 election, Dave Beckwith got a call from his old college friend George Covington, a visually impaired photographer. Covington made him the following proposition: "Dave, it took two hundred years for the American media to create negative images and stereotypes against disabled people in this country. It took them only two months to do the job on your boss. Do you think he would be willing to help us change our image if we help him change his?" George Covington became my special assistant for disability policy, and the approach he took was always unsentimental and competitive, the kind we'd taken for years at the *Huntington Herald-Press*, which made a point of hiring people with disabilities. To take an example, this is how George puts the case for "universal design" of home health care equipment: "Why do you think we're getting our butt kicked by the Japanese? They look at what we do and design it better; it's more applicable to more people. . . . There are billions of dollars to be made, and if the home-health-care industry does not wake up to that fact, it's going to turn around and its chief competitor is going to have a rising sun on it."

On balance, coverage of the council was a big plus for me. It gave me more clout with the President and the Cabinet, and just a little more standing with the public. My deregulating powers may have been exaggerated, but as political images go, dangerous is a lot better than stupid. As a *Wall Street Journal* editorial noted on November 25, 1991: "It wasn't long ago that Vice President Dan Quayle was said to be Washington's village idiot. All of a sudden he's becoming its scheming Rasputin. This can only mean he's begun to accomplish something."

29 | Too Many Lawyers

It's only logical: too much government regulation breeds too many lawyers. Since all professions, like all bureaucracies, want to perpetuate themselves, legions of American attorneys (more per capita than anywhere else in the world) keep creating new thickets of regulation which produce lucrative work for themselves. More important, they produce a society whose members are too quick to sue one another, without ever considering the costs to American productivity.

My interest in product liability reform went back to my first days in Congress, and by the time I was halfway through my vice-presidency the situation was even worse than it had been in the late 1970s. Product liability, by 1991, was costing American firms fifteen times what it was costing some of their foreign competitors, and the worst cost of all was a loss of jobs. That summer somebody in Columbus, Ohio, told me about the business he used to have making components for ladders and scaffolding. He'd been sued so many times that he could no longer afford the cost of defending himself. Finally, he just closed down. Now this fellow wasn't sued because he was a negligent manufacturer. In fact, he never lost a single one of those lawsuits. He was sued so much because that's the routine way of doing business in America: people look for any way to trap someone in the regulatory forest and squeeze some money out of him in an outrageous settlement just to end the expensive, emotionally draining litigation. *Nuisance suits* is the familiar term; *legalized extortion* might be an even better one.

We have become a crazily litigious country. Today a baseball comes crashing through a window, and instead of picking it up and returning it to the neighbor whose kid knocked it through— and who pays the glazier's bill in a reasonable, neighborly way— the "victim" hangs on to the baseball as evidence and sues the neighbor. (Or the baseball's manufacturer. Or the glass maker. Or usually all three.) Several lawyers are soon billing hours, and the civil docket has been further crowded by one more pointless case that's probably going to be part of the 92 percent of cases that get settled before they come to trial—but not before a huge amount of time and money has been wasted on everything from "discovery" to picking a jury that will be discharged before it ever deliberates this case that shouldn't have gotten started in the first place. In America we now sue first and ask questions later. The system—and the mind-set—are inefficient and anticompetitive. By not paying the huge legal costs their U.S. counterparts are bearing year after year, foreign companies have a tremendous advantage. American businesses and individuals spend more than $80 billion annually on the direct costs of litigation and higher insurance premiums. Include the extra costs and the figure can top $300 billion.

It was natural for the Competitiveness Council to look not only at laws but at lawyers as well. In Dick Thornburgh the administration was lucky to have an attorney general interested in seeing the legal system as a competitiveness issue, and he didn't want the question to die in some turf battle among the Competitiveness Council, the Economic Policy Council, and the Domestic Policy Council, which he headed. He wanted to see something actually get done. That's why in January 1991 he helped the Competitiveness Council put together an advisory group headed by Ken Starr, the U.S. solicitor general, whose charge it was to develop proposals for reforming the civil litigation system in the United States. By August they had come up with a list of fifty good ideas.

The American Bar Association is the chief professional organization for what, at that time, were the nation's 729,000 lawyers. Its annual convention was scheduled for mid-August in Atlanta, and I eagerly sought an invitation to pitch the proposals of Ken Starr's group to the delegates. Ken himself went down to Atlanta the day before I was scheduled to speak, and he warned me about what I might find. He said that many of the lawyers he was talking to were sympathetic to some of the reforms I would be proposing (such as alternative dispute resolution and reform of the discovery process) but that I should expect a reception more polite than enthusiastic.

As it turned out, the greeting I received wasn't even polite. I would soon come to realize that the ABA, dominated by liberal lawyers and a liberal staff, has become a partisan organization, out of touch not just with the American people but with many American lawyers as well. Its leaders tend to be glibly fond of the cameras. They're a noisy bunch, they raise a lot of money, and they contribute heavily to Democrats. (Bill Clinton would have no more loyal and lucrative constituency in 1992 than America's trial lawyers.)

I knew the speech—especially its line about America's having 70 percent of the world's lawyers—would be controversial, and that was fine with me. I didn't want controversy for controversy's sake. I wanted it because that's the way a new item gets onto the public agenda. Still, I didn't expect to get into quite the dustup I did with the lawyers, nor to experience something completely new to my vice-presidency: an avalanche of good press, the best I would have in my four years in office.

When I went in to address the House of Delegates, I was walking into a trap. Just before I went on, the ABA's president, John Curtin, Jr., came to me and said, "We would like for you to stay after your speech, so that I can respond." This was not the original plan, and I turned to Dave Beckwith and Craig Whitney, one of my advance men, and asked them what this was all about. They told me that they had already told Curtin I couldn't stay. Just by looking out to the stage, I could see that he was trying to set me up: there were no seats by the podium, which meant that, if I stayed to listen to Curtin's rebuttal, I would either have to stand by him at the lectern or go out and sit in the audience. Either way, he would have the last word and I would look like a schoolboy being reprimanded. I told him that once I had raised the issues in my speech, I wanted to continue the dialogue—but not in the format he was proposing. There would be other occasions and venues. First, I wanted the chance for my speech to be reported in the press, so that its ideas could get out to the general public. Then the lawyers could counterattack, and we could mix it up.

I went out and gave the speech, which boiled down to a set of specific proposals for reducing the eighteen million civil lawsuits being filed each year in America. Among the suggestions was a call to limit the discovery process, which is often used just as a means for delay and harassment. Unnecessary document requests and depositions can bring an expensive halt to much of a company's operation. I mentioned one judge who said his policy is "just to have the parties exchange filing cabinets," since that winds up being what happens anyway. What's needed instead are procedures requiring both sides in a civil suit to exchange certain core information, after which limits are put on further requests for documents and depositions. If one party wants to go beyond those limits, okay: he can pay the costs his adversary incurs producing the information. Along these same lines of fairness, I proposed adoption of the English Rule, which is used by most Western countries and requires the loser of a civil suit to pay the costs of his opponent. We would modify it and call it the Fairness Rule, stipulating that the loser's cost couldn't exceed what he'd spent on his own case. This would keep one side from overspending in the hope that a judgment in its favor would bankrupt the opposition. And we would provide for a certain amount of judicial discretion in the application of all this. Movement in this direction is absolutely essential if we're going to motivate disputing parties to think twice before they file a suit.

I also proposed to the ABA delegates a "multidoor courthouse," a means by which the courts can offer methods and forums for conflict resolution that stop short of actually trying a lawsuit. Wherever possible, litigation should be replaced by mediation. And where that is not possible, we should at least limit the amount of punitive damages that can be imposed on a losing party. As things now stand, these damages are often grotesquely out of proportion to any offense that's been committed. These were the most fundamental changes we were proposing, but there were many others as well—from changing the rules on experts' testimony, to reform of "summary judgment" procedures, to the institution of greater flexibility in judicial assignments so that the clogged civil litigation system at least has judges available in the places they're most needed. We had so many proposals, in fact, that they couldn't all fit into that speech, but I offered the lawyers, who listened more or less in silence, about as much meat as they could be expected to digest in a single sitting. Even so, as soon as I finished, I knew that John Curtin had a bad case of indigestion. He was moving right to the microphone I had just used, and I knew he was going to attack most of my proposals. So at that point I made a snap decision: I would stay and listen after all. I was going to stand there, right at his elbow, while he trashed what we'd worked so hard to develop. I would do it because, whether he knew it or not, I wasn't going to let him have the last word.

His "rebuttal" was more like a diatribe—a whole bushel of red herrings. "Anyone who believes a better day dawns when lawyers are eliminated bears the burden of explaining who will take their place—who will protect the poor, the injured, the victims of negligence, the victims of racial discrimination, and the victims of violence."

I stood and listened to this—as Curtin's cheering section applauded him—and I got furious. I'm sure he could see my face turning red, and I'm sure he was pleased with himself, too. As soon as he finished, he seemed sure that I was going to leave the stage with him. But I now had no intention of doing that. The microphone was free, and I was going to use it. Now he could stand there and take it.

"Nobody is talking about eliminating lawyers," I said. "Nobody is talking about not allowing individuals to have their day in court. So let's not be extreme. Let's focus on the very fundamental problem, and that is that we should challenge the status quo. I am convinced we can have a better legal system in America if we sit down and work together." Some of what he had said was so wild that it didn't deserve a response (such as the talk of "violence," as if that were primarily a matter for the civil courts and not the criminal ones). Some of the audience seemed to realize this, because my rejoinder got more applause than my speech had.

Suddenly, what would probably have been a page 20 story was page 1. And I had the extraordinary experience of enjoying the morning papers! The *New York Times* reported that Curtin's "dressing-down [of Quayle] was unusually sharp for such a noteworthy speaker to the bar group, and several past presidents of the association expressed uneasiness with it afterward." *USA Today* referred to an "ambushing" of the Vice President and quoted a lawyer from Shreveport, Louisiana, as saying, "I think it was discourteous, and I'd say 85 percent of the lawyers here thought it was discourteous." My line about the United States having 70 percent of the world's lawyers was the sound bite of the day, and over the next week or so, editorial pages took up the question of legal reform. They were almost unanimous in saying that our proposals were worthy of serious discussion. The cartoonists had a field day with the convention incident. (My favorite was in the *Albuquerque Journal,* where I was driving a little van labeled "Council on Competitiveness." It was giving a gentle nudge to the back bumper of a limousine marked "ABA." From inside the limo, four lawyers were screaming "Whiplash!!") I had long since given up on the idea that a single "defining moment" would recast my image, but this was as good as anything that had come along in two and a half years. In fact, for a politician it doesn't get any better than this: good press for doing something that he strongly believes in,

The few dissenting voices were pretty weak. The *New York Times* quoted Kristen Rand, counsel for Consumers Union, as saying that our initiatives would leave "more uncompensated victims and fewer incentives to make safer products." She should have been thinking of situations like the one involving an experimental vaccine that might reduce the incidence of HIV-positive babies born to mothers with AIDS: fearing lawsuits, companies had been reluctant to proceed with testing it.

The mail I got was as heartening as the press. Charles E. Stokes, Jr., wrote from San Antonio that "for some years, I ran and owned the largest sheepswool combing mill west of the Mississippi. Last year we endeavored to install a similar mill in Texas, but were told by insurance brokers that workmen's compensation, health and liability insurance would cost more than the cost of the machinery for such a plant! Obviously, we have opted not to build the plant in this country." Dr. David E. Ison, a dentist from

Manchester, Kentucky, wrote to say that he had "a substantial caseload of elderly patients, who desperately need dental care I could provide at much less expense to the patient and their families; but because of the certainty of lawsuits and the concomitant loss of my professional reputation if an unforeseen complication develops, I am totally unable to help these individuals. It is getting to the point that my staff and I cannot help anyone [elderly] into our operatory chairs for fear of negligence lawsuits if they fall."

The system isn't just hurting businesspeople and medical professionals. Other citizens, at moments in their lives when they need the courts the most, are being let down by them. Charla Snyder Toth wrote my office with the following story from Alexandria, Virginia: "Our house we were renting burned down last August due to faulty electrical wiring. We lost everything. Our landlord refused to give us our security deposit back. We took it to Small Claims Court, but our landlord had the right to have the case moved to General District Court—which required us to hire an attorney. We won the case. But our landlord has appealed. He knows that we won't spend another $1,000 in attorney fees to take it to Circuit Court—so even though we won, we lost! What a sad system. . . ."

Letters like these made me all the more determined to follow up on our proposals. I kept an eye out for outrageous examples of litigiousness, ones that could vividly illustrate my point. (Among the best of them: In October 1991, the *Wall Street Journal* reported that a legal frenzy had erupted among lawyers trying to "Line Up Teen 'Victims'" who would claim they had been injured as a result of buying records by the group Milli Vanilli, who were later revealed to have lip-synched their lyrics.) But we did more than keep the issue alive for discussion. We acted. We drafted some model statutes that the states could look at in their own attempts to reform their individual court systems, and President Bush signed an executive order that actually implemented some of the proposed reforms for civil litigation involving the U.S. government, which happens to be the largest single consumer of legal resources. We sent legislation to the Hill that would apply them to the rest of the system as well, but we were never able to get the bill out of the judiciary committees. Although there was a close vote on product liability legislation, the coalition supporting it did not support civil justice reform. It was not possible to get senior Republicans to push the bill either.

Powerful interests (chief among them the plaintiffs' bar of the trial lawyers' association) are blocking these sorely needed reforms. Nonetheless, this issue is not going to go away. It is too tied to fundamental questions of American competitiveness. What's more, the health care debate now under way in the country is going to keep the matter of legal reform front and center. Almost everyone agrees that the high cost of malpractice insurance is one of the villains driving up health costs, and almost every new health care proposal seeks a way of bringing them down. If limiting liability for physicians is good, then reforming the liability system for all kinds of other businesses and individuals is good as well. Bill Clinton and his trial lawyer supporters may not agree with our ideas for legal reform, but the President's health care plan is going to give supporters of our proposals a great big opening through which to drive home their point.

In 1993, two summers after my Atlanta encounter with John Curtin, Attorney General Janet Reno addressed the ABA convention in New York. "I love lawyers," she told the delegates, in an obvious reference to the "lawyer bashing" I had supposedly engaged in back in 1991. Well, I love lawyers, too. I even married one. But in the twenty years since Marilyn and I hung out our Quayle & Quayle shingle in Huntington, the legal profession has changed, and mostly for the worse. It's a much more cutthroat business now. Clients are less loyal to their law firms than they used to be, and the big firms will do whatever they can to keep their clients. The public good sometimes seems to be the lowest item on their list of priorities. It should and could be different, and I'm hopeful that our program of reform will help things along. But I know that changing the legal culture of our country will not happen quickly. The problems with it have been around too long to be easily uprooted, and I'm not the first Republican to take up the cry of reform. "Discourage litigation," wrote another one. "Persuade your neighbors to compromise whenever you can. Point out to them how the final winner is often a real loser—in fees, expenses, and waste of time. As a peace-maker the lawyer has a superior opportunity of being a good man." So, back around 1850, wrote a self-taught lawyer named Abraham Lincoln.

PART FIVE

Losing and Winning

1992

30 | Trouble on the Right

December 7, 1991, brought the fiftieth anniversary of the Japanese attack on Pearl Harbor, and no President could have presided more appropriately over the commemorations than George Bush. A half century after serving as one of America's youngest naval aviators, the President stood near the *Arizona* memorial to proclaim his country's triumph not only in World War II but in the cold war that had followed. Speaking of the sailors who perished in the Japanese attack, he said, "Don't you think they're saying: 'Fifty years have passed. Our country is the undisputed leader of the free world. We are at peace.' Don't you think each one is saying: 'I did not die in vain.'"

The ceremonies in Hawaii were an emotional time for the President, but he made it clear that he felt no rancor toward our former enemies. He also warned against a new isolationism, both economic and military, that was beginning to grow in the United States. Along with those who favored protectionism for American products (and minimized the disastrous effects a trade war would have) there were those who looked at the end of the Soviet threat and decided the United States could now pursue an isolationist "America first" foreign policy that had not had any serious advocates for a half century. Some of these new isolationists were in the Republican Party, and at Pearl Harbor the President challenged the seductive vision they offered of a "Fortress America."

The anniversary provided a chance for George Bush to look his presidential best, but his strong performance in Hawaii belied the disarray within his administration. With 1992 only weeks away, the internal White House was being torn apart.

John Sununu, who had gotten a wave of bad press about his personal travel at government expense and who was forced to take most of the blame for the President's falling popularity, had left the administration. It's true that John used perks. He never did anything his predecessors hadn't done. But you can't push the limits when there are so many people out there whom you've angered or who just don't like you. John gave them the rope, and they hung him. The last months of his tenure were chaotic. The Cabinet got into a mild state of revolt, going around the chief of staff and directly to the President.

I don't know who leaked the information about Sununu's travels, but it was an inside job and it was lethal. John had plenty of enemies within the administration and more in the campaign apparatus, especially Bob Teeter, who told people he wouldn't serve as campaign chairman if Sununu was chief of staff. This was a bluff, but it became a factor in forcing Sununu out. John was torn between leaving and doing what was even tougher—hanging in there. One of the tasks I least relished in my four years as Vice President was telling Sununu that he had to go, but that's what the President asked me to do after one of our weekly lunches late in 1991. Bush wanted this handled with the utmost care. He and Sununu had a special friendship. The President was naturally distressed that John's accumulating problems left him with only one option. However unpleasant it would be letting John go, though, it had to be done. The President's son George W. had already had a tough talk with John, but it fell to me to ask for his resignation— just as Vice President George Bush had had to ask for that of Don Regan, chief of staff in the Reagan White House.

"What?!" asked Sununu, when I gave him the news in his office. He was visibly upset and wanted to talk directly to the President. "When does he want it?"

"Today," I had to tell him.

"Today?"

This was an unexpected blow. He expressed concern about the timing of the announcement and the manner of his departure. My conversation with him, though brief, was cordial.

I got back to my own office, where Bush soon called me, wanting to know how John had taken it. "Not well," I said. "But he will be a good soldier. He just wants to talk to you about the details." The President couldn't have been surprised by John's reaction. He knew how much he owed Sununu for the revival of his own presidential campaign in New Hampshire four years earlier, and for his tough, loyal services as chief of staff.

Bill Kristol was sitting in my office when the President buzzed me, and he heard my part of this conversation. This was one of the times I had to rein him in in no uncertain terms: "This will not leak," I demanded—and it didn't. Later on, the President called again and I joined him and Sununu in the Oval Office. We worked out an arrangement by which John would stay on for a few months in the role of special counsel to the President. John was unusually subdued throughout the meeting.

In December 1991, the President asked Transportation Secretary Sam Skinner to replace Sununu. I had strongly recommended him. When he took over, there was at first a great sense of relief. He wanted the job, was loyal to the President, and got on well with Mrs. Bush. He and his wife had been close to the President's daughter, Doro, during the difficult period of her divorce, and that had helped bond him to the Bush family. Everyone in the West Wing looked forward to his coming in and getting things back on track.

But it didn't work out that way. Cabinet secretaries, like Sam, and Don Regan before him, have a hard time making the transition to the White House staff. As department secretaries they've gotten used to having their own chiefs of staff, and now they have to do the heavy administrative lifting and function as the President's gatekeeper. It's a transition that usually doesn't work, and it didn't work this time either. Skinner never really got the authority required for the job. Sununu's continuing presence in the White House as special counsel complicated matters, and Skinner ended up squandering precious time trying to dilute Darman's power and influence around the White House. The two of them clashed from the beginning and never developed the working relationship that Darman and Sununu had managed. Sam also hired a management guru to take a look at West Wing operations. The guy went around and interviewed everybody, getting them in an uproar, making them feel their jobs were threatened. When Sam did try to make personnel changes, they went over his head and appealed directly to the President. The end result of this whole efficiency review, predictably, was one more layer of bureaucracy. The new regime just didn't work, and during the first months of 1992, when the President should have been getting ready to mount a tough reelection drive, he was more or less serving as his own chief of staff, doing everything from scheduling to making foreign policy decisions.

Early in January, he suffered the most embarrassing episode of his four years in office, when he collapsed at a state dinner in Japan. The President had been scheduled to go there in December, but a number of his advisers convinced him to postpone, worried that the Christmas season economic news might provide a grim backdrop to the trip and that any more overseas travel would make Bush look more out of touch with domestic issues. They asserted it would be bad politics to go now. Brent Scowcroft was reluctant to join this chorus, but he eventually did. The President's own instincts were telling him to go, but he gave in to the postponement.

What I was seeing, though I didn't fully realize it, was George Bush's reluctance to assert his instincts on political matters. This hands-on policy President was deferring to campaign advisers because he lacked confidence as a politician. He didn't consider himself a good speaker and he didn't like the attack mode necessary for a bruising campaign. Having lost two Senate elections (one to Lloyd Bentsen in 1970) and the presidential nomination to Ronald Reagan in 1980, he thought of himself as a less than stellar campaigner. Actually, when his back was to the wall, he could be as good as any politician I've seen, but he detested what he perceived to be name-calling and ugliness.

What he never fully appreciated is the extent to which his opponents would say or do anything to get elected. Now that he was President he believed partisan politics could be left to others. This was a mistake. In politics, the candidate's instincts are crucial. It is the candidate who sets the tone and direction of the campaign. It is vital that he trust himself. Yet, as we approached the 1992 campaign it seemed that the President was beginning to hesitate.

He postponed the Japan trip, but he would still make it before the holiday season was completely over, while Congress was still out of town. No House or Senate members could fault him for paying too much attention to foreign policy, if he was working while they were still enjoying time with their families.

But it turned into a fiasco.

A month after the country had focused on America's triumphant comeback from Pearl Harbor, television was full of pictures of the President with his head cradled in the Japanese Prime Minister's lap—the worst kind of symbolism for a country that was becoming ever more anxious, even paranoid, about Japanese economic strength and business practices. From the beginning, the trip had seemed to proceed more from weakness than strength. The President brought with him a group of American CEOs—just as I had done the year before on a trip to South America and once after that on a second trip to Japan. There is nothing wrong with encouraging exports of American products. But this time it looked as if American business was begging for relief rather then seeking opportunities. Instead of seeing the mission as combative, the public got a hat-in-hand impression of it.

Bob Stempel, the chairman of General Motors, came to see me shortly before he left with the President and confessed his doubts about the whole undertaking. GM had fewer problems with Japan than the other automakers did, but Bob couldn't stay home if the rest of the Big Three were going. Aside from everything else, State and the NSC didn't like the idea of the CEOs from the auto industry making the trip. From the NSC's point of view, the President of the United States was going to visit our most powerful ally in the Pacific, with the whole thing looking as if it were being driven by the Commerce Department. Instead of dealing from the strength of our high-tech industries, we went with our struggling automotive companies, which had lost their market share by not keeping their products competitive. Aside from the Big Three, the business aspect of the trip was a success in that a number of historic business agreements were concluded. But in the public's mind the whole trip was a disaster—and January had a way of forecasting the year ahead of us.

The President never should have gone. He was tired before he set out for Tokyo, during a week when he should have been relaxing and preparing his agenda for the upcoming campaign. He was overworked, overscheduled, and exhausted, and finally he got sick. On the morning of January 8, I got a 5:45 A.M. phone call from Sam Skinner, telling me that Bush had collapsed. He said the President was all right: it was only the flu. But he warned me that the TV was likely to be reporting something different. Sure enough, I flipped on CNN, and there was a lot of speculation about the President's having suffered a heart attack. Before long the situation calmed down, and by 7:30 I was talking with Barbara Bush. I could tell from her voice, and by the fact that they weren't canceling the rest of the trip, that things were going to be okay. She talked to me as a wife who was annoyed by her husband's stubbornness: the President had overdone things, even playing tennis when he wasn't up to it. If he'd gone to bed instead, he might not have gotten so sick. She told me there was no need to be concerned.

If the President's collapse seemed to symbolize the country's economic anxieties, it also seemed a bad omen for the campaign we were beginning. The news came on the very day I was supposed to head up to New Hampshire and begin our reelection campaign in earnest. To make matters worse, we had a wreck on our way to the plane. My follow-up vehicle thought we were going through a light and didn't see our limo stop; they smashed into us and I had mild whiplash for two or three days. (No, I didn't think of calling a lawyer.) Ken Adelman, who was traveling with me, and I flashed back to the beginning of the 1988 campaign, which I'd started off with a pinched nerve from playing tennis with him. This time I just took Tylenol, and the pain went away after a few days, but it wasn't a very promising beginning. On top of everything else, I noticed, as soon as I arrived in New Hampshire, that the press contingent was larger than expected: the President's collapse was bringing them out, just as last May's atrial fibrillation had.

I was there to help stave off Pat Buchanan's primary challenge,

which he had launched with the claim that our administration
had betrayed the Reagan revolution, to which he was the true
conservative heir. I had had mixed feelings about Pat for some
time. I liked watching him on the political talk shows; he was a
no-nonsense conservative, fast and articulate, and he hit hard.
But there were things about him that bothered me deeply, and not
just his unrelenting and unjustified criticism of the President.
During Desert Shield, he had taken a position that was isolationist, and I thought some of his statements opposing Israeli policy
bordered on being anti-Semitic, especially his reference to Israel's
supporters as an "amen corner." During my Senate tenure he had
made some distasteful statements in the debate over sanctions
against South Africa, and he often used language about members
of Congress that was way out of bounds. There's a fine line
between the political cutting edge and what is objectionable, and
all too often Pat crossed it. The President was obviously no big
fan of his, but they had gotten along well enough when Buchanan
worked in the Reagan White House. Don Regan had brought him
in because Buchanan spoke a political language he understood,
but I think Regan realized that, once he was inside, Pat went
around making more trouble than he was worth. Ideology and
cultural warfare made him tick. Rather than the Oval Office,
Buchanan is much better suited to "Crossfire" (he and his cohort
Michael Kinsley are perfect for each other).

I was a little bit surprised when Buchanan decided to go ahead
with his campaign in 1992. Everyone knew it would be a futile
effort, but I underestimated his ego, as well as the drive of his sister, Bay, who had as much to do with his deciding to run as he
did. I also should have realized that Pat, a Washington insider,
knew full well the effect a presidential bid would have on his lecture fees and other celebrity income. Pete du Pont, who could
also have gotten in, running as an antitax candidate and pounding away at the 1990 budget deal, might have had a better chance
as an alternative to Bush. In 1990 he got as far as calling state
party chairmen all over the country to find out whether they
thought the tax increase had been a terrible mistake. The Gulf
War more or less scared him off, just as it scared off a number of
Democrats who might have made the race. Still, we were eventu-

ally so vulnerable that I have a feeling Pete du Pont is still kicking himself for not getting in.

There are ways an incumbent President can turn a modest primary challenge to his advantage. Back in 1972, Nixon, after going to China and imposing wage and price controls, had some opposition from conservative Congressman John Ashbrook, and a couple of primary victories allowed the President to look like a winner early in the election year. They also let him look—to those Democrats who might be thinking of voting for him—like a moderate, someone who was holding off the more conservative elements of his party. With the Buchanan challenge, things were a bit different. Primary-night victories didn't hurt the President's image, but every time his role as a moderate appealed to potential Democratic and Independent voters, he risked alienating a bloc of conservative Republicans who remained skeptical of him (more than those disappointed in Nixon) and whom he didn't want sitting out the fall election. Buchanan was a much different campaigner from John Ashbrook. Buchanan ran a tough, punch-'em-in-the-nose, take-no-prisoners race, and his attacks on the President were invariably sharp and quotable. We always knew we would beat him, but we couldn't be sure what damage he'd inflict along the way.

In any case, Pat wasn't our biggest problem in New Hampshire; the economy was. The Reagan Eighties had been very good to the state: its low-tax economy had continued to grow even during the 1982 recession; by early 1992 because of bad loans and a regulatory-induced recession, it was a basket case, an East Coast California. It had been the state to turn things around for George Bush in 1988, when with Governor John Sununu's help it handed him his key primary victory over Bob Dole. Bush had even made a point of saying "Thank you, New Hampshire" when he claimed final victory on election night in November. Over the next four years the bottom fell out of the state. Its citizens were aware of the President's frequent presence next door in Maine, when he was on vacation, and some of them felt they were being neglected. Some Republicans were not ruling out the possibility that Buchanan might actually come in first in New Hampshire; even Senator Warren Rudman, whom I campaigned with on that January 8 trip, was concerned about how well Pat might do there.

Inside the White House there were two schools of thought about how to deal with Buchanan. One said to leave him alone, not offend him, and avoid bringing him any more attention than he was already getting. These were the people who never understood conservatives and were scared of their reaction. Believing conservatives would never really accept George Bush as being "one of them," this group tended to duck instead of punching back. The other side—which I tended toward—said not to underestimate him: stick your nose in there and hit back. I felt we had to take this guy on, that the conservatives would eventually come back to us, even if we temporarily alienated them by attacking one of their favorites. I didn't want to get personal about it, either. We could engage him on the issues, about which we had huge, principled disagreements. Buchanan liked name-calling (I was the President's "pit puppy"), but we could make our case on substance.

Protectionism was a potent issue in New Hampshire, and it was understandable that people hurting economically might want to embrace it. But we were sure, whatever problems the economy might have, that free trade wasn't one of them. As a reporter for the *Christian Science Monitor* wrote that year: "The rise of exports has, in fact, been one of the few economic success stories of this administration." On that first January trip to New Hampshire I visited three different manufacturing plants and reminded voters that thirty-five thousand jobs in the state depended on exports. I kept hearing that New Hampshire's Republicans wanted to send us a message, so I told them: "We've got the message. The President understands the problem and is doing something about it. We have a growth agenda. Don't send us a message of protectionism. Don't send us a message of isolationism. Those policies will only make your problems worse." That was our other big disagreement with Buchanan. We believed in global leadership, not retreat. We believed in taking charge and being responsible.

I was looking forward to running on our outstanding foreign policy record. The cold war had been won; nuclear weapons dramatically reduced; Germany reunited; Eastern Europe made newly democratic; apartheid dismantled; Noriega put in jail; Kuwait made free; a Middle East peace settlement advanced;

GATT nearly completed; and NAFTA made ready for congressional approval. But when it came to economics, *had* we really gotten the message? Were we really offering a coherent vision that the voters could identify and, more important, identify *with*? The campaign people told George Bush that he was perceived as not really caring about voters' economic problems. To meet the problem head-on, they sent the President up to New Hampshire to say, "Message: I care." This only made matters worse. He often spoke in that funny, choppy way, and it could be both charming and memorable, but this particular sound bite was a small disaster. It sounded empty.

His New Hampshire operation was a mess. Nobody liked or trusted anybody. Republican Governor Judd Gregg was running for the Senate, while Gregg's father, who had also been Governor, was the de facto Bush campaign chairman. Both Greggs greatly disliked Sununu, and he returned the feeling. Sununu was still at the White House as special counsel, and he certainly knew New Hampshire, but the campaign didn't want him in the picture. Warren Rudman, who was getting ready to retire from the Senate, wanted to run the show, even though he'd been for Dole over Bush in 1988. He, too, found it difficult to get along with the Greggs. The whole thing was a recipe for pettiness and political disaster. Every bit of logistics (who traveled on the bus, who sat on the dais) turned into an endless negotiation and ultimately a crisis.

The President had barely recovered from his Japanese trip when he went up to the state to make eight speeches in a single day—and to pose beside a cow. They'd forgotten to mention agriculture in any of the speeches, so some genius of an advance person decided this would be a good form of substitute communication with the state's farmers. On top of everything, the ads the campaign was running were just awful. There was no message. There was no theme. Even the visual quality was third-rate. I dropped into the Oval Office early one morning to tell the President how bad I thought they were. I had the cassettes in my hands and I wanted the President to view them with me. But he begged off. He told me he didn't want to interfere. I had a visceral feeling that these idiotic ads were indicative of the campaign ahead. I should have insisted, but he was the boss and he was telling me he didn't want to "second-guess the campaign." He thought they were experts on campaigning and he was the expert on being President.

I couldn't believe what I was hearing. That was almost exactly the mistake I made in 1988: trusting the campaign experts instead of myself. The President was saying he didn't want to interfere with the campaign, but he *was* the campaign. They needed him. For the first time, I felt powerless. I knew in my heart and mind the campaign was seriously off track, but what could I do to convince the President? He wanted to delegate these responsibilities and there was a limit to how much I could protest. Unfortunately, I took his lead and let this pass—but not without a heavy heart. By the time the President was willing to admit how bad the campaign operation was, it was too late.

I enjoyed campaigning—any campaign was fun after 1988—but I couldn't get away from our political troubles, or the economic ones facing the voters. I remember one conversation I had in a restaurant with a woman who was employed at a high-tech company across the border in Massachusetts. Her husband had been out of work for a year. She was a Republican and still inclined to vote for us, but her husband, also a Republican, was very uncertain—not only about how he would vote but about how his whole future would shape up. Stories like this were too common, and we were not putting out a message that responded to them. We should have been pushing tax cuts and cuts in capital gains and hammering away at Congress, but the administration couldn't decide when or whether it should do anything. Some of us argued that we had to take action immediately. Others, like Darman, wanted to wait until the President gave his State of the Union address at the end of the month; they said he was best at big events like that. This was true. Darman always had the answers. But in this case we needed a whole new strategy that didn't just rely on big plays. We needed a sustained drive.

I always knew that I might become an election issue, but it would be months before I worried about being dropped from the ticket. For the time being, logic said that a conservative challenge like Buchanan's made me more valuable to Bush. Richard Nixon told Larry King, "For those that think George Bush has become a flaming liberal, Dan Quayle will be out there preaching the old-time religion."

During the New Hampshire campaigning, another boost came when Bob Woodward and David Broder finally published their seven-part series on me in the *Washington Post*. The two journalists spent six months on the story. It was the most extensive research ever done on a Vice President. According to *Newsweek*, the articles showed me passing "through a metal detector of political credibility set up by two of the paper's most formidable reporters." Of course, a lot of Woodward and Broder's colleagues could not bear this. The *Post*'s own media critic, Howard Kurtz, wrote that "the series has been vigorously debated in the *Post* newsroom. Most members of the national staff who were interviewed said they thought it was too favorable to Quayle. Some said readers had asked them whether the paper is cozying up to the Bush administration." Before the whole series had even run, Dan Rather trashed it in a radio commentary. Broder called him to ask why he didn't at least wait until all seven parts appeared, and Rather said he didn't need to; he could tell where it was going.

After I left office, Rather told me he thought the series was a "valentine" and that the *Washington Post* was trying to win favor with me because it looked like I might be the next President after Bush. Both of these assertions are pretty ridiculous. As for the first of them, I've since gone back and reread the Woodward-Broder series in book form, and that volume is not one I would recommend to my children or friends. Many people, not just friends and supporters, have said that in places it's far too critical of me, and it's clearly unfair to Marilyn.

In 1993, Broder told me that some of his colleagues in the press could not bring themselves to say anything about the series to him at the time it ran. The *Post*'s Ann Devroy told me that she remembered the way reporters had been expecting the series to be the final nail in my coffin—and lost interest when it turned out to be largely positive. "They worked too hard to make it balanced," some of them complained. Woodward and Broder—two of America's respected journalists—were "scorned" for being too kind, and the series' editors were blamed for not leading with the more negative parts. (Devroy says it made her regret not paying a little more attention to me all along.) Brit Hume says the media were "astonished" by the articles, and *U.S. News & World Report*'s Michael Barone says the press was so surprised by the series' content that it went into denial and just tried to keep it off the radar screen of presidential politics that year. Dan Rather has told me that he got over a dozen requests (from people in the *Post* newsroom) for his commentary attacking the series; and Kay Graham, who generally avoided interfering with her editorial product, let Woodward know that her friends were complaining about the articles. All in all, not a pretty story—but a revealing one. As Ann Devroy recently explained it to me, reporters wanted to rely on their first impressions of me. They didn't want to complicate them with any new, positive information from the series. They didn't want evidence that they had been wrong.

On February 18, 1992, Pat Buchanan received 37 percent of the vote—enough to keep his challenge alive and to highlight the President's problems with conservative voters and, more important, the economy. For the next couple of months I found myself chasing Pat, campaigning against him on the President's behalf from Georgia to South Dakota. Some people viewed this as a kind of duel between the two of us, a rehearsal for 1996, when we might be challenging each other for the Republican nomination. That hypothetical race presupposed a Bush victory in 1992 (which most of us still believed was coming) and Buchanan's retaining a large following; neither turned out to be true. Pat may have his fans, but the "Buchanan brigades" he talked about were largely a myth. We beat him in every single primary, and by the time we got to the convention in Houston, there weren't any sizable brigades to be found inside or outside the hall.

Still, he remained a persistent irritant, bashing us over peripheral issues like the National Endowment for the Arts, where our own appointment, John Frohnmayer, was such a disaster. Frohnmayer had no clear vision for the agency (the arts community didn't like him any better than we did), and he was absolutely at odds with the spirit of the administration when it came to funding art that was at best sexually graphic and at worst obscene. I remember my legislative affairs assistant, Bill Gribbin, showing me the Robert Mapplethorpe pictures. I could not believe the government was helping to underwrite a museum showing of them. I even showed those pictures to the President, who could barely bring himself to look at them. He said something about how he thought the NEA was in the process of cleaning up its act, but that never really happened under Frohnmayer. For many months, everyone urged George Bush to fire him, but the President held onto him until the end of February 1992, giving him chance after chance to correct the situation. Buchanan continued to make an issue of Frohnmayer, and the NEA, even after he was gone. Frohnmayer's thanks for George Bush's patience and misplaced loyalty was an endorsement of Bill Clinton. Obviously, on Frohnmayer, Buchanan was right.

Maybe the biggest problem with our campaign was having a pollster, Bob Teeter, in charge. Pollsters are trained to give information and advice in response to polling data, not to make the proactive management decisions essential to a good campaign. Teeter didn't like people with an edge, and that included savvy media strategist and Bush loyalist Roger Ailes, who had done an end run around him during the 1988 campaign. This time Teeter refused to lose control, and Ailes was out of the picture. Like Sununu and Atwater, Ailes had been totally loyal to George Bush, willing to catch any spear headed his way. In 1992 all three of these men were absent, and as the months went by, George Bush was more and more vulnerable. As we got close to the convention, there was almost unanimous sentiment for turning the operation over to Jim Baker. Even I, despite my history of problems with him, recommended that course to the President, but even after Baker arrived, wedge issues (where there is a clear difference between Republicans and Democrats) were not sufficiently stressed. The hand-wringers prevailed.

I never had any fear that, for me, 1992 would turn out to be a repeat of 1988. There was no way I was going to let myself get trapped by "handlers" this time. From the start, I told Teeter that I was going to operate on my own. At one point we heard they wanted to put someone on our plane, but if they'd come to me and asked to do so, my response would have been, "Forget it." As it was, they seemed to drop the idea and leave us alone. I guess they figured they could only screw up one campaign at a time.

31 | Clinton and Perot

John Sununu and I usually held the same political convictions, but we didn't always make the same predictions. Still, early in 1992, as the Democratic primary was taking shape in New Hampshire (before the Gennifer Flowers episode), we were pretty sure that Arkansas Governor Bill Clinton would be the party's candidate. Sununu had known him from his own gubernatorial days and been impressed by his political skills, and he thought they were likely to lead him to victory over a very weak Democratic field. Presidential campaigns really have to get going almost two years before the election, and early in 1991, most of the strongest Democrats had been scared off by President Bush's popularity. They decided to sit things out until 1996. Some of the remaining contenders did have a certain appeal, of course. Former Massachusetts Senator Paul Tsongas, who would actually finish first in New Hampshire, was a politician who tried to create the image of speaking the truth and never hedging. But he lacked stature and staying power, and his frequent cough always reminded voters of his battle with cancer. Bob Kerrey, a Vietnam veteran and Medal of Honor recipient who had had his leg amputated, should have been more formidable, but he somehow never caught on. Reporters might have been intrigued by him, but they were more comfortable with Clinton, whose Vietnam protesting resonated more strongly with their own experience.

I was always hoping that the Democrats' *most* interesting, formidable-looking candidate, someone with real stature, would get into the race. I'm talking about Mario Cuomo. It would have been beautiful. He and Clinton would have gone at it hammer and tongs, each one softening the other up. And if Cuomo emerged as the nominee, we would have been able to run against him as one more traditional left-wing eastern Democratic candidate. He would never have been able to paint himself as a "New" centrist Democrat the way Clinton did. For all his eloquence, Cuomo is very thin-skinned, and it would have been a real treat to see him respond to the assault we could have launched from the center and the conservative side of the political spectrum. Aside from many other things, he was vulnerable on the Gulf War, having suggested during Desert Shield that we appease Saddam Hussein by offering him a piece of Kuwait.

I first met Bill Clinton during the 1980s, when Indiana Governor Bob Orr hosted a conference on educational issues. I can remember Clinton talking about his daughter, who would be attending the public schools in Little Rock; he intended to treat his commitment to educational reform as a personal matter. He appeared well informed and committed. And he almost never stopped talking. I remember thinking he would have fit right in at the Senate. He's a good pol—a natural—who knows how to win elections. He's got a good memory and conveys knowledgeability. He chooses words carefully when describing his programs. But he shades the truth, and he has a tendency to lash out when he gets into a box.

Early in the New Hampshire campaign, Clinton's vulnerabilities became obvious, particularly as they involved his private life and draft history. I didn't have much taste for discussing the former, and on the latter I resented the parallels that the media drew between the two of us. I had served in the military, and Clinton had energetically avoided doing so. But that wasn't the issue, and I never tried to make it into one. (Nor did the President, who was never especially bothered by Clinton's not having served. What did bother him later in the campaign—much more than it bothered me—was Clinton's having organized demonstrations against U.S. policy while he was on foreign soil.) There was, however, an issue about Clinton's draft history that I didn't even have to frame myself. Bob Kerrey did that during the primary battle in New Hampshire: "When Dan Quayle went through his stuff, Bill Clinton said: What matters is not what you did. What matters is [that you] just level and tell us exactly what it was you did. We asked that of Dan Quayle, and I think we have an obligation to ask it of him." Bill Clinton never leveled with the American voter.

Even so, there was plenty else on which to run against him. He had raised taxes in Arkansas without raising the people's quality of life, something our campaign should have made clear, just as we had punctured the myth of Dukakis's "Massachusetts miracle" in 1988. From the start I said that he would raise taxes on the middle class, though he never conceded that they would go up on anyone making less than $200,000 a year. He even promised the middle class a tax cut. We found out how long it took him to break that promise once he got elected. The middle class is now getting clobbered under his administration. I was also eager to get the debate focused on foreign policy. Clinton had relatively little interest in that area. I thought that, if he won, he would be content to react to circumstances, instead of trying to shape a real policy, and recent events—from Bosnia to Somalia—have borne out our arguments on that, too.

Basically, I thought the campaign would come down to taxes and trust. As the months went on, it did; the only problem was that Clinton's people were smart enough to turn those issues against us. And they needed only one stone to hit both birds: the 1990 budget deal. There was no way to deny that we'd broken the read-my-lips pledge—and given away the game on taxes *and* trust. Clinton managed some major waffling in the course of the campaign, but by the end of it (incredibly, to me), some polls would show the American people had more trust in his character than they did in the President's.

I was only vaguely familiar with Ross Perot before the roller-coaster ride he took the country on in 1992.

Before he blurted out his candidacy on Larry King's show, we had heard some rumors about his intention to run. The President picked them up first: some of his Texas friends would tell him what Ross Perot had been telling *his* Texas friends. I didn't take it all that seriously, but I remember my good friend Norm Brinker, a Dallas businessman, telling me to hang onto my hat. He knew

Ross Perot well, knew he was cunning, tough, and fanatically goal-oriented. Still, what would have best prepared me for his entry into the race was knowing just how much Perot despised the President—something I was unaware of until his hat was in the ring.

That animosity went back to the early 1980s, when President Reagan asked Vice President Bush to thank Ross Perot for his services when it came to the POW and MIA issue—and to tell him that those services were no longer needed. A task like this would have been more appropriate for the White House chief of staff to perform, but Bush drew the short straw: he had to tell Ross Perot not to do something, and Perot never forgave him for it. Perot is a complicated, intense person, and many of his motivations are deep-seated and entirely personal, including the one that made him run for President; I have no doubt that his extreme dislike for George Bush was the primary factor pushing him into the race. I don't think he ever harbored any illusions that he could be elected, but he does like the limelight and has virtually unlimited resources (money largely made off government contracts) to spend on promoting himself. His campaign for President was a personal vendetta against George Bush. Buchanan had drawn first blood; Perot wanted to go in for the kill.

The President considered himself the expert on Perot. He'd say, "I know this guy. I know him well. And when the media start going after him, he won't be able to handle it." He was partially right: after one wave of negative coverage, Perot got out as suddenly as he had gotten in. Even so, his first candidacy hurt us, perhaps irreparably. Not just in the polls, either. During all the weeks when the media were trying to figure out how the "Perot factor" would cut, he was demoralizing the White House and the campaign in a personal sort of way. When Ed Rollins, Reagan's 1984 campaign manager, teamed up with Hamilton Jordan, Jimmy Carter's chief of staff, and went to work for Perot, gloom settled over the Bush camp. Rollins's wife, Sherrie, was working in the White House for Sam Skinner. She was—and remained—personally close to the President and Barbara Bush. She handled her inevitable departure with grace, but the episode was another kick in the stomach for the President and his team at a time when they could ill afford any more of them.

I always thought Rollins was one of the more overrated consultants. His claim to fame was having been Ronald Reagan's campaign manager in 1984, but Bugs Bunny could have gotten Reagan reelected that year. Still, Rollins got great media coverage until his Waterloo in 1993, when he fabricated a story about helping to suppress the black vote in the New Jersey Governor's race between Democrat Jim Florio and Republican Christine Todd Whitman. Rollins had been popular because he was a "megaleaker" and willing to publicly attack George Bush. He would give the press inside campaign information and in return they would exaggerate his abilities. After Christie Whitman's victory, a front-page story in the *New York Times* gave Rollins credit for beating Florio's strategist, James Carville, instead of emphasizing the real story, that *Whitman* had won the race by calling for a tax cut. That same month, Rollins was quoted in a *New York Times* editorial as an authority on the upcoming NAFTA debate between Al Gore and Ross Perot: he predicted that Perot would eat Gore alive. After that didn't happen and the Rollins scandal broke, the *Times* editorial writers said we shouldn't believe anything Ed Rollins says. Maybe it's the *Times* and the rest of the media that we should be listening to with skepticism, since they were the ones that helped create the Rollins image.

During the (first) 1992 Perot campaign, I argued that we shouldn't just wait for him to self-destruct; we should assist the process a little. I had a sense that the media, though they wanted us to lose, were eager to write the story of Perot's collapse, and I told people in the Bush campaign that we ought to help them get to that story. I kept pounding this point to Teeter, and finally the campaign agreed it was time to do something.

This was the prologue to my June 12 speech to the Federalist Society, during which I called Perot a "temperamental tycoon" with "contempt for the Constitution." Those sound bites left some teeth marks, and the media kept repeating the phrases all week. Perot didn't like having to respond to something I'd said, and he tried being dismissive, but we forced him onto the defensive for the first time, because what I said was accurate. His brief campaign had already given plenty of evidence of his personal volatility and political demagoguery.

When Perot dropped out of the race, on the very day Clinton was to accept the Democratic nomination, the President was out in Wyoming. He made a mad scramble to interrupt his two-day fishing trip for a call to Perot and some comments to the press, about how, despite their differences, Ross had made a big contribution to democracy by exciting a lot of disaffected voters back into the system. It was the only response the President could make, politically, at that moment, but I'm sure it made his stomach churn. As I looked at the press conference on television, I watched for any signs of body language that might betray his discomfort. I had to hand it to him—I couldn't find any.

Immediately there was intense speculation about how this development would play. Some believed that Perot's departure would help us: the story of his exit would siphon news coverage away from Clinton's acceptance speech, and with just a two-man race we would have a cleaner shot. How wrong this theory was became clear almost instantly, when Clinton's poll numbers skyrocketed. All of a sudden the Perot voters had been sprung loose and were looking for a new place to go. They had declared their allegiance to Perot in the first place because they didn't like us, so it was hardly likely they'd return to us now—particularly with Perot telling them that Clinton had "revitalized" the Democratic Party. He was giving them permission to go over to Clinton, something they had had a hard time doing before.

I believe Perot hurt us and helped Clinton throughout 1992—when he was in the race and when he was out of it. When he first got in, he took a lot of dissatisfied Republicans into his camp. They were looking for someone else but did not like Clinton. So they went with Perot; and once they had gone from us, we were hard pressed to get them back. Dropping out of the race was the second step. That's when Perot ushered those voters over to Clinton. This still served his purpose: the defeat of George Bush. He was never in the race with clean hands.

Of course, there would be a third phase—Perot Redux—but that wouldn't come until the end of September, a political lifetime away from the primaries and conventions.

Obviously, I have no respect for Ross Perot, though he attracted dedicated supporters who cared deeply about their country. But even I would have to admit that, motivations aside, he wasn't entirely wrong in some of the things he talked about. In fact, some of them were things we were also talking about, just not so vividly and relentlessly. He had a way of making people wake up to the extent to which Congress was a problem. During the primary campaign I'd said it was the members of the Democratic Congress who were really beholden to the special interest groups. They were the ones unable to pass anything but bad checks. Throughout 1992 it was fashionable to talk about "gridlock," as if the last time the President and both houses of Congress had all belonged to the same party (Jimmy Carter's administration) was some golden era of progress. In fact, the biggest problem with Congress is its members' way of getting used to sitting up on the Hill forever, with little fear of being defeated for reelection.

Term limitation was now a hot item on the national agenda, but I'd been talking about it for fifteen years. In fact, back in 1977 I gave my very first speech in the U.S. House of Representatives on the subject. It was something I believed in then and believe in now. If we limit our President to two terms for the good reason that power shouldn't be concentrated in one person any longer than that, it is logical to believe that, even in its smaller measures, power should not be held, decade after decade, by the same individuals. Members of the House should be limited to six terms (twelve years) and Senators to two (twelve years)—which means that people who move, as they often do now, from the House to the Senate could still serve in Congress for a total of twenty-four consecutive years. Or even more: they could come *back* to the Senate, so long as they took some time off after their twelve years and had a chance to get reacquainted with life as a "civilian." Certainly, the Founding Fathers never intended that serving in Congress be a lifetime profession and that members ensconce themselves in Washington for periods of up to forty or fifty years. That kind of prolonged exposure to the air inside the Beltway necessarily causes them to think and act as Washingtonians rather than in a way that is representative of the folks back home.

Those against the idea argue that term limits deny voters a choice. But they're already denied a choice, given the incumbent's tremendous advantages. Incumbents get reelected almost 90 percent of the time. If good, qualified people realize they have only a 10 percent chance of winning, how many of them will risk it? Term limits will bring back genuine competition. Those who oppose them argue that they will force good Senators—the Dick Lugars and Sam Nunns—from office. But those Senators could come back after sitting out a cycle. A surprising supporter of term limits is Senate Majority Leader George Mitchell, who, as I mentioned earlier, shocked Washington with his retirement, stating that serving in Congress should not be a lifetime job.

Not many people remember this, but term limitation was part of the 1988 Republican platform. Lee Atwater was a big proponent of the idea, and he sort of snuck it in there. It didn't really attract much attention at the time, but the idea took off during the midterm elections of 1990, when the protracted wrangling that followed the budget deal showed the public how much was wrong with Congress. The House Post Office and check-writing scandals followed. I talked about term limitation in 1990, and what I said caught the disapproving eye of Jamie Whitten, chairman of the House Appropriations Committee. He had first been elected to Congress in 1942, nearly a half century before. Now his committee was quietly telling Dick Darman that unless Quayle got off the term limitation kick, and stopped using the chairman as an example, Mrs. Quayle would not get the funds she'd requested for repairs at the Vice President's residence. Those funds were, in fact, held up and reduced. (But they would be substantially increased for the Gores two years later.) By trying to get at me in this petty way, they were making a more powerful argument for term limits than I ever could. I didn't back down, and I came back to the issue in 1992. I always found it to be well received by the people, and where it has been on the ballot in individual states it has almost always fared well. New York City and the state of Maine (two places that have little in common except cynicism about our public officials) recently said yes to term limits. Polls show 70 percent of the people support the idea. Congress will be the last bastion of resistance, but term limits is an idea that is not going to go away, and when it develops new converts, I'll be quick to welcome them to the cause. When George Will changed his mind and began pushing for term limits (see his persuasive book, *Restoration*), I sent congratulations on his having joined the revolution.

Some political thinkers have taken to recommending single, six-year presidential terms, but the question seems a less urgent one than reform of the House and Senate. In any case, no one has argued that a President who's served just four years shouldn't be eligible for reelection, and getting George Bush a second term was our foremost concern by the middle of 1992, by which time it was clear he would be facing Bill Clinton on the Democratic side. Still, there were times when his supporters wondered if he wanted a second term for himself as much as they wanted one for him. They questioned just how much he'd ever wanted to be President in the first place—the degree to which he had "fire in the belly."

George Bush had given some serious thought to not running in 1988. Despite the Reagan landslide and his own besting of Geraldine Ferraro in their televised debate, he had not had a good campaign for reelection as Vice President in 1984. There had been much negative reporting by the media. I was among the first to call him after that 1984 election, partly because I was looking toward my own Senate race in 1986. Along with giving him my congratulations, I asked him if he would come into Indiana and campaign for me in two years. He said that he couldn't tell me right then and there; he would get back to me. Three weeks later, he called to say he would be glad to stump for me. (I presume he had decided to make the run for President.)

It was Bush's longtime friend Nick Brady who put together a group of people to help convince Bush to run in 1988. I strongly believe, and history should record, that the country is better off for his having said yes. But there is little doubt in my mind that George Bush never had the same kind of single-minded desire to be President that, say, Lyndon Johnson and Richard Nixon had. He had a wonderful life outside politics. Nixon had no real interests beyond politics; Bob Dole, to take one more example, doesn't either. I think Bush's lack of obsession made him a better President, because he was able to behave and think like a person, not just a politician. But in an election year, a little single-mindedness is not a bad thing, and there were times in 1992 when I could understand how others might question whether the President really hungered for another four years in the White House. I know that Mrs. Bush was philosophical about it all. I remember her musing on the election during a state dinner that spring. "We'll just do what we can," she said, "and if we don't win, we don't win." She was saying she'd be content either way. That she could view the situation with such equanimity showed her strength, wisdom, and stability. She would campaign her heart out for her husband, but if he lost there was life after the White House.

I never heard Barbara Bush raise the possibility of the President's not running, and I don't think that was ever seriously considered. Certainly, Bush, more than anyone else, was convinced he would win. Up until Election Day he honestly believed the American people would go into the voting booth and check their gut about whom they trusted the most. Right up until the end he didn't believe that people would really pull the lever for Bill Clinton.

32 | Murphy and Me

I was at the White House when the verdict in the Rodney King trial came down. Everyone was shocked by the acquittal, including the President, since we had seen the videotape of the beating. But once the riots began in Los Angeles, our revulsion was vastly magnified. The riots were a disgusting display of wanton violence that accomplished absolutely nothing. Without them, the federal government would still have filed the civil rights charges on which the police officers were eventually convicted; those charges had deliberately been withheld pending the outcome of the state proceedings.

Once the riots were under way, our first priority was restoring law and order, but we were not going to send federal troops to quell the situation unless we retained complete command and control over them. As it turned out, Governor Pete Wilson and Mayor Tom Bradley seemed relieved when President Bush more or less federalized Los Angeles; I thought they might raise objections about jurisdiction, but the situation was too far out of control for that to be a concern.

A year earlier, when videotaped evidence of the beating came to light, Daryl Gates, the Los Angeles police chief, should have taken matters firmly into his own hands. If he had aggressively cleaned up his own department without relying on the court system, a lot of grief might have been avoided. Even so, the responsibility for the riots has to be placed squarely and solely with the rioters. The knee-jerk search for "root causes" and the clamor for federal programs to make up for "twelve years of Republican neglect" were as predictable as they were wrong. The effect was to shift blame away from the thugs and murderers who were destroying the neighborhoods of people just as disadvantaged as themselves.

The administration's response to the riots was confused. One day Press Secretary Marlin Fitzwater would blame them on the culture of dependency created by Great Society–style welfare programs, and the next, someone else in the administration would try to dampen liberal criticism by claiming that spending for such programs had actually gone up during the Bush years. I was uncomfortable talking about "programs" of any kind, for fear of giving the riots a certain legitimacy. But if we had to talk about programs to combat urban poverty—and politically we had no choice—then I wanted to talk about new ones to empower the individual, not ones that would further bloat the already failed welfare bureaucracies. On "Face the Nation" I said that the President would make a new push for urban enterprise zones, for the conversion of public housing to private ownership, and for school choice.

The President did make an honest push for enterprise zones, but the Democrats were more interested in scoring political points than in doing anything useful for the people they claimed to represent. They loaded up the President's bill with lard, making it into a hugely expensive—and unimaginative—urban renewal package. Of course, they didn't want to pass the bill as much as they wanted to force the President to veto it so that they could make him appear "insensitive" (a favorite word of the Democrats), just as they had tried to earlier, when they labeled him the first President to veto a civil rights bill. By summertime we managed to get a piece of legislation enacted.

Three weeks after the riots, I was ready to talk about my own sense of their "root causes." Instead of the speech on U.S.–Japanese trade relations that I'd planned to give the Commonwealth Club of California, I decided to talk about a fundamental "poverty of values," which, more than anything else, was the real cause of the lawlessness we'd seen in Los Angeles. I made the speech in San Francisco on Tuesday, May 19, citing both American success and American failure. I noted how in the last quarter of a century an entirely new black middle class had emerged (since 1967 the median income of black two-parent families has risen by 60 percent in real terms) but also how an underclass had been left behind without the values of family, hard work, and, above all, personal responsibility, which the black writer Shelby Steele, in his book, *The Content of Our Character,* calls "the brick and mortar of power." "Our inner cities," I said, "are filled with children having children, with people who have not been able to take advantage of educational opportunities, with people who are dependent on drugs or the narcotic of welfare."

I made a special point of expressing concern over how, "if a single mother raising her children in the ghetto has to worry about drive-by shootings, drug deals, or whether her children will join gangs and die violently, her difficult task becomes impossible." That remark came pages before the single sentence that would create the real ideological firestorm of my vice-presidency: "It doesn't help matters," I said, "when prime time TV has Murphy Brown—a character who supposedly epitomizes today's intelligent, highly paid, professional woman—mocking the importance of fathers, by bearing a child alone, and calling it just another 'lifestyle choice.'"

Although I'd sometimes glanced at it while my children watched, I had never seen a whole episode of "Murphy Brown." Even so, the reference was my idea. What had really gotten my attention were all the press stories about the season's final episode, on which real-life network personalities like Katie Couric and Joan Lunden would show up and celebrate the birth of a child to their fictional colleague, Murphy. The Hollywood spin was that there was no downside to having a child out of wedlock, whereas the reality is that children born in these circumstances— and their mothers—face economic hardship or even outright poverty.

I was bothered by all the cute glamour with which the episode (sure to be seen by millions of young girls and boys) was being surrounded. I talked about it to Connie Horner, the director of presidential personnel and a serious thinker about social issues. I told her I was considering mentioning my objections in a speech I was preparing, and she told me they needed saying. So when I met with my staff to exchange ideas for the Commonwealth Club speech, Murphy Brown was discussed. I put the reference to the show in my first draft, and it stayed in the several rewrites I would do before I was satisfied with the wording. I knew the line would be controversial—in fact, we didn't try to get the text over to the White House until a few hours before the speech was delivered.

Just *how* controversial that line would be was something I couldn't predict, not even from the press conference immediately following the speech. I remember a question about my reference to Shelby Steele (one reporter tartly stated that he doesn't speak for a majority of black people), but I'm not sure Murphy Brown even came up. Still, within a few hours it was clear that something was happening. From San Francisco we flew to Palm Springs to a campaign fundraiser. Once we got there, Dave Beckwith came into my room and said, "Hey, I've got great news. You're on ABC, CBS, and NBC."

"What did they pick up?" I asked. "The Murphy Brown thing?"

The answer was, to put it mildly: yes. Our last stop that day was Los Angeles—home of Hollywood itself—and when we landed, we found the airport lit up for live coverage of our arrival. I avoided mentioning Murphy Brown to the waiting reporters but did make the larger point about Hollywood versus traditional morality, as a way of getting back to the general "poverty of values" that had been my subject in San Francisco. Still, by Wednesday morning the country was plastered with screaming Murphy headlines (New York's *Daily News:* QUAYLE TO MURPHY BROWN: YOU TRAMP!) and involved in the kind of loud national quarrel it had had eight months before over Clarence Thomas and Anita Hill. Most newspapers actually covered it as a fairly straight story, with some serious attention to the issues I was trying to raise. But the networks, which are part of the same entertainment industry that produces "Murphy Brown," went ballistic. The electronic media was in a meltdown.

That morning we went to visit a school in south central Los Angeles, which had taken the brunt of the riots. By this time we realized the White House staff was in total panic. Bill Kristol was on the car phone with them and getting absolutely nowhere. I told him to give me the phone. I needed to talk to the President. As it happened, he was in a meeting with Canadian Prime Minister Brian Mulroney, but I did get hold of Sam Skinner and told him that the White House ought to be supporting me.

"But this thing's a loser," said Sam.

"That's what you think," I argued back. "It's not a loser. If you handle it right, it's a winner."

"Well, you're a minority of one," he shot back. "Everybody around here is concerned about it. It looks like you're criticizing single mothers."

"But I'm not!"

"They're even worried it looks as if you're indirectly criticizing Doro Bush."

To which I could only respond: "Give me a break. This is absolutely ridiculous."

While still in the car, I got through to the President and told him I didn't intend to keep talking about Murphy Brown, who had been the subject of just one sentence of a speech about the poverty of values. "I just felt that you needed to know this, and I hope all the hand-wringers over there will settle down."

"There are a lot of nervous people over here," the President said. "The problem I have is that I've never seen 'Murphy Brown.'"

"Neither have I."

"You haven't?"

"No, I haven't seen the show. But it doesn't make any difference. Forget about Murphy Brown. The issue is the poverty of values."

"Okay," he said. "I'm glad you checked in."

The President's joint press conference with Mulroney turned comical. The Canadian Prime Minister had expected the questions to revolve around trade issues, but when the reporters' first question to the President was about Murphy Brown, Bush said to him, "See? I told you that would be the question."

As usual, the President was better than his team. Marlin Fitzwater's first remark was supportive of my values-oriented speech, but when Teeter and the campaign folks decided that no one should be criticizing a popular show in the middle of an election year, they made Marlin go back out and praise "Murphy Brown" for exhibiting "pro-life" values. As if anyone was arguing that the character should have had an abortion. My main objection was to how the show deemed fathers irrelevant—in a way that was damaging

above all to our children. Fathers are important to a child's life—
both financially and emotionally. A society that promotes the idea
that a father's role is irrelevant breeds irresponsibility.

It didn't help that Murphy's tony circumstances bore little
resemblance to the economic situation in which most unwed
mothers and their children find themselves. But instead of supporting me and trying to focus the country on an important issue,
the White House went into a crazy campaign spin cycle, dragging
me into what looked like a debate with the same administration I
was part of.

The media coverage became more and more beside the point.
In an effort to show that the Murphy character was more typical
than I'd admit, one news outfit went to find an unwed mother
who was also an anchorwoman. They came up with one in the
Midwest, who two years later told Marilyn that I was right. Governor Cuomo accused me of trivializing a serious issue, to which I
would respond by saying it was the media who trivialized it, by
refusing to see the larger purpose of that reference in the speech.
I also wonder how much attention anyone would have given the
issue without this allusion to popular culture. Sam Donaldson
even asked me if the whole thing didn't rank as another "gaffe."
His blatant bias was never more in evidence. A year later, when
Bill Clinton raised the issue as President, Donaldson would discuss it respectfully.

The editorials, the call-in shows devoted to the subject, the cartoons, and even the serious commentaries—all of them went on
for weeks. What I said had struck a national nerve, and the better
political writers knew it. "The journalistic mockers of the Murphy
Brown speech are wrong," wrote David Broder. "The values
debate is important. But it can't be allowed to stop at the level of
once-every-four-years rhetoric, whether it's Spiro Agnew, Dan
Quayle or George Bush doing the orations." Point taken. In fact,
the response to that speech convinced me that a sustained debate
about values and responsibility could finally move this country
forward toward real, imaginative solutions to its toughest social
problems. I continued to speak out on family values but the campaign people refused to put the issue front and center.

In the four years that I was Vice President, nothing generated more mail and phone calls to my office than the Murphy Brown speech. These communications ranged from fierce denunciations to hallelujahs, with every shade of opinion and tone in between. You could make a whole book out of just those letters, which taken together show that, when it comes to talking to their elected officials, Americans are anything but shy. One would begin, "Dear Mr. Vice President: Hooray for you!" and another, "Dan—Get a Clue." The overwhelming number of letters were supportive.

The favorable letters ("Don't retract. Don't apologize. Repeat it at every opportunity") not only kept me going but also gave me a variety of perspectives on the problem. I heard from a Head Start volunteer who said that in twenty years with the program she could see "the tragic results of these four-year-olds not having a father in the home. . . . We do what we can to help and love them while they are in Head Start, but some of them are already lost. It is so sad!" A county prosecutor told me that in his experience "babies born to young mothers have a much poorer quality of life, suffer a greater variety of serious illnesses, and are much more likely to be the recipient of child abuse and child neglect." Two high school teachers from Brooklyn, New York, wrote: "As educators working in the New York City public school system we see our students receiving the message that having children borne by children is acceptable in too many subtle ways." A pro-life Catholic Democrat (who told us she would vote Bush–Quayle) said that while she was glad Murphy Brown didn't opt for an abortion, she still thought the show had been damaging: "I was a single mother once, due to divorce, and it was a very hard life, certainly not an ideal situation." And one man from Florida wrote: "Don't be surprised [if] with that line of thought you may well have gained allies among black male dads. Until your statement, myself and some other black males have had the opinion 'the system' was trying to keep us from having any say in raising our children."

My favorite letter of all may have been from Mrs. Erma Mitchell-Phelps of Harlem, who sent me a copy of a Letter to the Editor that she'd written: "Mr. Quayle is not criticizing 'the show' Murphy Brown but rather asking us to consider the tragedies we can mindlessly cause by glamorizing a way of life that . . . has proved for the most part to be disastrous." Mrs. Mitchell-Phelps enclosed this letter in a cheerful card to me and Marilyn. "Dear Folks," she wrote. "I'm a Democrat and will probably die a Democrat, but in spite of our political beliefs we are all brothers and sisters in a wonderful, patient God. I'm so grateful for this. So sorry you are having to endure such meanness of spirit—but just know that God is always there for us. If you're ever in Harlem please visit our church. Fr. Castle is very militant, not too keen on Republicans—but he is a Good Shepherd and even if you find you disagree with him, you'll like him and especially his beautiful wife Katie. Keep the Faith. This Democrat loves you." I still plan to take Mrs. Mitchell-Phelps up on her invitation.

One Erma Mitchell-Phelps can make up for an awful lot of late-night monologues and editorial cartoons, but I paid as much attention to the negative letters as to the encouraging ones. A number of people reminded me that the Murphy character chose to have her baby instead of an abortion, and one writer, a single mother of three children who had been abandoned by her husband, warned me: "I'm afraid by the stand that you took many women may choose abortion because you made [single motherhood] sound like such a disgrace!"

I was especially moved by a letter I got from Tracy Kelly of Milford, Connecticut, which with her permission I want to reproduce in full:

> August 22, 1992
>
> Dear Mr. Vice President:
>
> Enclosed please find two pictures of my son. In one he is posing for the camera, sitting on top of a ball in the backyard of my daycare worker's house. In the other he is being comforted by me after he woke up from a bad dream.
>
> He is a well cared for, much-loved two-year-old of a full-time working single mother. I, like Murphy Brown, became pregnant unexpectedly and *"chose"* to raise my son alone. Unlike Murphy Brown, the show doesn't end after 30 minutes. My life is difficult and decisions are tough ones.
>
> Working 40 hours, paying taxes, cleaning house, reading the

evening paper, preparing healthy meals and balancing the check-book all must fit into a tight schedule. But the simplest thing I do is love my child. We laugh together, read together, learn about nature, accept disappointments and rejoice with successes.

He learns about family values through my examples and those of others. My brother, with whom I live, dresses his nephew every day before rushing off to work himself. I drive him to day-care, where he spends time with his playmates running after balls, climbing jungle gyms, laughing under the sprinkler, and learning about colors. Life can be confusing for a small boy, though.

My mother, who has Alzheimer's disease, frightens my son when she yells. And he grows sad when he can't find his "Pop-Pop" (my father) who died of cancer last month.

It's difficult for me not to continue to take your insults toward single parents personally. But I don't want to harbor resentment, because that interferes with the values I try to teach my son; those of love, equality for all, justice and honesty.

You don't understand my life, Mr. Vice President. Please don't lay judgment on something you don't comprehend.

Sincerely,

Tracy Kelly

What distressed me about Tracy's heartfelt letter, and others like it that I received, was its sense that I had attacked single mothers. If anything, I was trying to be their champion, to point out the distinction between real life and what was being shown on "Murphy Brown." The last thing in the world I wanted to do was leave people like Tracy Kelly (who sounds to me like a terrific mother) feeling insulted. I want to see policies—from job train-ing, to cracking down on "deadbeat dads," to creating a robust economy—that will make their lives easier, not harder. My hope is that those who influence the culture will be more sensitive to the hardships faced by unwed mothers and their children.

I can't pretend to understand all the burdens Tracy Kelly is bearing, but I do want to correct the widespread impression that the extended Quayle family has lived a life—if I can use one last sitcom example—out of "Ozzie and Harriet." The facts are these: My maternal grandmother, divorced from my grandfather at a time when divorce was severely stigmatized, was a single mother. My sister, who has two children, has gotten divorced. Of the five cousins on my mother's side who married, three have been divorced. As you can see, my family has known plenty of the troubles I read about in the mountain of Murphy mail. I don't judge the people who disagreed with me any more than I judge those family members I love no matter what. And I certainly don't live in a fantasy world: I leave that to the creators of "Murphy Brown."

In May 1992 I was talking about reality, and by every statistical yardstick that reality is terrible. In 1990, 29.8 percent of fatherless white families were living below the poverty line; for blacks the rate was 50.6 percent. By every measure, children raised with both their parents do better than those raised with only one: they are treated less frequently for emotional problems, have more success in school, experience fewer troubles with the law, and as adults get further ahead economically. Sometimes divorce is inevitable, but all children deserve two parents to love and nurture them.

As 1992 rolled on, the Murphy controversy did, too. The twisted response to what I said led me, in a speech to the Southern Baptist convention in Indianapolis, to attack the "cultural elite," who "sneer at the simple but hard virtues—modesty fidelity, integrity." I attacked the cynicism that allowed Time Warner to profit from the rap song "Cop Killer," and I didn't wilt when, that September, Hollywood turned the Emmy Awards into one big Quayle joke. Even some of my liberal critics thought that evening was an exercise in wretched excess. When Diane English, the creator of "Murphy Brown," got her award, her brother, the Rev. Rick English of Buffalo, New York, couldn't bring himself to call with congratulations, even though he'd done that in the past. "I guess what's been bothering me," he told the *Buffalo News,* "is that I've been working with youth for ten years and I see firsthand the problems they face. I don't believe that the media is promoting family values and

I think a large segment of media is out of contact with real-life situations."

When "Murphy Brown" had its season premiere, after a whole summer of national debate, I wrote a letter addressed to "Dear Baby Brown," in which I said: "It's important to me that you know the respect and personal understanding I have for single mothers, who work hard to do their best for their children, often against the odds." This letter was the campaign's idea, and along with it we sent Baby Brown a good Republican stuffed elephant. As campaign ideas go, this one was all right—I thought we might as well create some good feelings that would diminish one more night of Quayle bashing—but Marilyn was opposed to it. She didn't want stories about me watching the season premiere and suggested I put in an appearance at the Monday night football game instead. That turned out to be impossible, since we found out Bill Clinton was going to be there in Chicago with Mayor Daley. So Marilyn and I ended up watching the show—with press and protesters outside—at the Washington home of our friend Zora Brown, who had worked with Marilyn and me in the fight against breast cancer. Zora invited a number of her friends, including some single parents, to watch with us. As she pointed out to the *Washington Post*: "This is not a trivial matter to us. In the black community, this is a major problem. . . . I thought the vice president should have an opportunity to talk to some of my friends and hear what they had to say."

That conversation on family values is still going on, all across the country, with increased attention to the kind of statistics I've quoted. In their forthcoming book, *Fatherless America*, David Blankenhorn, Barbara Dafoe Whitehead, and David Popenoe make a powerful case for the two-parent family. When a portion of Whitehead's findings were published in the April 1993 *Atlantic*, the cover story (titled "Dan Quayle Was Right") received more mail from readers than any other piece in the history of the magazine.

The most significant convert to the family-values issue is Bill Clinton, who late in 1993 went to the Memphis church where Dr. Martin Luther King preached just before his assassination and spoke about the responsibility parents have to nurture the children they bring into the world. He lamented teenage pregnancies and criticized young fathers who abandon their children—or don't even stay around long enough to see them born. In a subsequent television interview, the President said: "I read [Dan Quayle's] whole speech, his Murphy Brown speech. I thought there were a lot of very good things in that speech."

I believe that Clinton is genuinely moved by the plight of his poor neighbors in decaying parts of Washington, D.C., and by all those children so much less fortunate than his daughter, Chelsea. But I predict that whatever solutions he offers will end up involving more government intervention and spending, which won't work (just as his surgeon general's belief that our social breakdown is somehow related to a shortage of condoms won't help matters). Still, it is imperative that he keep raising the issue of family values. We are more accustomed to discussing these matters in private than in public, but it is time to bring the coffee table into the political arena. Our country's health, maybe even its survival, depends on continuing this difficult conversation.

Many have asked me, "Can we do more than *talk* about family values?"

Of course we can. There is an agenda we should advance:

Increase the tax exemption for our children.

Eliminate the "marriage tax" penalty, which pools the income of married wage earners, putting them in a higher tax bracket than if they were single.

Radically reform the welfare system to reward marriage, eliminate incentives for mothers receiving assistance to have additional children, eliminate disincentives for absentee fathers to rejoin their families, and require unwed minor children to live with their parents. A minor and her offspring are a parent's responsibility, not the state's.

Change the divorce law so that the needs of our children are given priority.

Begin public service announcements that underscore the enormous responsibilities of being a parent.

Reform the education system by giving all parents the right to choose their children's school and insist on a value-based education where virtues such as integrity, responsibility, industry, morality, and courage are taught.

It is time we put our children first. Our families and our nation depend on it.

33 | Baked, Mashed, and Fried

On June 15, at 8:30 A.M., I took off from Andrews Air Force Base for a busy day of campaigning in hostile territory. I was headed for that ultimate Democratic stronghold and media capital, New York, to give a speech about everything that was wrong with that city.

Addressing the Manhattan Institute at the Waldorf-Astoria, I talked about how New York is a great city in spite of itself. "Here is what's right with New York: the decent, hard-working people who live here," I said. "Here's what's wrong with New York: the entrenched government establishment and its liberal ideology that have failed them." For a half century the city has been an overtaxed, bureaucratized laboratory for one bad liberal social policy experiment after another, from rent control (a 1940s emergency measure that still continues and ensures the decay of the most lopsidedly priced housing stock in the country) to, in 1991, condom distribution in the schools. Whatever the city's woes, from crime to the steady flight of manufacturing jobs, its leaders never failed to blame years of "federal neglect" by the Reagan and Bush administrations. In fact, New York's decline had been going on for decades and represented a massive failure of the liberal imagination.

From New York it was on to Trenton, New Jersey, to celebrate Weed and Seed, the kind of urban program that can help reverse some of the decay. Digger Phelps had just retired as one of Notre Dame's great basketball coaches and was giving much of his time to promoting the project. As Digger explains it, "the 'weed' is cleaning up the neighborhood, and the 'seed' is giving people help to find jobs, provide decent housing and health care and other basic needs." The program depends on federal and state money, but not nearly as much as it does on individual initiative and hard work. Trenton was a place where it had had some impact, and on that day in June, Digger took me into a neighborhood where it was operating. Before visiting the Luis Munoz Rivera School (a designated "safe haven" for kids living in a community constantly jeopardized by drug-related crime), I spoke with some of the neighborhood women about the program. Inside the school, some of them joined me and community leaders for a discussion of the drug problem. While there, I saw a drill-team performance and dropped in on some classes in self-esteem, before heading off to watch a spelling bee.

You know what I'm getting to.

"What are we supposed to do?" I asked Keith Nahigian, the advance man who had prepared this little photo op.

"Just sit there and read these words off some flash cards," he explained, "and the kids will go up and spell them at the black-board."

Bill Kristol was with us, and he asked Keith, "Has anyone checked the cards?"

"Oh, yeah," Keith answered. "We looked at them and they're just very simple words. It's no big deal."

No one ever actually asked me to spell *potato* that afternoon. If they had, I imagine I'd have gotten it right, though I wouldn't swear to it. I'm not the world's greatest speller, and while I could bore you with a lot of stories about other politicians' deficiencies in this area, I'm going to try to concentrate on the ridiculous facts. We got to the point where it was twelve-year-old William Figueroa's turn to go to the board and spell whatever was on the next card, which was the word *potato*—except that the card, prepared by the school, read *potatoe*, with an *e*. I can't remember if the spelling struck me as odd or not, but William spelled it correctly on the blackboard—no *e*. I noticed the discrepancy, showed the card to the other adults with me, and as they nodded in agreement, I gently said something about how he was close but had left a little something off. So William, against his better judgment and trying to be polite, added an *e*. The little audience down in front applauded him, and that was it.

A minute or so later, we were back in the holding room awaiting a press conference. We anticipated questions about Cardinal O'Connor, with whom I'd met in the morning and discussed abortion, and about New York politicians who might already have reacted to my speech—especially Governor Mario Cuomo. We got those questions and were near to winding up the press conference, when one reporter asked, "How do you spell potato?" I gave him a puzzled look, and then the press started laughing. It wasn't until that moment that I realized anything was wrong. None of the staff people had told me. Caught off guard, I just rattled on a little to fill the air—something about how I wasn't going to get into spelling matters—but I knew that something was really amiss. After one more question, we wrapped it up, and I went back into the holding room to ask the staffers just what was going on.

When you make a mistake in the "image is all" world of politics, you want to recover from it as fast as you can. Get out in front of it. And we could have done that with this particularly ridiculous one. If somebody had even nudged me while I was still in that classroom, I could have gone up to William in front of everyone and told him that it had just been pointed out to me how, when it came to potatoes, he was a better speller than both the card preparer and the Vice President of the United States. We could have ended the thing by giving him a much bigger round of applause than the one he'd gotten. Not an ideal situation, but certainly a better one than my standing up in front of the press and not knowing what they were talking about.

This was one of those rare times when I felt like exploding at the staff. I can hardly expect them to be responsible for my spelling, but I still don't know why I was kept in the dark during the several minutes we'd prepared for the press conference. Only now did they remind me that *potato* is spelled without an *e*. I told them that the card had said otherwise, and Keith Nahigian went off to find it; but all of this was pointless.

I knew that this was going to be big—certainly the story of the day, and maybe of the next few days. I could feel myself getting increasingly angry as we rode to our next stop, a fundraiser. Bill

Kristol tried to cheer me up, saying he didn't think it would be such a big story after all, but I knew better than that. I went over and over the incident in my mind, wondering what the videotape of it looked like, hoping that maybe it wasn't so bad.

If I lost some sense of proportion over the incident, my only defense is that everyone else was about to do that, too.

"How did it go, Dan?" asked Marilyn, when I got back home that night.

"There was one small problem with spelling." I told her the story, and for a moment she was puzzled, unsure herself (and Marilyn *is* a good speller) that the word didn't have an *e* after all.

The fact is that the press wasn't sure how to spell it either. Once the question was asked at the news conference, some reporters were seen heading out of the room to get a school dictionary to check on the spelling. And a month later, by which time this story still wasn't dead, the *New York Post* ran a "Correction": "Due to an editing error in late editions of yesterday's Post, the word 'potato' was misspelled. . . . Ironically, the error occurred in a reference to Vice President Quayle's infamous misspelling of the same word. The *Post* regrets the error. The outpouring of phone calls from literate readers has helped us to be a little more understanding about Quayle's goof."

But this wasn't a goof. In the language of media politics, this was a gaffe—the perfect gaffe from four years of the press's patrolling for them. It was more than a gaffe; in the language of Lee Atwater, it was a "defining moment," of the worst kind imaginable. Over the next several weeks, continuing through the Democratic Convention and beyond (to this day, in fact), there was an avalanche of late-night jokes and Democratic sound bites. QUAYLE GETS BAKED, MASHED AND FRIED, said one tabloid headline.

There's something crazy about our national life, or let's say our national discourse, when something as trivial as this incident becomes a major event—yes, an entire chapter—in a political figure's life. But that's the way things work. I've mentioned how some people say I trivialized the issue of single motherhood by using Murphy Brown as an example. But is there anyone who would claim my speech would have gotten one percent of the attention it did if I hadn't used an example from pop culture? The two incidents aren't directly analogous, but there is a connection. Politicians live and die by the symbolic sound bite.

Howard Kurtz, the *Washington Post*'s media critic, did a story on the whole episode, and he pointed out that the incident got so much play because it seemed like a perfect illustration of what people thought about me anyway. I wasn't alone in this sort of thing, he argued. "Bill Clinton's 'didn't inhale' comment about marijuana seemed to underscore his reputation for slick evasiveness. And the disputed incident in which President Bush appeared unfamiliar with a supermarket scanner brought Bush weeks of ridicule as an out-of-touch patrician." It's an interesting argument, and correct up to a point, but—to borrow an image from Saddam Hussein—potato was the mother of all gaffes. I don't think the inhaling or the supermarket scanner got a tenth as much play. An even more important argument, quoted by Kurtz in his piece, came from Robert Lichter, director of the Center for Media and Public Affairs, who said: "Quayle is getting beaten up because a lot of people are upset that he's being treated much more seriously."

The media had been infuriated with me for a month, ever since the Murphy Brown speech. I handed them a perfect opportunity to strike back. The potato gaffe helped them undo the positive image I had recently earned, not only with that speech but with my fairly aggressive campaigning throughout the primary season. *Time* had even run a picture that suggested the President was riding on my shoulders. Now, after potato, it was back to the same old cartoons.

I can't overstate how discouraging and exasperating the whole event was. It put Marilyn into a state of what she called "complete and total irritation." Her husband could make "five speeches a day for twenty-five months," she explained to a CNN reporter, "and never make a mistake; he makes one mistake, it's aired and aired and aired and aired."

It was a tough week. But even though the press was trying to make me out as a fool, I ignored them and went about the business of government. I met in Washington with Boris Yeltsin. We talked about the space program, and I offered to help broker his upcoming trip to Japan, since on my own trips there I'd made many connections that would be valuable to him.

My next public appearance was before a group of radio talk-show hosts, a pretty rambunctious bunch. I was warned that I would be presented with a dictionary. I was happy to go along with the joke. I planned to say something like how I felt "humble—with an *e*." In the end, the host got cold feet and never gave me the book, which made me even more certain this was one gaffe I wouldn't be able to laugh off. I spoke for twenty minutes about Yeltsin's visit and then took questions. I sat on a stool with a hand mike and no notes, just the opposite of the formal style imposed on me in the 1988 campaign. If I made a mistake, it would be big news.

There were no mistakes, and the press coverage was favorable. But the *Washington Post* couldn't resist running the kind of picture they really wanted. I had allowed my head to drop while listening to a question and considering my answer. The picture made me look out of it, disengaged from an audience with whom I'd actually connected quite well.

In 1994 I finally got the last laugh. I made a cameo appearance in a TV commercial for Wavy Lay's Potato Chips, which aired only once during half-time at the Super Bowl (the net proceeds I earned from the appearance went to charity). But there was one letter I got in 1993 that really put the incident into perspective better than anything else. Jolene M. Holaday wrote me from Burke County, Georgia, where she was about to graduate from high school. She enclosed a letter that I had written to her mother, Carolyn, back in 1985, when the two of them were living in Noblesville, Indiana, after being abandoned by Jolene's father. Mrs. Holaday had no job skills, and when she wrote my office for help, I put her in touch with someone who could give her information about how she might make use of the Job Training Partnership Act. Eight years later, she was employed as a secretary in a law office and completing studies as a paralegal—as a result of the start she got through JTPA. "It hurts to talk about it," her daughter Jolene wrote, "but I want you to appreciate the effects of your political action in our home." She explained that while her mom was taking the JTPA training, "a neighbor for whom Mom did child care brought potatoes for Mom to use in preparing a hot lunch for his children under Mom's care. At the end of the day, the only thing Mom had to serve me for dinner was the fried peelings left over from those potatoes." In 1992, they were in a comfortable cottage in Georgia, eating a dinner of hot corn, fried chicken, and mashed potatoes—not just skins—when the potato story came on the television news. "My mom and I abruptly stopped chewing, looked at each other. . . . 'With an e or without an e is not important. Having potatoes to eat. Now that's important.'"

34 | Dump Quayle

I didn't think it would be Al Gore.

When it came time for Bill Clinton to pick his running mate, I thought he might turn to one of his primary opponents, Nebraska's Senator Bob Kerrey, whose record as a Vietnam War hero could offset Clinton's image problems with the draft. All vice-presidential choices come with liabilities, and Kerrey's may have been his being divorced and single, or just some things he'd said during the primary campaign that Bill Clinton had a hard time getting over. In any case, he didn't get it. But I wouldn't have predicted Gore, who gave the ticket no real geographic or ideological balance. He gave it no generational balance either, but the Democrats obviously wanted to emphasize the country's chance to shift power, all at once, to the baby boomers. Gore was like Bill Clinton in everything but his personality, which is Clinton's opposite.

Al and I both came to the House in 1977. We never got to be particular friends, but we did play pick-up basketball from time to time; as a matter of fact, I think we may have guarded each other on a couple of occasions. Marilyn and I would run into him and Tipper at congressional family social functions now and then, but I never got to know him well, and I don't think he ever had many close friends in the Senate. He takes himself with tremendous seriousness. In person he's not as stiff, as his image has it; but he's always "on," always working each situation to his advantage. Sometimes he comes over to shake your hand and inhales a great big gulp of air—presumably, to expand his chest and make himself look intimidating.

Clinton is altogether warmer and more natural. It was reported that the first time the two really became acquainted was when Clinton spent three hours interviewing him about the job. Warren Christopher, a friend of Gore's father, is probably the one who pushed Clinton toward him. Christopher is, like Al Gore's parents, a Washington insider. For that matter, so is Al Gore himself, who has spent most of his life in the District of Columbia.

I must admit, I did envy the way he was introduced to the American people in 1992. Having run in the presidential primaries four years earlier, he wasn't a complete stranger, but the announcement of his selection was still going to bring him more media attention than he'd ever gotten in his life, and it was handled perfectly. It came well before the Democratic Convention and was done in an orderly way outside the Governor's mansion in Little Rock. The candidate and his running mate had thoroughly prepared themselves to answer questions from any angle the press wanted to throw them. It was hard for me to watch Gore's unveiling without thinking back to the chaos of Spanish Plaza in New Orleans and shaking my head.

Now that I would be running against him, I looked for weak spots. There were certainly a few. Early on Gore made a point of saying that he had not sought the second spot and that everyone—except for his own parents—would agree that Clinton was the best man to be our next President. The constant suggestion, if only subliminal, was that Clinton was lucky to have him and that he was every bit as presidential. I suspected from the start that, if pressed, Gore would have trouble defending Bill Clinton's character. Hillary Clinton was also going to cause Al some discomfort. At the time of his selection, the Clinton campaign was in a phase of downplaying Hillary's potential power, trying to keep her in the background and depict her as a traditional candidate's wife. But Gore knew how important she was—he had to know, in fact, that he was really running for the number three job in a Clinton administration.

For a time during the mid-1980s, Al's wife, Tipper, had been better known than he was. Along with Jim Baker's wife, Susan, she campaigned for a warning label on record albums with sexually explicit and violent lyrics, thereby earning the ire of the entertainment industry. When Al needed funding for his 1988 campaign, Tipper and Al agreed to drop her campaign about the family values that the Democrats and their Hollywood friends would love to mock me for supporting in 1992. Then, later, when the Democrats' polls indicated that a majority of Americans were concerned about values, they changed their strategy and immediately began showcasing the formerly muzzled Tipper. There was a little hypocrisy here. Al's future was apparently more important than fighting for what Tipper thought was right.

In 1992 the Democrats finally learned to run a convention. Their gatherings in 1984 and 1988 had done more to showcase a losing candidate, Jesse Jackson, than the one they were nominating. Both times, Jackson's fiery partisan oratory managed to dismay millions of the moderate voters the party needed to win. Clinton was obviously determined that this not happen a third time. Not long before the convention, he picked a fight with Jackson over the racial comments made by rap singer Sister Souljah and so avoided looking like Mondale and Dukakis, who had always been afraid to offend Reverend Jackson. Clinton limited Jackson's convention role, just as he permitted his last defeated rival, California's Jerry Brown, to speak only after negotiations that maintained the winner's tight control over the podium and schedule.

The convention as a whole was masterfully produced. The Clinton people kept the left-wing, special interest crowd (the party's financial and media backbone) largely out of the public spotlight. The Democratic Congress, still under the cloud of the banking scandal, was rarely mentioned, and the delegates managed for once to stress common ground instead of leftover primary squabbles. Moderation was the order of the day. They even succeeded in presenting Al Gore as a middle-of-the-roader, although his voting record made him right at home in the party's liberal wing, whose members he outdid with an environmentalism that was rooted far more in personal emotions than science (not to mention economic reality).

The main speeches were good. Clinton's, predictably, went on too long, but it was effective in its own way. When Jesse Jackson

did speak, he compared me with King Herod—the biblical nemesis of mothers. This was the most grotesquely offensive, below-
the-belt piece of rhetoric I can recall being directed my way in sixteen years of politics, and the media's double standard allowed
Jackson's slur to pass with hardly a murmur. Although they would
portray the Republicans' convention as hate mongering, Jesse
Jackson's speech was more full of hate and fear than all the
Republican speeches combined.

As expected, throughout the four days the Democrats were at
New York's Madison Square Garden, I came in for a steady
pounding. The potato jokes became pretty monotonous (they even
got young William Figueroa to recite the Pledge of Allegiance) but
there wasn't much to do but take it. We would have the chance to
turn things around at our own convention in Houston. Or so I
thought.

By the time the Democrats left New York they were, by some
estimates, more than twenty points in front of us. They owed
their sudden look of invincibility to a number of factors, among
them the skillful convention, the still-limping economy, and the
drift that then seemed to characterize both our administration
and the reelection campaign. Above all, they were indebted to
Ross Perot, whose withdrawal from the presidential race on the
very day Bill Clinton was nominated threw an army of disaffected
voters into the Democratic ranks. Perot pronounced the Democratic Party to have been "revitalized" and seemed, for the
moment, to be all but endorsing their nominee.

The gap in the polls was so huge that I began recalling a dinner
table conversation I'd had back around January with our son Ben,
who this time would be the best political prognosticator in the
family. "Dad, you're going to lose the election," he'd told me.

"Why?" I asked.

"Because you raised taxes."

I had begged to differ with my fifteen-year-old son, but he kept
coming back at me, telling me that all his friends at school were
saying the same thing.

By July you could lose count of how many albatrosses we had
around our neck. I still thought we could win, but I knew that it
would now take two enormous pieces of luck. First, we would

have to run a letter-perfect campaign; second, Clinton would have to make a couple of big mistakes.

In the month between the conventions, there was no sign that either one of these was about to happen. Our own campaign remained inexplicably complacent. I can remember Bob Teeter coming in one day, when we were still down by more than twenty points, to tell us the supposedly good news that we were in a better position than Gerald Ford had been at this point in the 1976 campaign. Oh, great! An appointed President who'd pardoned Nixon, raised taxes—and lost in November. And this was the *good* news. There were times, I thought, when Teeter and Baker would be satisfied with coming close, as Ford did, so that political historians would praise them for turning a potential debacle into a squeaker.

I didn't want to come close. I wanted to win. But right after the Democratic Convention we let the Clinton campaign keep the offensive, with their bus rides through those "heartland" areas that were ours to lose. I called the bus trips "slick" when I appeared on Larry King's show, but that was just a politician saying what a politician has to. The fact is that Clinton's people were smart and effective in setting the agenda and in defining him as he wished to be seen, not as he was. We remained reactive, letting him define himself—and us. Clinton looked as if he were playing by Lee Atwater's book. Every day he was avoiding stumbles, hitting solid singles.

Still, in the latter part of July, his campaign was really hoping for an early home run. More specifically, they wanted to knock me out of the park. If President Bush dropped me from the ticket, they would claim credit for forcing him to do so, and even if—in Nixonian terms—they would no longer have me to kick around, they'd be able to accuse the President of panic and disloyalty and of bad judgment back in 1988. As the month went on I was eager for us to fight back against the Democrats with everything we had—but first I had to spend a week or two just fighting to stay on the ticket.

I was no longer protected by the President's high poll numbers. Those were long since gone. I thought back to historical precedents. There had been some strong "dump Nixon" sentiment back in 1956, which he survived. But I wondered if he would have survived had Eisenhower's reelection prospects been as weak as Bush's.

I had watched the conclusion of the Democrats' convention with Marilyn and Ben in the library of the VP residence. As the balloons were coming down, ABC ran an instant poll showing us behind by twenty-six points. I looked over to Marilyn and told her that they would now be coming after me in a big way. Ben asked why, and I told him that there would be a push for a bold stroke. Marilyn thought dropping me would be a foolish political move for the President, but I wanted my family to be ready for anything. The children tried to take it in stride (Ben acted nonchalant, as though this was just Dad talking), but they were undoubtedly rattled. By now even Corinne had gotten used to the house and her school and all the things that went with my being Vice President. What had been so unfamiliar back in 1988 and 1989 was now their normal life.

I never really expected to be dropped. I knew what my relationship with the President was, and I knew he felt I'd gotten a bum rap for four years. He had supported me in difficult times, and I was sure he would calculate the cost of a switch, however low my poll numbers, to be prohibitive. Above all, the conservatives, who still didn't regard him as a true believer, would be howling.

As it was, the only rumblings I got involved the "Wednesday Group" of Senate Republicans, to which I'd once belonged. I called some of my friends up there to check on rumors and ascertain if they were putting together some little delegation that was going to try to persuade me to quit, but they just reassured me. "No, no, I was at the last meeting," they'd say, "and nobody is thinking that." Jim Jeffords, a first-term liberal Republican from Vermont, had actually gone public with a suggestion that I get off the ticket, but I thought he was such a wobbly sort of Republican that it might do me some good to have him out there flapping his wings against me.

But I still needed to be ready for anything. The town was full of rumors, a lot of them malicious, and most of them just crazy: the President wasn't well; Marilyn was seriously ill; Mrs. Bush was sick. There was an atmosphere of panic, and a lot of people were convincing themselves it would subside only when Jim Baker finally took over the campaign. I don't know what Baker himself was telling the President about me. I suspect it was that dumping me would create more problems than it would solve. I'm sure the President saw some campaign polls, which indicated that he ran only very slightly stronger—a statistically insignificant amount—if he was paired with Colin Powell or any other hypothetical replacement.

But a small "dump Quayle" movement began to gather steam in the media. George Will's July 23 column in the *Washington Post* prescribed five things the President could do to salvage his campaign, and one of them was: "Replace Quayle. Yes, he is the darling of the very conservatives who most despise Bush; and Bush has said he would keep Quayle; and this change might present a picture of an administration in turmoil, as did Carter's personnel changes in the summer of 1979. Therefore Quayle's replacement must be so exciting he becomes the topic of conversation. The choice is obvious: Colin Powell would be good for the country and would scramble the political equation, perhaps for a generation." The next day, William F. Buckley was suggesting Jack Kemp be sent in for me, no matter what friction might exist between Bush and his HUD secretary. Former Reagan speech writer Peggy Noonan was part of the chorus, and there was one report that Gerald Ford was urging the President to go for the long ball and find a new running mate.

The knives were out. The potato incident had whetted my opponents' appetites, and they were waiting to finish me off. On his program Larry King asked me a hypothetical question about what I would do if my daughter (presumably as an adult) got pregnant and wanted an abortion. I answered, as any father might, that I would counsel her and hope she chose life over abortion, but that in the end I would support her decision. Parents should always love their children even if they make a mistake. The press, and my nemesis Governor Cuomo, said this was hypocritical, and the media went on to try and drive a wedge between me and Marilyn on the issue, even though no disagreement existed.

William Buckley began his July 24 "dump Quayle" column by saying that word had reached him from a trusted source that "last week Vice President Dan Quayle went to President Bush and offered to withdraw as a candidate for re-election." Not true. I didn't need to. The President always knew that I wanted to serve only at his pleasure. As I told Larry King, if I was hurting the ticket, I would be gone. Bush told reporters on Wednesday, July 22, that my place on it was "very certain," and he told me the same on Friday morning the 24th. I had an early meeting with him in the Oval Office, and as he was getting ready to leave and go over to the residence, he just turned to me and said, "All this stuff about dumping you from the ticket, just don't pay any attention to it. I think you're doing a good job." From there I went to a breakfast meeting with some of my own staff and Mitch Daniels, who had been the White House's political director under Reagan, and I told them what the President had told me. Later in the day, I answered with a simple yes the *Washington Post*'s question about whether I'd be on the ticket, and that pretty much closed the matter.

During this period, Bill Kristol fought hard for me with the press. He went so far as to hint that the problem this time around was not Quayle, but Bush. This was what I'd lacked four years ago—somebody out there defending me aggressively. There's no question that Bill's work helped keep Jim Baker and Bob Teeter from going too far. Baker was so conscious of how formidable Bill was, and so aware of his reputation as a leaker, that once Baker began running the campaign in late summer, he wouldn't allow me to send Bill to the top strategy meetings. Baker said I could send Al Hubbard, but he wasn't going to have Kristol leaking campaign secrets to the press. I told Baker that Bill's leaking was exaggerated and that it wasn't fair to shut Bill out. Sending the deputy chief of staff in his place would be a slap in Kristol's face. The fact that the meetings had turned into mere handwringing sessions convinced me not to compromise.

On July 29, Evans and Novak wrote that the 1992 Bush operation was "the worst-conceived incumbent presidential campaign in memory." In fact, things were beginning to look so bad that in the two weeks before the Houston convention, some of the commentators, including longtime Bush critic George Will, changed their prescription from "dump Quayle" to "dump Bush." There was talk that this President who a year ago had a 91 percent approval rating, and who had beaten his recent opponent in every single primary, should, for the good of the party and country, take himself out of the race. People were wondering whether he really wanted a second term or had any vision of how he would use it. Earlier in the campaign, a reporter at one of his press conferences had asked the President, out of the blue, about what he wanted to accomplish in the next four years. Some considered the President's answer vague and compared it to Ted Kennedy's response when he was asked by Roger Mudd, back in 1980, why he wanted to be President. Ted never really found a coherent answer.

I can remember, early on, telling Teeter that the American people knew Bush was a better man than Clinton but that they needed a positive—not just comparative—reason to keep him in charge for four more years. Teeter and the rest of the campaign people would always say not to worry, that the reason would be coming in the next big speech, either the State of the Union or, as the months went on (with each of them wasted), the acceptance speech in Houston. But they never succeeded in concentrating the campaign—or the President—on a big theme. They got bogged down in minutiae: focus groups, chit-chat with the press, gossip mongering. They lacked fire, and as the economy just stayed where it was, floating dead in the water, the campaign stayed with it. It was now clear that any economic growth was going to show up too late for people to believe we had turned the corner. Still, no one wanted to try anything. The President had a vision and a bold program but it was never effectively communicated.

We could have pushed for a new capital-gains cut and called it a jobs bill. We could have pushed for school choice and revolutionized the bureaucratic education system. We could have demanded the line-item veto. We could have become zealots for enterprise zones and hit hard on family values. We could have beat the drum for term limits. We could have blasted the daylights out of the Democratic Congress every day they didn't pass our agenda. At least some Perot voters were now up for grabs; they were as disaffected with Congress as with the executive branch, and we could have tried to appear their allies in an assault on the bloated, inactive House and Senate. But our faint hearts in the Republican ranks would warn the President, "When you start bashing Congress, you're also talking about some of your good Republican friends."

I exploded every time I heard this. "When are you guys going to realize you don't have any say up there? In the Senate you can only filibuster, and in the House you've got absolutely zero power, zilch. It's the Democrats' Congress. And why did the Democrats hide their own congressional leadership at their convention? Because they understand how unpopular Congress is; they know it's a huge liability to Clinton's campaign. But you guys aren't willing to exploit it." At least not beyond a few timid references in the occasional speech.

The betting was that the President, if he were to preserve any chance of reelection, needed what the *Wall Street Journal* called a "knockout" at his own convention. So off the party went to Houston, trying to steal the Democrats' playbook. Which is just what we did—except the edition we got hold of was the one from 1984 and 1988.

35 | How to Lose an Election

It looked pretty well organized—at least before we got to Houston. Craig Fuller, who had been George Bush's vice-presidential chief of staff, was in charge of coordinating the convention, and in the days leading up to it, I thought he did a good job. To me and Marilyn as well as the President and Mrs. Bush, he made a slide presentation of what he had in mind for the four evenings. I was pleased to see that one night would be devoted to showcasing the family values I had been talking about for months, and that it would feature the candidates' wives front and center. Barbara Bush and Marilyn Quayle wouldn't just be waving to the crowd in the time-honored manner. They'd be making speeches, though the campaign wanted them to confine their remarks to the night's theme.

Pat Buchanan did not seem to be much of a consideration. The President said he didn't much care whether his defeated rival spoke or not, but Pat and his sister, Bay, were bent on getting prime-time prominence. Bay tried to get my office to negotiate things, but I refused to have anything to do with the matter. Just how Pat ended up dominating the convention's second night still isn't clear to me, but I assume Bob Teeter okayed the setup. It still seems unbelievable that nobody insisted on clearing Buchanan's text in advance. All Pat had to promise was that in the course of the speech he would endorse the President for reelection.

Tuesday, August 18, was supposed to be Ronald Reagan's night, but some speakers early in the evening went on too long, and the former President's speech, which was to end the session, got started later than planned—leaving the middle portion of the program, and the juiciest slice of prime time, to Pat. We ended up repeating the Democrats' mistake from 1984 and 1988. We showcased the candidate who had been repeatedly rejected in the primaries, and in the process we scared off the party's moderates and some independent voters. The strident behavior of others also hurt us. Had George Bush not changed his position on abortion years before, going from pro-choice to pro-life, he might have been able to negotiate with the right-to-life community in 1992 and get it to take a more politically reasonable approach toward compromise at the convention. But having once changed his mind, however sincerely, the President was not credible to them.

Buchanan's speech itself was probably not as bad as it was made out to be by media analysts; Pat's rhetorical bark is usually worse than his bite. But his tone quickly alienated many in the hall and many of those watching at home. Pat talked about a "cultural war" with such relish that you wondered how he'd ever cope with harmony. In my own speech I would talk about a "cultural divide"—something whose existence in the country is undeniable—but the difference in our phrasing was no small thing. Our business in Houston was to help reelect George Bush, but Pat just wanted to draw blood, and he ended up hurting the President once again. I was in the Astrodome for his speech. After it, Dave Beckwith complained to me that the cameras were panning over to me every so often and that I didn't look as if I was enjoying what I was hearing. I knew I was more representative of the party's conservatives than Pat, and I could not understand why the convention organizers hadn't reined him in. They were overestimating the strength of the phantom Buchanan brigades. Political reality was that, insofar as they existed at all, Pat's voters had little choice but to march with us in November.

The following night, the media took some thoughtful remarks from Marilyn celebrating both working women and mothers at home and attacked them as an antifeminist diatribe. In fact, when she said that "women do not wish to be liberated from their essential natures as women," she was agreeing in part with pioneering feminists like Betty Friedan. As Marilyn wrote in a follow-up article that tried to set the record straight, feminists like

Friedan have argued that "liberation wouldn't be worthwhile if it simply turned women into clones of men." Marilyn never attacked career mothers; she only expressed gratitude for having had enough economic security herself to make the choice she did, which was to interrupt her career as a lawyer and stay home— raising our children, doing volunteer work, and helping her husband's career. She asked that stay-at-home moms be accorded the same respect for their contributions as women in the work force.

On Thursday night, August 20, 1992, I wanted to reintroduce myself to the American people, to come before them with four years of accomplishment and confidence under my belt rather than as what they'd seen in 1988—an unknown man in the crisis of his life. Rush Limbaugh, the most influential conservative in America today, sat in the audience with Marilyn, and my friend Jack Danforth put my name in nomination. One of my seconders was Donna Simms, a single mother from Houston who'd written a supportive letter during the Murphy Brown controversy. There was also the by-now ritual video introduction, complete with an old home-movie clip that showed me as a kid, getting back up onto my roller skates every time I fell down, and a more recent bit of tape, which had me saying that I wore my critics' scorn—particularly when it came to family values—as a badge of honor.

I'd never prepared so hard for a speech. My devoted speech writer, John McConnell, and I reworked the text many different times, and the weekend before, at the VP residence, I must have practiced delivering it three or four times into a Teleprompter. Jon Kraushar was my coach, and he did a great job. My delivery was much more forceful than it had been four years before. I'd always rejected the idea that I needed much coaching—even when Roger Ailes suggested it after the 1988 election. I thought I was all right at extemporaneous speaking and just wanted to get on with the real work of the vice-presidency. So I never made much time for coaching, and over the next few years many of my speeches—and their messages—suffered. I should have gotten coaching sooner, because when I did, it made a difference.

My message this time was that I hadn't been undone by four years of media pounding. I told the delegates that I came before them "unbowed, unbroken, and ready to keep fighting for our beliefs." Even more important, I told the television audience that I was not the rich-boy caricature some of them still imagined. "I come from Huntington," I told them, "a small farming community in Indiana. I had an upbringing like many in my generation—a life built around family, public school, Little League, basketball and church on Sunday. My brother and I shared a room in our two-bedroom house. We walked to school together." I hit a lot of political buttons, too, of course—attacking the Democratic congressional leadership and declaring that "if [Bill Clinton and Al Gore] are moderates, I'm a world champion speller." But my chief mission, after four years of hard work and ridicule, was to seize this chance to redefine myself, on my own terms. The speech was well received by the delegates and even most of the press. The best measure of its success was that I became a nonissue. The media focused, as the voters would, on the President instead of his running mate.

I left Houston in a completely different state of mind from the one I'd been in departing New Orleans in 1988. But as then, we now returned to Huntington, to a crowd that wasn't nearly as large—or as loaded for bear. "You'll notice this time around there's a different crowd of reporters," I told the folks who came out to see us. "The ones from 1988, they said they wouldn't come back unless they had police protection, and the police said no." The *Washington Post* reported that I was "four years older, with a touch of gray and crow's feet and the confidence of a man who suspects the worst might be past."

In one sense, that was true. The nightmarish aspects of 1988 were never there in 1992, and yet now, for the first time in my sixteen-year political career, I realized I might be on the losing side. The Bush–Quayle ticket got only a very temporary bounce in the postconvention polls, and by Labor Day—a traditional political benchmark, when the seasons change, the kids go back to school and people turn more serious attention to politics—things were not good. The polls had us down by as much as fifteen points, whereas four years before we'd been holding a lead over Dukakis.

The campaign was prone to gaffes, and this time none of them were being charged to me. The President's people made him look foolish by having him say, when he was in Atlanta, that the

Democrats had left the three letters G-O-D out of their platform. Later on he made a mistake of his own when, in a moment of frustration, he called Clinton and Gore "bozos." The campaign had become frantic and it was beginning to affect the President.

It appeared as if the Republicans couldn't wait to lose, so that they could get on with the blame game. Jim Baker told people what an impossible job he had. He set things up so that, if we managed to win, he would look like Houdini, whereas if we lost, as he seemed to expect, nobody would be able to blame him. (It was the same thing he had subtly tried to do with my selection in 1988.) George Bush had actually had to ask his old friend to return as chief of staff. Everyone knew the switch was inevitable, but Baker never volunteered to make it. When he returned to the West Wing, he removed the couch in his outer office so that people couldn't hang around. He and his staff dealt with one another behind closed doors, excluding others, which gave the place an us-versus-them atmosphere. A month before the election, Darman was telling Bob Woodward why he thought we might lose the election. Here he was, helping George Bush prepare for his debates against Clinton, and already he was analyzing the President's election defeat!

When I traveled around the country, I would hit the regional issues hard. In Michigan one day I'd point out Gore's environmental hysteria (he insisted that the nation had to eliminate the internal combustion engine), and then, out in California, I'd warn against the way Clinton would gut the defense budget.

As for campaign themes, I focused on taxes and trust, the only two bases, however damaged, on which we might still win it. I was scheduled to debate Al Gore in Atlanta on October 13, and as I prepared, I concentrated on getting him to play our game. I decided to ignore him and direct all my fire toward Clinton. I always felt that if I could put Gore in a position where he'd have to defend Clinton's character, he'd be unable to do it. I also wanted to highlight a few issues that the President could carry to Richmond two nights later, where he would debate Clinton and Perot, who by then was back in the race and once more hurting us, not Clinton.

I didn't especially care which format they picked—a panel of questioners; one moderator; with Admiral Stockdale (Perot's running mate and Vietnam War hero) or without him. But Baker made a big mistake in turning the debate negotiations over to Teeter. Baker was a skilled negotiator who superbly handled the debating schedule for Bush in 1988. But 1992 was different. The odds against winning were greater. Thus it was easier for Baker to let Teeter handle it. But Teeter turned it over to somebody else. So essentially we had our third team negotiating the details of the debate, which was really our only hope for winning. Pathetic.

Instead of using my flexibility about format to their advantage—making concessions in the vice-presidential bargaining in order to get a format for Richmond that the President really wanted—the Bush campaign people got their lunch handed to them. They came back with a single moderator (Hal Bruno) for the vice-presidential debate, which was all right with me, but the President got locked into a sort of talk-show format (audience question-and-answer) for Richmond. This was Clinton's dream format, and the President didn't realize he'd been had until it was too late.

There's a small myth floating around that we asked if I could bring Gore's book on the environment (*Earth in the Balance*) to the debate, and that we dropped the request when the Gore people said sure, so long as we can bring a potato. Nice story, but one the Gore people leaked to the *New York Times*. The truth is I said I would be happy to have Al Gore show up with a potato. I can't think of anything that would have looked less presidential than a display like that. But there was never any trade-off. There was no way they were going to let me bring his book onto the debate stage. Period. And I don't blame them. What I was able to cite from it from memory was bad enough.

Warren Rudman and Bob Grady (Dick Darman's deputy at OMB) stood in for Gore during our rehearsals in the office, and they asked tough questions. In fact, when the debate itself was over, my staffers told me that of the three debates (the two dry-runs and the real thing), the only one I won handily was against Senator Gore.

I believe I won it, too. In preparing for it, I remembered our joint service on the Senate Armed Services Committee from 1984 to 1988. I knew Gore's argumentative skills were overrated. I was convinced that, once we really got going, I could beat him. And, boy, did we get going. The format allowed for so much give-and-take that some commentators called it a free-for-all, a "tabloid debate" or a schoolyard scrap. I think many of them took that line (although they usually complain about the straitjacketed format of candidates' debates) because I did better than they wanted me to. At least this time no one was accusing me of being a "deer caught in the headlights." Charles Krauthammer's assessment was typical of the grudging compliments I got: "The performance was shrill and annoying. Yet one must admit it was nervy. His party facing annihilation, his colleagues deserting, his ammunition gone, Quayle seemed determined to go down fighting. It was a display of frantic combativeness that verged on courage. Such a performance does not add dignity or gravitas to his public persona, but it does add guts."

Compared with 1988, I was better prepared and the questions were fairer. And we weren't *quite* out of ammo. I was able to tell viewers that Bill Clinton would raise their taxes, make their government bigger, and go in woefully unprepared to whatever foreign crises lay ahead. After the debate, Tom Brokaw (who according to press reports after the election seriously considered joining the Clinton administration) and ABC's Jeff Greenfield both said I was being misleading when I said Clinton would raise taxes on almost everyone making over $36,000 a year. Less than a month after Clinton took office, *USA Today* reported: "Looks like Quayle was right. Last year's vice presidential debate . . . produced an accurate prediction for Quayle about the Clinton budget plan. . . . The final plan, according to Clinton officials, will hit those making $30,000 and above." When Gore flip-flopped, I accused him of "pulling a Clinton," and when I reminded him that the Governor of Arkansas "has trouble telling the truth," he never really rose to his running mate's defense.

The next day Gore and I continued our debate on all three morning talk shows. He still refused to defend Clinton. I could hardly contain myself. Hadn't anyone talked to him, clued him in as to what really happened? I later learned that the Clintons were quite upset, but the campaign wanted to get on to other matters. So they let Gore be Gore.

That same morning after the debate I flew to a rally at Auburn University in Alabama, where Marilyn and I were given a reception that made us realize the debate had excited people, gotten them out of the doldrums. Back at the White House that afternoon, we got another terrific welcome, this time from the President himself, who came out to the lawn to greet us with great fanfare. I was on a high, feeling like a winner, and the clearest sign that some Democrats felt I'd won the debate was the speed with which Gore changed the subject away from everything we'd argued about, by making the outrageous statement that "Iraqgate" was bigger than Watergate. The media had no interest in talking about my debate performance, so they helped him to change the focus.

The President had only one more day until he faced Clinton and Perot in Richmond, and some commentators were going as far as to urge him to "pull a Quayle." I got involved in his debate preparations on Wednesday afternoon. Everybody was there—Baker, Fitzwater, Teeter, Darman, Scowcroft, and Tutwiler—making suggestions. I told the President that if they got on him about breaking the no-new-taxes pledge, he ought to point out that he had been willing to take the political heat when it came to doing what's best for the country, whereas the only time Bill Clinton takes any political risk is when it's in the interest of Bill Clinton.

I had a bad feeling about Richmond. As I've said, the format was Clinton's, not the President's. Most of the preparations I witnessed seemed to focus on minutiae. When moderator Carole Simpson took the character issue off the table by suggesting it wasn't an important matter, the debate was over. Her admonition represented a huge lost opportunity. After that, the President seemed disengaged. His worst moment came when the cameras caught him looking at his watch; my speech writer John McConnell remembers seeing me put my head into my hands as we watched the proceedings on television in North Carolina.

It isn't easy to campaign when you're pretty sure you're going to lose. My Senate friends from different spectrums of our party, like Don Nickles and Bill Cohen, were telling me of the impossible road ahead. Even so, the fall of 1992 provided me with some pleasant memories. Driving into a rural Georgia community, I was greeted by a banner that thanked me for standing up for families. I went to Cape Girardeau, Missouri—Rush Limbaugh's home town—with a rather mundane, vanilla speech for what I thought would be a bipartisan audience (I was dedicating a grant to their port authority), but when I said, "I'm not here to give a partisan speech," they booed. So I gave them as partisan a speech as I could deliver, and they kept chanting, "Hit 'em again, harder, harder." This was shortly before the Gore debate, and I called Rush from the airport tarmac, asking if he'd like to act as moderator. He accepted the offer, but the Gore people, not too surprisingly, said no.

For the last few weeks we had Debbie Ross's great little rock band traveling from rally to rally with us. It was one of the things keeping people's spirits up, but things were hopeless. The Friday before the election a well-known liberal Democratic lawyer, Craig Gillen, one of Lawrence Walsh's team investigating the Iran-contra affair, brought an indictment against Caspar Weinberger. The timing was motivated solely by politics: the Clinton people knew about the indictment a day ahead of time. Their point was to remind the public of lingering questions about the President's alleged part in the affair. (Lawrence Walsh's whole investigation was just like his final report and last press conference: pathetic.) They were trying to take away the last card we had to play: the character issue. Several days before, Bill Kristol had proposed the "Tower test" for Bill Clinton, saying that any candidate for President should be held to the same standards of conduct the Democratic Senate had applied to John Tower three and a half years earlier.

We were going to lose because we were unable to argue convincingly that the economy was recovering—even though that was true. Another key factor was that, after twelve years of Republican rule, the media was on the side of Bill Clinton. They too wanted a change. A third and perhaps most decisive factor was that for too long we had adopted our opponents' agenda: compromised on taxes, run away from our foreign policy accomplishments, and let ourselves speak timidly about family values. This was the most poorly planned and executed incumbent presidential campaign in this century. All the negatives piled up against us overshadowed the first-rate character of President Bush and the extraordinary job he had done leading America into a completely new global arrangement.

On Tuesday, November 3, Marilyn and I voted in Huntington. I made my usual stops in town: getting my teeth cleaned in Dr. John Regan's dental chair, dropping in at the *Huntington Herald-Press*, and stopping for a cup of coffee at Nick's Kitchen. Along the way I ran into Ed Roush, whom I'd beaten in my first congressional campaign sixteen years before. He's always been very gracious, and we exchanged some pleasant words. But the chance encounter contributed to a feeling that my decade and a half in politics was coming full circle.

After voting at the Huntington courthouse, we headed down to Indianapolis. I played a little basketball with Tucker and Ben against some of our advance people—the only contest I would win that day. Over the weekend I had told the kids to be prepared, that we needed a miracle to win. I'm not sure they really believed me, since up until then I'd tried to be confident, telling them we were going to keep pushing ahead and pull this thing out. But it wasn't going to work out that way. Back at the White House the exit polls were showing how bad it was: I was told that, late in the morning, the President, who expected to win right up until Election Day, looked at those polls and asked the people in the room: "Do you think we've been kidding ourselves?"

When it was over, I called Bill Clinton to congratulate him. His voice was just terrible, completely worn out, but he did go out of his way to say how he admired the way I had always hung in there during some very rough treatment. He had had his own struggles that year, and I think he meant it sincerely. I responded with weary admiration: "You hung in there pretty good yourself." I called Al Gore the next day, and our conversation was a little more formal and very brief.

My staff had two speeches ready for election night. But I'd long since known which one I'd need to give. In the end, instead of reading it, I spoke in my own words, from the heart, without a text and without a podium. This was the way I spoke when I was twenty-nine, running for Congress; I *had* come full circle. I told people it was Bill Clinton's night, that he deserved our support and congratulations. I said that "if he runs the country as well as he ran this campaign, we'll be all right." I wanted to be gracious because he had earned that, and I also wanted to set him a high mark for what his presidency should be. I remembered how angry Nixon had been after his 1962 gubernatorial defeat, and even though I had had my own stormy time with the press, I didn't want to go out the way he had. How you exit is important—especially if you're thinking of coming back.

36 | Keeping Faith

We went back to Washington the next day. I had two and a half months left to serve as Vice President—and the children had to be back at school. On the tarmac at the Indianapolis airport we got an emotional farewell from our old friend and associate Mary Moses Cochran (still wearing her Bush–Quayle campaign sweatshirt), whose beeper Marilyn had borrowed four years before in New Orleans, so we wouldn't miss the call that began it all.

We arrived back on the South Lawn of the White House in time to join the arrival ceremony for President and Mrs. Bush, who were returning from Houston. The White House staff and campaign people cheered them from the heart, and they carried off a difficult moment with real dignity. The President spoke only briefly, and when he was through he turned to me to ask if I wanted to say anything myself. I almost picked up the microphone to say something about the great contribution he had made to the country, but I finally decided the most fitting thing to do was practice some vice-presidential deference and let him have the only word.

I saved my words for the private moment the President and I shared once we got back inside the White House. I shook my head, still disbelieving. I started to mention the way the campaign had been run, but he didn't want to talk about that. He was steeling himself to go in and face all the stewards and White House personnel who had been so good to him and Barbara and who, however quietly, had rooted for them in the election. Mrs. Bush is in some ways more resilient than the President; it was he who most dreaded the long transition and its ordeal of good-byes.

On Thursday morning (Ben's birthday) I had my usual CIA briefing at 7:40 and the NSC one at 8:45. The Cabinet met at 10:00, and during the day I did a couple of newspaper interviews. The normal routine continued, but the calendar began to thin, and there was finally some time for reflection. I kept going back to the incompetent way the campaign had been conducted. Some late successes for the administration made me feel even worse: the military mission to Somalia, begun to feed a starving population, quickly began saving countless lives. It was the last big foreign policy achievement of an administration that had been full of them. In addition to this, new statistics showed that the economy was at last beginning to grow. But it was too late for us to reap political benefit from any of this.

The President went out of office as he came in: a gentleman who sometimes suffered from what Roger Ailes called "terminal politeness." He did the right thing in pardoning Caspar Weinberger, whose indictment by Lawrence Walsh was motivated by politics. But Bush felt he had to go further than that. He pardoned a number of others, which brought him one last hail of unjustified criticism.

If substance was the criterion, it seemed clear that we deserved to win. I still feel that. But if the criterion was campaigning, you had to say we deserved to lose. For all my talk about the need to look forward, which is what I told the Republican Governors Association on November 16, I remained preoccupied by my own failure to convince the President early on—from the time of John Sununu's departure a year before—that the campaign organization taking shape was going to cause problems. He continued to rely on it until much too late, and after November 3 I realized I should have done more to dissuade him from that. For four years I had stood firm for my principles and tried to inject some ideology into a nonideological administration. This was the one time I wasn't as forceful as I should have been. To this day I ask myself: If I had been more adamant, could our defeat have been averted?

I found it hard to move on. I loved the job I was doing, felt we were accomplishing great things, and enjoyed the people with whom I was working. I also knew how much I'd grown in it. In January 1993 I had lunch with Richard Nixon, and this time, unlike during our transition meeting four years before, I found myself doing half the talking. After sixteen years in Washington, it was emotionally difficult to go, but the calendar wasn't going to wait until I was ready. January 20 approached at its own speed.

The night before the Clinton–Gore inaugural, we had one last dinner at the vice-presidential residence. Our guests, our Washington friends and supporters, both Republican and Democrat, included Clarence and Virginia Thomas, *U.S. News & World Report*'s Michael Barone (for whose balanced coverage, from 1988 on, I remain grateful), and our friends Dick and Deana Freeland, to whose home in Naples, Florida, we'd be traveling the next day for an overdue vacation. Corinne had three of her friends over to spend one last night at the house, and I took a last jog around the grounds.

The next morning Marilyn and I arrived at the White House at 10:05 for the awkward ordeal of transferring power. The weather was just beautiful, and almost everyone tried their best to be cheerful, but there was no avoiding the fact that you had a room half filled with people who had won and half filled with the people they'd beaten. Even in victory, Hillary Clinton was cold and distant, but I exchanged some friendly words with the incoming President and Mack McLarty, his chief of staff. "You don't know what you're getting yourself into," I told the new chief of staff. "You're not the first person who's said that," he replied. Even so, I congratulated him.

Bill Clinton and I exchanged pleasantries. I gave him some golf advice. In Kennebunkport, President Bush had always played on a public course with a small army of reporters tailing him, so I recommended that, when in Washington, Clinton go out to the Robert Trent Jones Club, where access to the media can be cut off and he could play in peace.

I rode to the Capitol for the swearing in with Senator Ted Stevens of Alaska, Congressman Dick Gephardt, and my successor, Al Gore. I pointed out to Ted that Al and Dick and I were all members of the class of 1976, having been elected as freshmen Congressmen that year. Dick and Jane Gephardt had lived out by Marilyn and me in those days, and on occasion Dick would even drive me in to the Hill. "Who'd have guessed it would work out this way?" I said. Certainly none of us had foreseen that in the course of sixteen years, both Al and I would become Vice President and Dick a serious presidential candidate and House majority leader.

It was a pleasant enough conversation, but I really felt the strain once I was on the platform with people like Jimmy Carter and Walter Mondale, who represented all the failed policies the Reagan revolution had tried to undo. Now the pendulum was swinging back once more. Clinton's speech was well delivered but not especially inspiring. He stuck to general themes and offered little specific indication of what he would do. It was noteworthy for being only eighteen minutes long, a fact Clinton boasted about.

On the Capitol steps the Bushes and Quayles said good-bye to the Clintons and Gores, as well as to some members of the outgoing administration. We helicoptered to Andrews Air Force Base, after circling the great buildings of Washington. When we were over the White House, Mrs. Bush pointed out that she could see the moving vans in the driveway. At Andrews I joined a receiving line of people offering the President their farewells. Even here, politics intruded. Jack Kemp, despite his public differences with George Bush, put himself front and center. I was amazed at his chutzpah.

We flew to Florida with our friends the Freelands. Reality was sinking in. Only Ben was with Marilyn and me. Tucker was at college and Corinne didn't want to miss a day of school. The conversation deliberately avoided the emotions of the moment. We looked forward to going out on the boat once we were down there, and talked about the golf and tennis we would play. We exchanged a few impressions of Bill and Hillary Clinton but otherwise tried to stay off the subject of the inaugural.

Months would pass before we moved home to Indiana. Tucker was now a freshman at Lehigh University in Pennsylvania, but Ben and Corinne were in high school in Washington, and we didn't want to uproot them in the middle of the year. Going "home" would be a big enough adjustment after the term was finished: they'd spent their whole lives in McLean and Washington, not Indiana. For the first half of 1993 we moved into my aunt's house in suburban Maryland, where years ago I sometimes stayed when my Guard unit was training at Aberdeen Proving Ground. It was in her home that we made the transition back to private life and I began working on this book.

The perks—and confinements—of office were gone; I was even driving my own car again and stopping by the grocery store on the way home from the office. I could move around freely. On one trip, Karl Jackson, my good friend and national security adviser, persuaded me to walk with him around Berkeley, where he used to teach. (Berkeley not being Quayle country, I wore dark glasses and kept a brisk pace.) Congress authorized Secret Service protection for six months, but after thirty days, the Service recommended that it be terminated. I had no argument with that. Ralph Basham, the agent who headed the detail, gave me a list with the names of people who, as he put it, "have an interest in you." He told me to notify the Service immediately if any of them called or wrote or otherwise attempted to contact us. Some of the names had an "O" next to them, and some an "I," so he enlightened me about the code. "O" meant "out," while "I" meant "incarcerated." Oh, great.

Marilyn began commuting a few days a week to Indianapolis, where she had joined the law firm of Krieg, DeVault, Alexander & Capehart. There is speculation that she might run for Governor of Indiana in 1996, but that's the subject of another time. She adjusted to the defeat, and looked forward to what lay ahead, much more quickly than I did. I kept as much in the background as I could, and journalists wondered about my plans. Stories circulated that I was about to join a big Washington law firm as a "rainmaker" whose "name" would bring in clients; or that I would run the family newspapers; or even that I would become the next commissioner of the PGA Tour.

The only thing I wanted to do was get back to Indiana. My immediate future—like the GOP's—lay outside the Washington Beltway, and I was glad when June came around and we were able to move into our new home in suburban Indianapolis. Everyone who aspires to public office should spend some time in the private sector (a lot of the Clinton people, including the President, have never given it a try), and now I had an opportunity to do that. I convinced my public affairs director, Anne Hathaway, to come back to Indianapolis and work for me there. I'm now making speeches around the country, pursuing some business opportunities, working with the Hudson Institute, and writing a syndicated newspaper column. My base of support is fiercely loyal. Everywhere I go, I meet people who thank me for having taken up the causes they believe in. Last fall, when Marilyn and I were coming back from seeing Tucker at Lehigh's Sophomore Parents Weekend, the copilot of the flight we took home greeted us as we got off the aircraft. "Thank you," he said, "for standing firm, and showing some light in a time of darkness."

"There's your book title," said Marilyn.

Like George Bush, I stayed off Bill Clinton's case for the first several months of his term. It was only fair that he be allowed to put forward his first initiatives without constant carping from the sidelines. But by the fall of 1993 I was ready to speak out when things he was doing struck me as seriously wrong. By changing the nature of our mission in Somalia, for example, he botched the good work President Bush had begun. Instead of just trying to feed the hungry, which they'd done magnificently, the troops were now charged with "nation building," an impossible job in a land where there was no real tradition of central government. The UN had conned him into the change, needlessly costing American lives. The results of Clinton's on-the-job foreign policy training were becoming evident. Furthermore, he has assembled the weakest foreign policy team in this century. On the domestic front, I began to speak out against Clinton's proposals to change American health care—"reforms" that amounted to a federal takeover of the entire system and were guaranteed to make things worse. And on the social and cultural front, I've continued to point out all the ways that Hollywood fails to "get it." (My favorite 1993 tale of the extent to which the movie and TV establishment is out of touch with the country came when director Sydney Pollack accepted the bonus of a Mercedes on top of his whopping $5.5 million fee for directing *The Firm*—a film he said was about the greed of the Reagan years.)

The controversy surrounding my four years in office allows my comments on all these issues a little greater publicity, and I hope a bit more impact, than former Vice Presidents usually get. That's one lasting effect of the four years. But the question I'm frequently asked—"Would you do it all over again?"—is a complicated one. When people would ask it before and just after I'd left office, I'd answer with a firm and unequivocal yes. I had accomplished a great deal, and in some ways had been able to enlarge the scope of an awkward office. But now that I've once more been a private citizen for a year, I would have to qualify that yes. I would do it again, but there are things I would do differently. Writing this book has forced me to go back and re-live those four years day by day, sometimes even hour by hour. I've had to remember more unpleasant moments than I expected to. When I lived them, I was so caught up in political considerations and in doing the job that I didn't really have time to dwell on the pain and the ugliness. I was "in the bubble." It's only in the last year that I've been able to realize just how vicious so much of the ridicule directed at me really was and the toll it took on those closest to me.

Would I have been better off staying in the Senate, building up my experience and getting to know the national media better than I did in 1988? You could make a good argument for all that, but in politics you can't always pick the timing of your opportunities. When one comes your way, you have to seize it.

I don't know if my children will follow me into politics. On the whole, they're happy to be out of it, and I'm pleased that I can make time for them more easily than I did in the past. In redefining the role of a Vice President's wife, Marilyn broke some barriers, and she took uncalled-for abuse during the four years we lived in the VP residence. The media tried its best to create tension between the two of us, to make it seem as if she ran the show and I was just a tool for her agenda. The truth is she was my most important adviser, but that wasn't enough for the press. If Marilyn had been a liberal, the media would have canonized her. Together, she and I endured, and what had always been a strong marriage became even stronger.

During those four years, Marilyn and I came to realize the many ways in which the media are like sheep. The people in the upper echelons of the national press corps are very homogeneous. They hang around with one another, they think alike, and they have, to a great extent, come from the same backgrounds. A couple of generations ago, many of our political journalists had blue-collar origins—not the upper-middle-class, Ivy League sort that many of today's share. Journalists love to portray themselves as "afflicting the comfortable," but there's a tinge of hypocrisy to that. Most of them have never been anything but comfortable themselves.

I entered politics because I thought I could make a difference. And during the sixteen years I was in Washington, I did make a difference. I helped to change the country as I myself changed. When the media say that a politician has "grown," they usually mean he's moved leftward. In my own case, I've never strayed from my basic principles, but I know that I grew in the true senses of the word. My experience deepened; my character was proved; my faith was tested and enlarged.

Many in the media have commented that I have a sunny disposition. That's generally true. A friend of mine once remarked that Dan Quayle didn't know that people could look him in the eye and lie to him. He was right. After all these years in politics, though, a touch of skepticism lies beneath my often-remarked-upon sunny disposition. I still give people the benefit of the doubt, but I no longer greet them with my former openness. After four years of relentless public abuse, I'm just relieved that that skepticism hasn't hardened into cynicism. That would be the worst thing of all. I have been too blessed—with encouraging parents, a strong, loving wife, loyal children, and devoted friends—to let the hardest blows of public life harden my heart. I remain a true believer—in my principles, in my country, and in my God and Savior. I have, as the psalmist said, been tested in my heart and mind.

With all my being, I have tried to stand firm, without wavering, for what I believe.

I remain confident and unbowed: I have much yet to do.

Appendix: Selected Speeches

Address to Faculty and Students at
Seton Hall University, November 29, 1990
(On the Persian Gulf Crisis)

Thank you. As always, I am happy to once again talk with the student body of an outstanding American university—I did so last month at DePauw. As Vice President, I do a lot of international travel. Nothing makes me more proud than to hear the international community rave about America's colleges and universities.

Our finest schools have kept firmly in mind what Dr. Samuel Johnson, the great eighteenth-century British man of letters, termed the "supreme end of education: expert discernment in all things—the power to tell the good from the bad, the genuine from the counterfeit, and to prefer the good and the genuine to the bad and the counterfeit."

I am honored to have the opportunity to address the Seton Hall community—a community which truly strives to promote "expert discernment in all things." Since your founding in 1856 by Bishop James Roosevelt Bayley, you have understood that questions of good and bad, right and wrong, are not just minor add-ons to the serious business of life. Rather, they constitute its very core. As the eighth largest Catholic university in the U.S., you have drawn on a rich tradition to promote a greater sense of moral discernment throughout your community and your country. Your motto puts it in perspective: "Advance despite diffi culties."

As all of you know, our country, along with the rest of the international community, currently faces a grave crisis in the Persian Gulf. This crisis carries with it the risk of war. Some in this country have questioned whether the U.S. has any interest in the Gulf that is worth fighting for. Today, I would like to step back a bit from the current debate. I'd like to speak to the larger perspectives of the subject that is too often presented in ten second sound bites on television. Why is the region so important? What have the strategic goals of the U.S. Middle East policy been over the last forty years? And how do these goals apply in the current crisis?

The Middle East, as everyone knows, is the source of much of the oil on which the industrialized world and developing nations depend. It is a region of striking contrasts: vast wealth and grinding poverty; secular radicalism and religious fundamentalism; hatred of the West and emulation of the West. Most importantly, perhaps, the Middle East is caught up in a vast process of change, as ancient societies and cultures strive to adapt to the modern world. This process of adaptation, which entails much turmoil and instability, is what makes the Middle East such an interesting place. Unfortunately, it also makes the Middle East a dangerous place.

Since the onset of the Cold War, the United States has had three strategic objectives in the region. The first objective was to contain Soviet expansionism. In 1947, the Soviet threat to one regional state, Turkey, played a role in President Truman's decision to issue the doctrine that bears his name. Thirty-three years later, the threat of Soviet encroachment on another region of the Middle East—the Persian Gulf—led President Carter to proclaim the equivalent of the Truman Doctrine for the Gulf. The Carter Doctrine, which was also reinforced by President Reagan, warned that, "Any attempt by *any* outside force to gain control of the Persian Gulf region will be regarded as an assault on the vital interests of the United States of America, and such an assault will be repelled by any means necessary, including military force."

But the Cold War is over. And because it is over, because *one* of America's strategic objectives has been realized, some commentators have assumed that *all* of our objectives have been realized. They could not be more mistaken. For in addition to containing the Soviets, American foreign policy has traditionally pursued two other strategic objectives in the Middle East. It has sought to prevent any local Middle East power from achieving hegemony over its neighbors; and it has sought to secure the uninterrupted supply of oil at a reasonable price. Let me describe both of these objectives in greater detail.

Today, all the states of the Middle East face a major threat in Saddam Hussein's Iraq. Saddam's ambitions are not confined to Kuwait. Rather, his goal is to dominate the Persian Gulf region and use its vast wealth to become the greatest Arab hero of modern times, the leader of a new Arab superpower. To that end, he spent some fifty billion dollars on arms imports during the 1980s alone. He has launched two wars of aggression during this period, against Iran and against Kuwait, at a cost of some one million lives—thus far. He has built the sixth largest military force in the world. He has acquired a sizeable stockpile of both chemical and biological weapons, and is estimated to have employed several thousand tons of chemical agents against Iranians and against his own people— Iraqi Kurds—in the 1980s. And he has launched a massive program to acquire nuclear weapons.

The United States opposes Saddam Hussein's bid for regional hegemony for the same reasons that we have opposed other bids. We do not think any government has the right to impose its political will on other

countries through subversion or conquest. We do not think Israel's existence, or the existence of other friendly regional states, should be threatened. And, of course, the prospect of Saddam Hussein strutting across
the world stage at the head of a malevolent global power, armed to the
teeth with weapons of mass destruction, and controlling a large portion
of the world's energy supplies, is something no sane person would welcome. That is why we are working to contain Saddam Hussein's bid for
hegemony today—just as we worked to contain other bids for hegemony
yesterday.

Of course, no discussion of America's strategic objectives in the region
is complete without mention of oil, so let me turn to that issue now. A
key strategic goal of U.S. Middle East policy has been to assure the uninterrupted flow of oil at reasonable prices. This does not mean, as some
cynics have suggested, that we are risking war to prevent the price of oil
from going up a few cents a gallon. During the Arab oil embargo of
1973–74, and during the 1979 oil price shock that came in the wake of
the Iranian revolution, the price of oil went up much more than that.
But we never thought of going to war because the price of oil was too
high. We were confident that market forces would eventually bring the
price of oil down—and we were right.

We did prepare for all contingencies, however, when the Soviet invasion of Afghanistan, coupled with instability in Iran, brought Soviet
forces within striking distance of the Persian Gulf—hence the Carter
Doctrine. For if "any outside force," as the Carter Doctrine put it, could
control the flow of Persian Gulf oil it would, as President Bush said,
place our independence and way of life at risk. No nation should be willing to tolerate such a state of affairs, just as no individual should be willing to allow anyone to hold a gun to his or her head.

That is why President Carter was willing to commit the United States
to preventing a single power—the Soviet Union—from controlling the
Gulf. And that is why President Bush has dispatched American troops to
Saudi Arabia to prevent another power—Iraq this time—from doing like-
wise. Neither President was prepared to jeopardize American security by
permitting, in President Bush's words, "a resource so vital to be dominated by one so ruthless"—either Leonid Brezhnev of Moscow, or Saddam Hussein of Baghdad.

So far, I have talked about traditional U.S. strategic objectives in the
Middle East. But there is another strategic American objective in the current crisis that is not traditional—that has only emerged, in fact, as a
result of the end of the Cold War. This objective might be described as
strengthening the foundations of world order. Let me explain what I mean.

When the Cold War was still raging, any regional crisis in the Third World contained within it the seeds of a possible Soviet-American confrontation. That is why, in the Middle East and elsewhere, both the United States and the Soviet Union often made significant efforts to restrain the clients from rash behavior. These efforts were part of the unwritten "rules of the game" that prevented Soviet-American competition from getting out of hand during the Cold War.

With the end of the Cold War, the chances of a Soviet-American clash in any Third World conflict, including the Middle East, have greatly diminished. Unfortunately, so have the traditional restraints that the superpowers used to impose on their regional clients. As a result, unless the U.N. Charter's rules about using force are not reaffirmed and defended fairly quickly, we face the dangerous prospect of a new, post-Cold War world that is actually more anarchic, and more violence-prone, than the world which preceded it.

Iraq's invasion of Kuwait is the first crisis of the post-Cold War world. One way or another, it is bound to set a precedent—either on behalf of greater world order or on behalf of greater chaos. If Saddam Hussein succeeds in his aggression, it is likely that his success will embolden other dictators to emulate his example. But if he fails—and believe me, he will fail—others will draw the lesson that might does not make right and that aggression will not be allowed to succeed.

This is why President Bush has sought to rally the international community against Iraq's aggression. This is why the U.N. Security Council has passed ten resolutions condemning Iraq, and is considering yet another resolution today. This is why scores of nations have agreed to contribute economically or militarily to the joint effort against Saddam Hussein. And this is why twenty-seven nations have sent troops or military materiel to the Persian Gulf. Everyone recognizes that this is a test case. Everyone can see that, beyond America's traditional objectives in the region, what is at stake is nothing less than the shape of tomorrow.

None of these considerations, of course, frees us from the responsibility to proceed carefully. The moral and human implications of war—any war—are very grave. No reasonable effort should be spared in the quest for a peaceful solution. That is why, despite the use of American hostages as human shields, despite the outrages against our embassy, despite Iraq's continued barbarism in Kuwait, we have refrained from military action against Saddam Hussein.

But even as we exercise patience and restraint, we must also be alert to the moral costs of such a course. Consider, for example, the fate of the people of Kuwait. With every day that passes, their plight grows more desperate. Being patient with Iraq allows Saddam Hussein to prolong their agony. Is this a moral course of action?

Or consider the fate of American military personnel in Saudi Arabia. The longer we refrain from action against Iraq, the more time Saddam Hussein has to tighten his grip on Kuwait, and the harder it may be to break that grip, if and when war comes. Does patience today risk greater American casualties tomorrow? And if so, is this a moral course of action?

Or consider Iraq's drive for nuclear weapons. As President Bush told American troops in Saudi Arabia during Thanksgiving, "Each day that passes brings Saddam one day closer to realizing his goal of a nuclear weapons arsenal. . . . And we do know this for sure: He has never possessed a weapon that he didn't use." Will continued patience with Iraq help make the world vulnerable to nuclear blackmail by Saddam Hussein? And if so, is this a moral course of action?

Please don't misunderstand me. I believe that every reasonable effort must be made to resolve this crisis peacefully. I also think that there must be limits to our patience. And those limits are reached when our restraint threatens to undermine other, equally moral goals. These goals, as I said, include ending Kuwait's agony as soon as possible; minimizing American casualties in the event of war; and preventing Saddam Hussein from adding nuclear weapons to his already formidable arsenal of mass destruction. It is in order to prevent Saddam Hussein from thwarting these goals that the U.N. Security Council is expected to adopt a resolution today endorsing the use of force against Iraq if Saddam does not withdraw his forces from Kuwait.

The challenge the civilized world faces today is very grave. But it is not unprecedented. In 1936, the world faced a rather similar challenge when Adolf Hitler, who had only recently come to power, moved German troops into the Rhineland, in open defiance of the treaties of Versailles and Locarno. British and French leaders faced a major dilemma. To confront Hitler militarily could mean war. Not to confront him meant acquiescing in a cynical breach of international law. What to do?

But while British and French leaders vacillated between their hopes and their fears, one voice rang out loud and clear. On March 13, 1936, Winston Churchill called on the League of Nations to take tough action against German aggression. His words deserve to be quoted at some length:

"If no means of lawful redress can be offered to the aggrieved party," Churchill wrote, "the whole doctrine of international law and cooperation upon which the hopes of the future are based would lapse ignominiously . . .

"But the risk! No one must ignore it. How can it be minimized? There is a simple method: the assembly of an overwhelming force, moral and physical, in support of international law. . . . If the forces at the disposal of the League of Nations are four or five times as strong as those that the aggressor can yet command, the chances of a peaceful and friendly solution are very good . . .

"The constabulary of the world is at hand. On every side of Geneva stand great nations, armed and ready, whose interests as well as whose obligations bind them to uphold, and in the last resort enforce, the public law. This may never come to pass again. The fateful moment has arrived for choice between the New Age and the Old."

Tragically, most leaders did not see the stakes as clearly as Churchill did. They did not force the issue to a head in the League of Nations. Instead, they acquiesced in Hitler's aggression. When, many years later, Churchill called World War II the "unnecessary war," it was the failure of British and French statesmanship during the Rhineland crisis that he had in mind.

Today, the U.N. Security Council stands poised at an historic juncture not unlike that faced by the League of Nations in 1936. We are hopeful—indeed, we are confident—that it will not fail the test. Some will thoughtlessly say that a vote for today's U.N. resolution is a vote for war. We reject this idea. Saddam has shown that he understands no language other than the language of force. Today's U.N. resolution is our last and best hope for peace—for a genuine peace, not the false peace that is only a prelude to another "unnecessary war."

Thank you, and God bless you.

ADDRESS TO THE ANNUAL MEETING OF THE
AMERICAN BAR ASSOCIATION, AUGUST 13, 1991
(ON LEGAL REFORM)

The ABA is the largest voluntary professional association in the world. And you have many things to be proud of: from your early leadership in reforming and unifying American law, to your longstanding commitment to service through pro bono activities. Through his "Points of Light" program, the President has tried to reinvigorate the great American spirit of volunteerism. Many members of the ABA have been points of light since the day this organization was formed.

It is in the spirit of the early reformers in the ABA that I join you here today. Our goal, as was theirs, is to improve the administration of justice. Chief Justice Burger once termed this "a task never finished," and that is especially so in a country like ours. Madison's "vast and extended commercial Republic" is now more complex, diverse, and mobile than he could have ever imagined. But the ideals of the republic remain unchanged: the rights of the individual are fundamental in America. We take rights seriously.

So when we think about the command of our Constitution's Preamble, to "establish Justice," we have to start at the doors to the courthouse, and keep them open to every American. We owe them a system in which they can resolve their conflicts promptly, effectively, and fairly. And from the hundreds of county courts throughout America, to the Supreme Court in Washington, we also owe it to the people to maintain the independence and excellence of the third branch of government.

That is why we view it as so important that the Senate confirm President Bush's Supreme Court nominee, Judge Clarence Thomas. The ABA knows Judge Thomas. In fact, you've already considered his fitness to sit on the federal bench, and found him qualified just last year. And the Senate has confirmed him no less than four times for high positions in the federal government.

As you know, there's been a bit of opposition to Judge Thomas's confirmation from some interest groups. But in spite of this ideological opposition, I'm confident that my former colleagues in the Senate will consider this nomination fairly and on the merits. I think the great majority of senators will end up agreeing with the former national board chair of the NAACP, Margaret Bush Wilson, who wrote last week that Judge Thomas's "record will speak for itself and will impress those willing to listen and look beyond misinformed rhetoric." Ladies and gentlemen, Judge Clarence Thomas is an outstanding nominee. He deserves to be confirmed, and I believe he will be.

Today I want to talk about our legal system's impact on the American economy, on our ability to compete. Through the 1990s, we're going to face many obstacles in the global marketplace. Some will come from the outside; we're still seeing unfair practices on the part of some trading partners—subsidies, nontariff trade barriers, and the like. But there are other stumbling blocks that we can't make excuses for—because they're our own fault. And that's the way I think we should look at litigation in America today. Our system of civil justice is, at times, a self-inflicted competitive disadvantage.

Every year in America, individuals and businesses spend more than 80 billion dollars on direct litigation costs and higher insurance premiums. When you include the indirect costs, it may add up to more than 300 billion.

This is just one part of the problem. Look at the sheer number of disputes now flowing through our judicial system. One of the most insightful studies of the system is aptly titled, *The Litigation Explosion*. In 1989 alone, more than 18 million civil suits were filed in this country—one for every ten adults—making us the most litigious society in the world. Once in court, many litigants face excessive delays—some caused by overloaded court dockets, others by adversaries seeking tactical advantage. In addition, many of the costs confronting our citizens are enormous, and often wholly unnecessary. And in resolving conflicts, Americans don't have enough access to avenues other than the formal process of litigation.

Isn't our legal system in need of reform? Can't we improve the delivery of justice to American citizens? With these questions in mind, the President's Council on Competitiveness, which I chair, assembled a Working Group on Civil Justice Reform. I was pleased that the Solicitor General, Ken Starr, agreed to serve as chairman, and he and his colleagues have done a wonderful job. Their Report, which was endorsed unanimously by the Council, puts forward solid reform proposals in a number of areas. We have 50 recommendations in all; some ambitious, others more narrow. But each will help reduce cost and delay in the system, and make it easier for citizens to vindicate their legal rights.

Many of the Working Group's deliberations centered on the issue of Discovery under Rule 26. This reflects the view of many that, as one corporate counsel told us, "discovery is 80 percent of the problem." Anyone who has ever sued or been sued knows discovery too often becomes an instrument of delay and even harassment. Unnecessary document requests and depositions can disrupt or put on hold a company's entire research and development program, and the very idea of limits on discovery is outdated. I'm told of one judge who has said his policy is "just to have the parties exchange filing cabinets."

Worse yet, discovery can be a virtually cost-free weapon for the requesting party. That is what we want to change. The Council suggests the following reform. First, to require disclosure of some basic, core information on both sides. Then, to have the parties meet to formulate a discovery plan, with preset quantitative limits, approved by the court and changeable only with good cause. Discovery beyond the set limits is permissible—but only so long as the requesting party pays his adversary's production costs. We serve no purpose by allowing the extreme waste and expense of marginal and abusive discovery under the federal rules. It is time that we bring it to an end.

It's also time to give people a greater right to choose among methods of resolving disputes. We believe the system should provide a "multidoor courthouse," where parties have options other than formal litigation. This idea builds on much of the ABA's important work on this subject. The Council's recommendation is that before the machinery of litigation kicks in, both sides sit down together—with a mediator, or in a conference where they tell their stories to an experienced lawyer volunteering his or her time. The object would be to probe the issues carefully but informally, and to weigh the chances for concluding the matter as quickly as possible and without a trial. In line with this procedure, alternative dispute resolution would be made more widely available.

Now, this idea will, of course, empower people with disputes, and it'll help unclog the courts. But it will also help preserve relationships that might be destroyed by the stresses of a courtroom fight, and this is something we should all take very seriously. The great Judge Learned Hand once said that he dreaded a lawsuit "beyond almost anything short of sickness and death." A lot of Americans see things the same way. They find the system bewildering, a little intimidating, and frightfully expensive. That is why the Council advises that we do our best to give the American people a multidoor courthouse. After all, the system belongs to them, and it ought to respond to their needs.

On the question of financing litigation, there's been a lot of discussion on the relative merits of a "loser pays" rule. From our law school days, we know it goes by the name, the English Rule. But in fact, it's the rule in virtually every other western country.

The English Rule is grounded in fairness—in the equitable principle that a party who suffers should be made whole. Where the Rule operates, the parties are encouraged to look more carefully at the merits of their cases. And there's no doubt that it weeds out a lot of frivolous claims and specious defenses.

On the other hand, to apply the rule too broadly could discourage some suits with true merit—in civil rights and the environment, to name two areas. For that reason, we propose an experiment: to apply the English Rule in federal diversity cases where the plaintiff elects diversity.

There would be two important features to this experiment with the English Rule. First, the amount to be paid by the losing party would not exceed the amount he spent on his own case. This will keep the other side from loading up expenses to penalize the loser. Second, the rule won't be a guillotine; there will be an element of judicial discretion in its application.

Another item of great concern to the Council is punitive damages. These damages, of course, become an issue only after an injury is found and a compensatory sum is calculated. By definition, punitives aren't essential to compensation; in fact, some jurisdictions don't even have them. Most do, though, because for centuries they've been viewed, I think properly, as an effective punishment and deterrent for outrageous conduct.

The problem is that the method of assessing punitive damages has developed over the years without any real structure or limits. Even a casual observer knows that, in the last several decades, punitive damages have grown dramatically in both frequency and size. What began as a sanction only for the most reprehensible conduct has now become almost routine. In California, estimates are that one in every ten jury awards now includes punitive damages, in amounts averaging more than $3 million. And as these awards become more common, so do the instances of their arbitrary, even freakish application.

Now, as Justice Blackmun wrote in the *Pacific Mutual* case, there are only modest due process limitations on punitive damages. So the tough issues of reform are left to the political branches. Here is the proposal agreed to by the Council. First, to restore the quasi-criminal nature of punitive damages, they should be awarded in a separate proceeding after the jury has determined liability, and only where there is some element of intent involved. Second, and most importantly, the trial judge would set punitive damages at an amount not to exceed the amount of the plaintiff's actual harm.

This reform will be good in every respect. For starters, it will preserve the rights of plaintiffs to collect punitive damages in egregious cases, and continue to serve the goals of punishment and deterrence. But it will curtail the randomness of the system—and restore some measure of certainty to commercial transactions. And, of course, it will leave unchanged the law of compensation.

I've covered for you only some of the high points of the Working Group's report. But the 50 recommendations touch quite a few other aspects of the administration of justice. For example:

- Changing the rules on expert evidence. We recommend that expert testimony be admissible only as far as it relates to a community of opinion or scientific thought. We think it is time to reject the notion that "junk science" is truly relevant evidence. We're also recommending that contingency fees for experts be eliminated. An expert witness should not be an advocate.

- Reforming summary judgment. Where it is appropriate to grant summary judgment, it should be mandatory.

- Instituting greater flexibility in judicial assignments—to ensure that we have the judges in the places we need them.

A word now about implementation. The Working Group was formed in response to a system we believe is in danger of spinning out of control. For that reason, the Group worked intensively these last eight months, and received input from state and federal judges, scholars, practitioners, and laymen of varying backgrounds. And for the same reason, we have a strong plan for action on the recommendations.

Some of the proposals envision formal legislation, and we will take that to the Congress. In the same vein, we'll be making contact with appropriate officials at the state level, and encouraging them to adopt reforms in their systems. In fact, I'll be presenting some of our recommendations later today to the National Conference of State Legislators. We'll also be communicating with relevant policy groups, and proposed changes in the federal rules will be taken through the proper channels.

And in the executive branch, we intend to take our own advice. The President will soon be issuing an executive order that will apply some of these proposals to the federal government when it engages in litigation. Specifically: to follow the recommendations on expert witnesses; to allow parties in disputes with the government to elect the English Rule; and to require a policy-level review of discovery requests.

I'm personally optimistic—and I know Judge Starr and his colleagues share this view—that many if not all of the Council's ideas will be adopted. Our inspiration came from the American people: they've seen the problems, they've told us to act, and now they expect us to follow through.

After all, let's ask ourselves: Does America really need 70 percent of the world's lawyers? Is it healthy for our economy to have 18 million new lawsuits coursing through the system annually? Is it right that people with disputes come up against staggering expense and delay?

The answer is no. We are serious about challenging the status quo, and the proposals I've just outlined are offered to inspire dialogue, discussion, and action. Should we succeed, the American people will be the beneficiaries. And so, too, I suggest, will be the legal profession.

This is no time to be timid. If we believe in progress, we must not fear change. And on this bicentennial of the Bill of Rights, we should remind ourselves of the memorable words of Justice Robert Jackson: "Civil liberties had their origin and must find their ultimate guaranty in the faith of the people." Our job in government, and your job as leaders in the law, is to strengthen the faith of the people—in the resolute protection of their rights, and in the effective delivery of justice.

ADDRESS TO THE COMMONWEALTH CLUB OF CALIFORNIA, MAY 19, 1992
(ON FAMILY VALUES)

As you may know, I've just returned from a week-long trip to Japan. I was there to commemorate the 20th anniversary of the reversion of Okinawa to Japan by the United States, an act that has made a lasting impression on the Japanese.

While I was there, Japan announced its commitment to join with the United States in assisting Eastern and Central Europe with a 400 million dollar aid package. We also announced a manufacturing technology initiative that will allow American engineers to gain experience working in Japanese businesses.

Japan and the United States are allies and partners. Though we have our differences, especially in the area of trade, our two countries—with 40 percent of the world's GNP—are committed to a global partnership in behalf of peace and economic growth.

But in the midst of all of these discussions of international affairs, I was asked many times in Japan about the recent events in Los Angeles. From the perspective of many Japanese, the ethnic diversity of our culture is a weakness compared to their homogenous society. I begged to differ with my hosts. I explained that our diversity is our strength. And I explained that the immigrants who come to our shores have made, and continue to make, vast contributions to our culture and our economy.

It is wrong to imply that the Los Angeles riots were an inevitable outcome of our diversified society. But the question that I tried to answer in Japan is one that needs answering here: What happened? Why? And how do we prevent it in the future?

One response has been predictable: Instead of denouncing wrongdoing, some have shown tolerance for rioters; some have enjoyed saying "I told you so"; and some have simply made excuses for what happened. All of this has been accompanied by pleas for more money.

I'll readily accept that we need to understand what happened. But I reject the idea we should tolerate or excuse it.

When I have been asked during these last weeks who caused the riots and the killing in L.A., my answer has been direct and simple: Who is to blame for the riots? The rioters are to blame. Who is to blame for the killings? The killers are to blame. Yes, I can understand how people were shocked and outraged by the verdict in the Rodney King trial. But there is simply no excuse for the mayhem that followed. To apologize or in any way to excuse what happened is wrong. It is a betrayal of all those people equally outraged and equally disadvantaged who did not loot and did not riot—and who were in many cases victims of the rioters. No matter how much you may disagree with the verdict, the riots were wrong. And if we as a society don't condemn what is wrong, how can we teach our children what is right?

But after condemning the riots, we do need to try to understand the underlying situation.

In a nutshell: I believe the lawless social anarchy which we saw is directly related to the breakdown of family structure, personal responsibility and social order in too many areas of our society. For the poor the situation is compounded by a welfare ethos that impedes individual efforts to move ahead in society, and hampers their ability to take advantage of the opportunities America offers.

If we don't succeed in addressing these fundamental problems, and in restoring basic values, any attempt to fix what's broken will fail. But one reason I believe we won't fail is that we have come so far in the last 25 years.

There is no question that this country has had a terrible problem with race and racism. The evil of slavery has left a long legacy. But we have faced racism squarely, and we have made progress in the past quarter century. The landmark civil rights bills of the 1960s removed legal barriers to allow full participation by blacks in the economic, social and political life of the nation. By any measure the America of 1992 is more egalitarian, more integrated, and offers more opportunities to black Americans—and all other minority group members—than the America of 1964. There is more to be done. But I think that all of us can be proud of our progress.

And let's be specific about one aspect of this progress: This country now has a black middle class that barely existed a quarter century ago. Since 1967 the median income of black two-parent families has risen by 60 percent in real terms. The number of black college graduates has skyrocketed. Black men and women have achieved real political power— black mayors head 48 of our largest cities, including Los Angeles. These are achievements.

But as we all know, there is another side to that bright landscape. During this period of progress, we have also developed a culture of poverty— some call it an underclass—that is far more violent and harder to escape than it was a generation ago.

The poor you always have with you, Scripture tells us. And in America we have always had poor people. But in this dynamic, prosperous nation, poverty has traditionally been a stage through which people pass on their way to joining the great middle class. And if one generation didn't get very far up the ladder—their ambitious, better-educated children would.

But the underclass seems to be a new phenomenon. It is a group whose members are dependent on welfare for very long stretches, and whose men are often drawn into lives of crime. There is far too little upward mobility, because the underclass is disconnected from the rules of American society. And these problems have, unfortunately, been particularly acute for Black Americans.

Let me share with you a few statistics on the difference between black poverty in particular in the 1960s and now.

- In 1967 68% of black families were headed by married couples. In 1991, only 48% of black families were headed by both a husband and wife.

- In 1965 the illegitimacy rate among black families was 28%. In 1989, 65%—two thirds—of all black children were born to never-married mothers.

- In 1951 9.2% of black youth between 16–19 were unemployed. In 1965, it was 23%. In 1980 it was 35%. By 1989, the number had declined slightly, but was still 32%.

- The leading cause of death of young black males today is homicide.

It would be overly simplistic to blame this social breakdown on the programs of the Great Society alone. It would be absolutely wrong to blame it on the growth and success most Americans enjoyed during the 1980s. Rather, we are in large measure reaping the whirlwind of decades of changes in social mores.

I was born in 1947, so I'm considered one of those "Baby Boomers" we keep reading about. But let's look at one unfortunate legacy of the "Boomer" generation. When we were young, it was fashionable to declare war against traditional values. Indulgence and self-gratification seemed to have no consequences. Many of our generation glamorized casual sex and drug use, evaded responsibility and trashed authority. Today the "Boomers" are middle-aged and middle class. The responsibility of having families has helped many recover traditional values. And, of course, the great majority of those in the middle class survived the turbulent legacy of the 60s and 70s. But many of the poor, with less to fall back on, did not.

The intergenerational poverty that troubles us so much today is pre-dominantly a poverty of values. Our inner cities are filled with children having children; with people who have not been able to take advantage of educational opportunities; with people who are dependent on drugs or the narcotic of welfare. To be sure, many people in the ghettos struggle very hard against these tides—and sometimes win. But too many feel they have no hope and nothing to lose. This poverty is, again, fundamentally a poverty of values.

Unless we change the basic rules of society in our inner cities, we cannot expect anything else to change. We will simply get more of what we saw three weeks ago. New thinking, new ideas, new strategies are needed.

For the government, transforming underclass culture means that our policies and programs must create a different incentive system. Our policies must be premised on, and must reinforce, values such as: family, hard work, integrity and personal responsibility.

I think we can all agree that government's first obligation is to maintain order. We are a nation of laws, not looting. It has become clear that the riots were fueled by the vicious gangs that terrorize the inner cities. We are committed to breaking those gangs and restoring law and order. As James Q. Wilson has written, "Programs of economic restructuring will not work so long as gangs control the streets."

Some people say "law and order" are code words. Well, they are code words. Code words for safety, getting control of the streets, and freedom from fear. And let's not forget that, in 1990, 84 percent of the crimes committed by blacks were committed against blacks.

We are for law and order. If a single mother raising her children in the ghetto has to worry about drive-by shootings, drug deals, or whether her children will join gangs and die violently, her difficult task becomes impossible. We're for law and order because we can't expect children to learn in dangerous schools. We're for law and order because if property isn't protected, who will build businesses?

As one step on behalf of law and order—and on behalf of opportunity as well—the President has initiated the "Weed and Seed" program—to "weed out" criminals and "seed" neighborhoods with programs that address root causes of crime. And we have encouraged community-based policing, which gets the police on the street so they interact with citizens.

Safety is absolutely necessary. But it's not sufficient. Our urban strategy is to empower the poor by giving them control over their lives. To do that, our urban agenda includes:

• Fully funding the Home-ownership and Opportunity for People Everywhere program. HOPE—as we call it—will help public housing residents become home-owners. Subsidized housing all too often merely made rich investors richer. Home ownership will give the poor a stake in their neighborhoods, and a chance to build equity.

• Creating enterprise zones by slashing taxes in targeted areas, including a zero capital gains tax, to spur entrepreneurship, economic development, and job creation in inner cities.

• Instituting our education strategy, AMERICA 2000, to raise academic standards and to give the poor the same choices about how and where to educate their children that rich people have.

• Promoting welfare reform to remove the penalties for marriage, create incentives for saving, and give communities greater control over how the programs are administered.

These programs are empowerment programs. They are based on the same principles as the Job Training Partnership Act, which aimed to help disadvantaged young people and dislocated workers to develop their skills to give them an opportunity to get ahead. Empowering the poor will strengthen families. And right now, the failure of our families is hurting America deeply. When families fail, society fails. The anarchy and lack of structure in our inner cities are testament to how quickly civilization falls apart when the family foundation cracks. Children need love and discipline. They need mothers and fathers. A welfare check is not a husband. The state is not a father. It is from parents that children learn how to behave in society; it is from parents above all that children come to understand values and themselves as men and women, mothers and fathers.

And for those concerned about children growing up in poverty, we should know this: marriage is probably the best anti-poverty program of all. Among families headed by married couples today, there is a poverty rate of 5.7 percent. But 33.4 percent of families headed by a single mother are in poverty today.

Nature abhors a vacuum. Where there are no mature, responsible men around to teach boys how to be good men, gangs serve in their place. In fact, gangs have become a surrogate family for much of a generation of inner-city boys. I recently visited with some former gang members in Albuquerque, New Mexico. In a private meeting, they told me why they had joined gangs. These teenage boys said that gangs gave them a sense of security. They made them feel wanted, and useful. They got support from their friends. And, they said, "It was like having a family." "Like family"—unfortunately, that says it all.

The system perpetuates itself as these young men father children whom they have no intention of caring for, by women whose welfare checks support them. Teenage girls, mired in the same hopelessness, lack sufficient motive to say no to this trap.

Answers to our problems won't be easy.

We can start by dismantling a welfare system that encourages dependency and subsidizes broken families. We can attach conditions—such as school attendance, or work—to welfare. We can limit the time a recipient gets benefits. We can stop penalizing marriage for welfare mothers. We can enforce child support payments.

Ultimately, however, marriage is a moral issue that requires cultural consensus, and the use of social sanctions. Bearing babies irresponsibly is, simply, wrong. Failing to support children one has fathered is wrong. We must be unequivocal about this.

It doesn't help matters when prime time TV has Murphy Brown—a character who supposedly epitomizes today's intelligent, highly paid, professional woman—mocking the importance of fathers, by bearing a child alone, and calling it just another "lifestyle choice."

I know it is not fashionable to talk about moral values, but we need to do it. Even though our cultural leaders in Hollywood, network TV, the national newspapers routinely jeer at them, I think that most of us in this room know that some things are good, and other things are wrong. Now it's time to make the discussion public.

It's time to talk again about family, hard work, integrity and personal responsibility. We cannot be embarrassed out of our belief that two parents, married to each other, are better in most cases for children than one. That honest work is better than hand-outs—or crime. That we are our brothers' keepers. That it's worth making an effort, even when the rewards aren't immediate.

So I think the time has come to renew our public commitment to our Judeo-Christian values—in our churches and synagogues, our civic organizations and our schools. We are, as our children recite each morning, "one nation under God." That's a useful framework for acknowledging a duty and an authority higher than our own pleasures and personal ambitions.

If we lived more thoroughly by these values, we would live in a better society. For the poor, renewing these values will give people the strength to help themselves by acquiring the tools to achieve self-sufficiency, a good education, job training, and property. Then they will move from permanent dependence to dignified independence.

Shelby Steele, in his great book, *The Content of Our Character*, writes, "Personal responsibility is the brick and mortar of power. The responsible person knows that the quality of his life is something that he will have to make inside the limits of his fate. . . . The quality of his life will pretty much reflect his efforts."

I believe that the Bush administration's empowerment agenda will help the poor gain that power, by creating opportunity, and letting people make the choices that free citizens must make.

Though our hearts have been pained by the events in Los Angeles, we should take this tragedy as an opportunity for self-examination and progress. So let the national debate roar on. I, for one, will join it. The President will lead it. The American people will participate in it. And as a result, we will become an even stronger nation.

Index